Planning Guide for Balanced Literacy

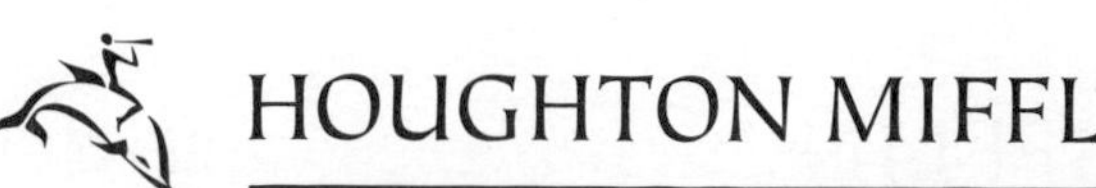

BOSTON

Printed in the U.S.A.

ISBN: 0-618-61910-0

1 2 3 4 5 6 7 8 9-KDL-12 11 10 09 08 07 06 05

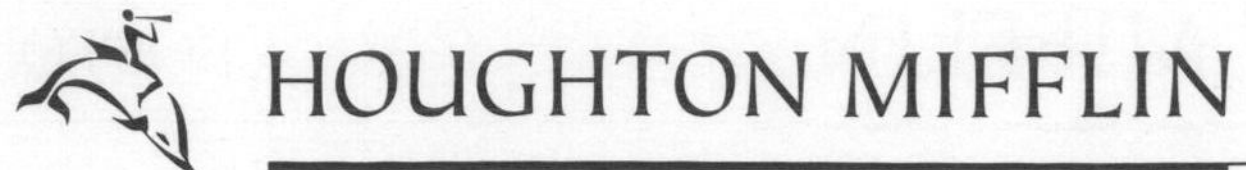

BOSTON

Table of Contents

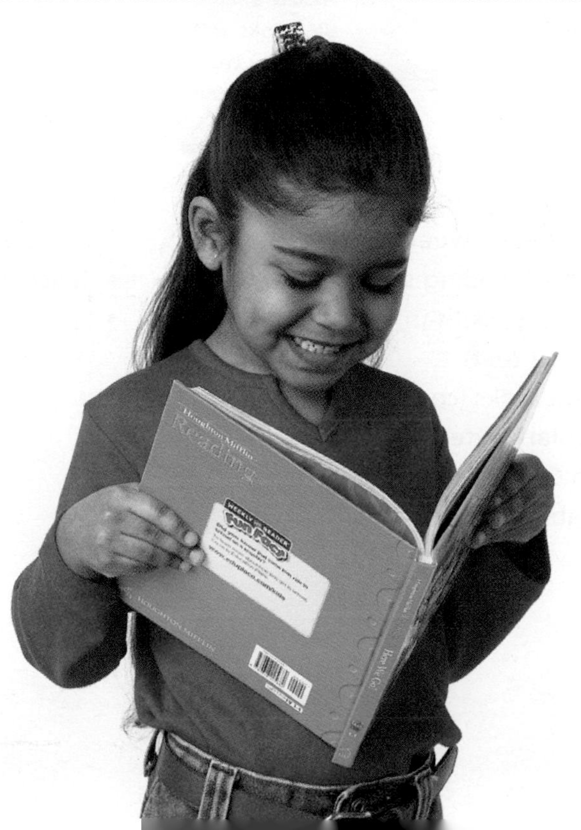

Introduction and Resources

Planning Guide for Balanced Literacy

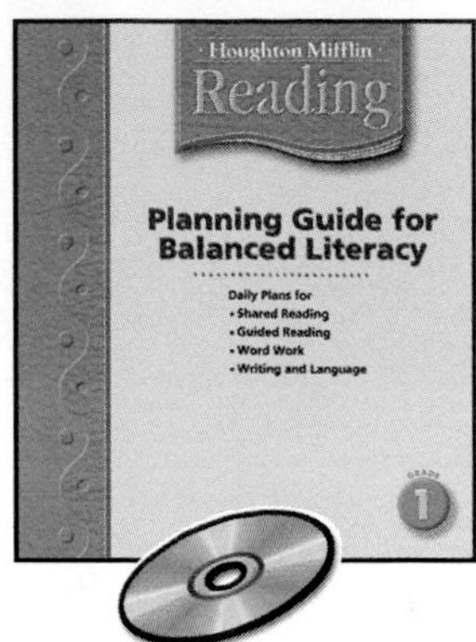

Teacher's Resource CD-ROM
- Practice Book pages
- Lesson transparencies

Introduction

The ***Planning Guide for Balanced Literacy*** provides daily lesson plans that combine *Houghton Mifflin Reading's* core instruction and leveled reading resources to support teachers in reaching all learners.

Four-part lesson plans show the resources you will need each day for
- whole-group instruction for Reading and Comprehension, Word Work, and Writing and Language
- small-group Options for Guided Reading, using leveled books

The plan also provides ideas for independent and cooperative work.

With the ***Planning Guide,*** you can access *Houghton Mifflin Reading's* comprehensive, research-based instruction, meet and assess state standards, *and* address the needs of all learners through small-group Guided Reading.

For Whole-Group Instruction

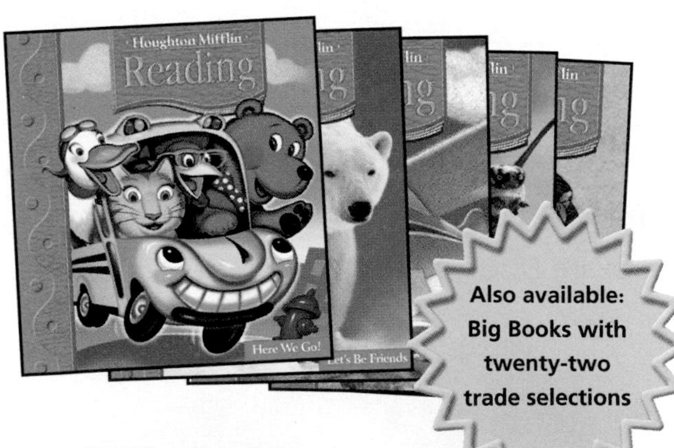

Anthologies
- Award-winning literature
- Three texts each week:
  - ✓ Get Set (decoding skills)
  - ✓ Main Story (skills in extended text)
  - ✓ Content Links (concepts, vocabulary extensions)
- Focus on Genre sections

Also available on Audio CD

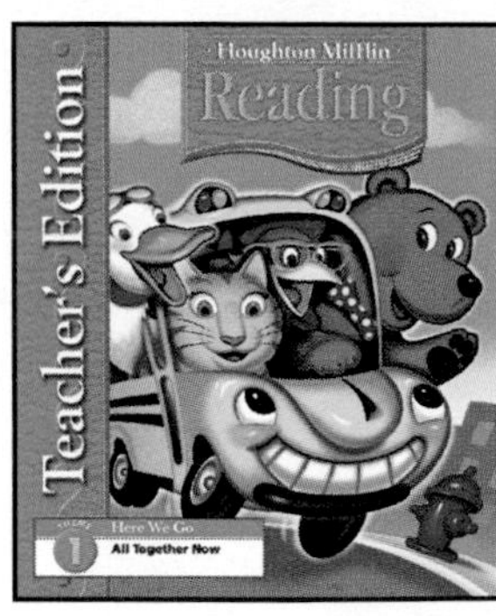

Teacher's Editions
- Lessons to support reading comprehension and skill instruction
- Teacher Read-Aloud selections
- Special sections to focus on genres

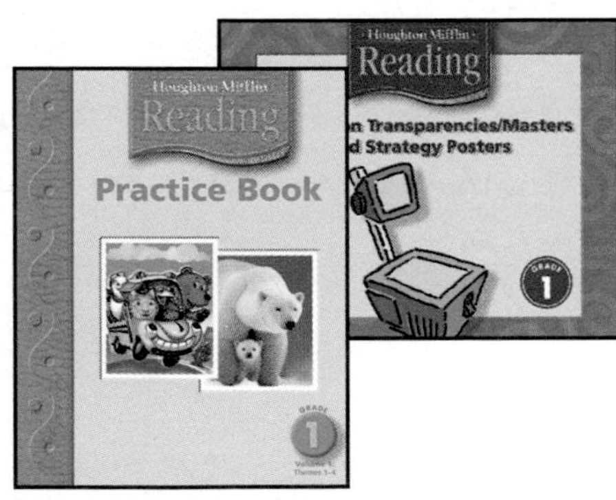

Practice Book and Transparencies
- Transparencies for lesson support
- Independent practice for all skills
- Test-taking practice
- Punch-out letter and word cards
- Sound-Spelling Cards

For Small-Group Guided Reading

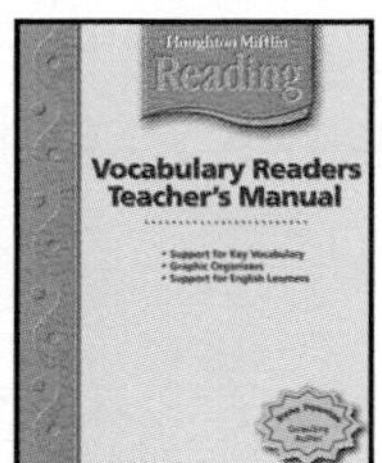

Leveled Readers

- Four levels: Below, On, Above, and Language Support
- Lesson support in the Teacher's Editions
- **Teaching Resource Kit** available for each level; provides lessons and blackline masters for all Leveled Reader titles

Vocabulary Readers

- Key vocabulary and comprehension support for the main Anthology selections
- Below grade level text
- Lesson support in separate Teacher's Manual

Readers available on Audio CD

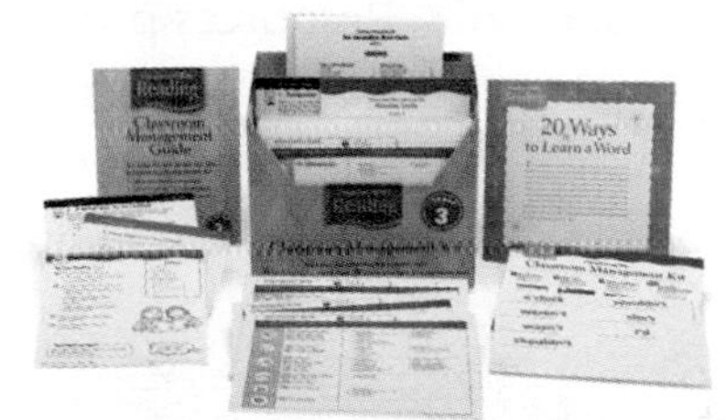

Theme Paperbacks

- Three levels: Below, On, and Above
- Theme-related reading
- Lesson support in the Teacher's Editions

Phonics Library Stories

Practice for decoding, high-frequency words, and fluency

Classroom Management Kit

Activities for independent and partner work

Additional Resources

Assessment Resources

- Weekly Skills Tests
- Alternative Assessments on Teacher's Resource Blackline Masters
- Integrated Theme Tests

Technology

Education Place Website

www.eduplace.com

Activities related to the Anthology selections, including vocabulary support

Edusoft Assessment Platform

Online assessment: rapid scoring, reports, and support for grouping and differentiating instruction

Preview: Day 1

To the Teacher

This preview of two sample days will familiarize you with the ***Planning Guide for Balanced Literacy.*** The lesson plan combines whole-class reading and skill instruction from *Houghton Mifflin Reading* with small-group Guided Reading using Houghton Mifflin leveled books. The plan is flexible and easily adaptable to your personal style and scheduling needs.

Shared Reading

Each day read a shared text with the whole class to prompt discussion, introduce vocabulary, or teach/review comprehension strategies and skills. Resources provided include Big Books, Teacher Read Alouds, and Anthology selections. Choose the best way to share each text (partner reading, independent reading, or audio CD).

Word Work

On Days 1–5, provide whole-group instruction and individual practice with word skills: phonemic awareness, phonics, high-frequency words, spelling, and vocabulary. The week's phonics and spelling skills are related.

Guided Reading: Small Groups

Organize children in flexible groups according to instructional needs. Help them apply the week's reading skills with leveled texts.

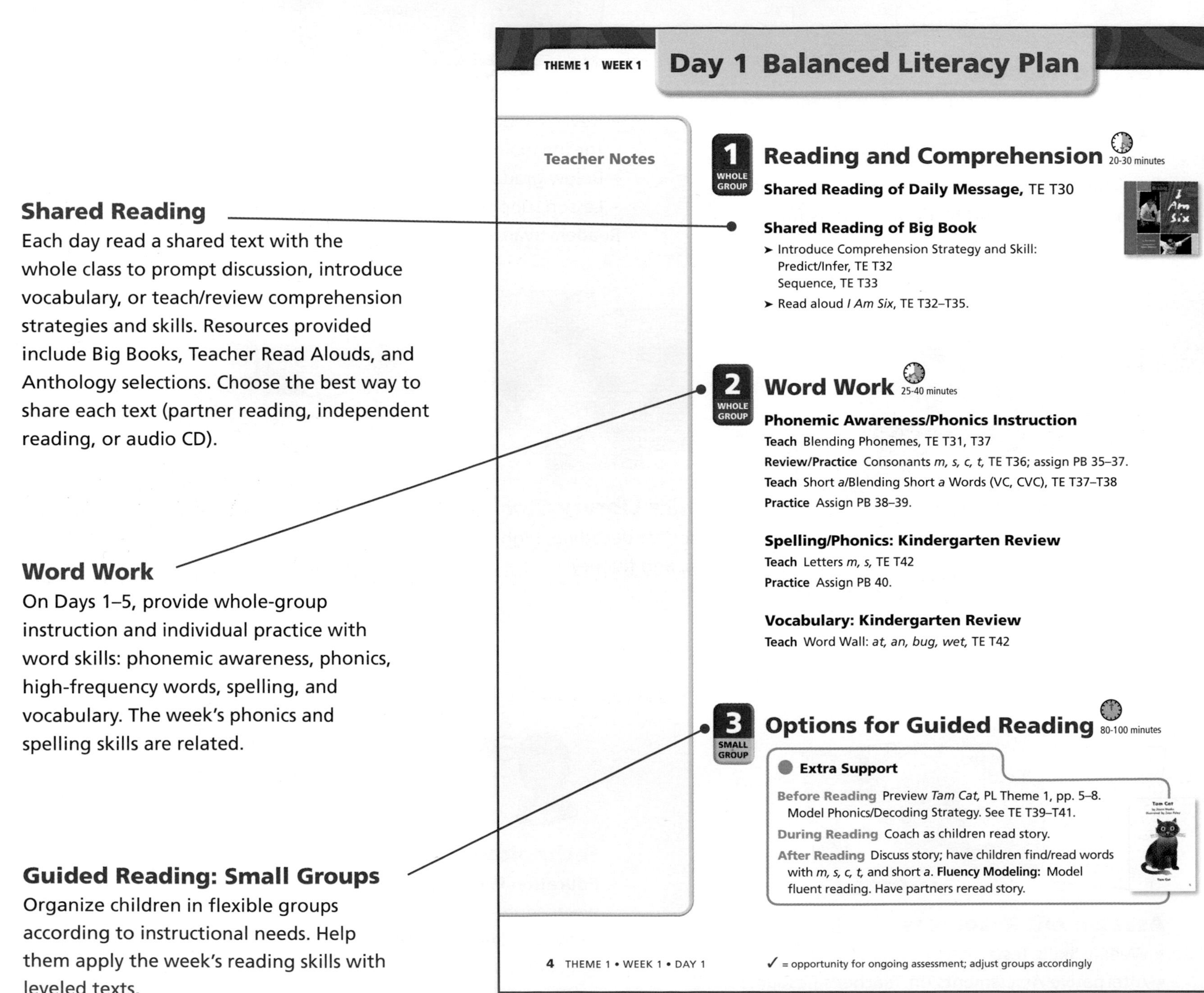

Managing Guided Reading

Daily lesson options are provided for every group.

- Be flexible. Some groups may not need to meet every day.
- Adjust group times according to the tasks and children's needs.
- Regroup children when they show progress or need to work with easier text.

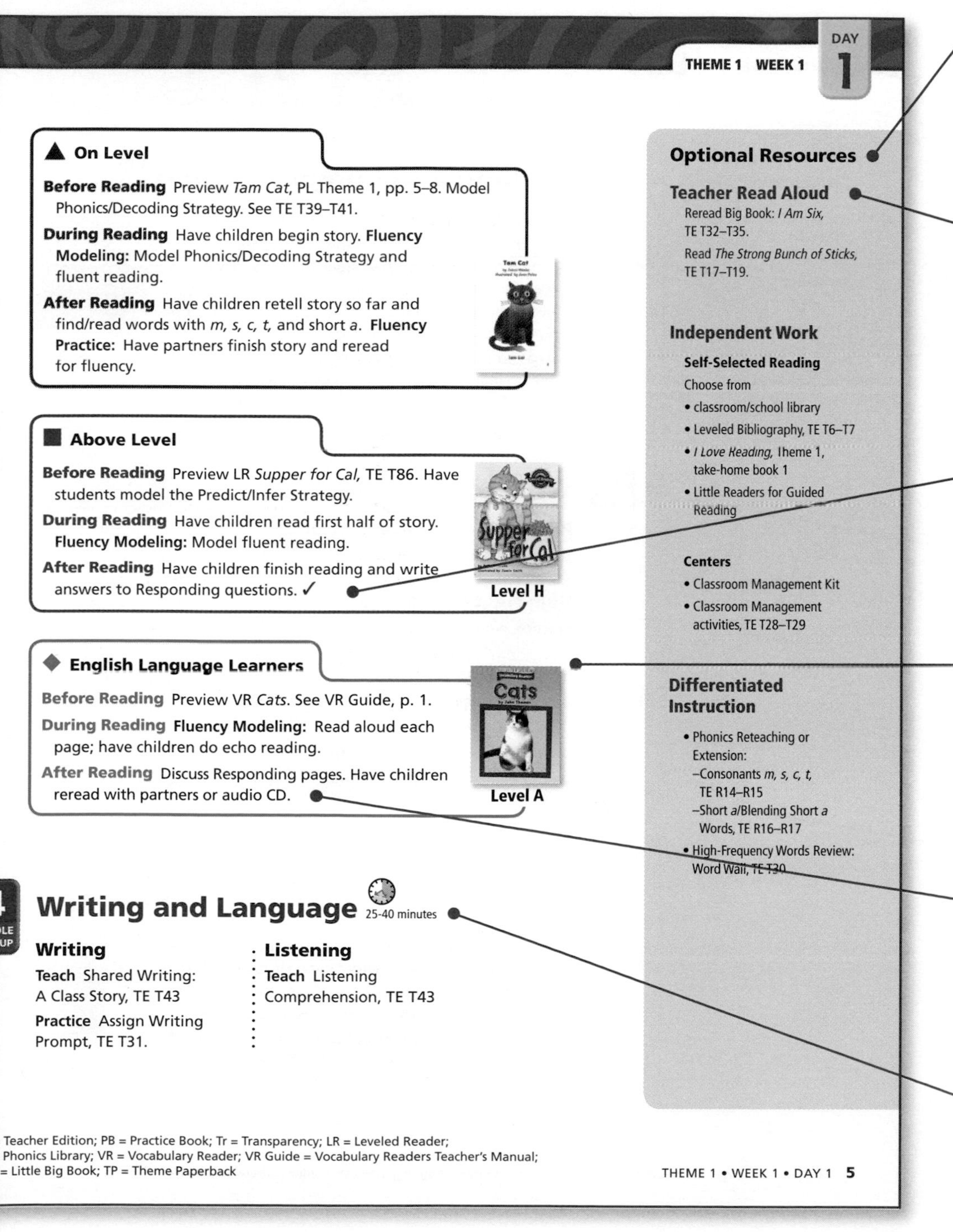

THEME 1 WEEK 1 DAY 1

▲ On Level

Before Reading Preview *Tam Cat*, PL Theme 1, pp. 5–8. Model Phonics/Decoding Strategy. See TE T39–T41.

During Reading Have children begin story. **Fluency Modeling:** Model Phonics/Decoding Strategy and fluent reading.

After Reading Have children retell story so far and find/read words with *m, s, c, t,* and short *a*. **Fluency Practice:** Have partners finish story and reread for fluency.

■ Above Level

Before Reading Preview LR *Supper for Cal*, TE T86. Have students model the Predict/Infer Strategy.

During Reading Have children read first half of story. **Fluency Modeling:** Model fluent reading.

After Reading Have children finish reading and write answers to Responding questions. ✓

Level H

◆ English Language Learners

Before Reading Preview VR *Cats*. See VR Guide, p. 1.

During Reading **Fluency Modeling:** Read aloud each page; have children do echo reading.

After Reading Discuss Responding pages. Have children reread with partners or audio CD.

Level A

Optional Resources

Teacher Read Aloud

Reread Big Book: *I Am Six*, TE T32–T35.

Read *The Strong Bunch of Sticks*, TE T17–T19.

Independent Work

Self-Selected Reading

Choose from

- classroom/school library
- Leveled Bibliography, TE T6–T7
- *I Love Reading*, Theme 1, take-home book 1
- Little Readers for Guided Reading

Centers

- Classroom Management Kit
- Classroom Management activities, TE T28–T29

Differentiated Instruction

- Phonics Reteaching or Extension:
  - –Consonants *m, s, c, t*, TE R14–R15
  - –Short *a*/Blending Short *a* Words, TE R16–R17
- High-Frequency Words Review: Word Wall, TE T30

4 WHOLE GROUP

Writing and Language 25-40 minutes

Writing

Teach Shared Writing: A Class Story, TE T43

Practice Assign Writing Prompt, TE T31.

Listening

Teach Listening Comprehension, TE T43

= Teacher Edition; PB = Practice Book; Tr = Transparency; LR = Leveled Reader; = Phonics Library; VR = Vocabulary Reader; VR Guide = Vocabulary Readers Teacher's Manual; B = Little Big Book; TP = Theme Paperback

THEME 1 • WEEK 1 • DAY 1 5

Optional Resources

Suggestions for read alouds and independent work are provided each day.

Teacher Read Aloud

A Read Aloud is provided in the Teacher's Edition for modeling fluency and building listening comprehension.

Comprehension Check

In each Guided Reading group, both oral and written work provide opportunities to check comprehension.

English Language Learners

Lessons focus on developing English language proficiency as well as on strengthening reading skills.

Fluency

Fluency modeling, practice, and checks are suggested for every group during the week.

Writing and Language

Across the week, whole-class instruction and individual practice focus on writing, grammar, and oral language. Lessons for shared, interactive, and independent writing are included.

Preview: Day 5

Managing Independent Work

- The Classroom Management Kit provides you with routines and ready-made materials.
- Post the daily schedule for whole- and small-group work.
- Organize the classroom to foster independence.
- Teach children to work independently, with partners, and in groups.

Book Share

In preparation for Literature Circles, guide a whole-class discussion of books that children have read this week. Focus on the week's comprehension skills.

Word Work

On Day 5, children review and extend the phonics/decoding and word skills practiced during the week.

Small-Group Options

As needed, additional instruction is provided for Extra Support and English Language Learners on Day 5. Have these groups also participate in the Literature Circles.

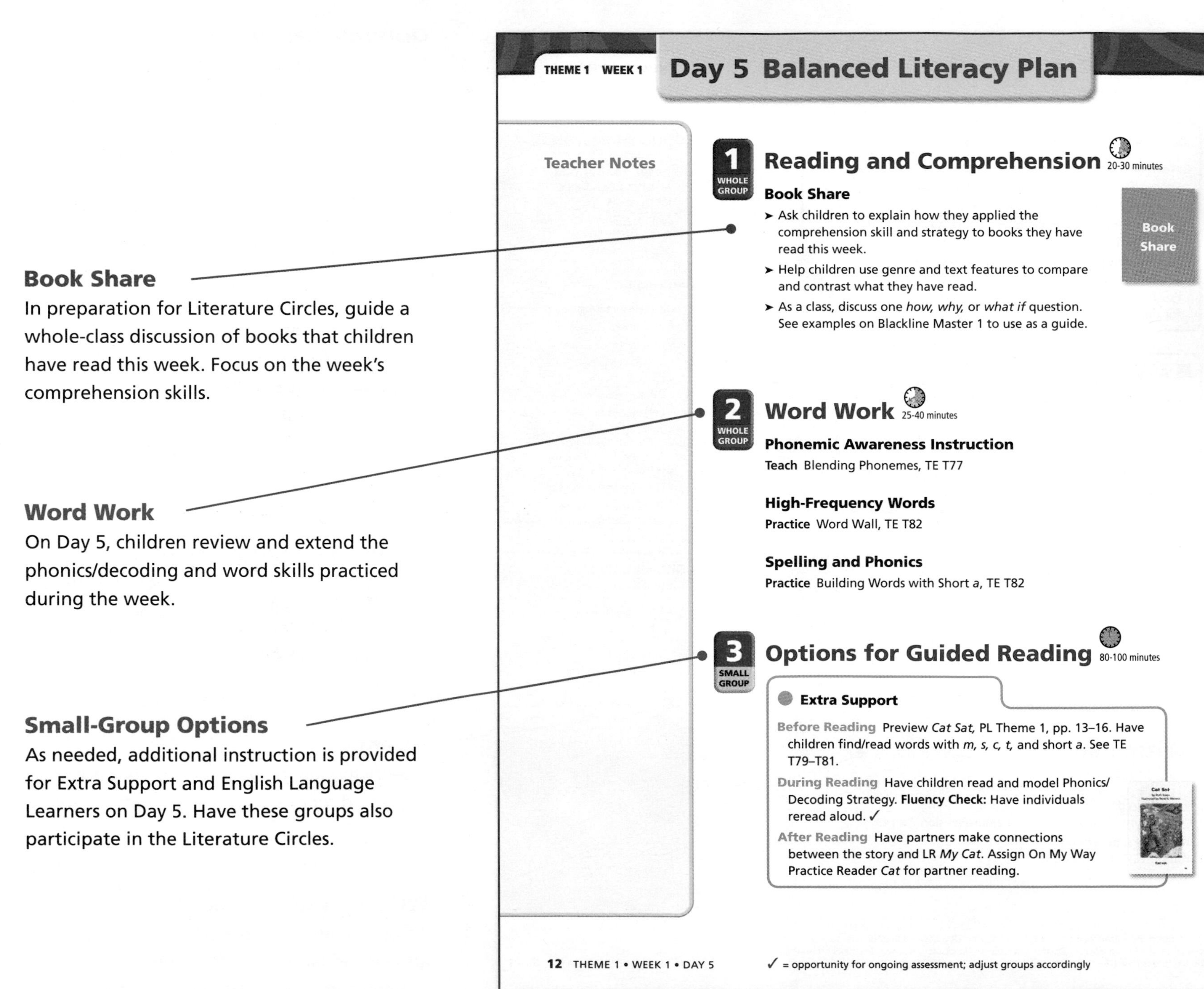

THEME 1 WEEK 1 **Day 5 Balanced Literacy Plan**

Teacher Notes

1 WHOLE GROUP **Reading and Comprehension** 20-30 minutes

Book Share

- Ask children to explain how they applied the comprehension skill and strategy to books they have read this week.
- Help children use genre and text features to compare and contrast what they have read.
- As a class, discuss one *how, why,* or *what if* question. See examples on Blackline Master 1 to use as a guide.

Book Share

2 WHOLE GROUP **Word Work** 25-40 minutes

Phonemic Awareness Instruction
Teach Blending Phonemes, TE T77

High-Frequency Words
Practice Word Wall, TE T82

Spelling and Phonics
Practice Building Words with Short *a*, TE T82

3 SMALL GROUP **Options for Guided Reading** 80-100 minutes

Extra Support

Before Reading Preview *Cat Sat,* PL Theme 1, pp. 13–16. Have children find/read words with *m, s, c, t,* and short *a*. See TE T79–T81.

During Reading Have children read and model Phonics/Decoding Strategy. **Fluency Check:** Have individuals reread aloud. ✓

After Reading Have partners make connections between the story and LR *My Cat*. Assign On My Way Practice Reader *Cat* for partner reading.

12 THEME 1 • WEEK 1 • DAY 5

✓ = opportunity for ongoing assessment; adjust groups accordingly

◆ **English Language Learners**

Before Reading Review LR *10 Cats,* TE T87.

During Reading Coach rereading of book. **Fluency Check:** Have individuals reread aloud. ✓

After Reading Help children summarize LR story events in sequence. Have children draw/caption a picture about a book they read this week. ✓

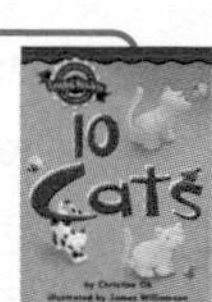
Label Book

●▲■◆ **Mixed Ability Levels**

Literature Circles Form small, mixed-ability groups. Ask groups to discuss the main Anthology selection, Link, Leveled Readers, and other books they have read this week. Pose questions or topics for each group, and circulate among groups to offer support. Suggested group activities:

- Respond to specific Literature Discussion questions on Blackline Master 13.
- Discuss story or text elements, authors' choice of language, and/or illustrations.
- Connect book topics or themes to personal experiences or other reading.

Literature Circle

Writing and Language

30-40 minutes

Writing

Practice Assign Writing Prompt, TE T77.

Grammar

Review Using Capital Letters, TE T83

Viewing

Practice Compare and Contrast, TE T83

Optional Resources

Teacher Read Aloud
Choose a nonfiction book related to Social Studies or Science unit.

Independent Work

Self-Selected Reading
Choose from
- classroom/school library
- Leveled Bibliography, TE T6–T7
- children's magazines
- consumer texts such as maps, recipes, charts

Centers
- Classroom Management Kit
- Classroom Management activities, TE T28–T29
- Responding activities, TE T63

Differentiated Instruction
- Vocabulary: Speed Drill, TE T76
- Comprehension Review: sequence TET78

End-of-Week Assessment
- Weekly Skills Tests for Theme 1, Week 1
- Fluency Assessment, *Cat Sat,* PL Theme 1, pp. 13–16, TE T79–T81
- Alternative Assessment, Teacher's Resource Blackline Master 12

TE = Teacher Edition; PB = Practice Book; Tr = Transparency; LR = Leveled Reader; PL = Phonics Library; VR = Vocabulary Reader; VR Guide = Vocabulary Readers Teacher's Manual; LBB = Little Big Book; TP = Theme Paperback

Independent Work

As you meet with small groups each day, provide these activities for other children to complete independently, cooperatively, and creatively.

Literature Circles

Vary your Guided Reading groups to form several Literature Circles, mixing ability levels within each group. Encourage each child to contribute to a discussion of books read this week. Suggest questions and circulate to offer guidance, or have each group meet separately so you can guide and observe.

Differentiated Instruction

To address children's varying needs and strengths, choose among these options for reteaching or extending skills.

Assessment

In addition to ongoing comprehension and fluency checks, end-of-week assessments focus on targeted skills. The new Phonics Library story provides an additional fluency check. Use the results to modify further instruction.

Theme 1 Overview

	Week 1
Reading and Comprehension	**Shared Reading** Main Selection: *Mac the Cat* Science Link: "Pet Cats and Big Cats" Book Share **Comprehension** Strategy: Predict/Infer Skill: Sequence Content Skill: How to Read a Science Article
Word Work	**Phonemic Awareness:** Blending Phonemes **Phonics:** Kindergarten Review: *m, s, c, t* **Phonics:** Short *a*/Blending Short *a* Words (VC, CVC) **Kindergarten Review:** Alphabet Letters **Vocabulary:** Names for Animals; Animal Sounds **High-Frequency Words:** *go, the, on* **Spelling and Phonics:** Kindergarten Review: Words with *m, s, c, t,* and Short *a*
Options for Guided Reading	**Big Book** *I Am Six* **Vocabulary Reader** *Cats* **Leveled Readers:** Extra Support: *My Cat* On Level: *Cat and Dog* Above Level: *Supper for Cal* ELL: *10 Cats* **Phonics Library** *Tam Cat* *Cat on the Mat* *Cat Sat* **Theme Paperbacks** **Literature Circles**
Writing and Oral Language	**Shared Writing:** A Class Story **Interactive Writing:** A Class Story **Independent Writing:** Writing About Animals **Grammar:** Using Capital Letters **Listening:** Listening Comprehension **Viewing:** Compare and Contrast
Assessment Options	• Weekly Skills Test for Theme 1, Week 1 • Fluency Assessment: Phonics Library

- Use **Back to School** to review Kindergarten skills, introduce strategies, diagnose children's needs, and plan instruction.
- Use **Launching the Theme** on pages T16–T17 of the Teacher's Edition to introduce the theme.

Week 2

Shared Reading
Main Selection: *A Day at School*
Poetry Link: "School"
Book Share

Comprehension
Strategy: Summarize
Skill: Compare and Contrast
Content Skill: How to Read Poetry

Phonemic Awareness: Blending Phonemes
Phonics: Kindergarten Review: *n, f, p*
Phonics: Short *a*/Blending Short *a* Words (VC, CVC)
Kindergarten Review: Words with *a, c, m, s, t*
Vocabulary: Rhyming Words; School Words
High-Frequency Words: *and, here, jump, not, too, we*
Spelling and Phonics: Words with *n, f, p,* and Short *a*

Big Book
Ten Dogs in the Window

Vocabulary Reader
At School

Leveled Readers:
Extra Support: *Nat, Nan, and Pam*
On Level: *Fun, Fun, Fun*
Above Level: *Meet the Feet*
ELL: *Colors*

Phonics Library
Nan Cat
Fat Cat
Tap Tap

Literature Circles

Shared Writing: Writing About a Topic
Interactive Writing: A Class Story
Independent Writing: Writing About School
Grammar: Beginning Sentences with Capital Letters
Viewing: Using Nonverbal Cues
Listening: Listening to a Story

- Weekly Skills Test for Theme 1, Week 2
- Fluency Assessment: Phonics Library

Week 3

Shared Reading
Main Selection: *Pigs in a Rig*
Social Studies Link: "Let's Go to the Fair"
Book Share

Comprehension
Strategy: Evaluate
Skill: Cause and Effect
Content Skill: How to Read

Phonemic Awareness: Blending Phonemes
Phonics: Kindergarten Review: *b, r, h, g*
Phonics: Short *i*/Blending Short *i* Words (VC/CVC)
Kindergarten Review: Words with Short *a*
Vocabulary: Shape Words; Words for Feelings
High-Frequency Words: *a, find, have, one, to, who*
Spelling and Phonics: Kindergarten Review: Words with *b, r, h, g,* and Short *i*

Big Book
Charles Tiger

Vocabulary Reader
Sit, Pig!

Leveled Readers:
Extra Support: *Pat and Pig*
On Level: *Gram's Hat*
Above Level: *Kit Finds a Mitt*
ELL: *Here Is Hen*

Phonics Library
Can It Fit?
Who Can Hit?
On Big Fat Fig

Literature Circles

Shared Writing: A Class Story
Interactive Writing: A Class Story
Independent Writing: Creating a New Ending
Grammar: Using Punctuation
Listening and Speaking: Choral Reading
Listening and Speaking: Singing Songs

- Weekly Skills Test, Theme 1, Week 3
- Fluency Assessment: Phonics Library

Day 1 Balanced Literacy Plan

Teacher Notes

Reading and Comprehension

20-30 minutes

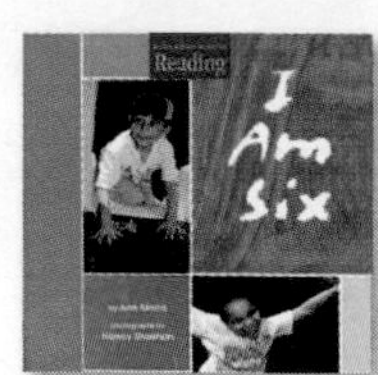

Shared Reading of Daily Message, TE T30

Shared Reading of Big Book

- Introduce Comprehension Strategy and Skill:
  Predict/Infer, TE T32
  Sequence, TE T33
- Read aloud *I Am Six*, TE T32–T35.

Word Work

25-40 minutes

Phonemic Awareness/Phonics Instruction

Teach Blending Phonemes, TE T31, T37

Review/Practice Consonants *m, s, c, t,* TE T36; assign PB 35–37.

Teach Short *a*/Blending Short *a* Words (VC, CVC), TE T37–T38

Practice Assign PB 38–39.

Spelling/Phonics: Kindergarten Review

Teach Letters *m, s,* TE T42

Practice Assign PB 40.

Vocabulary: Kindergarten Review

Teach Word Wall: *at, an, bug, wet,* TE T42

Options for Guided Reading

80-100 minutes

Extra Support

Before Reading Preview *Tam Cat,* PL Theme 1, pp. 5–8. Model Phonics/Decoding Strategy. See TE T39–T41.

During Reading Coach as children read story.

After Reading Discuss story; have children find/read words with *m, s, c, t,* and short *a*. **Fluency Modeling:** Model fluent reading. Have partners reread story.

✓ = opportunity for ongoing assessment; adjust groups accordingly

▲ On Level

Before Reading Preview *Tam Cat*, PL Theme 1, pp. 5–8. Model Phonics/Decoding Strategy. See TE T39–T41.

During Reading Have children begin story. **Fluency Modeling:** Model Phonics/Decoding Strategy and fluent reading.

After Reading Have children retell story so far and find/read words with *m, s, c, t,* and short *a*. **Fluency Practice:** Have partners finish story and reread for fluency.

■ Above Level

Before Reading Preview LR *Supper for Cal,* TE T86. Have students model the Predict/Infer Strategy.

During Reading Have children read first half of story. **Fluency Modeling:** Model fluent reading.

After Reading Have children finish reading and write answers to Responding questions. ✓

Level H

◆ English Language Learners

Before Reading Preview VR *Cats*. See VR Guide, p. 6.

During Reading **Fluency Modeling:** Read aloud each page; have children do echo reading.

After Reading Discuss Responding pages. Have children reread with partners or audio CD.

Level A

4 WHOLE GROUP

Writing and Language

25-40 minutes

Writing

Teach Shared Writing: A Class Story, TE T43

Practice Assign Writing Prompt, TE T31.

Listening

Teach Listening Comprehension, TE T43

Optional Resources

Teacher Read Aloud

Reread Big Book: *I Am Six,* TE T32–T35.

Read *The Strong Bunch of Sticks,* TE T17–T19.

Independent Work

Self-Selected Reading

Choose from

- classroom/school library
- Leveled Bibliography, TE T6–T7
- *I Love Reading,* Theme 1, take-home book 1
- Little Readers for Guided Reading

Centers

- Classroom Management Kit
- Classroom Management activities, TE T28–T29

Differentiated Instruction

- Phonics Reteaching or Extension:
  - –Consonants *m, s, c, t,* TE R14–R15
  - –Short *a*/Blending Short *a* Words, TE R16–R17
- High-Frequency Words Review: Word Wall, TE T30

TE = Teacher Edition; PB = Practice Book; Tr = Transparency; LR = Leveled Reader; PL = Phonics Library; VR = Vocabulary Reader; VR Guide = Vocabulary Readers Teacher's Manual; LBB = Little Big Book; TP = Theme Paperback

Day 2 Balanced Literacy Plan

Teacher Notes

Reading and Comprehension

Shared Reading of Get Set Story

➤ Build Background and Vocabulary, TE T48

➤ Read *On the Go!* Anthology pp. 13–19.

▼ Anthology Selection

Words to Know

go
on
the
cat
sat

Comprehension Skill Instruction

Teach Sequence, TE T50

Word Work

25-40 minutes

Phonemic Awareness

Teach Blending Phonemes, TE T45

High-Frequency Words

go
on
the

High-Frequency Words Instruction

Teach TE T46–T47, Tr 1-1; Practice PB 41.

Spelling and Phonics: Kindergarten Review

Teach Letters *c, t,* TE T52; Practice PB 42.

Vocabulary: Kindergarten Review

Practice Building Words, TE T52

Options for Guided Reading

Extra Support

Before Reading Preview VR *Cats*. See VR Guide, p. 6.

During Reading Read the book together; coach reading. Help children apply Predict/Infer Strategy.

After Reading Discuss the book and Responding questions. **Fluency Practice:** Have children reread VR with a partner. Assign *Cat on the Mat,* PL Theme 1, pp. 9–12, for partner reading.

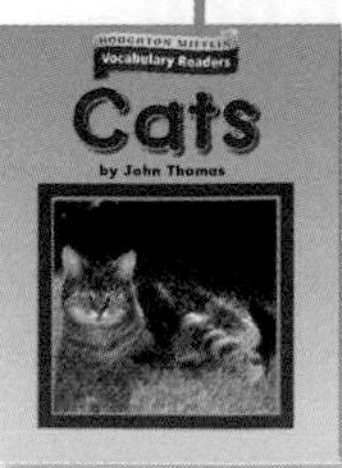

Level A

✓ = opportunity for ongoing assessment; adjust groups accordingly

▲ On Level

Before Reading Discuss PL *Tam Cat,* TE T40. Preview LR *Cat and Dog,* TE T85.

During Reading Coach reading as children begin story. **Fluency Modeling:** Model fluent reading, then have children model it. ✓

After Reading Discuss the sequence of events in the story. Then have children write answers to Responding questions. ✓ Assign *Cat on the Mat,* PL Theme 1, pp. 9–12, for partner reading.

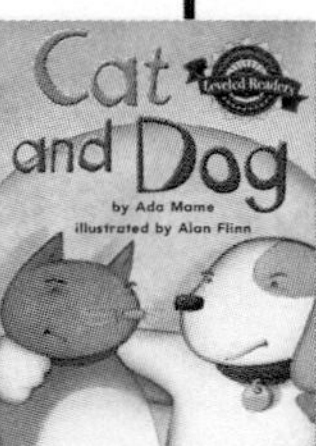

Level A

■ Above Level

Before Reading Have children model the Predict/Infer Strategy and discuss Responding questions for LR *Supper for Cal,* TE T86.

During Reading **Fluency Check:** Monitor children's oral reading. ✓

After Reading Have children summarize for a partner, telling story events in order. Assign *Cat on the Mat,* PL Theme 1, pp. 9–12, for partner reading.

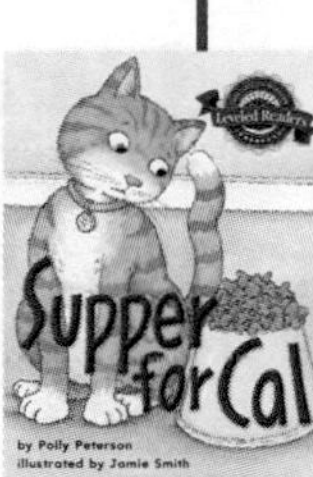

Level H

◆ English Language Learners

Before Reading To review VR vocabulary, have children demonstrate or give examples. See VR Guide, p. 6.

During Reading **Fluency Practice:** Have children reread book. Option: Preview and coach reading of *Tam Cat,* PL Theme 1, pp. 5–8, TE T39–T41.

After Reading Help children summarize VR. Have partners discuss, draw, or write facts they learned. ✓

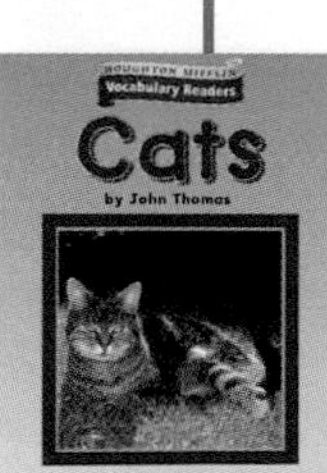

Level A

4 WHOLE GROUP Writing and Language

25-40 minutes

Writing

Teach Interactive Writing: A Class Story, TE T53

Practice Assign Writing Prompt, TE T45.

Optional Resources

Teacher Read Aloud

Reread Big Book: *I Am Six,* TE T32–T35.

Independent Work

Self-Selected Reading

Choose from

- classroom/school library
- Leveled Bibliography, TE T6–T7
- *I Love Reading,* Theme 1, take-home book 1
- Little Readers for Guided Reading

Centers

- Classroom Management Kit
- Classroom Management activities, TE T28–T29

Differentiated Instruction

- High-Frequency Words
  –Word Wall, TE T112
  –Reteaching or Extension, TE R26–R27

TE = Teacher Edition; PB = Practice Book; Tr = Transparency; LR = Leveled Reader; PL = Phonics Library; VR = Vocabulary Reader; VR Guide = Vocabulary Readers Teacher's Manual; LBB = Little Big Book; TP = Theme Paperback

Day 3 Balanced Literacy Plan

Teacher Notes

Reading and Comprehension

20-30 minutes

Shared Reading of *Mac the Cat*

▼ Anthology Selection

Mac the Cat

- Set Purpose; Review Comprehension Strategy and Skill, TE T56–T57
- Read Anthology Selection pp. 22–31 (independent, partner, or audio CD).
- Discuss questions; retell the story, TE T63.

Comprehension Skill Instruction

Teach Sequence, TE T64–T65, Tr 1-2

Practice Assign PB 45.

Words to Know

New This Week

go	cat
on	sat
the	

Kindergarten Review

a	bat
and	can
have	get
is	hug
my	jam
see	lap

Word Work

25-40 minutes

Phonemic Awareness Instruction

Teach Blending Phonemes, TE T55

Spelling and Phonics Instruction

Teach Words with Short *a,* TE T66

Vocabulary Instruction

Teach Names for Animals, TE T66

Options for Guided Reading

80-100 minutes

● Extra Support

Before Reading Review Responding questions from VR *Cats*. Preview LR *My Cat,* TE T84. Have children model Predict/Infer.

During Reading Coach as children read story. **Fluency Modeling:** Model fluent reading; have children model.

After Reading **Fluency Practice:** Have partners reread story. Have children answer Responding questions. ✓

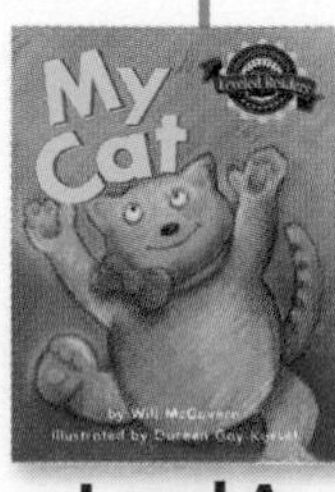

Level A

✓ = opportunity for ongoing assessment; adjust groups accordingly

▲ On Level

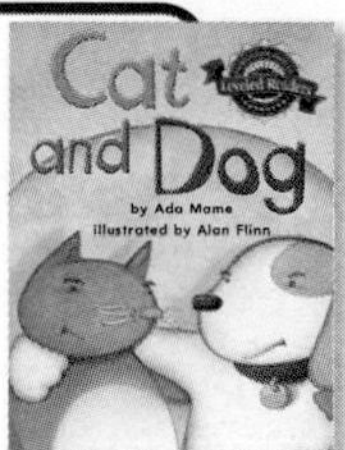
Level A

Before Reading Discuss Responding questions for LR *Cat and Dog,* TE T85.

During Reading **Fluency Check:** Ask individuals to read story aloud. ✓

After Reading Have children summarize story for a partner, telling events in order.

■ Above Level

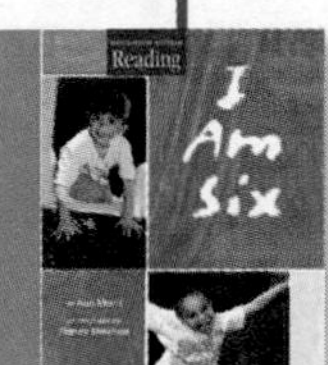
Level D

Before Reading Review LBB *I Am Six.* See TE T32–T35, R4–R5.

During Reading **Fluency Modeling:** Model fluent reading, then have children model it. Have them read first half of story independently.

After Reading Ask questions; have children cite text to support answers. Have partners summarize story events in order.

◆ English Language Learners

Before Reading Preview *Cat on the Mat,* PL Theme 1, pp. 9–12. Model Phonics/Decoding Strategy.

During Reading **Fluency Modeling:** Read aloud each page; have children do echo reading.

After Reading Discuss story; help children find/read words with short *a* and consonants *m, s, c, t.* Have children use illustrations to retell story to partners.

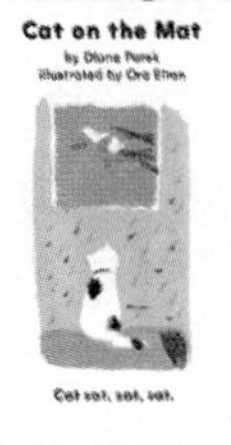

Writing and Language

30-40 minutes

Writing

Practice Assign Write a Label, Anthology p. 33.

Grammar

Teach Using Capital Letters, TE T67

Optional Resources

Teacher Read Aloud

Choose a book from your class/school library or from the Leveled Bibliography, TE T6–T7.

Suggestion: *Swimmy* by Leo Lionni

Independent Work

Self-Selected Reading

Choose from

- classroom/school library
- Leveled Bibliography, TE T6–T7
- *I Love Reading,* Theme 1, take-home book 1
- Little Readers for Guided Reading

Centers

- Classroom Management Kit
- Classroom Management activities, TE T28–T29
- Responding activities, TE T63

Differentiated Instruction

- Comprehension Reteaching and Extension: Sequence, TE R32–R33
- High-Frequency Word Review: Word Wall, TE T54

TE = Teacher Edition; PB = Practice Book; Tr = Transparency; LR = Leveled Reader; PL = Phonics Library; VR = Vocabulary Reader; VR Guide = Vocabulary Readers Teacher's Manual; LBB = Little Big Book; TP = Theme Paperback

Day 4 Balanced Literacy Plan

Teacher Notes

Reading and Comprehension

20-30 minutes

Shared Reading of Science Link

- "Pet Cats and Big Cats," Anthology pp. 34–37, TE T70–T71 (independent, partner, or group)
- Skill: How to Read a Science Article, TE T70
- Introduce Concept Vocabulary, TE T70.

Concept Vocabulary

lions
tigers
leopard
cubs

Word Work

25-40 minutes

Phonemic Awareness/Phonics Instruction

Teach Blending Phonemes, TE T69

Review Alphabet Letters, TE T72; Matching Letters, TE T73

Spelling and Phonics

Practice Word Slides with Short *a*, TE T74

Vocabulary Instruction

Teach Animal Sounds, TE T74

3 SMALL GROUP

Options for Guided Reading

80-100 minutes

Extra Support

Before Reading Review Responding questions for LR *My Cat,* TE T84.

During Reading Have children reread story. **Fluency Check:** Have individuals read aloud. ✓

After Reading Model using the words *first, next,* and *last* to summarize story events. Have children retell the story to a partner.

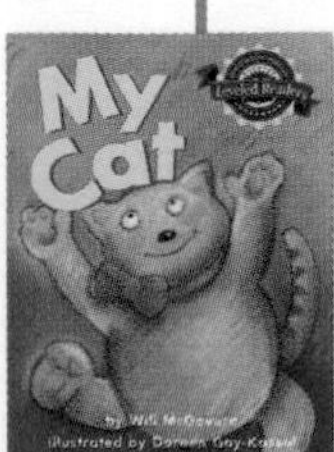

Level A

✓ = opportunity for ongoing assessment; adjust groups accordingly

▲ On Level

Before Reading Have children summarize LR *Cat and Dog,* telling story events in sequence. ✓ Preview a teacher-selected book or TP *Bear Play,* TE R3. Have children make predictions about the story.

During Reading Have children begin story and model Phonics/Decoding Strategy.

After Reading Discuss the story so far. Have children finish story.

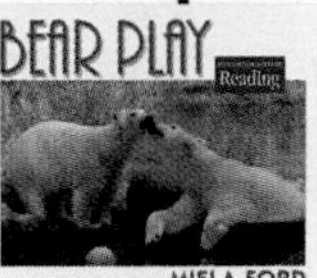

Level D

■ Above Level

Before Reading Review first half of LBB *I Am Six,* TE T32–T33.

During Reading Have children finish book.

After Reading Discuss how book connects to theme. Have children write journal entries to connect it to personal experience or other reading.

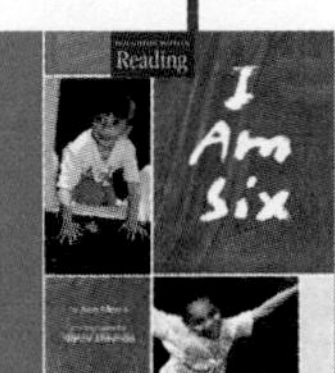

Level D

◆ English Language Learners

Before Reading Build background and preview LR *10 Cats,* TE T87. Have children make predictions about the story.

During Reading Share story. **Fluency Modeling:** Review each page; have children discuss it. Reinforce Phonics/Decoding Strategy.

After Reading Discuss Responding questions, TE T87. **Fluency Practice:** Have children retell to partners or listen to the audio CD.

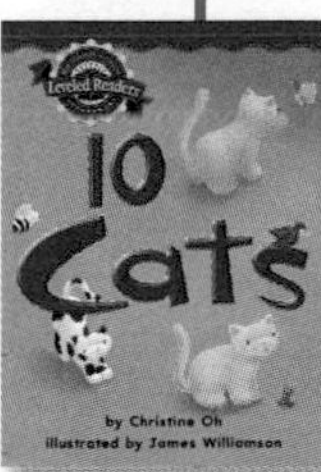

Label Book

4 WHOLE GROUP

Writing and Language

30-40 minutes

Writing

Practice Independent Writing: Writing About Animals; assign PB 47.

Optional Resources

Teacher Read Aloud

Continue selected Read Aloud book from Day 3 or choose a new one from your class or school library.

Independent Work

Self-Selected Reading

Choose from

- classroom/school library
- Leveled Bibliography, TE T6–T7
- children's magazines
- *I Love Reading,* Theme 1, take-home book 1
- Little Readers for Guided Reading

Centers

- Classroom Management Kit
- Classroom Management activities, TE T28–T29
- Responding activities, TE T63

Differentiated Instruction

- Visual Literacy: Using Photographs, TE T71
- High-Frequency Words: Word Wall, TE T68
- Study Skills: Parts of a Book, TE R38

TE = Teacher Edition; PB = Practice Book; Tr = Transparency; LR = Leveled Reader; PL = Phonics Library; VR = Vocabulary Reader; VR Guide = Vocabulary Readers Teacher's Manual; LBB = Little Big Book; TP = Theme Paperback

Day 5 Balanced Literacy Plan

Teacher Notes

Reading and Comprehension

20-30 minutes

Book Share

- Ask children to explain how they applied the comprehension skill and strategy to books they have read this week.
- Help children use genre and text features to compare and contrast what they have read.
- As a class, discuss one *how, why,* or *what if* question. See examples on Blackline Master 1 to use as a guide.

Word Work

25-40 minutes

Phonemic Awareness Instruction

Teach Blending Phonemes, TE T77

High-Frequency Words

Practice Word Wall/Vocabulary Speed Drill, TE T82

Spelling and Phonics

Practice Building Words with Short *a*, TE T82

Options for Guided Reading

80-100 minutes

Extra Support

Before Reading Preview *Cat Sat,* PL Theme 1, pp. 13–16. Have children find/read words with *m, s, c, t,* and short *a*. See TE T79–T81.

During Reading Have children read and model Phonics/Decoding Strategy. **Fluency Check:** Have individuals reread aloud. ✓

After Reading Have partners make connections between the story and LR *My Cat*. Assign On My Way Practice Reader *Cat* for partner reading.

✓ = opportunity for ongoing assessment; adjust groups accordingly

English Language Learners

Before Reading Review LR *10 Cats,* TE T87.

During Reading Coach retelling of book. **Fluency Check:** Have individuals describe a page. ✓

After Reading Help children share personal responses to LR. Have children draw/caption a picture about a book they read this week. ✓

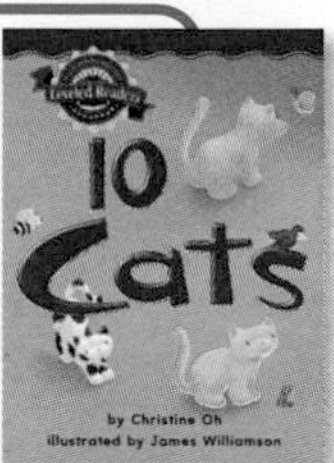

Label Book

Mixed Ability Levels

Literature Circles Form small, mixed-ability groups. Ask groups to discuss the main Anthology selection, Link, Leveled Readers, and other books they have read this week. Pose questions or topics for each group, and circulate among groups to offer support. Suggested group activities:

- Respond to specific Literature Discussion questions on Blackline Master 1.
- Discuss story or text elements, authors' choice of language, and/or illustrations.
- Connect book topics or themes to personal experiences or other reading.

Writing and Language

30-40 minutes

Writing

Practice Assign Writing Prompt, TE T77.

Grammar

Review Using Capital Letters, TE T83

Viewing

Practice Compare and Contrast, TE T83

Optional Resources

Teacher Read Aloud

Choose a nonfiction book related to Social Studies or Science unit.

Independent Work

Self-Selected Reading

Choose from

- classroom/school library
- Leveled Bibliography, TE T6–T7
- children's magazines
- consumer texts such as maps, recipes, charts

Centers

- Classroom Management Kit
- Classroom Management activities, TE T28–T29
- Responding activities, TE T63

Differentiated Instruction

- Vocabulary: Speed Drill, TE T76
- Comprehension Review: sequence TET78

End-of-Week Assessment

- Weekly Skills Tests for Theme 1, Week 1
- Fluency Assessment, *Cat Sat,* PL Theme 1, pp. 13–16, TE T79–T81
- Alternative Assessment, Teacher's Resource Blackline Master 12

TE = Teacher Edition; PB = Practice Book; Tr = Transparency; LR = Leveled Reader; PL = Phonics Library; VR = Vocabulary Reader; VR Guide = Vocabulary Readers Teacher's Manual; LBB = Little Big Book; TP = Theme Paperback

Day 1 Balanced Literacy Plan

Teacher Notes

Reading and Comprehension

20-30 minutes

Shared Reading of Daily Message, TE T98

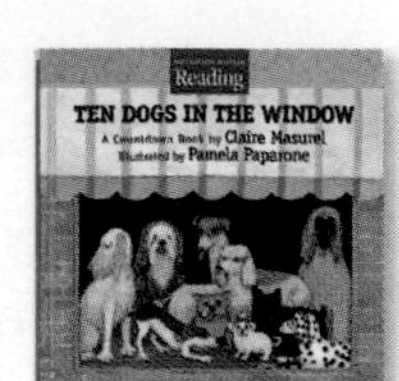

Shared Reading of Big Book

- Introduce Comprehension Strategy and Skill:
  Summarize, TE T100
  Compare and Contrast, TE T101
- Read aloud *Ten Dogs in the Window,* TE T100–T103.

Word Work

25-40 minutes

Phonemic Awareness/Phonics Instruction

Teach Blending Phonemes, TE T99, T105

Review/Practice Consonants *n, f, p,* TE T104; assign PB 48–50.

Teach Short *a*/Blending Short *a* Words (VC, CVC), TE T105–T106

Practice Assign PB 51–52.

Spelling/Phonics: Kindergarten Review

Teach Letters *f, n,* TE T110

Practice Assign PB 53.

Vocabulary: Kindergarten Review

Teach Word Wall: *hen, cut,* TE T110

Options for Guided Reading

80-100 minutes

Extra Support

Before Reading Preview *Nan Cat,* PL Theme 1, pp. 17–20. Model Phonics/Decoding Strategy. See TE T107–T109.

During Reading Coach as children read story.

After Reading Discuss story; have children find/read words with *n, f, p,* and short *a.* **Fluency Modeling:** Model fluent reading. Have partners reread story.

✓ = opportunity for ongoing assessment; adjust groups accordingly

 **On Level**

Before Reading Preview *Nan Cat,* PL Theme 1, pp. 17–20. Model Phonics/Decoding Strategy. See TE T107–T109.

During Reading Have children begin story. **Fluency Modeling:** Model Phonics/Decoding Strategy and fluent reading.

After Reading Have children retell story so far and find/read words with *n, f, p,* and short *a.* **Fluency Practice:** Have partners finish story and reread for fluency.

Above Level

Before Reading Preview LR *Meet the Feet,* TE T158. Have students model the Summarize Strategy.

During Reading Have children read first half of story. **Fluency Modeling:** Model fluent reading.

After Reading Have children finish reading and write answers to Responding questions. ✓

Level J

 **English Language Learners**

Before Reading Preview VR *At School.* See VR Guide, p. 7.

During Reading **Fluency Modeling:** Read aloud each page; have children do echo reading.

After Reading Discuss Responding pages. Have children reread with partners or audio CD.

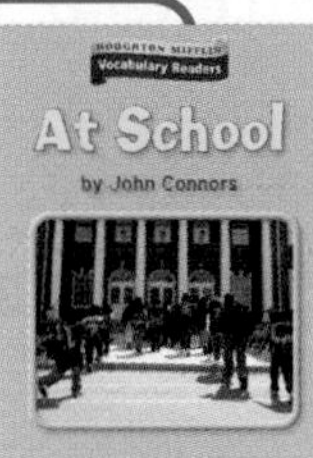

Level B

Optional Resources

Teacher Read Aloud

Reread Big Book: *Ten Dogs in the Window,* TE T100–T103.

Independent Work

Self-Selected Reading

Choose from

- classroom/school library
- Leveled Bibliography, TE T6–T7
- *I Love Reading,* Theme 1, take-home books 2–4
- Little Readers for Guided Reading

Centers

- Classroom Management Kit
- Classroom Management activities, TE T96–T97

Differentiated Instruction

- Phonics Reteaching or Extension:
  - –Consonants *n, f, p,* TE R18–R19
  - –Short *a*/Blending Short *a* Words (VC, CVC), TE R20–R21
- High-Frequency Words Review: Word Wall, TE T98

Writing and Language

 25-40 minutes

Writing

Teach Shared Writing: Writing About a Topic, TE T111

Practice Assign Writing Prompt, TE T99.

Viewing

Teach Using Nonverbal Cues, TE T111

TE = Teacher Edition; PB = Practice Book; Tr = Transparency; LR = Leveled Reader; PL = Phonics Library; VR = Vocabulary Reader; VR Guide = Vocabulary Readers Teacher's Manual; LBB = Little Big Book; TP = Theme Paperback

Day 2 Balanced Literacy Plan

Teacher Notes

Reading and Comprehension

20-30 minutes

▼ Anthology Selection

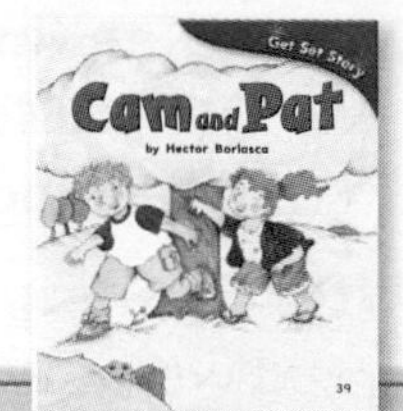

Shared Reading of Get Set Story

- Build Background and Vocabulary, TE T116
- Read *Cam and Pat,* Anthology pp. 40–45.

Comprehension Skill Instruction

Teach Compare and Contrast, TE T118

Words to Know

and	can
here	fan
jump	nap
not	Pat
too	tap
we	

Word Work

25-40 minutes

Phonemic Awareness

Teach Blending Phonemes, TE T113

High-Frequency Words Instruction

Teach TE T114, Tr 1-5; **Practice** PB 54–55.

High-Frequency Words

and	not
here	too
jump	we

Spelling and Phonics: Kindergarten Review

Teach Letter *p,* TE T120; **Practice** PB 57.

Vocabulary: Kindergarten Review

Practice Building Words, TE T120

Options for Guided Reading

80-100 minutes

● Extra Support

Before Reading Preview VR *At School.* See VR Guide, p. 7.

During Reading Read the book together; coach reading. Help children apply Summarize Strategy.

After Reading Discuss the book and Responding questions. **Fluency Practice:** Have children reread VR with a partner. Assign *Fat Cat,* PL Theme 1, pp. 21–24, for partner reading.

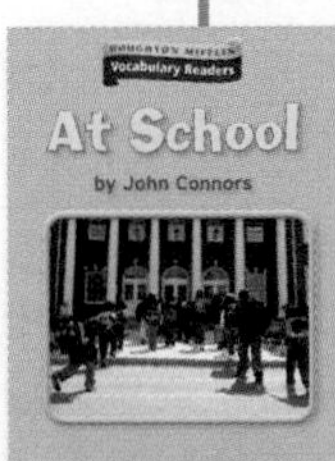

Level B

✓ = opportunity for ongoing assessment; adjust groups accordingly

▲ On Level

Before Reading Discuss PL *Nan Cat,* TE T107. Preview LR *Fun, Fun, Fun,* TE T157.

During Reading Coach reading as children begin story. **Fluency Modeling:** Model fluent reading, then have children model it.

After Reading Discuss the sequence of events in the story. Then have children write answers to Responding questions. ✓ Assign *Fat Cat,* PL Theme 1, pp. 21–24, for partner reading.

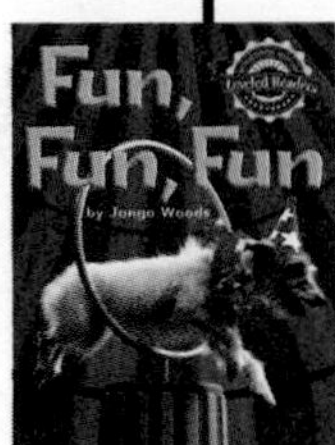

Level C

■ Above Level

Before Reading Have children model the Summarize Strategy and discuss Responding questions for LR *Meet the Feet,* TE T158.

During Reading **Fluency Check:** Monitor children's oral reading. ✓

After Reading Have children summarize for a partner, telling story events in order. Assign *Fat Cat,* PL Theme 1, pp. 21–24, for partner reading.

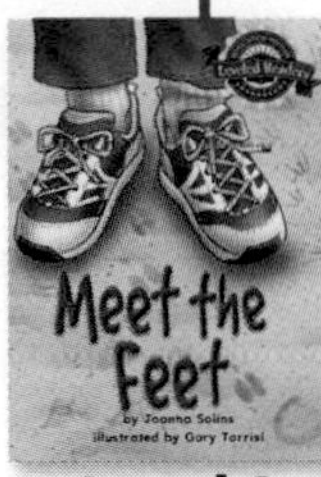

Level J

◆ English Language Learners

Before Reading To review VR vocabulary, have children demonstrate or give examples. See VR Guide, p. 7.

During Reading **Fluency Practice:** Have children reread book. Option: Preview and coach reading of *Nan Cat,* PL Theme 1, pp. 17–20, TE T107–T109.

After Reading Help children summarize VR. Have partners discuss, draw, or write facts they learned. ✓

Level B

4 WHOLE GROUP

Writing and Language  25-40 minutes

Writing

Teach Interactive Writing: A Class Story, TE T121

Practice Assign Writing Prompt, TE T113.

Optional Resources

Teacher Read Aloud

Reread Big Book: *Ten Dogs in the Window,* TE T100–T103.

Independent Work

Self-Selected Reading

Choose from

- classroom/school library
- Leveled Bibliography, TE T6–T7
- *I Love Reading,* Theme 1, take-home books 2–4
- Little Readers for Guided Reading

Centers

- Classroom Management Kit
- Classroom Management activities, TE T96–T97

Differentiated Instruction

- High-Frequency Words
  - –Word Wall, TE T112
  - –Reteaching or Extension, TE R28–R29

TE = Teacher Edition; PB = Practice Book; Tr = Transparency; LR = Leveled Reader; PL = Phonics Library; VR = Vocabulary Reader; VR Guide = Vocabulary Readers Teacher's Manual; LBB = Little Big Book; TP = Theme Paperback

Day 3 Balanced Literacy Plan

Teacher Notes

Reading and Comprehension

Shared Reading of *A Day at School*

- Introduce Key Vocabulary, TE T124, Tr 1-6
  add, read, sing, playground, school, teacher
- Set Purpose; Review Comprehension Strategy and Skill, TE T124–T125
- Read Anthology Selection pp. 47–63 (independent, partner, or audio CD).
- Discuss questions; retell the story, TE T135.

▼ **Anthology Selection**

A Day at School

Words to Know

New This Week

and	can
here	fan
jump	nap
not	pat
too	tap
we	

Kindergarten Review

a	to
have	cut
is	Jen
like	let
play	

Comprehension Skill Instruction

Teach Compare and Contrast, TE T136–T137, Tr 1-7

Practice Assign PB 60.

Word Work

25-40 minutes

Phonemic Awareness Instruction

Teach Blending Phonemes, TE T123

Spelling and Phonics Instruction

Teach Words with Short *a,* TE T138

Vocabulary Instruction

Teach Rhyming Words, TE T138

3
SMALL GROUP

Options for Guided Reading

80-100 minutes

● Extra Support

Before Reading Review Responding questions from VR *At School.* Preview LR *Nat, Nan, and Pam,* TE T156. Have children model Summarize.

During Reading Coach as children read story. **Fluency Modeling:** Model fluent reading; have children model.

After Reading **Fluency Practice:** Have partners reread story. Have children answer Responding questions. ✓

Nat, Nan, and Pam

Level C

✓ = opportunity for ongoing assessment; adjust groups accordingly

 **On Level**

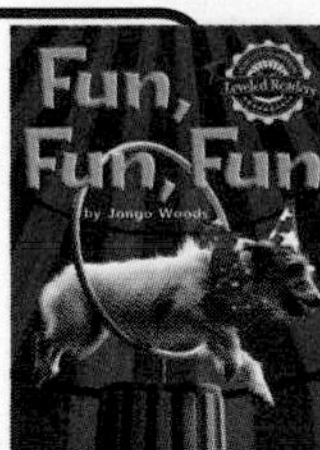

Level C

Before Reading Discuss Responding questions for LR *Fun, Fun, Fun,* TE T157.

During Reading **Fluency Check:** Ask individuals to read story aloud. ✓

After Reading Have children summarize story for a partner, telling events in order.

 **Above Level**

Level D

Before Reading Review LBB *Ten Dogs in the Window.* See TE T100–T103, R8–R9.

During Reading **Fluency Modeling:** Model fluent reading, then have children model it. Have them read first half of story independently.

After Reading Ask questions; have children cite text to support answers. Have partners summarize story events in order.

◆ **English Language Learners**

Before Reading Preview *Fat Cat,* PL Theme 1, pp. 21–24. Model Phonics/Decoding Strategy.

During Reading **Fluency Modeling:** Read aloud each page; have children do echo reading.

After Reading Discuss story; help children find/read words with *n, f, p,* and short *a.* Have children use illustrations to retell story to partners.

Writing and Language

 30-40 minutes

Writing

Practice Assign Write a List, Anthology p. 65.

Grammar

Teach Beginning Sentences with Capital Letters, TE T139

Optional Resources

Teacher Read Aloud

Choose a book from your class/school library or from the Leveled Bibliography, TE T6–T7.

- Suggestion: *Just a Little Bit* by Ann Tompert

Independent Work

Self-Selected Reading

Choose from

- classroom/school library
- Leveled Bibliography, TE T6–T7
- *I Love Reading,* Theme 1, take-home books 2–4
- Little Readers for Guided Reading

Centers

- Classroom Management Kit
- Classroom Management activities, TE T96–T97
- Responding activities, TE T134

Differentiated Instruction

- Comprehension Reteaching and Extension: Compare and Contrast, TE R34–R35
- High-Frequency Word Review: Word Wall, TE T122

TE = Teacher Edition; PB = Practice Book; Tr = Transparency; LR = Leveled Reader; PL = Phonics Library; VR = Vocabulary Reader; VR Guide = Vocabulary Readers Teacher's Manual; LBB = Little Big Book; TP = Theme Paperback

Day 4 Balanced Literacy Plan

Teacher Notes

Reading and Comprehension

Shared Reading of Poetry Link

- School poems, Anthology pp. 66–69, TE T142–T143 (independent, partner, or group)
- Skill: How to Read Poetry, TE T142
- Introduce Concept Vocabulary, TE T142.

Concept Vocabulary

wide
narrow
muddy
squish

Word Work

Phonemic Awareness/Phonics Instruction

Teach Blending Phonemes, TE T141

Review Consonants *m, s, c, t,* TE T144; Short *a* Words, TE T145

Spelling and Phonics

Practice Word Slides with Short *a*, TE T146

Vocabulary Instruction

Teach School Words, TE T146

3
SMALL
GROUP

Options for Guided Reading

80-100 minutes

Extra Support

Before Reading Review Responding questions for LR *Nat, Nan, and Pam,* TE T156.

During Reading Have children reread story. **Fluency Check:** Have individuals read aloud. ✓

After Reading Model using the words *first, next,* and *last* to summarize story events. Have children retell the story to a partner.

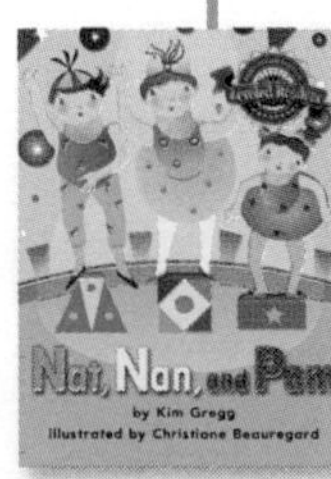

Level C

✓ = opportunity for ongoing assessment; adjust groups accordingly

▲ On Level

Before Reading Have children summarize LR *Fun, Fun, Fun,* telling story events in sequence. ✓ Preview a teacher-selected book or TP *Dan and Dan,* TE R7. Have children make predictions about the story.

During Reading Have children begin story and model Phonics/Decoding Strategy.

After Reading Discuss the story so far. Have children finish story.

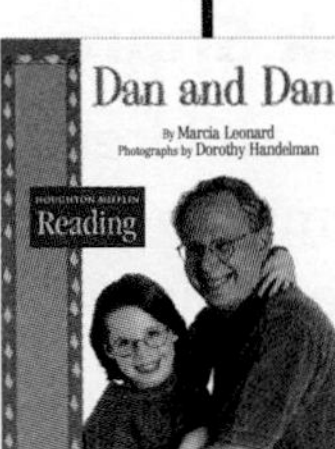

Level C

■ Above Level

Before Reading Review first half of LBB *Ten Dogs in the Window,* TE T100–T101.

During Reading Have children finish book.

After Reading Discuss how book connects to theme. Have children write journal entries to connect it to personal experience or other reading.

Level D

◆ English Language Learners

Before Reading Build background and preview LR *Colors,* TE T159. Have children point to various colors on the cover.

During Reading Share story. **Fluency Modeling:** Review each page; have children discuss it. Reinforce Phonics/Decoding Strategy.

After Reading Discuss Responding questions, TE T159. **Fluency Practice:** Have children retell to partners or listen to the audio CD.

Label Book

Writing and Language

30-40 minutes

Writing

Practice Independent Writing: Writing About School, TE T147; assign PB 61.

Optional Resources

Teacher Read Aloud

Continue selected Read Aloud book from Day 3 or choose a new one from your class or school library.

Independent Work

Self-Selected Reading

Choose from

- classroom/school library
- Leveled Bibliography, TE T6–T7
- children's magazines
- *I Love Reading,* Theme 1, take-home books 2–4
- Little Readers for Guided Reading

Centers

- Classroom Management Kit
- Classroom Management activities, TE T96–T97
- Responding activities, TE T134

Differentiated Instruction

- Genre: Rhyme in Poetry, TE T143
- High-Frequency Words: Word Wall, TE T140
- Study Skills: Parts of a Book, TE R38

TE = Teacher Edition; PB = Practice Book; Tr = Transparency; LR = Leveled Reader; PL = Phonics Library; VR = Vocabulary Reader; VR Guide = Vocabulary Readers Teacher's Manual; LBB = Little Big Book; TP = Theme Paperback

Day 5 Balanced Literacy Plan

Teacher Notes

Reading and Comprehension

20-30 minutes

Book Share

- Ask children to explain how they applied the comprehension skill and strategy to books they have read this week.
- Help children use genre and text features to compare and contrast what they have read.
- As a class, discuss one *how, why,* or *what if* question. See examples on Blackline Master 1 to use as a guide.

Word Work

25-40 minutes

Phonemic Awareness Instruction

Teach Blending Phonemes, TE T149

High-Frequency Words

Practice Word Wall/Vocabulary Speed Drill, TE T148

Spelling and Phonics

Practice Building Words with Short *a,* TE T154

Options for Guided Reading

80-100 minutes

● Extra Support

Before Reading Preview *Tap Tap,* PL Theme 1, pp. 25–28. Have children find/read words with *n, f, p,* and short *a*. See TE T151–T153.

During Reading Have children read and model Phonics/Decoding Strategy. **Fluency Check:** Have individuals reread aloud. ✓

After Reading Have partners make connections between the story and LR *Nat, Nan, and Pam.* Assign On My Way Practice Reader *Fan Cat Can Jump* for partner reading.

✓ = opportunity for ongoing assessment; adjust groups accordingly

◆ English Language Learners

Label Book

Before Reading Review LR *Colors,* TE T159.

During Reading Coach retelling of book. **Fluency Check:** Have individuals describe a page. ✓

After Reading Help children share personal responses to LR. Have children draw/caption a picture about a book they read this week. ✓

 Mixed Ability Levels

Literature Circles Form small, mixed-ability groups. Ask groups to discuss the main Anthology selection, Link, Leveled Readers, and other books they have read this week. Pose questions or topics for each group, and circulate among groups to offer support. Suggested group activities:

- Respond to specific Literature Discussion questions on Blackline Master 1.
- Discuss story or text elements, authors' choice of language, and/or illustrations.
- Connect book topics or themes to personal experiences or other reading.

Writing and Language

30-40 minutes

Writing

Practice Assign Writing Prompt, TE T149.

Grammar

Review Beginning Sentences with Capital Letters, TE T155

Listening

Practice Listening to a Story, TE T155

Optional Resources

Teacher Read Aloud

Choose a nonfiction book related to Social Studies or Science unit.

Independent Work

Self-Selected Reading

Choose from

- classroom/school library
- Leveled Bibliography, TE T6–T7
- children's magazines
- consumer texts such as poetry books, magazines
- *I Love Reading,* Theme 1, take-home books 2–4
- Little Readers for Guided Reading

Centers

- Classroom Management Kit
- Classroom Management activities, TE T96–T97
- Responding activities, TE T134

Differentiated Instruction

- Vocabulary: Speed Drill, TE T148
- Comprehension Review: Compare and Contrast, TE T150

End-of-Week Assessment

- Weekly Skills Tests for Theme 1, Week 2
- Fluency Assessment, *Tap Tap,* PL Theme 1, pp. 25–28, TE T151–T153
- Alternative Assessment, Teacher's Resource Blackline Master 16

TE = Teacher Edition; PB = Practice Book; Tr = Transparency; LR = Leveled Reader; PL = Phonics Library; VR = Vocabulary Reader; VR Guide = Vocabulary Readers Teacher's Manual; LBB = Little Big Book; TP = Theme Paperback

Day 1 Balanced Literacy Plan

Teacher Notes

Reading and Comprehension

Shared Reading of Daily Message, TE T170

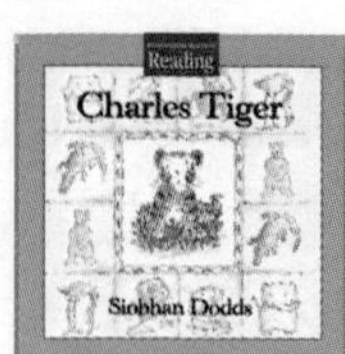

Shared Reading of Big Book

- Introduce Comprehension Strategy and Skill:
  Evaluate, TE T172
  Cause and Effect, TE T173
- Read aloud *Charles Tiger,* TE T172–T175.

Word Work

Phonemic Awareness/Phonics Instruction

Teach Blending Phonemes, TE T171, T177

Review/Practice Consonants *b, r, h, g,* TE T176; assign PB 63–65.

Teach Short *i*/Blending Short *i* Words (VC, CVC), TE T177–T178

Practice Assign PB 66–68.

Spelling/Phonics: Kindergarten Review

Teach Letters *b, h,* TE T182

Practice Assign PB 69.

Vocabulary: Kindergarten Review

Teach Word Wall: *a, have, to,* TE T170

Options for Guided Reading

Extra Support

Before Reading Preview *Can It Fit?* PL Theme 1, pp. 29–32. Model Phonics/Decoding Strategy. See TE T179–T181.

During Reading Coach as children read story.

After Reading Discuss story; have children find/read words with *b, r, h, g,* and short *i*. **Fluency Modeling:** Model fluent reading. Have partners reread story.

✓ = opportunity for ongoing assessment; adjust groups accordingly

On Level

Before Reading Preview *Can It Fit?* PL Theme 1, pp. 29–32. Model Phonics/Decoding Strategy. See TE T179–T181.

During Reading Have children begin story. **Fluency Modeling:** Model Phonics/Decoding Strategy and fluent reading.

After Reading Have children retell story so far and find/read words with *b, r, h, g,* and short *i.* **Fluency Practice:** Have partners finish story and reread for fluency.

Above Level

Before Reading Preview LR *Kit Finds a Mitt,* TE T230. Have students model the Evaluate Strategy.

During Reading Have children read first half of story. **Fluency Modeling:** Model fluent reading.

After Reading Have children finish reading and write answers to Responding questions. ✓

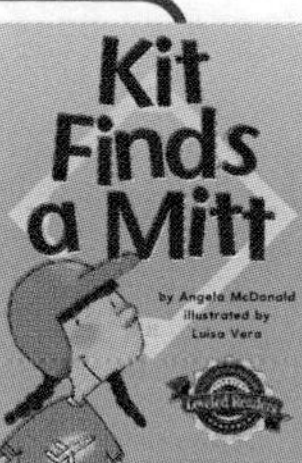

Level H

English Language Learners

Before Reading Preview VR *Sit, Pig!* See VR Guide, p. 8.

During Reading **Fluency Modeling:** Read aloud each page; have children do echo reading.

After Reading Discuss Responding pages. Have children reread with partners or audio CD.

Level A

4 WHOLE GROUP

Writing and Language

25-40 minutes

Writing

Teach Shared Writing: A Class Story, TE T183

Practice Assign Writing Prompt, TE T171.

Listening and Speaking

Teach Choral Reading, TE T183

Optional Resources

Teacher Read Aloud

Reread Big Book: *Charles Tiger,* TE T172–T175.

Independent Work

Self-Selected Reading

Choose from

- classroom/school library
- Leveled Bibliography, TE T6–T7
- *I Love Reading,* Theme 1, take-home books 5–9
- Little Readers for Guided Reading

Centers

- Classroom Management Kit
- Classroom Management activities, TE T168–T169

Differentiated Instruction

- Phonics Reteaching or Extension:
  - –Consonants *b, r, h, g,* TE R22–R23
  - –Short *i*/Blending Short *i* Words (VC, CVC), TE R24–R25
- High-Frequency Words Review: Word Wall, TE T170

TE = Teacher Edition; PB = Practice Book; Tr = Transparency; LR = Leveled Reader; PL = Phonics Library; VR = Vocabulary Reader; VR Guide = Vocabulary Readers Teacher's Manual; LBB = Little Big Book; TP = Theme Paperback

Day 2 Balanced Literacy Plan

Teacher Notes

Reading and Comprehension

20-30 minutes

Shared Reading of Get Set Story

- Build Background and Vocabulary, TE T188
- Read *A Big Hit,* Anthology pp. 71–77.

▼ Anthology Selection

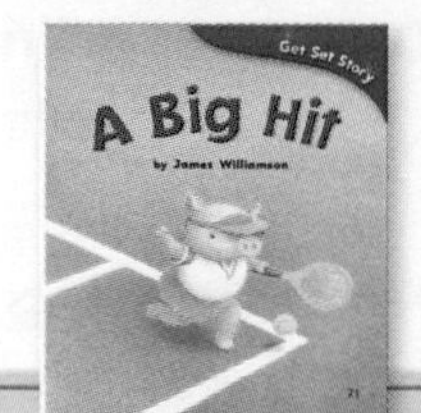

Comprehension Skill Instruction

Teach Cause and Effect, TE T190

Words to Know

a	big
find	hit
have	it
one	Pig
to	ran
who	sit

Word Work

25-40 minutes

Phonemic Awareness

Teach Blending Phonemes, TE T185

High-Frequency Words Instruction

Teach TE T186–T187, Tr 1-8; **Practice** PB 70–71.

High-Frequency Words

a	one
find	to
have	who

Spelling and Phonics: Kindergarten Review

Teach Letters *r, g,* TE T192; **Practice** PB 73.

Vocabulary: Kindergarten Review

Practice Building Words, TE T192

3 SMALL GROUP

Options for Guided Reading

80-100 minutes

Extra Support

Before Reading Preview VR *Sit, Pig!* See VR Guide, p. 8.

During Reading Read the book together; coach reading. Help children apply Evaluate Strategy.

After Reading Discuss the book and Responding questions. **Fluency Practice:** Have children reread VR with a partner. Assign *Who Can Hit?* PL Theme 1, pp. 33–36, for partner reading.

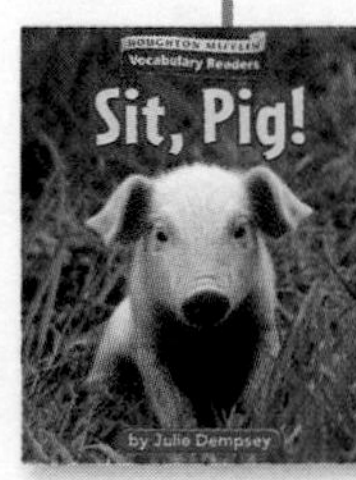

Level A

✓ = opportunity for ongoing assessment; adjust groups accordingly

▲ On Level

Before Reading Discuss PL *Can It Fit?* TE T179. Preview LR *Gram's Hat,* TE T229.

During Reading Coach reading as children begin story. **Fluency Modeling:** Model fluent reading, then have children model it.

After Reading Discuss the sequence of events in the story. Then have children write answers to Responding questions. ✓ Assign *Who Can Hit?* PL Theme 1, pp. 33–36, for partner reading.

Level D

■ Above Level

Before Reading Have children model the Evaluate Strategy and discuss Responding questions for LR *Kit Finds a Mitt,* TE T230.

During Reading **Fluency Check:** Monitor children's oral reading. ✓

After Reading Have children summarize for a partner, telling story events in order. Assign *Who Can Hit?* PL Theme 1, pp. 33–36, for partner reading.

Level H

◆ English Language Learners

Before Reading To review VR vocabulary, have children demonstrate or give examples. See VR Guide, p. 8.

During Reading **Fluency Practice:** Have children reread book. Option: Preview and coach reading of *Can It Fit?* PL Theme 1, pp. 29–32, TE T179–T181.

After Reading Help children summarize VR. Have partners discuss, draw, or write facts they learned. ✓

Level A

Writing and Language

25-40 minutes

Writing

Teach Interactive Writing: A Class Story, TE T193

Practice Assign Writing Prompt, TE T185.

Optional Resources

Teacher Read Aloud

Reread Big Book: *Charles Tiger,* TE T172–T175.

Independent Work

Self-Selected Reading

Choose from

- classroom/school library
- Leveled Bibliography, TE T6–T7
- *I Love Reading,* Theme 1, take-home books 5–9
- Little Readers for Guided Reading

Centers

- Classroom Management Kit
- Classroom Management activities, TE T168–T169

Differentiated Instruction

- High-Frequency Words
  - –Word Wall, TE T184
  - –Reteaching or Extension, TE R30–R31

TE = Teacher Edition; PB = Practice Book; Tr = Transparency; LR = Leveled Reader; PL = Phonics Library; VR = Vocabulary Reader; VR Guide = Vocabulary Readers Teacher's Manual; LBB = Little Big Book; TP = Theme Paperback

Day 3 Balanced Literacy Plan

Teacher Notes

Reading and Comprehension

Shared Reading of *Pigs in a Rig*

- Introduce Story Vocabulary, TE T196, Tr 1-9
  bump, mess, tub, goodbye, mud
- Set Purpose; Review Comprehension Strategy and Skill, TE T196–T197
- Read Anthology Selection pp. 80–95 (independent, partner, or audio CD).
- Discuss questions; retell the story, TE T206.

▼ Anthology Selection

Words to Know

New This Week

a	big
find	hit
have	it
one	pig
to	ran
who	sit

Kindergarten Review

are	the
here	go
see	and

Comprehension Skill Instruction

Teach Cause and Effect, TE T208–T209, Tr 1-10

Practice Assign PB 76.

2 WHOLE GROUP

Word Work

Phonemic Awareness Instruction

Teach Blending Phonemes, TE T195

Spelling and Phonics Instruction

Teach Words with Short *i*, TE T210

Vocabulary Instruction

Teach Shape Words, TE T210

Options for Guided Reading

Extra Support

Before Reading Review Responding questions from VR *Sit, Pig!* Preview LR *Pat and Pig*, TE T228. Have children model Evaluate.

During Reading Coach as children read story. **Fluency Modeling:** Model fluent reading; have children model.

After Reading **Fluency Practice:** Have partners reread story. Have children answer Responding questions. ✓

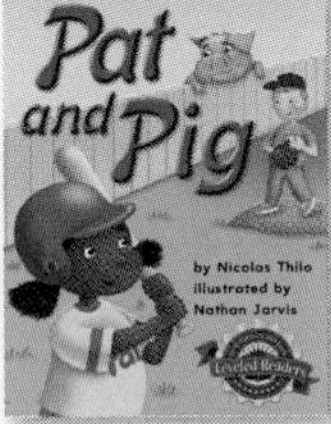

Level B

✓ = opportunity for ongoing assessment; adjust groups accordingly

▲ On Level

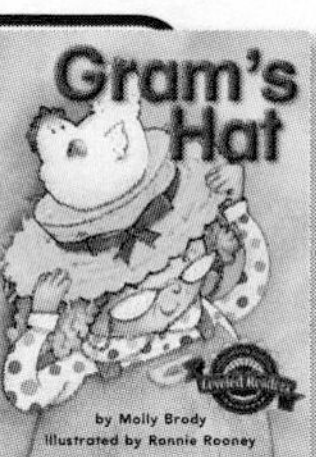
Level D

Before Reading Discuss Responding questions for LR *Gram's Hat,* TE T229.

During Reading **Fluency Check:** Ask individuals to read story aloud. ✓

After Reading Have children summarize story for a partner, telling events in order.

■ Above Level

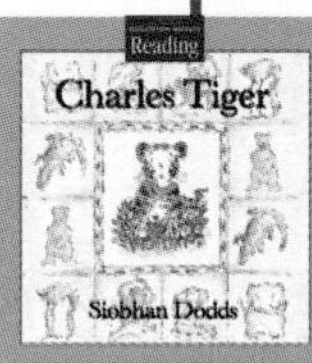
Level F

Before Reading Review LBB *Charles Tiger.* See TE T172–T181, R12–R13.

During Reading **Fluency Modeling:** Model fluent reading, then have children model it. Have them read first half of story independently.

After Reading Ask questions; have children cite text to support answers. Have partners summarize story events in order.

English Language Learners

Before Reading Preview *Who Can Hit?* PL Theme 1, pp. 33–36. Model Phonics/Decoding Strategy.

During Reading **Fluency Modeling:** Read aloud each page; have children do echo reading.

After Reading Discuss story; help children find/read words with *b, r, h, g,* and short *i*. Have children use illustrations to retell story to partners.

4 WHOLE GROUP Writing and Language

30-40 minutes

Writing

Practice Assign Describe a Character, Anthology p. 97.

Grammar

Teach Using Punctuation, TE T211

Optional Resources

Teacher Read Aloud

Choose a book from your class/school library or from the Leveled Bibliography, TE T6–T7.

Suggestion: *Is There Room on the Feather Bed?* by Libba Moore Gray

Independent Work

Self-Selected Reading

Choose from

- classroom/school library
- Leveled Bibliography, TE T6–T7
- *I Love Reading,* Theme 1, take-home books 5–9
- Little Readers for Guided Reading

Centers

- Classroom Management Kit
- Classroom Management activities, T168–T169
- Responding activities, TE T206–T207

Differentiated Instruction

- Comprehension Reteaching and Extension: Cause and Effect, TE R36–R37
- High-Frequency Word Review: Word Wall, TE T194

TE = Teacher Edition; PB = Practice Book; Tr = Transparency; LR = Leveled Reader; PL = Phonics Library; VR = Vocabulary Reader; VR Guide = Vocabulary Readers Teacher's Manual; LBB = Little Big Book; TP = Theme Paperback

Day 4 Balanced Literacy Plan

Teacher Notes

Reading and Comprehension

20-30 minutes

Shared Reading of Social Studies Link

- "Let's Go to the Fair," Anthology pp. 98–101, TE T214–T215 (independent, partner, or group)
- Skill: How to Read a Social Studies Article, TE T214
- Introduce Concept Vocabulary, TE T214.

Concept Vocabulary
county fairs
contests
blue ribbon
homemade

Word Work

25-40 minutes

Phonemic Awareness/Phonics Instruction

Teach Blending Phonemes, TE T213

Review Building Short *a* Words, TE T216; Rhyming Short *a* Words, TE T217

Spelling and Phonics

Practice Flip Books with Short *i* Words, TE T218

Vocabulary Instruction

Teach Words for Feelings, TE T218

3 SMALL GROUP

Options for Guided Reading

80-100 minutes

Extra Support

Before Reading Review Responding questions for LR *Pat and Pig,* TE T228.

During Reading Have children reread story. **Fluency Check:** Have individuals read aloud. ✓

After Reading Model using the words *first, next,* and *last* to summarize story events. Have children retell the story to a partner.

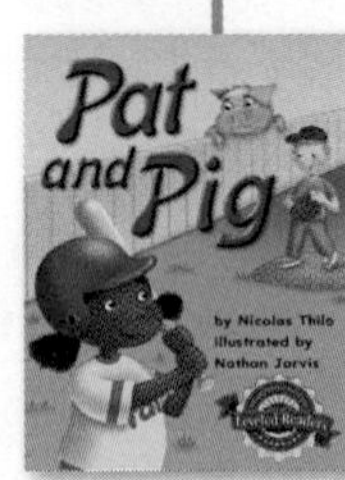

Level B

✓ = opportunity for ongoing assessment; adjust groups accordingly

▲ On Level

Before Reading Have children summarize LR *Gram's Hat,* telling story events in sequence. ✓ Preview a teacher-selected book or TP *I Had a Hippopotamus,* TE R11. Have children make predictions about the story.

During Reading Have children begin story and model Phonics/Decoding Strategy.

After Reading Discuss the story so far. Have children finish story.

Level D

■ Above Level

Before Reading Review first half of LBB *Charles Tiger,* TE T172–T173.

During Reading Have children finish book.

After Reading Discuss how book connects to theme. Have children write journal entries to connect it to personal experience or other reading.

Level F

◆ English Language Learners

Before Reading Build background and preview LR *Here Is Hen,* TE T231. Have children make predictions about the story.

During Reading Read story. **Fluency Modeling:** Reread each page; have children do echo reading. Reinforce Phonics/Decoding Strategy.

After Reading Discuss Responding questions, TE 231. **Fluency Practice:** Have children reread with partners or audio CD.

Level A

Writing and Language

30-40 minutes

Writing

Practice Independent Writing: Creating a New Ending, TE T219; assign PB 77.

Optional Resources

Teacher Read Aloud

Continue selected Read Aloud book from Day 3 or choose a new one from your class or school library.

Independent Work

Self-Selected Reading

Choose from

- classroom/school library
- Leveled Bibliography, TE T6–T7
- children's magazines
- *I Love Reading,* Theme 1, take-home books 5–9
- Little Readers for Guided Reading

Centers

- Classroom Management Kit
- Classroom Management activities, TE T168–T169
- Responding activities, TE T206–T207

Differentiated Instruction

- Visual Literacy: Using Photographs, TE T215
- High-Frequency Words: Word Wall, TE T212
- Study Skills: Parts of a Book, TE R38

TE = Teacher Edition; PB = Practice Book; Tr = Transparency; LR = Leveled Reader; PL = Phonics Library; VR = Vocabulary Reader; VR Guide = Vocabulary Readers Teacher's Manual; LBB = Little Big Book; TP = Theme Paperback

Day 5 Balanced Literacy Plan

Teacher Notes

Reading and Comprehension

20-30 minutes

Book Share

- Ask children to explain how they applied the comprehension skill and strategy to books they have read this week.
- Help children use genre and text features to compare and contrast what they have read.
- As a class, discuss one *how, why,* or *what if* question. See examples on Blackline Master 1 to use as a guide.

Word Work

25-40 minutes

Phonemic Awareness Instruction

Teach Blending Phonemes, TE T221

Vocabulary

Practice High-Frequency Word Speed Drill, TE T226

Spelling and Phonics

Practice Building Words with Short *i*, TE T226

Options for Guided Reading

80-100 minutes

Extra Support

Before Reading Preview *One Big Fat Fig,* PL Theme 1, pp. 37–40. Have children find/read words with *b, r, h, g,* and short *i*. See TE T223–T225.

During Reading Have children read and model Phonics/ Decoding Strategy. **Fluency Check:** Have individuals reread aloud. ✓

After Reading Have partners make connections between the story and LR *Pat and Pig.* Assign On My Way Practice Reader *One Big Hit* for partner reading.

✓ = opportunity for ongoing assessment; adjust groups accordingly

◆ English Language Learners

Before Reading Review LR *Here Is Hen,* TE T231.

During Reading Coach rereading of book. **Fluency Check:** Have individuals reread aloud. ✓

After Reading Help children summarize LR story events in sequence. Have children draw/caption a picture about a book they read this week. ✓

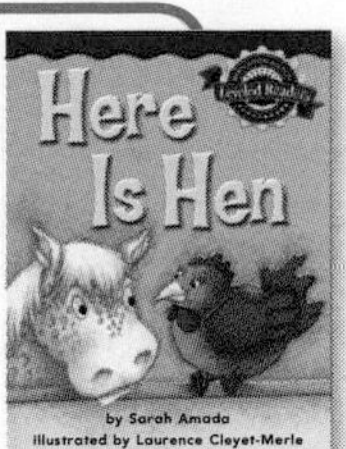

Level A

●▲■◆ Mixed Ability Levels

Literature Circles Form small, mixed-ability groups. Ask groups to discuss the main Anthology selection, Link, Leveled Readers, and other books they have read this week. Pose questions or topics for each group, and circulate among groups to offer support. Suggested group activities:

- Respond to specific Literature Discussion questions on Blackline Master 1.
- Discuss story or text elements, authors' choice of language, and/or illustrations.
- Connect book topics or themes to personal experiences or other reading.

Writing and Language

30-40 minutes

Writing

Practice Assign Writing Prompt, TE T221.

Grammar

Review Using Punctuation, TE T227

Listening and Speaking

Practice Singing Songs, TE T227

Optional Resources

Teacher Read Aloud

Choose a nonfiction book related to Social Studies or Science unit.

Independent Work

Self-Selected Reading

Choose from

- classroom/school library
- Leveled Bibliography, TE T6–T7
- children's magazines
- consumer texts such as social studies articles, books about fairs

Centers

- Classroom Management Kit
- Classroom Management activities, TE T168–T169
- Responding activities, TE T206–T207

Differentiated Instruction

- Vocabulary: Speed Drill, TE T220
- Comprehension Review: Cause and Effect, TE T222

Assessment

End-of-Week Assessment

- Weekly Skills Tests for Theme 1, Week 3
- Fluency Assessment, *One Big Fat Fig,* PL Theme 1, pp. 37–40, TE T223–T225
- Alternative Assessment, Teacher's Resource Blackline Master 19

End-of-Theme Assessment

- *See* Integrated Theme Tests for Theme 2.

TE = Teacher Edition; PB = Practice Book; Tr = Transparency; LR = Leveled Reader; PL = Phonics Library; VR = Vocabulary Reader; VR Guide = Vocabulary Readers Teacher's Manual; LBB = Little Big Book; TP = Theme Paperback

Theme 2 Overview

	Week 1
Reading and Comprehension	**Shared Reading** Main Selection: *A Party for Bob* Math Link: "Shapes Are Everywhere" Book Share **Comprehension** Strategy: Question Skill: Noting Details Content Skill: How to Read a Math Article
Word Work	**Phonemic Awareness:** Blending Phonemes **Phonics:** Kindergarten Review: *d, w, l, x* **Phonics:** Short *o*/Blending Short *o* Words (VC, CVC) **Kindergarten Review:** Words with Short *i* **Vocabulary:** Number Words; Fun Things **High-Frequency Words:** *five, four, in, once, three, two, upon, what* **Spelling and Phonics:** Kindergarten Review: Words with *d, w, l, x,* and Short *o*
Options for Guided Reading	**Big Book** *To Be a Kid* **Vocabulary Reader** *Happy Birthday, Brother!* **Leveled Readers:** Extra Support: *A Wig for Pig* On Level: *The Big Box* Above Level: *The Mixed Up Wigs* ELL: *The Box* **Phonics Library** *Dot Fox* *Bob Pig and Dan Ox* *Once Upon a Dig* Theme Paperbacks **Literature Circles**
Writing and Oral Language	**Shared Writing:** A Class Letter **Interactive Writing:** A Class Letter **Independent Writing:** Using Alliteration **Grammar:** Capitalizing Names; Word Order in Sentences **Listening and Speaking:** Sharing Information **Viewing:** Compare and Contrast
Assessment Options	• Weekly Skills Test for Theme 2, Week 1 • Fluency Assessment: Phonics Library

Use **Launching the Theme** on pages T16–T17 of the Teacher's Edition to introduce the theme.

Week 2

Shared Reading
Main Selection: *The Bunnies and the Fox*
Science Link: "Woodland Animals"
Book Share

Comprehension
Strategy: Monitor/Clarify
Skill: Fantasy and Realism
Content Skill: How to Read a Science Article

Phonemic Awareness: Blending Phonemes
Phonics: Kindergarten Review: *y, k, v*
Phonics: Short *e*/Blending Short *e* Words (VC, CVC)
Kindergarten Review: Words with Short *o*
Vocabulary: Opposites; Foods
High-Frequency Words: *do, for, I, is, me, my, said, you*
Spelling and Phonics: Kindergarten Review: Words with *y, k, v,* and Short *e*

Big Book
Minerva Louise at School

Vocabulary Reader
Outside the Window

Leveled Readers:
Extra Support: *In the Van*
On Level: *At the Vet*
Above Level: *Kenny's Big Present*
ELL: *Six Wet Pets*

Phonics Library
Not Yet!
Big Ben
Get Wet, Ken!

Literature Circles

Shared Writing: A Class Message
Interactive Writing: A Class Message
Independent Writing: Writing About Animals
Grammar: Using Naming Words
Viewing: Main Idea and Details
Speaking and Listening: Conflict Resolution

- Weekly Skills Test for Theme 2, Week 2
- Fluency Assessment: Phonics Library

Week 3

Shared Reading
Main Selection: *A Surprise for Zig Bug*
Science Link: "Insects"
Book Share

Comprehension
Strategy: Summarize
Skill: Story Structure
Content Skill: How to Read a Science Article

Phonemic Awareness: Blending Phonemes
Phonics: Kindergarten Review: *q, j, z*
Phonics: Short *u*/Blending Short *u* Words (VC, CVC)
Kindergarten Review: Words with Short *e*
Vocabulary: Days of the Week; Homographs
High-Frequency Words: *are, away, does, he, live, pull, they, where*
Spelling and Phonics: Kindergarten Review: Words with *q, j, z,* and Short *u*

Big Book
Jasper's Beanstalk

Vocabulary Reader
At the Pool

Leveled Readers:
Extra Support: *Where Is Zig?*
On Level: *Big Tug*
Above Level: *Let's Take a Trip*
ELL: *Slug and Bug*

Phonics Library
The Bug Kit
Quit It, Zig!
Rug Tug

Literature Circles

Shared Writing: A Class Diary
Interactive Writing: A Diary
Independent Writing: Writing About Bugs
Grammar: Using Action Words
Listening and Speaking: Retell/Summarize
Listening and Speaking: Reader's Theater

- Weekly Skills Test, Theme 2, Week 3
- Fluency Assessment: Phonics Library

Day 1 Balanced Literacy Plan

Teacher Notes

Reading and Comprehension

Shared Reading of Daily Message, TE T30

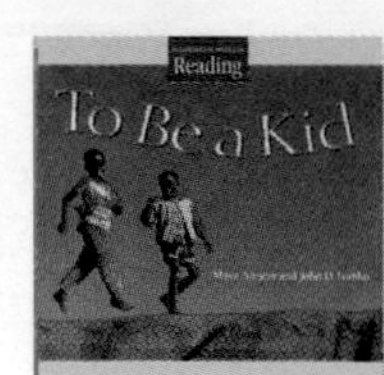

Shared Reading of Big Book

- Introduce Comprehension Strategy and Skill
  Question, TE T32
  Noting Details, TE T33
- Read aloud *To Be a Kid,* TE T32–T35.

Word Work

Phonemic Awareness/Phonics Instruction

Teach Blending Phonemes, TE T31, T37

Review/Practice Consonants *d, w, l, x,* TE T36; assign PB 79–81.

Teach Short *o*/Blending Short *o* Words (VC, CVC), TE T37–T38

Practice Assign PB 82–84.

Spelling/Phonics: Kindergarten Review

Teach Letters *d, l,* TE T42

Practice Assign PB 85.

Vocabulary: Kindergarten Review

Teach Word Wall: *have, a,* TE T30

Options for Guided Reading

Extra Support

Before Reading Preview *Dot Fox,* PL Theme 2, pp. 5–8. Model Phonics/Decoding Strategy. See TE T39–T41.

During Reading Coach as children read story.

After Reading Discuss story; have children find/read words with *s, w, l, x,* and short *o*.
Fluency Modeling: Model fluent reading. Have partners reread story.

✓ = opportunity for ongoing assessment; adjust groups accordingly

On Level

Before Reading Preview *Dot Fox,* PL Theme 2, pp. 5–8. Model Phonics/Decoding Strategy. See TE T39–T41.

During Reading Have children begin story.
Fluency Modeling: Model Phonics/Decoding Strategy and fluent reading.

After Reading Have children retell story so far and find/read words with *s, w, l, x,* and short *o*.
Fluency Practice: Have partners finish story and reread for fluency.

Above Level

Before Reading Preview LR *The Mixed Up Wigs,* TE T90. Have students model the Question Strategy.

During Reading Have children read first half of story.
Fluency Modeling: Model fluent reading.

After Reading Have children finish reading and write answers to Responding questions. ✓

Level I

English Language Learners

Before Reading Preview VR *Happy Birthday, Brother*. See VR Guide, p. 9.

During Reading **Fluency Modeling:** Read aloud each page; have children do echo reading.

After Reading Discuss Responding pages. Have children reread with partners or audio CD.

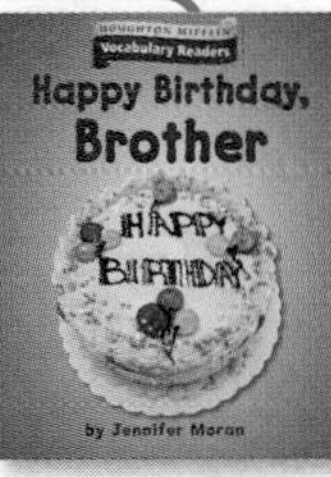

Level A

Optional Resources

Teacher Read Aloud

Reread Big Book: *To Be a Kid,* TE T32–T35.

Read *Jack and the Beanstalk,* TE T18–T19.

Independent Work

Self-Selected Reading

Choose from
- classroom/school library
- Leveled Bibliography, TE T6–T7
- *I Love Reading,* Theme 2, take-home books 11–14, 10
- Little Readers for Guided Reading

Centers
- Classroom Management Kit
- Classroom Management activities, TE T28–T29

Differentiated Instruction

- Phonics Reteaching or Extension:
  –*d, w, l, x,* TE R14–R15
  –Short *o*/Blending Short *o* Words (VC, CVC), TE R16–R17
- High-Frequency Words Review: Word Wall, TE T30

Writing and Language

25-40 minutes

Writing

Teach Shared Writing: A Class Letter, TE T43

Practice Assign Writing Prompt, TE T31.

Listening and Speaking

Teach Sharing Information, TE T43

TE = Teacher Edition; PB = Practice Book; Tr = Transparency; LR = Leveled Reader; PL = Phonics Library; VR = Vocabulary Reader; VR Guide = Vocabulary Readers Teacher's Manual; LBB = Little Big Book; TP = Theme Paperback

Day 2 Balanced Literacy Plan

Teacher Notes

Reading and Comprehension

Shared Reading of Get Set Story

- Build Background and Vocabulary, TE T48
- Read *A Lot! A Lot!,* Anthology pp. 104–111.

▼ Anthology Selection

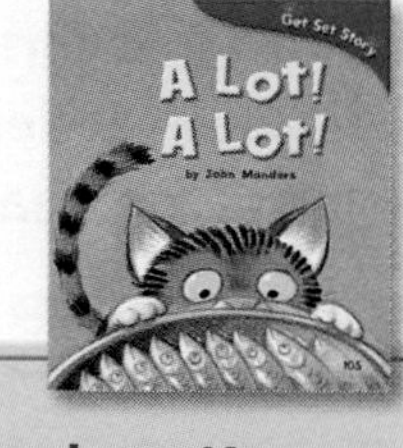

Comprehension Skill Instruction

Teach Noting Details, TE T50

Words to Know

five	what
four	box
in	did
once	got
three	hot
two	lot
upon	wag

2 WHOLE GROUP

Word Work

25-40 minutes

Phonemic Awareness

Teach Blending Phonemes, TE T45

High-Frequency Words Instruction

Teach TE T46–T47, Tr 2-1; Practice PB 86–87.

Spelling and Phonics: Kindergarten Review

Teach Letters *w, x,* TE T52; Practice PB 88.

Vocabulary: Kindergarten Review

Practice Building Words, TE T52

High-Frequency Words

five	three
four	two
in	upon
once	what

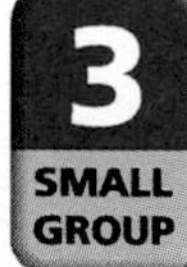

Options for Guided Reading

80-100 minutes

Extra Support

Before Reading Preview VR *Happy Birthday, Brother.* See VR Guide, p. 9.

During Reading Read the book together; coach reading. Help children apply Question Strategy.

After Reading Discuss the book and Responding questions. **Fluency Practice:** Have children reread VR with a partner. Assign *Bob Pig and Dan Ox,* PL Theme 2, pp. 9–12, for partner reading.

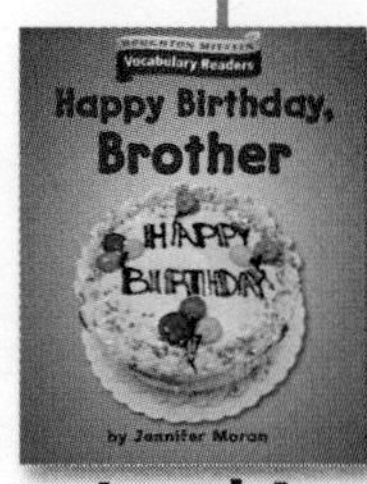

Level A

✓ = opportunity for ongoing assessment; adjust groups accordingly

▲ On Level

Before Reading Discuss PL *Dot Fox,* TE T39–T41. Preview LR *The Big Box,* TE T89.

During Reading Coach reading as children begin story. **Fluency Modeling:** Model fluent reading, then have children model it.

After Reading Discuss the sequence of events in the story. Then have children write answers to Responding questions. ✓ Assign *Bob Pig and Dan Ox,* PL Theme 2, pp. 9–12, for partner reading.

Level D

■ Above Level

Before Reading Have children model the Question Strategy and discuss Responding questions for LR *The Mixed Up Wigs,* TE T90.

During Reading **Fluency Check:** Monitor children's oral reading. ✓

After Reading Have children summarize for a partner, telling story events in order. Assign *Bob Pig and Dan Ox,* PL Theme 2, pp. 9–12, for partner reading.

Level I

◆ English Language Learners

Before Reading To review VR vocabulary, have children demonstrate or give examples. See VR Guide, p. 4.

During Reading **Fluency Practice:** Have children reread book. Option: Preview and coach reading of *Dot Fox,* PL Theme 2, pp. 5–8, TE T39–T41.

After Reading Help children summarize VR. Have partners discuss, draw, or write facts they learned. ✓

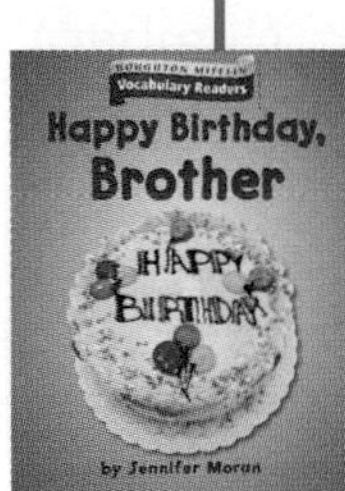

Level A

4 WHOLE GROUP Writing and Language

25-40 minutes

Writing

Teach Interactive Writing: A Class Letter, TE T53

Practice Assign Writing Prompt, TE T45.

Optional Resources

Teacher Read Aloud

Reread Big Book: *To Be a Kid,* TE T32–T35.

Independent Work

Self-Selected Reading

Choose from

- classroom/school library
- Leveled Bibliography, TE T6–T7
- *I Love Reading,* Theme 2, take-home books 11–14, 10
- Little Readers for Guided Reading

Centers

- Classroom Management Kit
- Classroom Management activities, TE T28–T29

Differentiated Instruction

- High-Frequency Words
  - –Word Wall, TE T44
  - –Reteaching or Extension, TE R26–R27

TE = Teacher Edition; PB = Practice Book; Tr = Transparency; LR = Leveled Reader; PL = Phonics Library; VR = Vocabulary Reader; VR Guide = Vocabulary Readers Teacher's Manual; LBB = Little Big Book; TP = Theme Paperback

Day 3 Balanced Literacy Plan

Teacher Notes

Reading and Comprehension

20-30 minutes

Shared Reading of *A Party for Bob*

▼ Anthology Selection

- Introduce Key Vocabulary, TE T56, Tr 2-2

  birthday cake happy party brother candles kids surprise

- Set Purpose; Review Comprehension Strategy and Skill, TE T56–T57
- Read Anthology Selection pp. 114–129 (independent, partner, or audio CD).
- Discuss questions; retell the story, TE T67.

Comprehension Skill Instruction

Teach Noting Details, TE T68–T69, Tr 2-3

Practice Assign PB 91.

Words to Know

New This Week

five	what
four	box
in	did
once	got
three	hot
two	lot
upon	Wag

Kindergarten Review

for	she
he	Ben
I	get
is	wet
my	

Word Work

25-40 minutes

Phonemic Awareness Instruction

Teach Blending Phonemes, TE T55

Spelling and Phonics Instruction

Teach Words with Short *o,* TE T70

Vocabulary Instruction

Teach Number Words, TE T70

3
SMALL GROUP

Options for Guided Reading

80-100 minutes

● Extra Support

Before Reading Review Responding questions from VR *Happy Birthday, Brother.* Preview LR *A Wig for Pig,* TE T88. Have children model Question.

During Reading Coach as children read story. **Fluency Modeling:** Model fluent reading; have children model.

After Reading **Fluency Practice:** Have partners reread story. Have children answer Responding questions. ✓

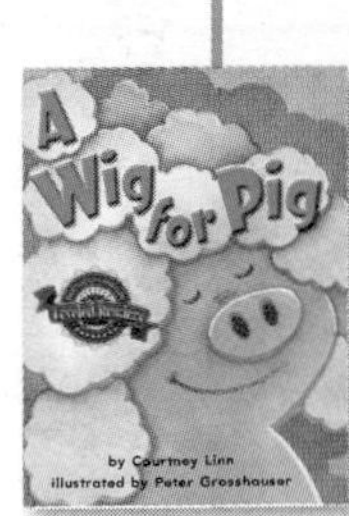

Level D

✓ = opportunity for ongoing assessment; adjust groups accordingly

▲ **On Level**

Before Reading Discuss Responding questions for LR *The Big Box,* TE T89.

During Reading **Fluency Check:** Ask individuals to read story aloud. ✓

After Reading Have children summarize story for a partner, telling events in order.

Level D

■ **Above Level**

Before Reading Review LBB *To Be a Kid.* See TE T32–T35, R4–R5.

During Reading **Fluency Modeling:** Model fluent reading, then have children model it. Have them read first half of story independently.

After Reading Ask questions; have children cite text to support answers. Have partners summarize story events in order.

Level F

◆ **English Language Learners**

Before Reading Preview *Bob Pig and Dan Ox,* PL Theme 2, pp. 9–12. Model Phonics/Decoding Strategy.

During Reading **Fluency Modeling:** Read aloud each page; have children do echo reading.

After Reading Discuss story; help children find/read words with *d, w, l, x,* and short *o.* Have children use illustrations to retell story to partners.

4 WHOLE GROUP

Writing and Language

30-40 minutes

Writing

Practice Assign Write a Sign, Anthology p. 131.

Grammar

Teach Capitalizing Names, TE T71

Optional Resources

Teacher Read Aloud

Choose a book from your class/school library or from the Leveled Bibliography, TE T6–T7.

Suggestion: *The Pig Is in the Pantry, the Cat Is on the Shelf* by Shirley Mozelle Clarion

Independent Work

Self-Selected Reading

Choose from

- classroom/school library
- Leveled Bibliography, TE T6–T7
- *I Love Reading,* Theme 2, take-home books 11–14, 10
- Little Readers for Guided Reading

Centers

- Classroom Management Kit
- Classroom Management activities, TE T28–T29
- Responding activities, TE T66–T67

Differentiated Instruction

- Comprehension Reteaching and Extension, Noting Details, TE R32–R33
- High-Frequency Word Review: Word Wall, TE T54

TE = Teacher Edition; PB = Practice Book; Tr = Transparency; LR = Leveled Reader; PL = Phonics Library; VR = Vocabulary Reader; VR Guide = Vocabulary Readers Teacher's Manual; LBB = Little Big Book; TP = Theme Paperback

Day 4 Balanced Literacy Plan

Teacher Notes

Reading and Comprehension

20-30 minutes

Shared Reading of Math Link

- "Shapes Are Everywhere," Anthology pp. 132–135, TE T74–T75 (independent, partner, or group)
- Skill: How to Read a Mathematics Article, TE T74
- Introduce Concept Vocabulary, TE T74.

Concept Vocabulary
triangle
rectangle
square
circle

Word Work

25-40 minutes

Phonemic Awareness/Phonics Instruction

Teach Blending Phonemes, TE T73

Review Building Short *i* Words, TE T76; Building Short *i* Words, TE T77

Spelling and Phonics

Practice Word Wheels with Short *o*, TE T78

Vocabulary Instruction

Teach Fun Things, TE T78

3 SMALL GROUP

Options for Guided Reading

80-100 minutes

Extra Support

Before Reading Review Responding questions for LR *A Wig for Pig,* TE T88.

During Reading Have children reread story. **Fluency Check:** Have individuals read aloud. ✓

After Reading Model using the words *first, next,* and *last* to summarize story events. Have children retell the story to a partner.

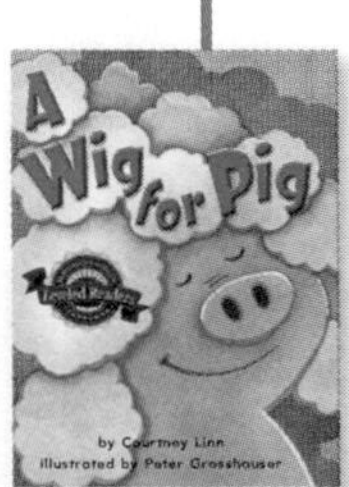

Level D

✓ = opportunity for ongoing assessment; adjust groups accordingly

▲ On Level

Before Reading Have children summarize LR *The Big Box,* telling story events in sequence. ✓ Preview a teacher-selected book or TP *"What is THAT?" Said the Cat,* TE R3. Have children make predictions about the story.

During Reading Have children begin story and model Phonics/Decoding Strategy.

After Reading Discuss the story so far. Have children finish story.

Level F

■ Above Level

Before Reading Review first half of LBB *To Be a Kid,* TE T32.

During Reading Have children finish book.

After Reading Discuss how book connects to theme. Have children write journal entries to connect it to personal experience or other reading.

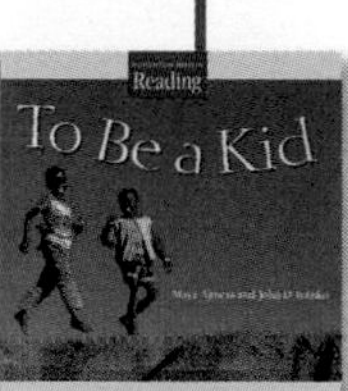

Level F

◆ English Language Learners

Before Reading Build background and preview LR *The Box,* TE 91. Have children make predictions about the story.

During Reading Read story. **Fluency Modeling:** Reread each page; have children do echo reading. Reinforce Phonics/Decoding Strategy.

After Reading Discuss Responding questions, TE 66. **Fluency Practice:** Have children reread with partners or audio CD.

Level C

Writing and Language

30-40 minutes

Writing

Practice Independent Writing: Using Alliteration; assign PB 93.

Optional Resources

Teacher Read Aloud

Continue selected Read Aloud book from Day 3 or choose a new one from your class or school library.

Independent Work

Self-Selected Reading

Choose from

- classroom/school library
- Leveled Bibliography, TE T6–T7
- children's magazines
- *I Love Reading,* Theme 2, take-home books 11–14, 10
- Little Readers for Guided Reading

Centers

- Classroom Management Kit
- Classroom Management activities, TE T28–T29
- Responding activities, TE T66–T67

Differentiated Instruction

- Visual Literacy: Using Photographs, TE T75
- High-Frequency Words: Word Wall, TE T72
- Study Skills: Following Instructions, TE R38

TE = Teacher Edition; PB = Practice Book; Tr = Transparency; LR = Leveled Reader; PL = Phonics Library; VR = Vocabulary Reader; VR Guide = Vocabulary Readers Teacher's Manual; LBB = Little Big Book; TP = Theme Paperback

Day 5 Balanced Literacy Plan

Teacher Notes

Reading and Comprehension

20-30 minutes

Book Share

Book Share

- ➤ Ask children to explain how they applied the comprehension skill and strategy to books they have read this week.
- ➤ Help children use genre and text features to compare and contrast what they have read.
- ➤ As a class, discuss one *how, why,* or *what if* question. See examples on Blackline Master 1 to use as a guide.

Word Work

25-40 minutes

Phonemic Awareness Instruction

Teach Blending Phonemes, TE T81

High-Frequency Words

Practice Word Wall/Vocabulary Speed Drill, TE T80

Spelling and Phonics

Practice Building Words with Short *o*, TE T86

Options for Guided Reading

80-100 minutes

● Extra Support

Before Reading Preview *Once Upon a Dig,* PL Theme 2, pp. 13–16. Have children find/read words with *d, w, l, x,* short *o*. See TE T83–T85.

During Reading Have children read and model Phonics/Decoding Strategy. **Fluency Check:** Have individuals reread aloud. ✓

After Reading Have partners make connections between the story and LR *A Wig for Pig.* Assign On My Way Practice Reader *Five Big Boxes* for partner reading.

✓ = opportunity for ongoing assessment; adjust groups accordingly

 **English Language Learners**

Before Reading Review LR *The Box,* TE T91.

During Reading Coach rereading of book. **Fluency Check:** Have individuals reread aloud. ✓

After Reading Help children summarize LR story events in sequence. Have children draw/caption a picture about a book they read this week. ✓

Level C

 **Mixed Ability Levels**

Literature Circles Form small, mixed-ability groups. Ask groups to discuss the main Anthology selection, Link, Leveled Readers, and other books they have read this week. Pose questions or topics for each group, and circulate among groups to offer support. Suggested group activities:

- Respond to specific Literature Discussion questions on Blackline Master 1.
- Discuss story or text elements, authors' choice of language, and/or illustrations.
- Connect book topics or themes to personal experiences or other reading.

Writing and Language

30-40 minutes

Writing

Practice Assign Writing Prompt, TE T81.

Grammar

Review Word Order in Sentences, TE T87

Viewing

Practice Compare and Contrast, TE T87

Optional Resources

Teacher Read Aloud

Choose a nonfiction book related to Social Studies or Science unit.

Independent Work

Self-Selected Reading

Choose from

- classroom/school library
- Leveled Bibliography, TE T6–T7
- children's magazines
- consumer text such as books about math, geometry, etc.

Centers

- Classroom Management Kit
- Classroom Management activities, TE T28–T29
- Responding activities, TE T66–T67

Differentiated Instruction

- Vocabulary: Speed Drill, TE T80
- Comprehension Review: Noting Details, TE T82

End-of-Week Assessment

- Weekly Skills Tests for Theme 2, Week 1
- Fluency Assessment: *Once Upon a Dig,* PL Theme 2, pp. 13–16, TE T83–T85
- Alternative Assessment, Teacher's Resource Blackline Master 27

TE = Teacher Edition; PB = Practice Book; Tr = Transparency; LR = Leveled Reader; PL = Phonics Library; VR = Vocabulary Reader; VR Guide = Vocabulary Readers Teacher's Manual; LBB = Little Big Book; TP = Theme Paperback

Day 1 Balanced Literacy Plan

Teacher Notes

Reading and Comprehension

20-30 minutes

Shared Reading of Daily Message, TE T102

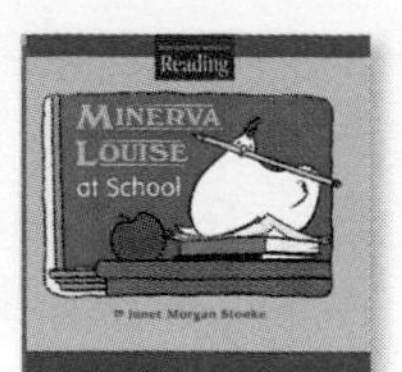

Shared Reading of Big Book

- Introduce Comprehension Strategy and Skill
  Monitor/Clarify, TE T104
  Fantasy and Realism, TE T105
- Read aloud *Minerva Louise at School,* TE T104–T107.

Word Work

25-40 minutes

Phonemic Awareness/Phonics Instruction

Teach Blending Phonemes, TE T103, T109

Review/Practice Consonants *y, k, v,* TE T108; assign PB 95–96.

Teach Short *e*/ Blending Short *e* Words (VC, CVC), TE T109–T110

Practice Assign PB 97–99.

Spelling/Phonics: Kindergarten Review

Teach Letters *y, v,* TE T114

Practice Assign PB 100.

Vocabulary: Kindergarten Review

Teach Word Wall: for, *is, a, I, my, and, to,* TE T102

Options for Guided Reading

80-100 minutes

Extra Support

Before Reading Preview *Not Yet!,* PL Theme 2, pp. 17–20. Model Phonics/Decoding Strategy. See TE T111–T113.

During Reading Coach as children read story.

After Reading Discuss story; have children find/read words with *y, k, v,* short *e.* **Fluency Modeling:** Model fluent reading. Have partners reread story.

✓ = opportunity for ongoing assessment; adjust groups accordingly

On Level

Before Reading Preview *Not Yet!,* PL Theme 2, pp. 17–20. Model Phonics/Decoding Strategy. See TE T111–T113.

During Reading Have children begin story. **Fluency Modeling:** Model Phonics/Decoding Strategy and fluent reading.

After Reading Have children retell story so far and find/read words with *y, k, v,* short *e*. **Fluency Practice:** Have partners finish story and reread for fluency.

Above Level

Before Reading Preview LR *Kenny's Big Present,* TE T162. Have students model the Monitor/Clarify Strategy.

During Reading Have children read first half of story. **Fluency Modeling:** Model fluent reading.

After Reading Have children finish reading and write answers to Responding questions. ✓

Level H

English Language Learners

Before Reading Preview VR *Outside the Window.* See VR Guide, p. 10.

During Reading **Fluency Modeling:** Read aloud each page; have children do echo reading.

After Reading Discuss Responding pages. Have children reread with partners or audio CD.

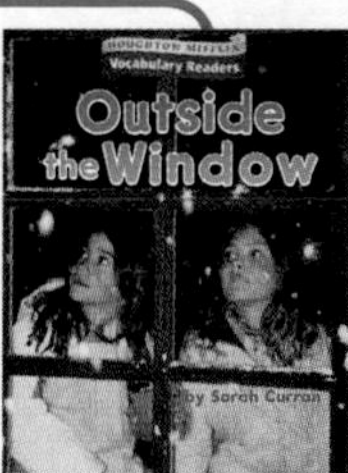

Level B

Writing and Language

 25-40 minutes

Writing

Teach Shared Writing: A Class Message, TE T115

Practice Assign Writing Prompt, TE T103.

Viewing

Teach Main Idea and Details, TE T115

Optional Resources

Teacher Read Aloud

Reread Big Book: *Minerva Louise at School,* TE T104–T107.

Read *Jack and the Beanstalk,* TE T18–T19.

Independent Work

Self-Selected Reading

Choose from

- classroom/school library
- Leveled Bibliography, TE T6–T7
- *I Love Reading,* Theme 2, take-home books 16–18, 15
- Little Readers for Guided Reading

Centers

- Classroom Management Kit
- Classroom Management activities, TE T100–T101

Differentiated Instruction

- Phonics Reteaching or Extension:
  –*y, k, v,* TE R18–R19
  –Short *e*/Blending Short *e* Words (VC, CVC), TE R20–R21
- High-Frequency Words Review: Word Wall, TE T102

TE = Teacher Edition; PB = Practice Book; Tr = Transparency; LR = Leveled Reader; PL = Phonics Library; VR = Vocabulary Reader; VR Guide = Vocabulary Readers Teacher's Manual; LBB = Little Big Book; TP = Theme Paperback

Day 2 Balanced Literacy Plan

Teacher Notes

Reading and Comprehension

20-30 minutes

Shared Reading of Get Set Story

- Build Background and Vocabulary, TE T120
- Read *Val Can Help,* Anthology pp. 137–143.

▼ Anthology Selection

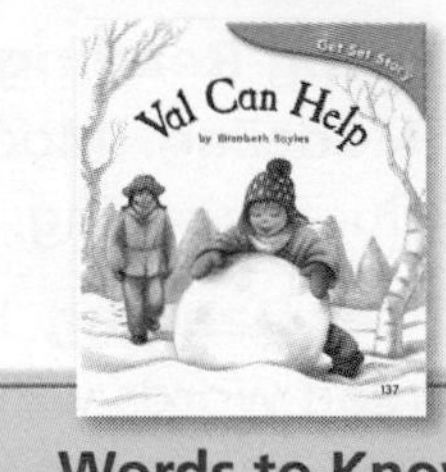

Comprehension Skill Instruction

Teach Fantasy and Realism, TE T122

Words to Know

do	you
for	get
I	help
is	kid
me	next
my	yes
said	yet

2
WHOLE GROUP

Word Work

25-40 minutes

Phonemic Awareness

Teach Blending Phonemes, TE T117

High-Frequency Words Instruction

Teach TE T118–T119, Tr 2-5, Practice PB 101, 102.

Spelling and Phonics: Kindergarten Review

Teach Letter *k,* TE T124; Practice PB 103.

Vocabulary: Kindergarten Review

Practice Read Rhyming Words, TE T124.

High-Frequency Words

do	me
for	my
I	said
is	you

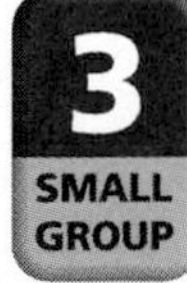

Options for Guided Reading

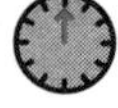
80-100 minutes

Extra Support

Before Reading Preview VR *Outside the Window.* See VR Guide, p. 10.

During Reading Read the book together; coach reading. Help children apply Monitor/Clarify Strategy.

After Reading Discuss the book and Responding questions. **Fluency Practice:** Have children reread VR with a partner. Assign *Big Ben,* PL Theme 2, pp. 21–24, for partner reading.

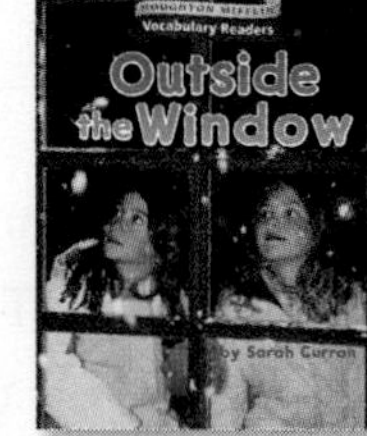

Level B

✓ = opportunity for ongoing assessment; adjust groups accordingly

▲ On Level

Before Reading Discuss PL *Not Yet!*, TE T111–T113. Preview LR *At the Vet*, TE T161.

During Reading Coach reading as children begin story. **Fluency Modeling:** Model fluent reading, then have children model it.

After Reading Discuss the sequence of events in the story. Then have children write answers to Responding questions. ✓ Assign *Big Ben*, PL Theme 2, pp. 21–24, for partner reading.

Level D

 Above Level

Before Reading Have children model the Monitor/Clarify Strategy and discuss Responding questions for LR *Kenny's Big Present*, TE T162.

During Reading **Fluency Check:** Monitor children's oral reading. ✓

After Reading Have children summarize for a partner, telling story events in order. Assign *Big Ben*, PL Theme 2, pp. 21–24, for partner reading.

Level H

◆ English Language Learners

Before Reading To review VR vocabulary, have children demonstrate or give examples. See VR Guide, p. 10.

During Reading **Fluency Practice:** Have children reread book. Option: Preview and coach reading of *Not Yet!*, PL Theme 2, pp. 17–20, TE T111–T113.

After Reading Help children summarize VR. Have partners discuss, draw, or write facts they learned. ✓

Level B

Writing and Language

25-40 minutes

Writing

Teach Interactive Writing: A Class Message, TE T125

Practice Assign Writing Prompt, TE T117.

Optional Resources

Teacher Read Aloud

Reread Big Book: *Minerva Louise at School*, TE T104–T107.

Independent Work

Self-Selected Reading

Choose from

- classroom/school library
- Leveled Bibliography, TE T6–T7
- *I Love Reading*, Theme 2, take-home books 16–18, 15
- Little Readers for Guided Reading

Centers

- Classroom Management Kit
- Classroom Management activities, TE T100–T101

Differentiated Instruction

- High-Frequency Words
  –Word Wall, TE T116
  –Reteaching or Extension, TE R28–R29

TE = Teacher Edition; PB = Practice Book; Tr = Transparency; LR = Leveled Reader; PL = Phonics Library; VR = Vocabulary Reader; VR Guide = Vocabulary Readers Teacher's Manual; LBB = Little Big Book; TP = Theme Paperback

Day 3 Balanced Literacy Plan

Teacher Notes

Reading and Comprehension

20-30 minutes

▼ Anthology Selection

Shared Reading of *The Bunnies and the Fox*

- Introduce Key Vocabulary, TE T128, Tr 2-6
  bear, bunny, snow, woods, bunnies, little, window,
- Set Purpose; Review Comprehension Strategy and Skill, TE T128–T129
- Read Anthology Selection pp. 146–161 (independent, partner, or audio CD).
- Discuss questions; retell the story, TE T138.

Comprehension Skill Instruction

Teach Fantasy and Realism, TE T140

Practice Assign PB 107.

Words to Know

New This Week

do	you
for	get
I	help
is	kids
me	next
my	yes
said	yet

Kindergarten Review

are	see
he	dug
play	

Word Work

25-40 minutes

Phonemic Awareness Instruction

Teach Blending Phonemes, TE T127

Spelling and Phonics Instruction

Teach Words with Short *e*, TE T142

Vocabulary Instruction

Teach Opposites, TE T142

3 SMALL GROUP

Options for Guided Reading

80-100 minutes

Extra Support

Before Reading Review Responding questions from VR *Outside the Window.* Preview LR *In the Van,* TE T160. Have children model Monitor/Clarify.

During Reading Coach as children read story.
Fluency Modeling: Model fluent reading; have children model.

After Reading **Fluency Practice:** Have partners reread story. Have children answer Responding questions. ✓

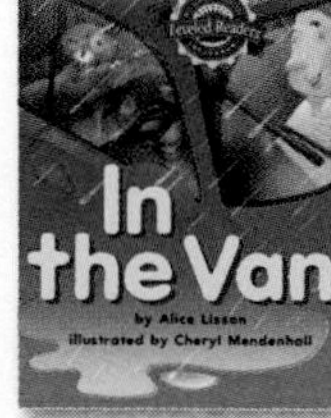

Level C

✓ = opportunity for ongoing assessment; adjust groups accordingly

▲ On Level

Before Reading Discuss Responding questions for LR *At the Vet,* TE T161.

During Reading **Fluency Check:** Ask individuals to read story aloud. ✓

After Reading Have children summarize story for a partner, telling events in order.

Level D

 Above Level

Before Reading Review LBB *Minerva Louise at School.* See TE T104–T105, R8–R9.

During Reading **Fluency Modeling:** Model fluent reading, then have children model it. Have them read first half of story independently.

After Reading Ask questions; have children cite text to support answers. Have partners summarize story events in order.

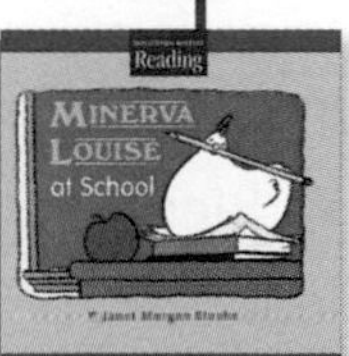

Level E

◆ English Language Learners

Before Reading Preview *Big Ben,* PL Theme 2, pp. 21–24. Model Phonics/Decoding Strategy.

During Reading **Fluency Modeling:** Read aloud each page; have children do echo reading.

After Reading Discuss story; help children find/read words with *y, k, v,* short *e*. Have children use illustrations to retell story to partners.

Writing and Language

30-40 minutes

Writing

Practice Assign Write a Description, Anthology p. 163.

Grammar

Teach Using Naming Words, TE T143

Optional Resources

Teacher Read Aloud

Choose a book from your class/school library or from the Leveled Bibliography, TE T6–T7.

Suggestion: *Possum's Harvest Moon* by Anne Hunter

Independent Work

Self-Selected Reading

Choose from

- classroom/school library
- Leveled Bibliography, TE T6–T7
- *I Love Reading,* Theme 2, take-home books 16–18, 15
- Little Readers for Guided Reading

Centers

- Classroom Management Kit
- Classroom Management activities, TE T100–T101
- Responding activities, TE T138–T139

Differentiated Instruction

- Comprehension Reteaching and Extension, Fantasy and Realism, TE R34–R35
- High-Frequency Word Review: Word Wall, TE T126

TE = Teacher Edition; PB = Practice Book; Tr = Transparency; LR = Leveled Reader; PL = Phonics Library; VR = Vocabulary Reader; VR Guide = Vocabulary Readers Teacher's Manual; LBB = Little Big Book; TP = Theme Paperback

Day 4 Balanced Literacy Plan

Teacher Notes

Reading and Comprehension

20-30 minutes

Shared Reading of Science Link

- "Woodland Animals," Anthology pp. 164–167, TE T146–T147 (independent, partner, or group)
- Skill: How to Read a Science Article, TE T146
- Introduce Concept Vocabulary, TE T146.

Concept Vocabulary

foxes
beavers
porcupines
lodge
quills

Word Work

25-40 minutes

Phonemic Awareness/Phonics Instruction

Teach Blending Phonemes, TE T145

Review Building Short *o* Words, TE T148; Reading and Writing Short *o* Words, TE T149

Spelling and Phonics

Practice Word Slides with Short *e,* TE T150

Vocabulary Instruction

Teach Foods, TE T150

Options for Guided Reading

80-100 minutes

Extra Support

Before Reading Review Responding questions for LR *In the Van,* TE T160.

During Reading Have children reread story.
Fluency Check: Have individuals read aloud. ✓

After Reading Model using the words *first, next,* and *last* to summarize story events. Have children retell the story to a partner.

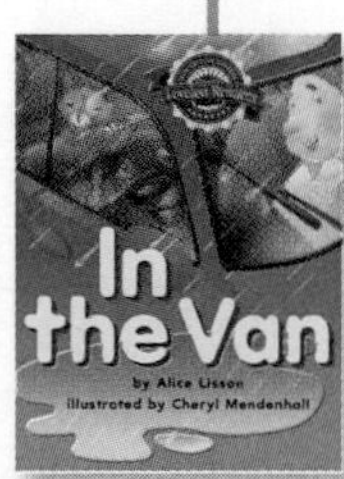

Level C

✓ = opportunity for ongoing assessment; adjust groups accordingly

▲ On Level

Before Reading Have children summarize LR *At the Vet,* telling story events in sequence. ✓ Preview a teacher-selected book or TP *The Pet Vet,* TE R7. Have children make predictions about the story.

During Reading Have children begin story and model Phonics/Decoding Strategy.

After Reading Discuss the story so far. Have children finish story.

Level D

■ Above Level

Before Reading Review first half of LBB *Minerva Louise at School,* TE T104–T107.

During Reading Have children finish book.

After Reading Discuss how book connects to theme. Have children write journal entries to connect it to personal experience or other reading.

Level E

◆ English Language Learners

Before Reading Build background and preview LR *Six Wet Pets,* TE T163. Have children make predictions about the story.

During Reading Read story. **Fluency Modeling:** Reread each page; have children do echo reading. Reinforce Phonics/Decoding Strategy.

After Reading Discuss Responding questions, TE T163. **Fluency Practice:** Have children reread with partners or audio CD.

Level B

Writing and Language

30-40 minutes

Writing

Practice Independent Writing: Writing About Animals; assign PB 108.

Optional Resources

Teacher Read Aloud

Continue selected Read Aloud book from Day 3 or choose a new one from your class or school library.

Independent Work

Self-Selected Reading

Choose from

- classroom/school library
- Leveled Bibliography, TE T6–T7
- children's magazines
- *I Love Reading,* Theme 2, take-home books 16–18, 15
- Little Readers for Guided Reading

Centers

- Classroom Management Kit
- Classroom Management activities, TE T100–T101
- Responding activities, TE T138–T139

Differentiated Instruction

- Visual Literacy: Using Photographs, TE T147
- High-Frequency Words: Word Wall, TE T144
- Study Skills: Following Instructions, TE R38

TE = Teacher Edition; PB = Practice Book; Tr = Transparency; LR = Leveled Reader; PL = Phonics Library; VR = Vocabulary Reader; VR Guide = Vocabulary Readers Teacher's Manual; LBB = Little Big Book; TP = Theme Paperback

Day 5 Balanced Literacy Plan

Teacher Notes

Reading and Comprehension

20-30 minutes

Book Share

- Ask children to explain how they applied the comprehension skill and strategy to books they have read this week.
- Help children use genre and text features to compare and contrast what they have read.
- As a class, discuss one *how, why,* or *what if* question. See examples on Blackline Master 1 to use as a guide.

Word Work

25-40 minutes

Phonemic Awareness Instruction

Teach Blending Phonemes, TE T153

High-Frequency Words

Practice Word Wall/Vocabulary Speed Drill, TE T152

Spelling and Phonics

Practice Building Words with Short *e*, TE T158

Options for Guided Reading

80-100 minutes

Extra Support

Before Reading Preview *Get Wet, Ken!*, PL Theme 2, pp. 25–28. Have children find/read words with *y, k, v,* short e. See TE T155–T157.

During Reading Have children read and model Phonics/Decoding Strategy. **Fluency Check:** Have individuals reread aloud. ✓

After Reading Have partners make connections between the story and LR *In the Van.* Assign On My Way Practice Reader *The Pet* for partner reading.

✓ = opportunity for ongoing assessment; adjust groups accordingly

◆ English Language Learners

Before Reading Review LR *Six Wet Pets,* TE T163.

During Reading Coach rereading of book. **Fluency Check:** Have individuals reread aloud. ✓

After Reading Help children summarize LR story events in sequence. Have children draw/caption a picture about a book they read this week. ✓

Level B

●▲■◆ Mixed Ability Levels

Literature Circles Form small, mixed-ability groups. Ask groups to discuss the main Anthology selection, Link, Leveled Readers, and other books they have read this week. Pose questions or topics for each group, and circulate among groups to offer support. Suggested group activities:

- Respond to specific Literature Discussion questions on Blackline Master 1.
- Discuss story or text elements, authors' choice of language, and/or illustrations.
- Connect book topics or themes to personal experiences or other reading.

Writing and Language

30-40 minutes

Writing

Practice Assign Writing Prompt, TE T153.

Grammar

Review Using Naming Words, TE T159

Speaking and Listening

Practice Conflict Resolution, TE T159

Optional Resources

Teacher Read Aloud

Choose a nonfiction book related to Social Studies or Science unit.

Independent Work

Self-Selected Reading

Choose from

- classroom/school library
- Leveled Bibliography, TE T6–T7
- children's magazines
- consumer text such as books about animals, books about forests, etc.
- *I Love Reading,* Theme 2, take-home books 16–18, 15
- Little Readers for Guided Reading

Centers

- Classroom Management Kit
- Classroom Management activities, TE T100–T101
- Responding activities, TE T138–T139

Differentiated Instruction

- Vocabulary: Speed Drill, TE T152
- Comprehensive Review: Fantasy and Realism, TE T154

End-of-Week Assessment

- Weekly Skills Tests for Theme 2, Week 2
- Fluency Assessment: *Get Wet, Ken!,* PL Theme 2, pp. 25–28, TE T155–T157
- Alternative Assessment, Teacher's Resource Blackline Master 31

TE = Teacher Edition; PB = Practice Book; Tr = Transparency; LR = Leveled Reader; PL = Phonics Library; VR = Vocabulary Reader; VR Guide = Vocabulary Readers Teacher's Manual; LBB = Little Big Book; TP = Theme Paperback

Day 1 Balanced Literacy Plan

Teacher Notes

Reading and Comprehension

20-30 minutes

Shared Reading of Daily Message, TE T174

Shared Reading of Big Book

- Introduce Comprehension Strategy and Skill
  Summarize, TE T176
  Story Structure, TE T177
- Read aloud *Jasper's Beanstalk,* TE T176–T179.

Word Work

25-40 minutes

Phonemic Awareness/Phonics Instruction

Teach Blending Phonemes, TE T175, T181

Review/Practice Consonants *q, j, z,* TE T180; assign PB 109.

Teach Short *u*/Blending Short *u* Words (VC, CVC), TE T181–T182

Practice Assign PB 110–112.

Spelling/Phonics: Kindergarten Review

Teach Letters *j, z,* TE T186

Practice Assign PB 113.

Vocabulary: Kindergarten Review

Teach Word Wall: *are, he, and, the, said,* TE T174

Options for Guided Reading

80-100 minutes

Extra Support

Before Reading Preview *The Bug Kit,* PL Theme 2, pp. 29–32. Model Phonics/Decoding Strategy. See TE T183–T185.

During Reading Coach as children read story.

After Reading Discuss story; have children find/read words with *q, j, z,* short *u.* **Fluency Modeling:** Model fluent reading. Have partners reread story.

✓ = opportunity for ongoing assessment; adjust groups accordingly

On Level

Before Reading Preview *The Bug Kit,* PL Theme 2, pp. 29–32. Model Phonics/Decoding Strategy. See TE T183–T185.

During Reading Have children begin story. **Fluency Modeling:** Model Phonics/Decoding Strategy and fluent reading.

After Reading Have children retell story so far and find/read words with *q, j, z,* short *u*. **Fluency Practice:** Have partners finish story and reread for fluency.

Above Level

Before Reading Preview LR *Let's Take a Trip,* TE T234. Have students model the Summarize Strategy.

During Reading Have children read first half of story. **Fluency Modeling:** Model fluent reading.

After Reading Have children finish reading and write answers to Responding questions. ✓

Level H

English Language Learners

Before Reading Preview VR *At the Pool.* See VR Guide, p. 11.

During Reading **Fluency Modeling:** Read aloud each page; have children do echo reading.

After Reading Discuss Responding pages. Have children reread with partners or audio CD.

Level A

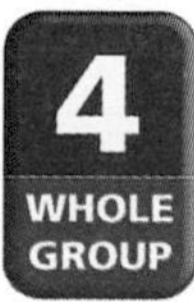

Writing and Language

 25-40 minutes

Writing

Teach Shared Writing: A Class Diary, TE T187

Practice Assign Writing Prompt, TE T175.

Listening and Speaking

Teach Retell/Summarize, TE T187

Optional Resources

Teacher Read Aloud

Reread Big Book: *Jasper's Beanstalk,* TE T176–T179.

Read *Jack and the Beanstalk,* TE T18–T19.

Independent Work

Self-Selected Reading

Choose from

- classroom/school library
- Leveled Bibliography, TE T6–T7
- *I Love Reading,* Theme 2, take-home books 20–22, 19
- Little Readers for Guided Reading

Centers

- Classroom Management Kit
- Classroom Management activities, TE T172–T173

Differentiated Instruction

- Phonics Reteaching or Extension:
  –*q, j, z,* TE R22–R23
  –Short *u*/Blending Short *u* Words (VC, CVC), TE R24–R25
- High-Frequency Words Review: Word Wall, TE T174

TE = Teacher Edition; PB = Practice Book; Tr = Transparency; LR = Leveled Reader; PL = Phonics Library; VR = Vocabulary Reader; VR Guide = Vocabulary Readers Teacher's Manual; LBB = Little Big Book; TP = Theme Paperback

Day 2 Balanced Literacy Plan

Teacher Notes

Reading and Comprehension

20-30 minutes

▼ Anthology Selection

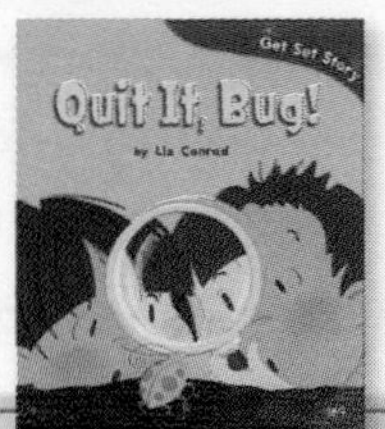

Shared Reading of Get Set Story

- ➤ Build Background and Vocabulary, TE T192
- ➤ Read *Quit It, Bug!,* Anthology pp. 169–175.

Comprehension Skill instruction

Teach Story Structure, TE T194

Words to Know

are	where
away	bug
does	jug
he	quit
live	up
pull	zag
they	zig

Word Work

25-40 minutes

Phonemic Awareness

Teach Blending Phonemes, TE T189

High-Frequency Words Instruction

Teach TE T190–T191, Tr 2-8; **Practice** PB 114, 115.

High-Frequency Words

are	live
away	pull
does	they
he	where

Spelling and Phonics: Kindergarten Review

Teach Letters *qu,* TE T196; **Practice** PB 117.

Vocabulary: Kindergarten Review

Practice Read Rhyming Words, TE T196.

Options for Guided Reading

80-100 minutes

Extra Support

Before Reading Preview VR *At the Pool.* See VR Guide, p. 11.

During Reading Read the book together; coach reading. Help children apply Summarize Strategy.

After Reading Discuss the book and Responding questions. **Fluency Practice:** Have children reread VR with a partner. Assign *Quit It, Zig!,* PL Theme 2, pp. 33–36, for partner reading.

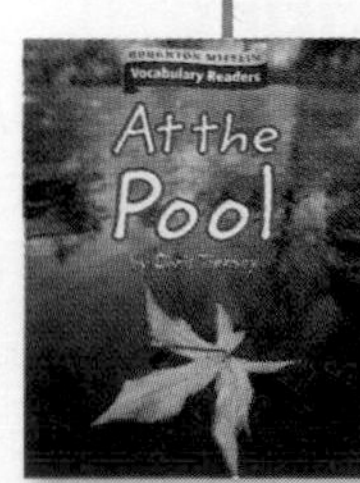

Level A

✓ = opportunity for ongoing assessment; adjust groups accordingly

▲ On Level

Before Reading Discuss PL *The Bug Kit,* TE T183–T185. Preview LR *Big Tug,* TE T233.

During Reading Coach reading as children begin story. **Fluency Modeling:** Model fluent reading, then have children model it.

After Reading Discuss the sequence of events in the story. Then have children write answers to Responding questions. ✓ Assign *Quit It, Zig!,* PL Theme 2, pp. 33–36, for partner reading.

Level D

■ Above Level

Before Reading Have children model the Summarize Strategy and discuss Responding questions for LR *Let's Take a Trip,* TE T234. ✓

During Reading **Fluency Check:** Monitor children's oral reading. ✓

After Reading Have children summarize for a partner, telling story events in order. Assign *Quit It, Zig!,* PL Theme 2, pp. 33–36, for partner reading.

Level H

◆ English Language Learners

Before Reading To review VR vocabulary, have children demonstrate or give examples. See VR Guide, p. 11.

During Reading **Fluency Practice:** Have children reread book. Option: Preview and coach reading of *The Bug Kit,* PL Theme 2, pp. 29–32, TE T183–T185.

After Reading Help children summarize VR. Have partners discuss, draw, or write facts they learned. ✓

Level A

4 WHOLE GROUP Writing and Language

25-40 minutes

Writing

Teach Interactive Writing: A Diary, TE T197

Practice Assign Writing Prompt, TE T189.

Optional Resources

Teacher Read Aloud

Reread Big Book: *Jasper's Beanstalk,* TE T176–T179.

Independent Work

Self-Selected Reading

Choose from

- classroom/school library
- Leveled Bibliography, TE T6–T7
- *I Love Reading,* Theme 2, take-home books 20–22, 19
- Little Readers for Guided Reading

Centers

- Classroom Management Kit
- Classroom Management activities, TE T172–T173

Differentiated Instruction

- High-Frequency Words
  - –Word Wall, TE T188
  - – Reteaching or Extension, TE R28–R29

TE = Teacher Edition; PB = Practice Book; Tr = Transparency; LR = Leveled Reader; PL = Phonics Library; VR = Vocabulary Reader; VR Guide = Vocabulary Readers Teacher's Manual; LBB = Little Big Book; TP = Theme Paperback

Day 3 Balanced Literacy Plan

Teacher Notes

Reading and Comprehension

20-30 minutes

Shared Reading of *A Surprise for Zig Bug*

- Introduce Key Vocabulary, TE T200, Tr 2-9
  leaf pool
- Set Purpose; Review Comprehension Strategy and Skill, TE T200–T201
- Read Anthology Selection pp. 178–193 (independent, partner, or audio CD).
- Discuss questions; retell the story, TE T210.

▼ Anthology Selection

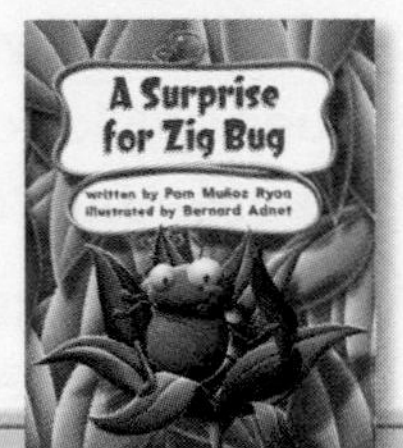

Words to Know

New This Week

are	where
away	bug
does	jug
he	quit
live	up
pull	zig
they	zag

Kindergarten Review

like	see
play	

Comprehension Skill Instruction

Teach Story Structure, TE T212–T213, Tr 2-10

Practice Assign PB 120.

2 WHOLE GROUP

Word Work

25-40 minutes

Phonemic Awareness Instruction

Teach Blending Phonemes, TE T199

Spelling and Phonics Instruction

Teach Words with Short *u,* TE T214

Vocabulary Instruction

Teach Days of the Week, TE T214

Options for Guided Reading

80-100 minutes

Extra Support

Before Reading Review Responding questions from VR *At the Pool.* Preview LR *Where Is Zig?,* TE T232. Have children model Summarize.

During Reading Coach as children read story. **Fluency Modeling:** Model fluent reading; have children model.

After Reading **Fluency Practice:** Have partners reread story. Have children answer Responding questions. ✓

Level D

✓ = opportunity for ongoing assessment; adjust groups accordingly

 **On Level**

Before Reading Discuss Responding questions for LR *Big Tug,* TE T233.

During Reading **Fluency Check:** Ask individuals to read story aloud. ✓

After Reading Have children summarize story for a partner, telling events in order.

Level D

■ **Above Level**

Before Reading Review LBB *Jasper's Beanstalk*. See TE T176–T179, R12–R13.

During Reading **Fluency Modeling:** Model fluent reading, then have children model it. Have them read first half of story independently.

After Reading Ask questions; have children cite text to support answers. Have partners summarize story events in order.

Level H

 **English Language Learners**

Before Reading Preview *Quit It, Zig!,* PL Theme 2, pp. 33–36. Model Phonics/Decoding Strategy. See TE T199.

During Reading **Fluency Modeling:** Read aloud each page; have children do echo reading.

After Reading Discuss story; help children find/read words with *q, j, z,* short *u*. Have children use illustrations to retell story to partners.

Writing and Language

30-40 minutes

Writing

Practice Assign Write a List, Anthology p. 195.

Grammar

Teach Using Action Words, TE T215

Optional Resources

Teacher Read Aloud

Choose a book from your class/school library or from the Leveled Bibliography, TE T6–T7.

Suggestion: *A Birthday Basket for Tia* by Pat Mora

Independent Work

Self-Selected Reading

Choose from

- classroom/school library
- Leveled Bibliography, TE T6–T7
- *I Love Reading,* Theme 2, take-home books 20–22, 19
- Little Readers for Guided Reading

Centers

- Classroom Management Kit
- Classroom Management activities, TE T172–T173
- Responding activities, TE T210–T211

Differentiated Instruction

- Comprehension Reteaching and Extension, Story Structure, TE R36–R37
- High-Frequency Word Review: Word Wall, TE T198

TE = Teacher Edition; PB = Practice Book; Tr = Transparency; LR = Leveled Reader; PL = Phonics Library; VR = Vocabulary Reader; VR Guide = Vocabulary Readers Teacher's Manual; LBB = Little Big Book; TP = Theme Paperback

Day 4 Balanced Literacy Plan

Teacher Notes

1 WHOLE GROUP

Reading and Comprehension

20-30 minutes

Shared Reading of Science Link

- "Insects," Anthology pp. 196–199, TE T218–T219 (independent, partner, or group)
- Skill: How to Read a Science Article, TE T218
- Introduce Concept Vocabulary, TE T218.

Concept Vocabulary

insects
wings
antennae
tubes

2 WHOLE GROUP

Word Work

25-40 minutes

Phonemic Awareness/Phonics Instruction

Teach Blending Phonemes, TE T217

Review Reading Short *e* Words, TE T220; Building Short *e* Words, TE T221

Spelling and Phonics

Practice Word Slides with Short *u*, TE T222

Vocabulary Instruction

Teach Homographs, TE T222

3 SMALL GROUP

Options for Guided Reading

80-100 minutes

Extra Support

Before Reading Review Responding questions for LR *Where Is Zig?*, TE T232.

During Reading Have children reread story. **Fluency Check:** Have individuals read aloud. ✓

After Reading Model using the words *first, next,* and *last* to summarize story events. Have children retell the story to a partner.

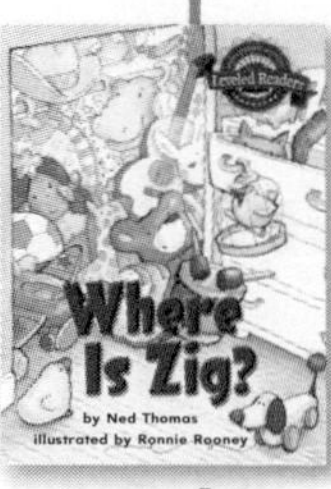

Level D

✓ = opportunity for ongoing assessment; adjust groups accordingly

▲ On Level

Before Reading Have children summarize LR *Big Tug,* telling story events in sequence. ✓ Preview a teacher-selected book or TP *Spots,* TE R11. Have children make predictions about the story.

During Reading Have children begin story and model Phonics/Decoding Strategy.

After Reading Discuss the story so far. Have children finish story.

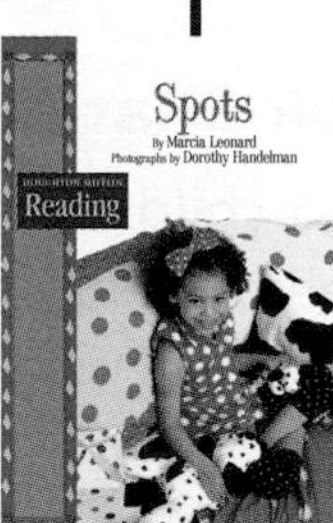

Level D

■ Above Level

Before Reading Review first half of LBB *Jasper's Beanstalk,* TE T176–T179.

During Reading Have children finish book.

After Reading Discuss how book connects to theme. Have children write journal entries to connect it to personal experience or other reading.

Level H

◆ English Language Learners

Before Reading Build background and preview LR *Slug and Bug,* TE T235. Have children make predictions about the story.

During Reading Read story. **Fluency Modeling:** Reread each page; have children do echo reading. Reinforce Phonics/Decoding Strategy.

After Reading Discuss Responding questions, TE T210. **Fluency Practice:** Have children reread with partners or audio CD.

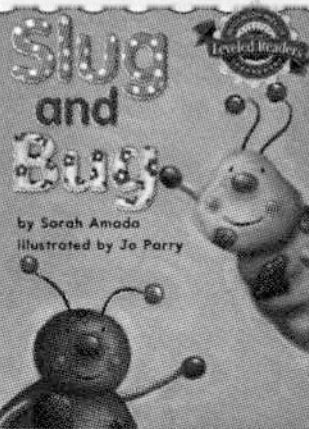

Level B

4 WHOLE GROUP

Writing and Language

30-40 minutes

Writing

Practice Independent Writing: Writing About Bugs; assign PB 121.

Optional Resources

Teacher Read Aloud

Continue selected Read Aloud book from Day 3 or choose a new one from your class or school library.

Independent Work

Self-Selected Reading

Choose from

- classroom/school library
- Leveled Bibliography, TE T6–T7
- children's magazines
- *I Love Reading,* Theme 2, take-home books 20–22, 19
- Little Readers for Guided Reading

Centers

- Classroom Management Kit
- Classroom Management activities, TE T172–T173
- Responding activities, TE T210–T211

Differentiated Instruction

- High-Frequency Words: Word Wall, TE T216
- Study Skills: Following Instructions, TE R38

TE = Teacher Edition; PB = Practice Book; Tr = Transparency; LR = Leveled Reader; PL = Phonics Library; VR = Vocabulary Reader; VR Guide = Vocabulary Readers Teacher's Manual; LBB = Little Big Book; TP = Theme Paperback

Day 5 Balanced Literacy Plan

Teacher Notes

Reading and Comprehension

20-30 minutes

Book Share

- Ask children to explain how they applied the comprehension skill and strategy to books they have read this week.
- Help children use genre and text features to compare and contrast what they have read.
- As a class, discuss one *how, why,* or *what if* question. See examples on Blackline Master 1 to use as a guide.

Word Work

25-40 minutes

Phonemic Awareness Instruction

Teach Blending Phonemes, TE T225

Vocabulary

Practice Speed Drill, TE T224

Spelling and Phonics

Practice Building Words with Short *u,* TE T230

Options for Guided Reading

80-100 minutes

Extra Support

Before Reading Preview *Rug Tug,* PL Theme 2, pp. 37–40. Have children find/read words with *q, j, z,* short *u.* See TE T227–T229.

During Reading Have children read and model Phonics/Decoding Strategy. **Fluency Check:** Have individuals reread aloud. ✓

After Reading Have partners make connections between the story and LR *Where Is Zig?* Assign On My Way Practice Reader *Where Is Tug Bug?* for partner reading.

✓ = opportunity for ongoing assessment; adjust groups accordingly

English Language Learners

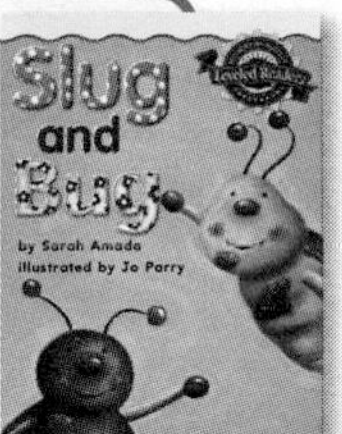

Level B

Before Reading Review LR *Slug and Bug,* TE T235.

During Reading Coach rereading of book. **Fluency Check:** Have individuals reread aloud. ✓

After Reading Help children summarize LR story events in sequence. Have children draw/caption a picture about a book they read this week. ✓

Mixed Ability Levels

Literature Circles Form small, mixed-ability groups. Ask groups to discuss the main Anthology selection, Link, Leveled Readers, and other books they have read this week. Pose questions or topics for each group, and circulate among groups to offer support. Suggested group activities:

- Respond to specific Literature Discussion questions on Blackline Master 1.
- Discuss story or text elements, authors' choice of language, and/or illustrations.
- Connect book topics or themes to personal experiences or other reading.

Literature Circle

4 WHOLE GROUP

Writing and Language

30-40 minutes

Writing

Practice Assign Writing Prompt, TE T225.

Grammar

Review Using Action Words, TE T231

Listening and Speaking

Practice Reader's Theater, TE T231

Optional Resources

Teacher Read Aloud

Choose a nonfiction book related to Social Studies or Science unit.

Independent Work

Self-Selected Reading

Choose from

- classroom/school library
- Leveled Bibliography, TE T6–T7
- children's magazines
- consumer text such as books about insects, books about animals, etc.

Centers

- Classroom Management Kit
- Classroom Management activities, TE T172–T173
- Responding activities, TE T210–T211

Differentiated Instruction

- Vocabulary: Speed Drill, TE T224
- Comprehension Review: Story Structure, TE T226

Assessment

End-of-Week Assessment

- Weekly Skills Tests for Theme 2, Week 3
- Fluency Assessment, *Rug Tug:* PL Theme 2, pp. 37–40, TE T227–T229
- Alternative Assessment, Teacher's Resource Blackline Master 34

End-of-Theme Assessment

- Integrated Theme Tests for Theme 2

TE = Teacher Edition; PB = Practice Book; Tr = Transparency; LR = Leveled Reader; PL = Phonics Library; VR = Vocabulary Reader; VR Guide = Vocabulary Readers Teacher's Manual; LBB = Little Big Book; TP = Theme Paperback

Theme 3 Overview

	Week 1
Reading and Comprehension	**Shared Reading** Main Selection: *Seasons* Language Arts Link: "Ha! Ha! Ha!" Book Share **Comprehension** Strategy: Evaluate Skill: Topic, Main Idea, Details/Summarizing Content Skill: How to Read Jokes and Lyrics
Word Work	**Phonemic Awareness:** Blending and Segmenting Phonemes **Phonics:** Double Final Consonants **Phonics:** Blending More Short *a* Words **Phonics:** Plurals with *-s* **Phonics Review:** Words with Short *u* **Vocabulary:** Seasons of the Year; Months of the Year **High-Frequency Words:** *animal, bird, cold, fall, flower, full, look, of, see* **Spelling:** The Short *a* Sound
Options for Guided Reading	**Big Book** *Counting on the Woods* **Vocabulary Reader** *Seasons* **Leveled Readers:** Extra Support: *A Summer Day* On Level: *Fun in the Snow* Above Level: *Fall Leaves* ELL: *Summer* **Phonics Library** *Cabs, Cabs, Cabs* *Fall Naps* *Pam Can Pack* Theme Paperbacks **Literature Circles**
Writing and Oral Language	**Shared Writing:** A Class Description **Interactive Writing:** A Class Description **Independent Writing:** Writing About Favorite Seasons **Grammar:** What Is a Sentence? **Listening:** Fact or Opinion?
Assessment Options	• Weekly Skills Test for Theme 3, Week 1 • Fluency Assessment: Phonics Library

Use **Launching the Theme** on pages T16–T17 of the Teacher's Edition to introduce the theme.

Week 2

Shared Reading
Main Selection: *Miss Jill's Ice Cream Shop*
Social Studies Link: "Making Ice Cream"
Book Share

Comprehension
Strategy: Predict/Infer
Skill: Making Predictions
Content Skill: How to Read a Social Studies Article

Phonemic Awareness: Blending and Segmenting Phonemes
Phonics: Verb Endings *-s, -ed, -ing*
Phonics: Blending More Short *i* Words
Phonics: Possessives with *'s*
Phonics Review: Double Final Consonants; Plurals with *-s;* Final Consonants *ck, s as /z/;* Short *a*
Vocabulary: Possessives; Words That Describe Size
High-Frequency Words: *all, call, eat, every, first, never, paper, shall, why*
Spelling: The Short *i* Sound

Big Book
Pearl's First Prize Plant

Vocabulary Reader
At the Ice Cream Shop

Leveled Readers:
Extra Support: *Tim's Pig*
On Level: *Mama and Kit Go Away*
Above Level: *Lazy Fox*
ELL: *Tim's Pig Eats*

Phonics Library
Lots of Picking
Bill Bird
Tim's Cat

Literature Circles

Shared Writing: A Persuasive Letter
Interactive Writing: A Persuasive Letter
Independent Writing: Writing About Favorite Foods
Grammar: Naming Part of a Sentence
Listening/Speaking: Retelling a Story

- Weekly Skills Test for Theme 3, Week 2
- Fluency Assessment: Phonics Library

Week 3

Shared Reading
Main Selection: *At the Aquarium*
Drama Link: "Why Sun and Moon Live in the Sky"
Book Share

Comprehension
Strategy: Question
Skill: Categorize and Classify
Content Skill: How to Read a Play

Phonemic Awareness: Blending and Segmenting Phonemes
Phonics: Clusters with *r*
Phonics: Contractions with *'s*
Phonics Review: Short *i;* Verbs Ending with *-s, -ed, -ing;* Possessives with *'s*
Vocabulary: Color Words; Words That Show Position
High-Frequency Words: *also, blue, brown, color, funny, green, like, many, some*
Spelling: Consonant Clusters with *r*

Big Book
Hilda Hen's Scary Night

Vocabulary Reader
Sea Animals

Leveled Readers:
Extra Support: *Let's Grab It!*
On Level: *Looking for Birds*
Above Level: *On the Beach*
ELL: *Grab It!*

Phonics Library
Let's Trim the Track!
Brad's Quick Rag Tricks
Fran Pig's Brick Hut

Literature Circles

Shared Writing: A Class Story
Interactive Writing: A Class Story
Independent Writing: Writing About Trips
Grammar: Action Part of a Sentence
Listening: To Gather Information

- Weekly Skills Test, Theme 3, Week 3
- Fluency Assessment: Phonics Library

Day 1 Balanced Literacy Plan

Teacher Notes

Reading and Comprehension

20-30 minutes

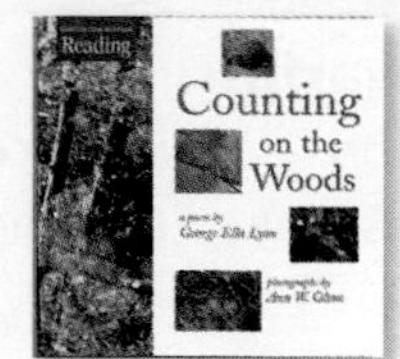

Shared Reading of Daily Message, TE T30

Shared Reading of Big Book

- Introduce Comprehension Strategy and Skill
  Evaluate, TE T32
  Topic, Main Idea, Details/Summarizing, TE T33
- Read aloud *Counting on the Woods,* TE T32–T35.

Word Work

25-40 minutes

Phonemic Awareness/Phonics Instruction

Teach Blending and Segmenting Phonemes, TE T31, T37

Teach Double Final Consonants; Blending More Short a Words; Plurals With -s, TE T36; T37; T38

Practice Assign PB 123–124; 125–126; 127

Spelling

Teach The Short *a* Sound, TE T42

Practice Assign PB 227.

Vocabulary

Teach Spelling Patterns *-ack, -ap,* TE T42

Options for Guided Reading

80-100 minutes

Extra Support

Before Reading Preview *Cabs, Cabs, Cabs,* PL Theme 3, pp. 5–8. Model Phonics/Decoding Strategy. See TE T39–T41.

During Reading Coach as children read story.

After Reading Discuss story; have children find/read words with double final consonants, short *a*, plurals with *-s.* **Fluency Modeling:** Model fluent reading. Have partners reread story.

✓ = opportunity for ongoing assessment; adjust groups accordingly

▲ On Level

Before Reading Preview *Cabs, Cabs, Cabs,* PL Theme 3, pp. 5–8. Model Phonics/Decoding Strategy. See TE T39.

During Reading Have children begin story. **Fluency Modeling:** Model Phonics/Decoding Strategy and fluent reading.

After Reading Have children retell story so far and find/read words with double final consonants, short *a,* plurals with *-s.* **Fluency Practice:** Have partners finish story and reread for fluency.

■ Above Level

Before Reading Preview LR *Fall Leaves,* TE T90. Have students model the Evaluate Strategy.

During Reading Have children read first half of story. **Fluency Modeling:** Model fluent reading.

After Reading Have children finish reading and write answers to Responding questions. 

Level J

◆ English Language Learners

Before Reading Preview VR *Seasons.* See VR Guide, p. 12.

During Reading **Fluency Modeling:** Read aloud each page; have children do echo reading.

After Reading Discuss Responding pages. Have children reread with partners or audio CD.

Level A

4 WHOLE GROUP Writing and Language

25-40 minutes

Writing

Teach Shared Writing: A Class Description, TE T43

Practice Assign Writing Prompt, TE T31.

Viewing

Teach Gathering Information, TE T43

Optional Resources

Teacher Read Aloud

Reread Big Book: *Counting on the Woods,* TE T32–T35.

Independent Work

Self-Selected Reading

Choose from

- classroom/school library
- Leveled Bibliography, TE T6–T7
- *I Love Reading,* Theme 3, take-home books 23–27
- Little Readers for Guided Reading

Centers

- Classroom Management Kit
- Classroom Management activities, TE T28–T29

Differentiated Instruction

- Phonics Reteaching or Extension:
  - –Double Final Consonants, TE R14–R15
  - –Blending More Short *a* Words, TE R16–R17
  - –Plurals with *-s,* TE R18–R19
- High-Frequency Words Review: Word Wall, TE T30

TE = Teacher Edition; PB = Practice Book; Tr = Transparency; LR = Leveled Reader; PL = Phonics Library; VR = Vocabulary Reader; VR Guide = Vocabulary Readers Teacher's Manual; LBB = Little Big Book; TP = Theme Paperback

Day 2 Balanced Literacy Plan

Teacher Notes

Reading and Comprehension

20-30 minutes

Shared Reading of Get Set Story

➤ Build Background and Vocabulary, TE T48

➤ Read *Animals in the Cold,* Anthology pp. 12–19.

Comprehension Skill Instruction

Teach Topic, Main Idea, Details/Summarizing, TE T50

▼ **Anthology Selection**

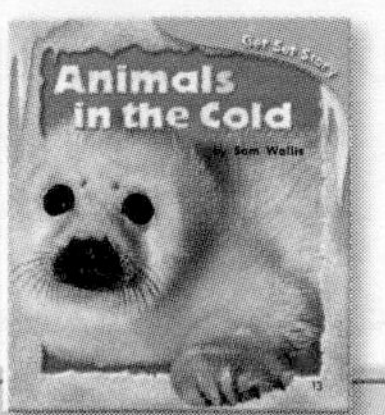

Words to Know

New This Week

animals	see
birds	buds
cold	is
fall	lots
flowers	pick
full	pups
look	will
of	

2 WHOLE GROUP

Word Work

25-40 minutes

Phonemic Awareness

Teach Blending and Segmenting Phonemes, TE T45

High-Frequency Word Instruction

Teach TE T46–T47, Tr 3-1; **Practice** PB 128–129.

Spelling

Teach The Short *a* Sound, TE T52; **Practice** PB 216–223.

Vocabulary

Review High-Frequency Words, TE T52

High-Frequency Words

animals	full
birds	look
cold	of
fall	see
flowers	

Options for Guided Reading

80-100 minutes

● Extra Support

Before Reading Preview VR *Seasons.* See VR Guide, p. 12.

During Reading Read the book together; coach reading. Help children apply Evaluate Strategy.

After Reading Discuss the book and Responding questions. **Fluency Practice:** Have children reread VR with a partner. Assign *Fall Naps,* PL Theme 3, pp. 9–12, for partner reading.

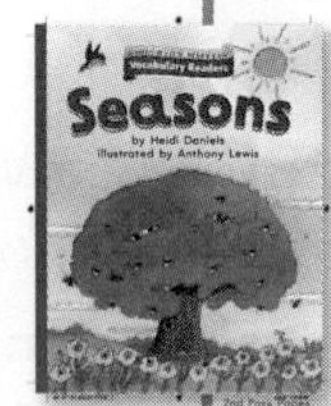

Level A

✓ = opportunity for ongoing assessment; adjust groups accordingly

▲ On Level

Before Reading Discuss PL *Cabs, Cabs, Cabs,* TE T39–T41. Preview LR *Fun in the Snow,* TE T89.

During Reading Coach reading as children begin story. **Fluency Modeling:** Model fluent reading, then have children model it.

After Reading Discuss the sequence of events in the story. Then have children write answers to Responding questions. ✓ Assign *Fall Naps,* PL Theme 3, pp. 9–12, for partner reading.

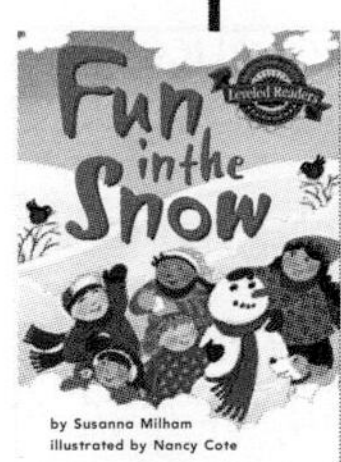

Level D

■ Above Level

Before Reading Have children model the Evaluate Strategy and discuss Responding questions for LR *Fall Leaves,* TE T90.

During Reading **Fluency Check:** Monitor children's oral reading. ✓

After Reading Have children summarize for a partner, telling story events in order. Assign *Fall Naps,* PL Theme 3, pp. 9–12, for partner reading.

Level J

◆ English Language Learners

Before Reading To review VR vocabulary, have children demonstrate or give examples. See VR Guide, p. 12.

During Reading **Fluency Practice:** Have children reread book. Option: Preview and coach reading of *Cabs, Cabs, Cabs,* PL Theme 13, pp. 5–8, TE T39–T41.

After Reading Help children summarize VR. Have partners discuss, draw, or write facts they learned. ✓

Level A

4 WHOLE GROUP

Writing and Language

25-40 minutes

Writing

Teach Interactive Writing: A Class Description, TE T53

Practice Assign Writing Prompt, TE T45.

Optional Resources

Teacher Read Aloud

Reread Big Book: *Counting on the Woods,* TE T32–T35.

Independent Work

Self-Selected Reading

Choose from

- classroom/school library
- Leveled Bibliography, TE T6–T7
- *I Love Reading,* Theme 3, take-home books 23–27
- Little Readers for Guided Reading

Centers

- Classroom Management Kit
- Classroom Management activities, TE T28–T29

Differentiated Instruction

- High-Frequency Words
  - –Word Wall, TE T44
  - –Reteaching or Extension, TE R14–R19

TE = Teacher Edition; PB = Practice Book; Tr = Transparency; LR = Leveled Reader; PL = Phonics Library; VR = Vocabulary Reader; VR Guide = Vocabulary Readers Teacher's Manual; LBB = Little Big Book; TP = Theme Paperback

Day 3 Balanced Literacy Plan

Teacher Notes

Reading and Comprehension

20-30 minutes

Shared Reading of *Seasons*

➤ Introduce Story Vocabulary, TE T56, Tr 3-2

bear	leaves	south	summer	winter
insects	rain	spring	trees	

➤ Set Purpose; Review Comprehension Strategy and Skill, TE T56–T57

➤ Read Anthology Selection pp. 20–41 (independent, partner, or audio CD).

➤ Discuss Responding questions; retell the story, TE T67.

▼ **Anthology Selection**

Words to Know

New This Week

animals	see
birds	buds
cold	is
fall	lots
flower	pick
full	pups
look	will
of	

Kindergarten Review

play

Comprehension Skill Instruction

Teach Topic, Main Idea, Details/Summarizing, TE T68–T69, Tr 3-3

Practice Assign PB 133.

Word Work

25-40 minutes

Phonemic Awareness Instruction

Teach Blending and Segmenting Phonemes, TE T55

Spelling

Teach The Short *a* Sound, TE T70

Vocabulary Instruction

Teach Seasons of the Year, TE T70

Options for Guided Reading

80-100 minutes

Extra Support

Before Reading Review Responding questions from VR Preview LR *A Summer Day,* TE T88. Have children model the Evaluate.

During Reading Coach as children read story. **Fluency Modeling:** Model fluent reading; have children model.

After Reading **Fluency Practice:** Have partners reread story. Have children write answers to Responding questions. ✓

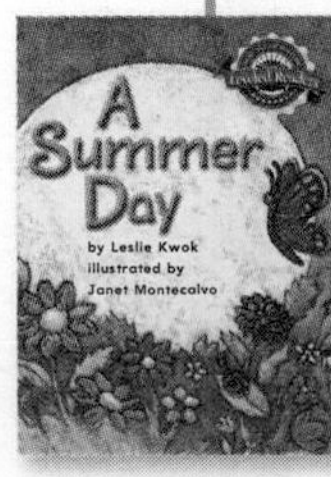

Level C

✓ = opportunity for ongoing assessment; adjust groups accordingly

▲ On Level

Before Reading Discuss Responding questions for LR *Fun in the Snow,* TE T89.

During Reading **Fluency Check:** Ask individuals to read story aloud. ✓

After Reading Have children summarize story for a partner, telling events in order.

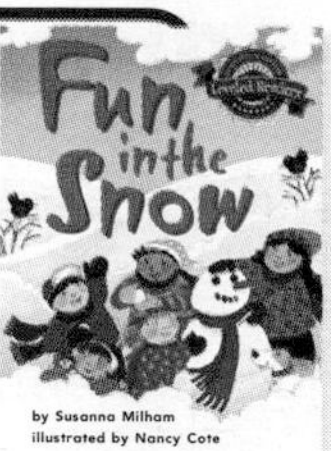

Level D

■ Above Level

Before Reading Review LBB *Counting on the Woods.* See TE T32–T35, R4–R5.

During Reading **Fluency Modeling:** Model fluent reading, then have children model it. Have them read first half of story independently.

After Reading Ask questions; have children cite text to support answers. Have partners summarize story events in order.

Level G

◆ English Language Learners

Before Reading Preview *Fall Naps,* PL Theme 3, pp. 9–12. Model Phonics/Decoding Strategy.

During Reading **Fluency Modeling:** Read aloud each page; have children do echo reading.

After Reading Discuss story; help children find/read words with short *a.* Have children use illustrations to retell story to partners.

4 WHOLE GROUP

Writing and Language

30-40 minutes

Writing

Practice Assign Think About the Story, Anthology p. 40.

Grammar

Teach What Is a Sentence?, TE T71

Optional Resources

Teacher Read Aloud

Choose a book from your class/school library or from the Leveled Bibliography, TE T6–T7.

- Suggestion: *Possum and the Peeper* by Anne Hunter

Independent Work

Self-Selected Reading

Choose from

- classroom/school library
- Leveled Bibliography, TE T6–T7
- *I Love Reading,* Theme 3, take-home books 23–27
- Little Readers for Guided Reading

Centers

- Classroom Management Kit
- Classroom Management activities, TE T28–T29
- Responding activities, TE T67

Differentiated Instruction

- Comprehension Reteaching and Extension: Topic, Main Idea, Details/Summarizing, TE R36–R37
- High-Frequency Word Review: Word Wall, TE T54

TE = Teacher Edition; PB = Practice Book; Tr = Transparency; LR = Leveled Reader; PL = Phonics Library; VR = Vocabulary Reader; VR Guide = Vocabulary Readers Teacher's Manual; LBB = Little Big Book; TP = Theme Paperback

Day 4 Balanced Literacy Plan

Teacher Notes

Reading and Comprehension

20-30 minutes

Shared Reading of Language Arts Link

- "Ha! Ha! Ha!," Anthology pp. 42–44, TE T74–T75 (independent, partner, or group)
- Skill: How to Read Jokes and Lyrics, TE T74
- Introduce Concept Vocabulary, TE T74.

Concept Vocabulary
planted
growing
corn
carrots

Word Work

25-40 minutes

Phonemic Awareness/Phonics Instruction

Teach Blending and Segmenting Phonemes, TE T73

Review Reading Short *u* Words, TE T76–T77

Spelling

Practice The Short *a* Sound, TE T78

Vocabulary Instruction

Teach Months of the Year, TE T78

Options for Guided Reading

80-100 minutes

Extra Support

Before Reading Review Responding questions for LR *A Summer Day,* TE T88.

During Reading Have children reread story. **Fluency Check:** Have individuals read aloud. ✓

After Reading Model using the words *first, next,* and *last* to summarize story events. Have children retell the story to a partner.

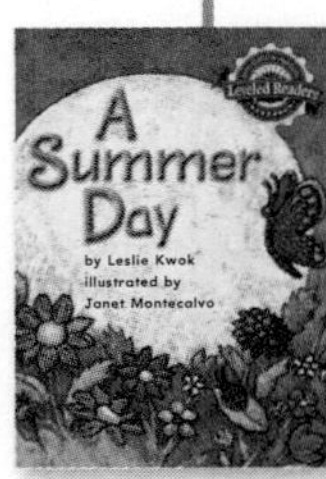

Level C

✓ = opportunity for ongoing assessment; adjust groups accordingly

▲ On Level

Before Reading Have children summarize LR *Fun in the Snow,* telling story events in sequence. ✓ Preview a teacher-selected book or TP *Barnyard Tracks,* TE R3. Have children make predictions about the story.

During Reading Have children begin story and model Phonics/Decoding Strategy.

After Reading Discuss the story so far. Have children finish story.

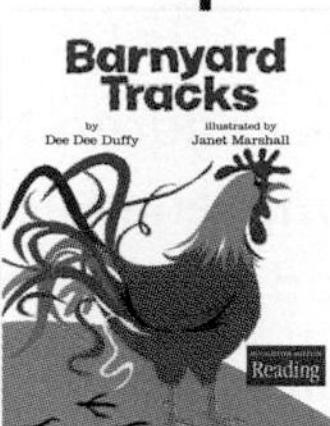

Level E

■ Above Level

Before Reading Review first half of LBB *Counting on the Woods,* TE T32–T35.

During Reading Have children finish book.

After Reading Discuss how book connects to theme. Have children write journal entries to connect it to personal experience or other reading.

Level G

 English Language Learners

Before Reading Build background and preview LR *Summer,* TE T91. Have children make predictions about the story.

During Reading Read story. **Fluency Modeling:** Reread each page; have children do echo reading. Reinforce Phonics/Decoding Strategy.

After Reading Discuss Responding questions, TE T91. **Fluency Practice:** Have children reread with partners or audio CD.

Level B

Writing and Language

30-40 minutes

Writing

Practice Independent Writing: Writing About Favorite Seasons, TE T79; assign PB 137.

Optional Resources

Teacher Read Aloud

Continue selected Read Aloud book from Day 3 or choose a new one from your class or school library.

Independent Work

Self-Selected Reading

Choose from

- classroom/school library
- Leveled Bibliography, TE T6–T7
- children's magazines
- *I Love Reading,* Theme 3 take-home books 23–27
- Little Readers for Guided Reading

Centers

- Classroom Management Kit
- Classroom Management activities, TE T28–T29
- Responding activities, TE T67

Differentiated Instruction

- High-Frequency Words: Word Wall, TE T72
- Study Skills: Topic, Main Idea, Details/Summarizing, TE R36–37

TE = Teacher Edition; PB = Practice Book; Tr = Transparency; LR = Leveled Reader; PL = Phonics Library; VR = Vocabulary Reader; VR Guide = Vocabulary Readers Teacher's Manual; LBB = Little Big Book; TP = Theme Paperback

Day 5 Balanced Literacy Plan

Teacher Notes

Reading and Comprehension

20-30 minutes

Book Share

Book Share

- Ask children to explain how they applied the comprehension skill and strategy to books they have read this week.
- Help children use genre and text features to compare and contrast what they have read.
- As a class, discuss one *how, why,* or *what if* question. See examples on Blackline Master 1 to use as a guide.

Word Work

25-40 minutes

Phonemic Awareness Instruction

Teach Blending and Segmenting Phonemes, TE T81

High-Frequency Words

Practice Word Wall, TE T86

Spelling

Practice The Short *a* Sound, TE T86

Options for Guided Reading

80-100 minutes

Extra Support

Before Reading Preview *Pam Can Pack,* PL Theme 3, pp. 13–16. Have children find/read words with double final consonants, short *a*, plurals with *-s*. See TE T83.

During Reading Have children read and model Phonics/Decoding Strategy. **Fluency Check:** Have individuals reread aloud. ✓

After Reading Have partners make connections between the story and LR *A Summer Day.* Assign On My Way Practice Reader *Mack* for partner reading.

✓ = opportunity for ongoing assessment; adjust groups accordingly

◆ English Language Learners

Level B

Before Reading Review LR *Summer,* TE T91.

During Reading Coach rereading of book. **Fluency Check:** Have individuals reread aloud. ✓

After Reading Help children summarize LR story events in sequence. Have children draw/caption a picture about a book they read this week. ✓

●▲■◆ Mixed Ability Levels

Literature Circles Form small, mixed-ability groups. Ask groups to discuss the main Anthology selection, Link, Leveled Readers, and other books they have read this week. Pose questions or topics for each group, and circulate among groups to offer support. Suggested group activities:

- Respond to specific Literature Discussion questions on Blackline Master 1.
- Discuss story or text elements, authors' choice of language, and/or illustrations.
- Connect book topics or themes to personal experiences or other reading.

Writing and Language

30-40 minutes

Writing

Practice Assign Writing Prompt, TE T81.

Grammar

Review What Is a Sentence?, TE T87

Listening

Practice Fact or Opinion?, TE T87

Optional Resources

Teacher Read Aloud

Choose a nonfiction book related to Social Studies or Science unit.

Independent Work

Self-Selected Reading

Choose from

- classroom/school library
- Leveled Bibliography, TE T6–T7
- children's magazines
- consumer text such as joke books, song books
- *I Love Reading,* Theme 3, take-home books 23–27
- Little Readers for Guided Reading

Centers

- Classroom Management Kit
- Classroom Management activities, TE T28–T29
- Responding activities, TE T67

Differentiated Instruction

- Vocabulary: Speed Drill, TE T80
- Comprehension Review: Topic, Main Idea, Details/ Summarizing, TE T82

End-of-Week Assessment

- Weekly Skills Tests for Theme 3, Week 1
- Fluency Assessment, *Pam Can Pack,* PL Theme 3, pp. 13–16, TE T83–T85
- Alternative Assessment, Teacher's Resource Blackline Master 39

TE = Teacher Edition; PB = Practice Book; Tr = Transparency; LR = Leveled Reader; PL = Phonics Library; VR = Vocabulary Reader; VR Guide = Vocabulary Readers Teacher's Manual; LBB = Little Big Book; TP = Theme Paperback

Day 1 Balanced Literacy Plan

Teacher Notes

Reading and Comprehension

20-30 minutes

Shared Reading of Daily Message, TE T102

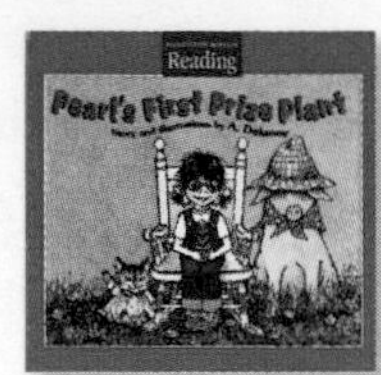

Shared Reading of Big Book

- Introduce Comprehension Strategy and Skill
  Predict/Infer, TE T104
  Making Predictions, TE T105
- Read aloud *Pearl's First Prize Plant,* TE T104–T107.

Word Work

25-40 minutes

Phonemic Awareness/Phonics Instruction

Teach Blending and Segmenting Phonemes, TE T103, T109

Teach Verb Endings *-s, -ed, -ing,* TE T108; assign PB 138.

Teach Blending More Short *i* Words, TE T109; assign PB 139–140.

Teach Possessives with *'s,* TE T110; assign PB 141.

Spelling

Teach The Short *i* Sound, TE T114

Practice Assign PB 227.

Vocabulary

Teach Word Wall: *go, here, is, a, and, have, I, said, to,* TE T102

Options for Guided Reading

80-100 minutes

Extra Support

Before Reading Preview *Lots of Picking,* PL Theme 3, pp. 17–20. Model Phonics/Decoding Strategy. See TE T111–T113.

During Reading Coach as children read story.

After Reading Discuss story; have children find/read words with *-s, -ed, -ing,* short *i* words, possessives with *'s.* **Fluency Modeling:** Model fluent reading. Have partners reread story.

✓ = opportunity for ongoing assessment; adjust groups accordingly

▲ On Level

Before Reading Preview *Lots of Picking,* PL Theme 3, pp. 17–20. Model Phonics/Decoding Strategy. See TE T111–T113.

During Reading Have children begin story. **Fluency Modeling:** Model Phonics/Decoding Strategy and fluent reading.

After Reading Have children retell story so far and find/read words with *-s, -ed, -ing,* short *i* words, possessives with *'s*. **Fluency Practice:** Have partners finish story and reread for fluency.

■ Above Level

Before Reading Preview LR *Lazy Fox,* TE T162. Have students model the Predict/Infer Strategy.

During Reading Have children read first half of story. **Fluency Modeling:** Model fluent reading.

After Reading Have children finish reading and write answers to Responding questions. ✓

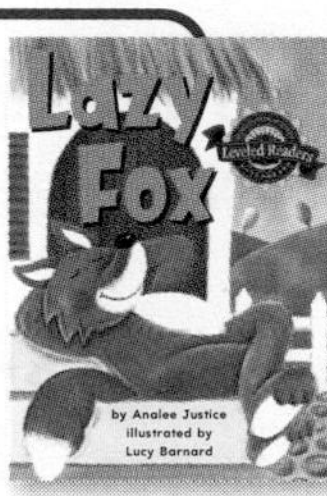

Level I

◆ English Language Learners

Before Reading Preview VR *At the Ice Cream Shop.* See VR Guide, p. 13.

During Reading **Fluency Modeling:** Read aloud each page; have children do echo reading.

After Reading Discuss Responding pages. Have children reread with partners or audio CD.

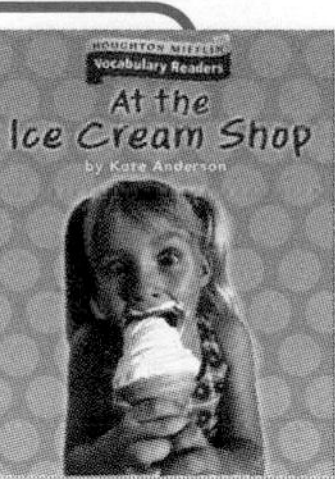

Level C

4 WHOLE GROUP Writing and Language

25-40 minutes

Writing

Teach Shared Writing: A Persuasive Letter, TE T115

Practice Assign Writing Prompt, TE T103.

Viewing

Teach Nonverbal Cues, TE T115

Optional Resources

Teacher Read Aloud

Reread Big Book: *Pearl's First Prize Plant,* TE T104–T107.

Independent Work

Self-Selected Reading

Choose from

- classroom/school library
- Leveled Bibliography, TE T6–T7
- *I Love Reading,* Theme 3, take-home books 28–30
- Little Readers for Guided Reading

Centers

- Classroom Management Kit
- Classroom Management activities, TE T100–T101

Differentiated Instruction

- Phonics Reteaching or Extension:
  –Verb Endings *-s, -ed, -ing,* TE R20–R21
  –Blending More Short *i* Words, TE R22–R23
  –Possessives with *'s*, TE R24–R25
- High-Frequency Words Review: Word Wall, TE T102

TE = Teacher Edition; PB = Practice Book; Tr = Transparency; LR = Leveled Reader; PL = Phonics Library; VR = Vocabulary Reader; VR Guide = Vocabulary Readers Teacher's Manual; LBB = Little Big Book; TP = Theme Paperback

Day 2 Balanced Literacy Plan

Teacher Notes

Reading and Comprehension

20-30 minutes

Shared Reading of Get Set Story

- ➤ Build Background and Vocabulary, TE T120
- ➤ Read *Ham and Eggs,* Anthology pp. 46–53.

▼ **Anthology Selection**

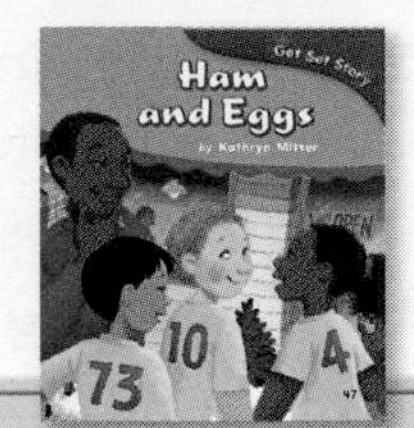

Comprehension Skill Instruction

Teach Making Predictions, TE T121

Words to Know

all	paper
called	shall
eat	why
eating	fixed
every	Jack's
first	licked
never	yelled

Word Work

25-40 minutes

Phonemic Awareness

Teach Blending and Segmenting Phonemes, TE T117

High-Frequency Word Instruction

Teach TE T118–T119, Tr 3-5; **Practice** PB 142–143.

Spelling

Teach The Short *i* Sound, TE T124; **Practice** PB 216–223.

Vocabulary

Practice High-Frequency Words, TE T124

High-Frequency Words

all	first
called	never
eat	paper
eating	shall
every	why

Options for Guided Reading

80-100 minutes

● Extra Support

Before Reading Preview VR *At the Ice Cream Shop.* See VR Guide, p. 13.

During Reading Read the book together; coach reading. Help children apply Predict/Infer Strategy.

After Reading Discuss the book and Responding questions. **Fluency Practice:** Have children reread VR with a partner. Assign *Bill Bird,* PL Theme 3, pp. 21–24, for partner reading.

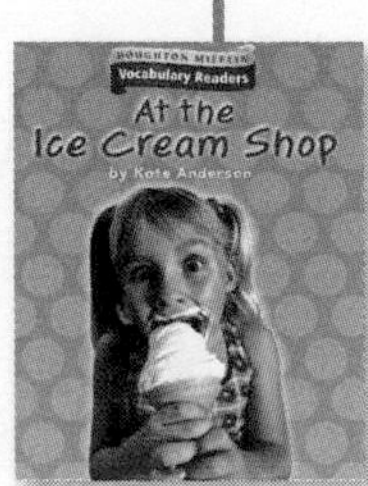

Level C

✓ = opportunity for ongoing assessment; adjust groups accordingly

On Level

Before Reading Discuss PL *Lots of Picking,* TE T111–T113. Preview LR *Mama and Kit Go Away,* TE T161.

During Reading Coach reading as children begin story. **Fluency Modeling:** Model fluent reading, then have children model it.

After Reading Discuss the sequence of events in the story. Then have children write answers to Responding questions. ✓ Assign *Bill Bird,* PL Theme 3, pp. 21–24, for partner reading.

Level D

Above Level

Before Reading Have children model the Predict/Infer Strategy and discuss Responding questions for LR *Lazy Fox,* TE T62.

During Reading **Fluency Check:** Monitor children's oral reading. ✓

After Reading Have children summarize for a partner, telling story events in order. Assign *Bill Bird,* PL Theme 3, pp. 21–24, for partner reading.

Level I

◆ English Language Learners

Before Reading To review VR vocabulary, have children demonstrate or give examples. See VR Guide, p. 13.

During Reading **Fluency Practice:** Have children reread book. Option: Preview and coach reading of *Lots of Picking,* PL Theme 3, pp. 17–20, TE T111–T113.

After Reading Help children summarize VR. Have partners discuss, draw, or write facts they learned. ✓

Level C

4 WHOLE GROUP

Writing and Language

25-40 minutes

Writing

Teach Interactive Writing: A Persuasive Letter, TE T125

Practice Assign Writing Prompt, TE T117.

Optional Resources

Teacher Read Aloud

Reread Big Book: *Pearl's First Prize Plant,* TE T104–T107.

Independent Work

Self-Selected Reading

Choose from

- classroom/school library
- Leveled Bibliography, TE T6–T7
- *I Love Reading,* Theme 3, take-home books 28–30
- Little Readers for Guided Reading

Centers

- Classroom Management Kit
- Classroom Management activities, TE T100–T101

Differentiated Instruction

- High-Frequency Words
  - –Word Wall, TE T118
  - –Reteaching or Extension, TE R32–R33

TE = Teacher Edition; PB = Practice Book; Tr = Transparency; LR = Leveled Reader; PL = Phonics Library; VR = Vocabulary Reader; VR Guide = Vocabulary Readers Teacher's Manual; LBB = Little Big Book; TP = Theme Paperback

Day 3 Balanced Literacy Plan

Teacher Notes

Reading and Comprehension

20-30 minutes

Shared Reading of *Miss Jill's Ice Cream Shop*

➤ Introduce Story Vocabulary, TE T128, Tr 3-6

cone	green	kind	shop	wish
dish	ice cream	napkins	try	

➤ Set Purpose; Review Comprehension Strategy and Skill, TE T128–T129

➤ Read Anthology Selection pp. 54–73 (independent, partner, or audio CD).

➤ Discuss Responding questions; retell the story, TE T138.

▼ Anthology Selection

Words to Know

New This Week

all	paper
call	shall
eat	why
eating	fixed
every	Jack's
first	licked
never	yelled

Kindergarten Review

she

Comprehension Skill Instruction

Teach Making Predictions, TE T140–T141

Practice Assign PB 147.

Word Work

25-40 minutes

Phonemic Awareness Instruction

Teach Blending and Segmenting Phonemes, TE T127

Spelling

Teach The Short *i* Sound, TE T142

Vocabulary Instruction

Teach Possessives, TE T142

3 SMALL GROUP

Options for Guided Reading

80-100 minutes

● Extra Support

Before Reading Review Responding questions from VR. Preview LR *Tim's Pig,* TE T160. Have children model the Predict/Infer.

During Reading Coach as children read story. **Fluency Modeling:** Model fluent reading; have children model.

After Reading **Fluency Practice:** Have partners reread story. Have children write answers to Responding questions. ✓

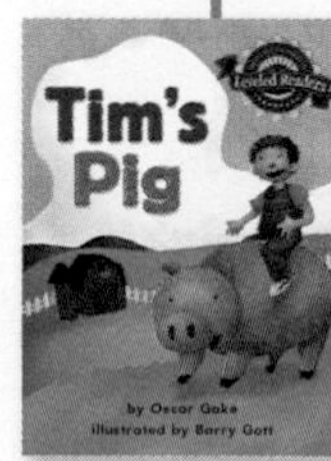

Level C

✓ = opportunity for ongoing assessment; adjust groups accordingly

▲ On Level

Before Reading Discuss Responding questions for LR *Mama and Kit Go Away,* TE T161.

During Reading **Fluency Check:** Ask individuals to read story aloud. ✓

After Reading Have children summarize story for a partner, telling events in order.

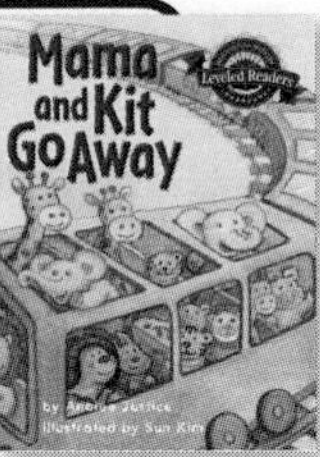

Level D

■ Above Level

Before Reading Review LBB *Pearl's First Prize Plant.* See TE T104–T107, R8–R9.

During Reading **Fluency Modeling:** Model fluent reading, then have children model it. Have them read first half of story independently.

After Reading Ask questions; have children cite text to support answers. Have partners summarize story events in order.

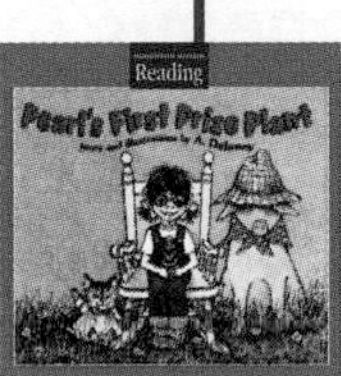

Level E

◆ English Language Learners

Before Reading Preview *Bill Bird,* PL Theme 3, pp. 21–24. Model Phonics/Decoding Strategy.

During Reading **Fluency Modeling:** Read aloud each page; have children do echo reading.

After Reading Discuss story; help children find/read words with short *i.* Have children use illustrations to retell story to partners.

Optional Resources

Teacher Read Aloud

Choose a book from your class/school library or from the Leveled Bibliography, TE T6–T7.

- Suggestion: *Red Is a Dragon* by Roseanne Thong

Independent Work

Self-Selected Reading

Choose from

- classroom/school library
- Leveled Bibliography, TE T6–T7
- *I Love Reading,* Theme 3, take-home books 28–30
- Little Readers for Guided Reading

Centers

- Classroom Management Kit
- Classroom Management activities, TE T100–T101
- Responding activities, TE T138–T139

Differentiated Instruction

- Comprehension Reteaching and Extension: Making Predictions, TE R38–R39
- High-Frequency Word Review: Word Wall, TE T126

4 WHOLE GROUP Writing and Language 30-40 minutes

Writing

Practice Assign Write a Menu, Anthology p. 73.

Grammar

Teach Naming Part of a Sentence, TE T143

TE = Teacher Edition; PB = Practice Book; Tr = Transparency; LR = Leveled Reader; PL = Phonics Library; VR = Vocabulary Reader; VR Guide = Vocabulary Readers Teacher's Manual; LBB = Little Big Book; TP = Theme Paperback

Day 4 Balanced Literacy Plan

Teacher Notes

Reading and Comprehension

20-30 minutes

Shared Reading of Social Studies Link

- "Making Ice Cream," Anthology pp. 74–77, TE T146–T147 (independent, partner, or group)
- Skill: How to Read a Social Studies Article, TE T146
- Introduce Concept Vocabulary, TE T146.

Social Studies Link

Concept Vocabulary

tank
blades
tubs
freezer

Word Work

25-40 minutes

Phonemic Awareness/Phonics Instruction

Teach Blending and Segmenting Phonemes, TE T145

Review More Short *a* Words, TE T148; Double Final Consonants, Final *ck,* Plurals with *-s,* TE T149

Spelling

Practice The Short *i* Sound, TE T150

Vocabulary Instruction

Teach Size Words, TE T150

Options for Guided Reading

80-100 minutes

Extra Support

Before Reading Review Responding questions for LR *Tim's Pig,* TE T160.

During Reading Have children reread story. **Fluency Check:** Have individuals read aloud. ✓

After Reading Model using the words *first, next,* and *last* to summarize story events. Have children retell the story to a partner.

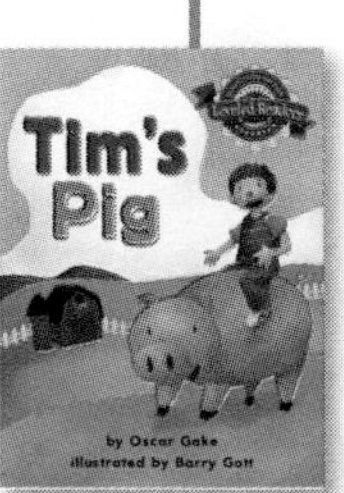

Level C

✓ = opportunity for ongoing assessment; adjust groups accordingly

▲ On Level

Before Reading Have children summarize LR *Mama and Kit Go Away,* telling story events in sequence. ✓ Preview a teacher-selected book or TP *Mud!*, TE R7. Have children make predictions about the story.

During Reading Have children begin story and model Phonics/Decoding Strategy.

After Reading Discuss the story so far. Have children finish story.

Level D

■ Above Level

Before Reading Review first half of LBB *Pearl's First Prize Plant,* TE T104–T107.

During Reading Have children finish book.

After Reading Discuss how book connects to theme. Have children write journal entries to connect it to personal experience or other reading.

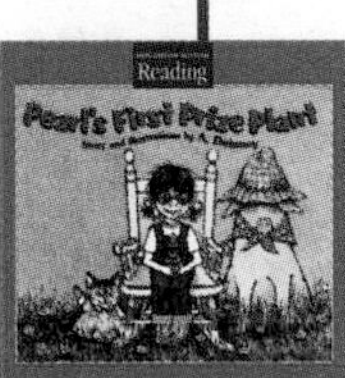

Level E

◆ English Language Learners

Before Reading Build background and preview LR *Tim's Pig Eats,* TE T163. Have children make predictions about the story.

During Reading Read story. **Fluency Modeling:** Reread each page; have children do echo reading. Reinforce Phonics/Decoding Strategy.

After Reading Discuss Responding questions, TE T163. **Fluency Practice:** Have children reread with partners or audio CD.

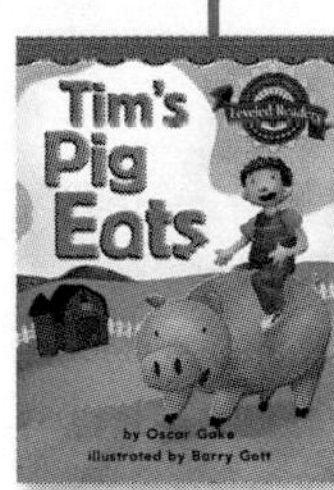

Level B

Optional Resources

Teacher Read Aloud

Continue selected Read Aloud book from Day 3 or choose a new one from your class or school library.

Independent Work

Self-Selected Reading

Choose from

- classroom/school library
- Leveled Bibliography, TE T6–T7
- children's magazines
- *I Love Reading,* Theme 3, take-home books 28–30
- Little Readers for Guided Reading

Centers

- Classroom Management Kit
- Classroom Management activities, TE T100–T101
- Responding activities, TE T138

Differentiated Instruction

- Visual Literacy: How to Read a Social Studies Article, TE T147
- High-Frequency Words: Word Wall, TE T144
- Study Skills: Making Predictions, TE R38–R39

4 WHOLE GROUP

Writing and Language

30-40 minutes

Writing

Practice Independent Writing: Writing About Favorite Foods, TE T151; assign PB 152.

TE = Teacher Edition; PB = Practice Book; Tr = Transparency; LR = Leveled Reader; PL = Phonics Library; VR = Vocabulary Reader; VR Guide = Vocabulary Readers Teacher's Manual; LBB = Little Big Book; TP = Theme Paperback

Day 5 Balanced Literacy Plan

Teacher Notes

Reading and Comprehension

20-30 minutes

Book Share

- Ask children to explain how they applied the comprehension skill and strategy to books they have read this week.
- Help children use genre and text features to compare and contrast what they have read.
- As a class, discuss one *how, why,* or *what if* question. See examples on Blackline Master 1 to use as a guide.

Word Work

25-40 minutes

Phonemic Awareness Instruction

Teach Blending Phonemes, TE T153

High-Frequency Words

Practice Word Wall, TE T158

Spelling

Practice The Short *i* Sound, TE T158

Options for Guided Reading

80-100 minutes

Extra Support

Before Reading Preview *Tim's Cat,* PL Theme 3, pp. 25–28. Have children find/read words with verb endings *-s, -ed, -ing,* short *i* words, possessives with *'s.* See TE T155–T157.

During Reading Have children read and model Phonics/Decoding Strategy. **Fluency Check:** Have individuals reread aloud. ✓

After Reading Have partners make connections between the story and LR *Tim's Pig.* Assign On My Way Practice Reader *Apple Picking* for partner reading.

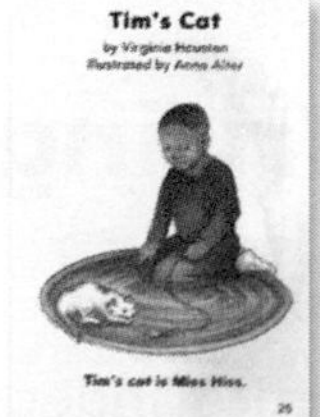

✓ = opportunity for ongoing assessment; adjust groups accordingly

◆ English Language Learners

Before Reading Review LR *Tim's Pig Eats,* TE T163.

During Reading Coach rereading of book. **Fluency Check:** Have individuals reread aloud. ✓

After Reading Help children summarize LR story events in sequence. Have children draw/caption a picture about a book they read this week. ✓

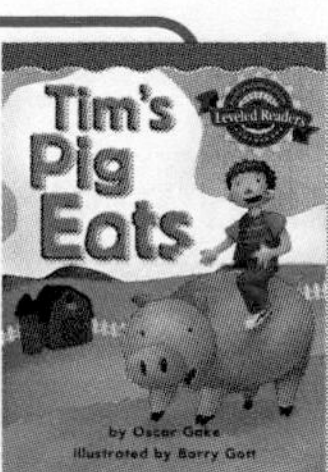

Level B

●▲■◆ Mixed Ability Levels

Literature Circles Form small, mixed-ability groups. Ask groups to discuss the main Anthology selection, Link, Leveled Readers, and other books they have read this week. Pose questions or topics for each group, and circulate among groups to offer support. Suggested group activities:

- Respond to specific Literature Discussion questions on Blackline Master 1.
- Discuss story or text elements, authors' choice of language, and/or illustrations.
- Connect book topics or themes to personal experiences or other reading.

Writing and Language

30-40 minutes

Writing

Practice Assign Writing Prompt, TE T153.

Grammar

Review Naming Part of a Sentence, TE T159

Listening and Speaking

Practice Retelling a Story, TE T159

Optional Resources

Teacher Read Aloud

Choose a nonfiction book related to Social Studies or Science unit.

Independent Work

Self-Selected Reading

Choose from

- classroom/school library
- Leveled Bibliography, TE T6–T7
- children's magazines
- consumer text such as children's newspapers and cookbooks
- *I Love Reading,* Theme 3, take-home books 28–30
- Little Readers for Guided Reading

Centers

- Classroom Management Kit
- Classroom Management activities, TE T100–T101
- Responding activities, TE T138–T139

Differentiated Instruction

- Vocabulary: Speed Drill, TE T152
- Comprehension Review: Making Predictions, TE T154

End-of-Week Assessment

- Weekly Skills Tests for Theme 3, Week 2
- Fluency Assessment, *Tim's Cat,* PL Theme 3, pp. 25–28, TE T155–T157
- Alternative Assessment, Teacher's Resource Blackline Master 43

TE = Teacher Edition; PB = Practice Book; Tr = Transparency; LR = Leveled Reader; PL = Phonics Library; VR = Vocabulary Reader; VR Guide = Vocabulary Readers Teacher's Manual; LBB = Little Big Book; TP = Theme Paperback

Day 1 Balanced Literacy Plan

Teacher Notes

Reading and Comprehension

20-30 minutes

Shared Reading of Daily Message, TE T174

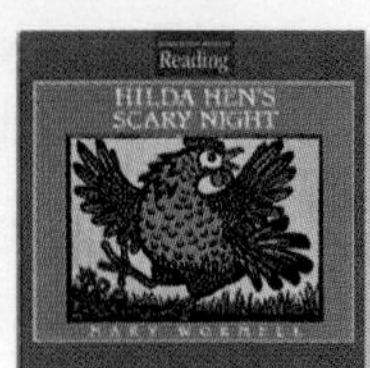

Shared Reading of Big Book

- Introduce Comprehension Strategy and Skill
  Question, TE T176
  Categorize and Classify, TE T177
- Read aloud *Hilda Hen's Scary Night,* TE T176–T179.

Word Work

25-40 minutes

Phonemic Awareness/Phonics Instruction

Teach Blending and Segmenting Phonemes, TE T175, T180

Review/Practice Clusters with *r,* TE T180–T181; assign PB 153–154.

Teach Contractions with *'s,* TE T182

Practice Assign PB 155.

Spelling

Teach Clusters with *r,* TE T186

Practice Assign PB 229.

Vocabulary

Practice Word Wall: *trick, grill,* TE T186

Options for Guided Reading

80-100 minutes

Extra Support

Before Reading Preview *Let's Trim the Track!,* PL Theme 3, pp. 29–32. Model Phonics/Decoding Strategy. See TE T183–T185.

During Reading Coach as children read story.

After Reading Discuss story; have children find/read words with clusters with *r,* contractions with *'s.* **Fluency Modeling:** Model fluent reading. Have partners reread story.

✓ = opportunity for ongoing assessment; adjust groups accordingly

▲ On Level

Before Reading Preview *Let's Trim the Track!,* PL Theme 3, pp. 29–32. Model Phonics/decoding Strategy. See TE T183–T185.

During Reading Have children begin story. **Fluency Modeling:** Model Phonics/Decoding Strategy and fluent reading.

After Reading Have children retell story so far and find/read words with clusters with *r,* contractions with *'s.* **Fluency Practice:** Have partners finish story and reread for fluency.

■ Above Level

Before Reading Preview LR *On the Beach,* TE T234. Have students model the Question Strategy.

During Reading Have children read first half of story. **Fluency Modeling:** Model fluent reading.

After Reading Have children finish reading and write answers to Responding questions. ✓

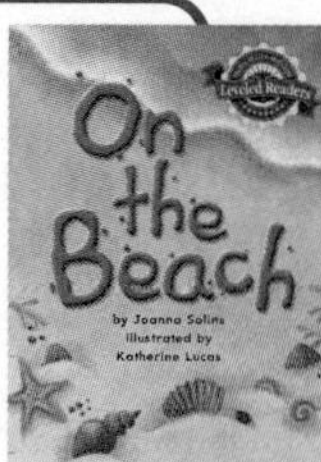

Level J

◆ English Language Learners

Before Reading Preview VR *Sea Animals.* See VR Guide, p. 14.

During Reading **Fluency Modeling:** Read aloud each page; have children do echo reading.

After Reading Discuss Responding pages. Have children reread with partners or audio CD.

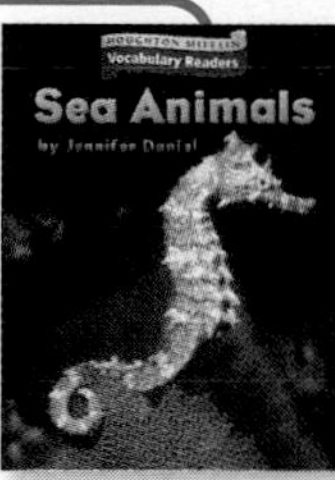

Level B

Optional Resources

Teacher Read Aloud

Reread Big Book: *Hilda Hen's Scary Night,* TE T176–T179.

Independent Work

Self-Selected Reading

Choose from

- classroom/school library
- Leveled Bibliography, TE T6–T7
- *I Love Reading,* Theme 3, take-home book 31
- Little Readers for Guided Reading

Centers

- Classroom Management Kit
- Classroom Management activities, TE T172–T173

Differentiated Instruction

- Phonics Reteaching or Extension:
  –Clusters with *r,* TE R26–R27
  –Contractions with *'s,* TE R28–R29
- High-Frequency Words Review: Word Wall, TE T174

4 WHOLE GROUP

Writing and Language

25-40 minutes

Writing

Teach Shared Writing: A Class Story, TE T187

Practice Assign Writing Prompt, TE T175.

Viewing

Teach Main Idea and Details, TE T187

TE = Teacher Edition; PB = Practice Book; Tr = Transparency; LR = Leveled Reader; PL = Phonics Library; VR = Vocabulary Reader; VR Guide = Vocabulary Readers Teacher's Manual; LBB = Little Big Book; TP = Theme Paperback

Day 2 Balanced Literacy Plan

Teacher Notes

1 WHOLE GROUP Reading and Comprehension

20-30 minutes

▼ Anthology Selection

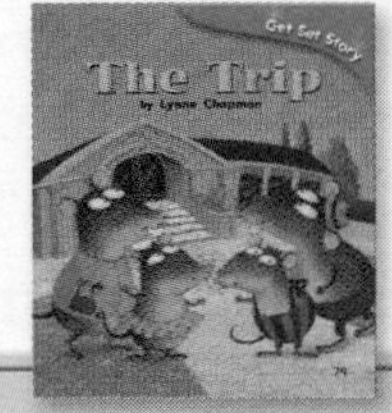

Shared Reading of Get Set Story

- ➤ Build Background and Vocabulary, TE T192
- ➤ Read *The Trip,* Anthology pp. 79–85.

Comprehension Skill Instruction

Teach Categorize and Classify, TE T194

Words to Know

also	many
blue	some
brown	grab
colors	grass
funny	it's
green	let's
like	trip

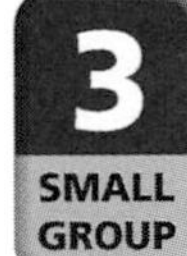

2 WHOLE GROUP Word Work

25-40 minutes

Phonemic Awareness

Teach Blending and Segmenting Phonemes, TE T189

High-Frequency Word Instruction

Teach TE T190–T191, Tr 3-7; Practice PB 156–157.

Spelling

Teach Clusters with *r,* TE T196; Practice PB 216–223.

Vocabulary

Practice High-Frequency Words, TE T196

High-Frequency Words

also	green
blue	like
brown	many
colors	some
funny	

3 SMALL GROUP Options for Guided Reading

80-100 minutes

Extra Support

Before Reading Preview VR *Sea Animals.* See VR Guide, p. 14.

During Reading Read the book together; coach reading. Help children apply Question Strategy.

After Reading Discuss the book and Responding questions. **Fluency Practice:** Have children reread VR with a partner. Assign *Brad's Quick Rag Tricks,* PL Theme 3, pp. 33–36, for partner reading.

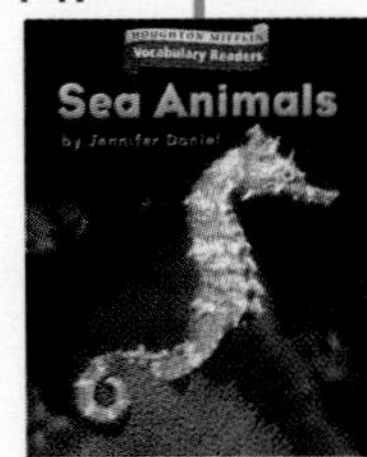

Level B

✓ = opportunity for ongoing assessment; adjust groups accordingly

▲ On Level

Before Reading Discuss PL *Let's Trim the Track!,* TE T183. Preview LR *Looking for Birds,* TE T233.

During Reading Coach reading as children begin story. **Fluency Modeling:** Model fluent reading, then have children model it.

After Reading Discuss the sequence of events in the story. Then have children write answers to Responding questions. ✓ Assign *Brad's Quick Rag Tricks,* PL Theme 3, pp. 33–36, for partner reading.

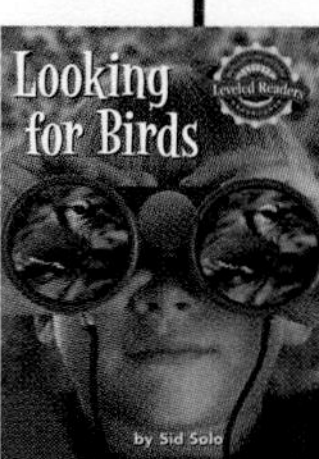

Level D

■ Above Level

Before Reading Have children model the Question Strategy and discuss Responding questions for LR *On the Beach,* TE T234.

During Reading **Fluency Check:** Monitor children's oral reading. ✓

After Reading Have children summarize for a partner, telling story events in order. Assign *Brad's Quick Rag Tricks,* PL Theme 3, pp. 33–36, for partner reading.

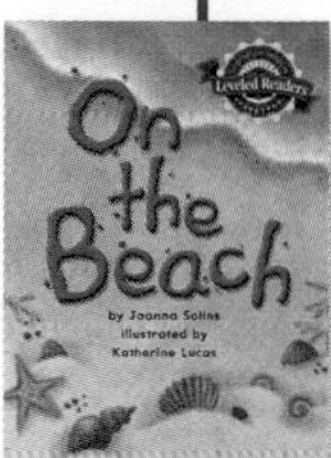

Level J

◆ English Language Learners

Before Reading To review VR vocabulary, have children demonstrate or give examples. See VR Guide, p. 14.

During Reading **Fluency Practice:** Have children reread book. Option: Preview and coach reading of *Let's Trim the Track!,* PL Theme 3, pp. 29–32, TE T183–T185.

After Reading Help children summarize VR. Have partners discuss, draw, or write facts they learned. ✓

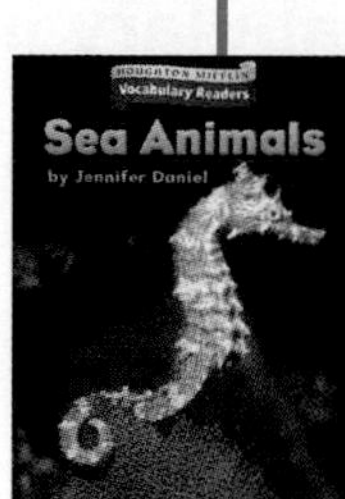

Level B

4 WHOLE GROUP Writing and Language

25-40 minutes

Writing

Teach Interactive Writing: A Class Story, TE T197

Practice Assign Writing Prompt, TE T189.

Optional Resources

Teacher Read Aloud

Reread Big Book: *Hilda Hen's Scary Night,* TE T176–T179.

Independent Work

Self-Selected Reading

Choose from
- classroom/school library
- Leveled Bibliography, TE T6–T7
- *I Love Reading,* Theme 3, take-home book 31
- Little Readers for Guided Reading

Centers
- Classroom Management Kit
- Classroom Management activities, TE T172–T173

Differentiated Instruction

- High-Frequency Words
  –Word Wall, TE T190
  –Reteaching or Extension, TE R34–R35

TE = Teacher Edition; PB = Practice Book; Tr = Transparency; LR = Leveled Reader; PL = Phonics Library; VR = Vocabulary Reader; VR Guide = Vocabulary Readers Teacher's Manual; LBB = Little Big Book; TP = Theme Paperback

Day 3 Balanced Literacy Plan

Teacher Notes

Reading and Comprehension

20-30 minutes

Shared Reading of *At the Aquarium*

- Introduce Story Vocabulary, TE T200, Tr 3-8

  breathe fish sea tails
  dolphins otter sea horse

- Set Purpose; Review Comprehension Strategy and Skill, TE T200–T201
- Read Anthology Selection pp. 86–107 (independent, partner, or audio CD).
- Discuss questions; retell the story, TE T211.

▼ Anthology Selection

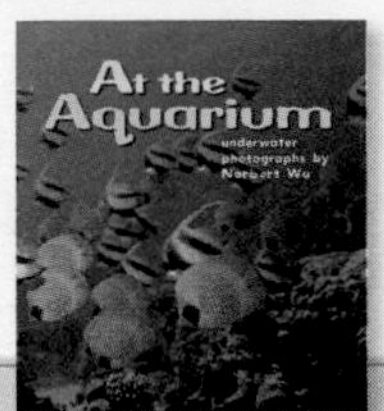

Words to Know

New This Week

also	many
blue	some
brown	grab
colors	grass
funny	it's
green	let's
like	trip

Comprehension Skill Instruction

Teach Categorize and Classify, TE T212–T213, Tr 3-9

Practice Assign PB 161.

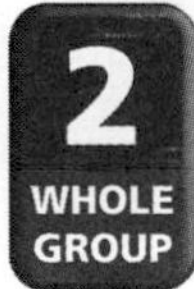

Word Work

25-40 minutes

Phonemic Awareness Instruction

Teach Blending and Segmenting Phonemes, TE T199

Spelling

Teach Clusters with *r*, TE T214

Vocabulary Instruction

Teach Color Words, TE T214

3 SMALL GROUP

Options for Guided Reading

80-100 minutes

● **Extra Support**

Before Reading Review Responding questions from VR. Preview LR *Let's Grab It!*, TE T232. Have children model the Question.

During Reading Coach as children read story. **Fluency Modeling:** Model fluent reading; have children model.

After Reading **Fluency Practice:** Have partners reread story. Have children answer Responding questions. ✓

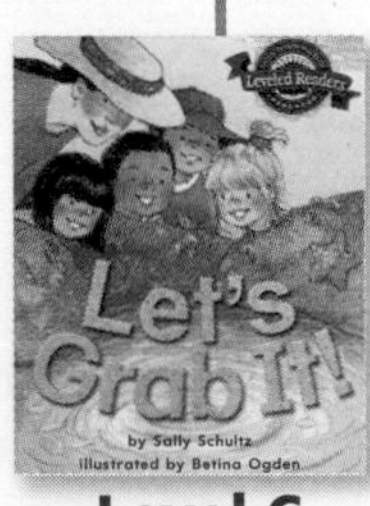

Level C

✓ = opportunity for ongoing assessment; adjust groups accordingly

▲ On Level

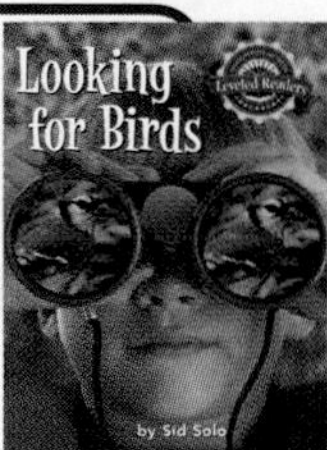
Level D

Before Reading Discuss Responding questions for LR *Looking for Birds,* TE T233.

During Reading **Fluency Check:** Ask individuals to read story aloud. ✓

After Reading Have children summarize story for a partner, telling events in order.

■ Above Level

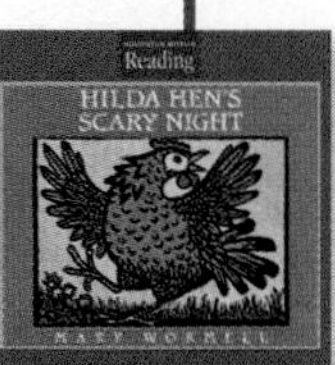
Level G

Before Reading Review LBB *Hilda Hen's Scary Night.* See TE T176–T179, R12–R13.

During Reading **Fluency Modeling:** Model fluent reading, then have children model it. Have them read first half of story independently.

After Reading Ask questions; have children cite text to support answers. Have partners summarize story events in order.

◆ English Language Learners

Before Reading Preview *Brad's Quick Rag Tricks,* PL Theme 3, pp. 33–36. Model Phonics/Decoding Strategy.

During Reading **Fluency Modeling:** Read aloud each page; have children do echo reading.

After Reading Discuss story; help children find/read words with clusters with *r.* Have children use illustrations to retell story to partners.

Writing and Language

30-40 minutes

Writing

Practice Assign Write a Description, Anthology p. 107.

Grammar

Teach Action Part of a Sentence, TE T215

Optional Resources

Teacher Read Aloud

Choose a book from your class/school library or from the Leveled Bibliography, TE T6–T7.

Suggestion: *Whales Passing* by Eve Bunting

Independent Work

Self-Selected Reading

Choose from

- classroom/school library
- Leveled Bibliography, TE T6–T7
- *I Love Reading,* Theme 3, take-home book 31
- Little Readers for Guided Reading

Centers

- Classroom Management Kit
- Classroom Management activities, TE T172–T173
- Responding activities, TE T211

Differentiated Instruction

- Comprehension Reteaching and Extension: Categorize and Classify, TE R40–R41
- High-Frequency Word Review: Word Wall, TE T198

TE = Teacher Edition; PB = Practice Book; Tr = Transparency; LR = Leveled Reader; PL = Phonics Library; VR = Vocabulary Reader; VR Guide = Vocabulary Readers Teacher's Manual; LBB = Little Big Book; TP = Theme Paperback

Day 4 Balanced Literacy Plan

Teacher Notes

1 WHOLE GROUP Reading and Comprehension

20-30 minutes

Shared Reading of Drama Link

- "Why Sun and Moon Live in the Sky," Anthology pp. 108–111, TE T218–T219 (independent, partner, or group)
- Skill: How to Read a Play, TE T218
- Introduce Concept Vocabulary, TE 218.

Concept Vocabulary

tale
characters
narrator

2 WHOLE GROUP Word Work

25-40 minutes

Phonemic Awareness/Phonics Instruction

Teach Blending and Segmenting Phonemes, TE 217

Review More Short *i* Words, TE T220; Verbs Ending with *-s, -ed, -ing;* Possessives with *'s,* TE T221

Spelling

Practice Clusters with *r,* TE T222

Vocabulary Instruction

Teach Words That Show Position, TE T222

3 SMALL GROUP Options for Guided Reading

80-100 minutes

Extra Support

Before Reading Review Responding questions for LR *Let's Grab It!,* TE T232.

During Reading Have children reread story. **Fluency Check:** Have individuals read aloud. ✓

After Reading Model using the words *first, next,* and *last* to summarize story events. Have children retell the story to a partner.

Level C

✓ = opportunity for ongoing assessment; adjust groups accordingly

▲ On Level

Before Reading Have children summarize LR *Looking for Birds,* telling story events in sequence. ✓ Preview a teacher-selected book or TP *When Tiny Was Tiny,* TE R11. Have children make predictions about the story.

During Reading Have children begin story and model Phonics/Decoding Strategy.

After Reading Discuss the story so far. Have children finish story.

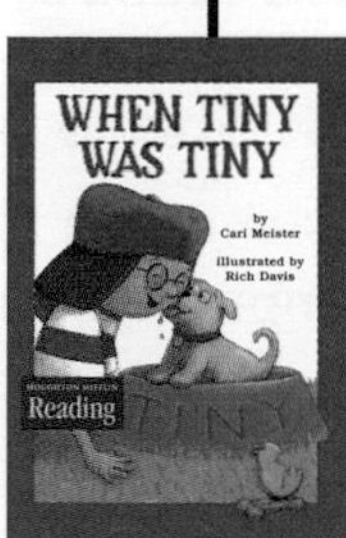

Level E

■ Above Level

Before Reading Review first half of LBB *Hilda Hen's Scary Night,* TE T176.

During Reading Have children finish book.

After Reading Discuss how book connects to theme. Have children write journal entries to connect it to personal experience or other reading.

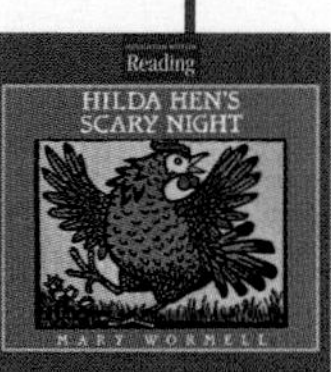

Level G

◆ English Language Learners

Before Reading Build background and preview LR *Grab It!,* TE T235. Have children make predictions about the story.

During Reading Read story. **Fluency Modeling:** Reread each page; have children do echo reading. Reinforce Phonics/Decoding Strategy.

After Reading Discuss Responding questions, TE T235. **Fluency Practice:** Have children reread with partners or audio CD.

Level C

Optional Resources

Teacher Read Aloud

Continue selected Read Aloud book from Day 3 or choose a new one from your class or school library.

Independent Work

Self-Selected Reading

Choose from

- classroom/school library
- Leveled Bibliography, TE T6–T7
- children's magazines
- *I Love Reading,* Theme 3, take-home book 31
- Little Readers for Guided Reading

Centers

- Classroom Management Kit
- Classroom Management activities, TE T172–T173
- Responding activities, TE T211

Differentiated Instruction

- Genre: How to Read a Play, TE T219
- High-Frequency Words: Word Wall, TE T216
- Study Skills: Categorize and Classify, TE R40

4 WHOLE GROUP

Writing and Language

30-40 minutes

Writing

Practice Independent Writing: Writing About Trips, TE T223; assign PB 165.

TE = Teacher Edition; PB = Practice Book; Tr = Transparency; LR = Leveled Reader; PL = Phonics Library; VR = Vocabulary Reader; VR Guide = Vocabulary Readers Teacher's Manual; LBB = Little Big Book; TP = Theme Paperback

Day 5 Balanced Literacy Plan

Teacher Notes

1 Reading and Comprehension

20-30 minutes

WHOLE GROUP

Book Share

Book Share

- Ask children to explain how they applied the comprehension skill and strategy to books they have read this week.
- Help children use genre and text features to compare and contrast what they have read.
- As a class, discuss one *how, why,* or *what if* question. See examples on Blackline Master 1 to use as a guide.

2 Word Work

25-40 minutes

WHOLE GROUP

Phonemic Awareness Instruction

Teach Blending and Segmenting Phonemes, TE T225

Vocabulary

Practice Speed Drill, TE T224

Spelling

Practice Clusters with *r,* TE T230

3 Options for Guided Reading

80-100 minutes

SMALL GROUP

Extra Support

Before Reading Preview *Fran Pig's Brick Hut,* PL Theme 3, pp. 37–40. Have children find/read words with clusters with *r,* contractions with *'s.* See TE T227–T229.

During Reading Have children read and model Phonics/Decoding Strategy. **Fluency Check:** Have individuals reread aloud. ✓

After Reading Have partners make connections between the story and LR *Let's Grab It!* Assign On My Way Practice Reader *The Crab* for partner reading.

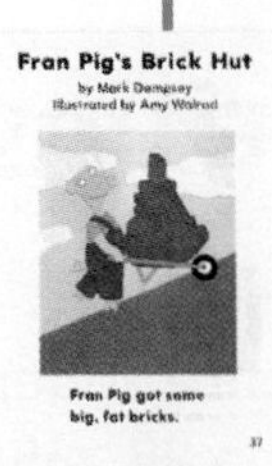

✓ = opportunity for ongoing assessment; adjust groups accordingly

◆ English Language Learners

Level C

Before Reading Review LR *Grab It!*, TE T235.

During Reading Coach rereading of book. **Fluency Check:** Have individuals reread aloud. ✓

After Reading Help children summarize LR story events in sequence. Have children draw/caption a picture about a book they read this week. ✓

●▲■◆ Mixed Ability Levels

Literature Circles Form small, mixed-ability groups. Ask groups to discuss the main Anthology selection, Link, Leveled Readers, and other books they have read this week. Pose questions or topics for each group, and circulate among groups to offer support. Suggested group activities:

- Respond to specific Literature Discussion questions on Blackline Master 1.
- Discuss story or text elements, authors' choice of language, and/or illustrations.
- Connect book topics or themes to personal experiences or other reading.

Writing and Language

30-40 minutes

Writing

Practice Assign Writing Prompt, TE T225.

Grammar

Review Action Part of a Sentence, TE T231

Listening

Practice To Gather Information, TE T231

Optional Resources

Teacher Read Aloud

Choose a nonfiction book related to Social Studies or Science unit.

Independent Work

Self-Selected Reading

Choose from

- classroom/school library
- Leveled Bibliography, TE T6–T7
- children's magazines
- consumer text such as books of plays and theater magazines

Centers

- Classroom Management Kit
- Classroom Management activities, TE T172–T173
- Responding activities, TE T211

Differentiated Instruction

- Vocabulary: Speed Drill, TE T224
- Comprehension Review: Rereading for Understanding, TE T226

Assessment

End-of-Week Assessment

- Weekly Skills Tests for Theme 3, Week 3
- Fluency Assessment, *Fran Pig's Brick Hut*, PL Theme 3, pp. 37–40, TE T227–T229
- Alternative Assessment, Teacher's Resource Blackline Master 45

End-of-Theme Assessment

- Integrated Theme Tests for Theme 3

TE = Teacher Edition; PB = Practice Book; Tr = Transparency; LR = Leveled Reader; PL = Phonics Library; VR = Vocabulary Reader; VR Guide = Vocabulary Readers Teacher's Manual; LBB = Little Big Book; TP = Theme Paperback

Theme 4 Overview

	Week 1
Reading and Comprehension	**Shared Reading** Main Selection: *Go Away, Otto!* Social Studies Link: "Helping at Home" Book Share **Comprehension** Strategy: Summarize Skill: Drawing Conclusions Content Skill: How to Read a Social Studies Article
Word Work	**Phonemic Awareness:** Blending and Segmenting Phonemes **Phonics:** Clusters with *l* **Phonics:** Blending More Short *o* Words **Phonics Review:** Clusters with *r;* Contractions with *'s* **Vocabulary:** Family Words; Exclamatory Words **High-Frequency Words:** *children, come, family, father, love, mother, people, picture, your* **Spelling:** The Short *o* Sound
Options for Guided Reading	**Big Book** *An Egg Is An Egg* **Vocabulary Reader** *Grandpa's Visit* **Leveled Readers:** Extra Support: *Jobs* On Level: *My Family* Above Level: *Shopping* ELL: *Jobs at Home* **Phonics Library** *Hot Dog* *Tom's Plan* *Jock's Hut* **Theme Paperbacks** **Literature Circles**
Writing and Oral Language	**Shared Writing:** A Class Album **Interactive Writing:** A Class Album **Independent Writing:** Writing Answers to Questions **Grammar:** Is It a Sentence? **Viewing:** Compare and Contrast **Listening and Speaking:** Conversation
Assessment Options	• Weekly Skills Test for Theme 4, Week 1 • Fluency Assessment: Phonics Library

Use **Launching the Theme** on pages T16–T17 of the Teacher's Edition to introduce the theme.

Week 2

Shared Reading
Main Selection: *Two Best Friends*
Social Studies Link: "How Mail Gets to You"
Book Share

Comprehension
Strategy: Evaluate
Skill: Compare and Contrast
Content Skill: How to Read a Social Studies Article

Phonemic Awareness: Blending and Segmenting Phonemes
Phonics: Clusters with *s*
Phonics: Blending Short *e* Words
Phonics: Silent Letters in *kn, wr, gn*
Phonics Review: Clusters with *l;* Words with Short *o*
Vocabulary: Sensory Words; Words and Symbols on Signs
High-Frequency Words: *friend, girl, know, play, read, she, sing, today, write*
Spelling: The Short *e* Sound

Big Book
The Secret Code

Vocabulary Reader
A New School

Leveled Readers:
Extra Support: *Sit, Ned!*
On Level: *Pets for the Twins*
Above Level: *Happy Birthday, Sam!*
ELL: *Ned*

Phonics Library
Knock, Knock
Miss Nell
Deb and Bess

Literature Circles

Shared Writing: A Class Message
Interactive Writing: A Class Message
Independent Writing: Writing Sentences on a Topic
Grammar: Telling Sentences
Viewing: Retelling/Summarizing
Listening and Speaking: Reader's Theater

- Weekly Skills Test for Theme 4, Week 2
- Fluency Assessment: Phonics Library

Week 3

Shared Reading
Main Selection: *Dog School*
Social Studies Link: "Daycare for Dogs"
Book Share

Comprehension
Strategy: Monitor/Clarify
Skill: Sequence of Events
Content Skill: How to Read a Social Studies Article

Phonemic Awareness: Blending and Segmenting Phonemes
Phonics: Triple Clusters
Phonics: Blending More Short *u* Words
Phonics Review: Clusters with *s;* Silent Letters in *kn, wr, gn;* Words with Short *e*
Vocabulary: Question Words; Noise Words
High-Frequency Words: *car, down, hear, hold, hurt, learn, their, walk, would*
Spelling: The Short *u* Sound

Big Book
Caribbean Dream

Vocabulary Reader
Dogs Learn Every Day

Leveled Readers:
Extra Support: *My Pup*
On Level: *A Bird on the Bus*
Above Level: *Scruffy*
ELL: *Me and My Pup*

Phonics Library
Buzzing Bug
Duff in the Mud
Jess and Mom

Literature Circles

Shared Writing: A Class Letter
Interactive Writing: A Class Letter
Independent Writing: Writing Questions
Grammar: Asking Sentences
Viewing: Looking at Fine Art

- Weekly Skills Test, Theme 4, Week 3
- Fluency Assessment: Phonics Library

Day 1 Balanced Literacy Plan

Teacher Notes

Reading and Comprehension

20-30 minutes

Shared Reading of Daily Message, TE T30

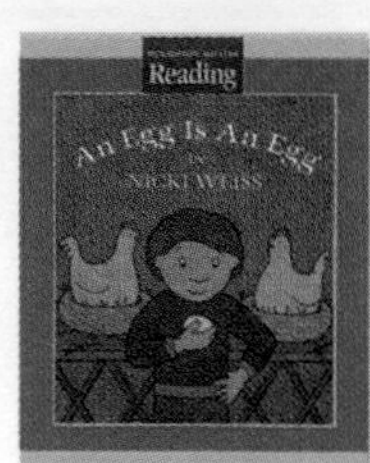

Shared Reading of Big Book

➤ Introduce Comprehension Strategy and Skill
Summarize, TE T32
Drawing Conclusions, TE T33

➤ Read aloud *An Egg Is An Egg,* TE T32–T35.

Word Work

25-40 minutes

Phonemic Awareness/Phonics Instruction

Teach Blending and Segmenting Phonemes, TE T31

Teach Clusters with *l,* TE T36; assign PB 167–168.

Teach Blending More Short *o* Words, TE T37–T38

Practice Assign PB 169–170.

Spelling

Teach The Short *o* Sound, TE T42

Practice Assign PB 229.

Vocabulary: Kindergarten Review

Teach Word Wall: *he, for, I, my, is, the, to, and, a, said,* TE T30

Options for Guided Reading

80-100 minutes

Extra Support

Before Reading Preview *Hot Dog,* PL Theme 4, pp. 5–8. Model Phonics/Decoding Strategy. See TE T39–T41.

During Reading Coach as children read story.

After Reading Discuss story; have children find/read words with *l,* short *o.* **Fluency Modeling:** Model fluent reading. Have partners reread story.

✓ = opportunity for ongoing assessment; adjust groups accordingly

▲ On Level

Before Reading Preview *Hot Dog,* PL Theme 4, pp. 5–8. Model Phonics/Decoding Strategy. See TE T39–T41.

During Reading Have children begin story. **Fluency Modeling:** Model Phonics/Decoding Strategy and fluent reading.

After Reading Have children retell story so far and find/read words with *l,* short *o.* **Fluency Practice:** Have partners finish story and reread for fluency.

■ Above Level

Before Reading Preview LR *Shopping,* TE T90. Have students model the Summarize Strategy.

During Reading Have children read first half of story. **Fluency Modeling:** Model fluent reading.

After Reading Have children finish reading and write answers to Responding questions. ✓

Level J

◆ English Language Learners

Before Reading Preview VR *Grandpa's Visit.* See VR Guide, p. 15.

During Reading **Fluency Modeling:** Read aloud each page; have children do echo reading.

After Reading Discuss Responding pages. Have children reread with partners or audio CD.

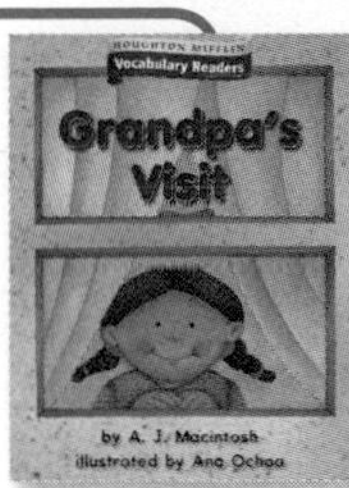

Level C

4 WHOLE GROUP

Writing and Language

25-40 minutes

Writing

Teach Shared Writing: A Class Album, TE T43

Practice Assign Writing Prompt, TE T31.

Viewing

Teach Compare and Contrast, TE T43

Optional Resources

Teacher Read Aloud

Reread Big Book: *An Egg Is An Egg,* TE T32–T35.

Read *Too Much Noise!,* TE T18–T19.

Independent Work

Self-Selected Reading

Choose from

- classroom/school library
- Leveled Bibliography, TE T6–T7
- *I Love Reading,* Theme 4, take-home book 32
- Little Readers for Guided Reading

Centers

- Classroom Management Kit
- Classroom Management activities, TE T28–T29

Differentiated Instruction

- Phonics Reteaching or Extension:
  - Consonant Clusters with *l,* TE R14–R15
  - Blending More Short *o* Words, TE R16–R17
- High-Frequency Words Review: Word Wall, TE T30

TE = Teacher Edition; PB = Practice Book; Tr = Transparency; LR = Leveled Reader; PL = Phonics Library; VR = Vocabulary Reader; VR Guide = Vocabulary Readers Teacher's Manual; LBB = Little Big Book; TP = Theme Paperback

Day 2 Balanced Literacy Plan

Teacher Notes

Reading and Comprehension

20-30 minutes

Shared Reading of Get Set Story

- Build Background and Vocabulary, TE T48
- Read *Fluff Is Missing!* Anthology pp. 115–121.

▼ Anthology Selection

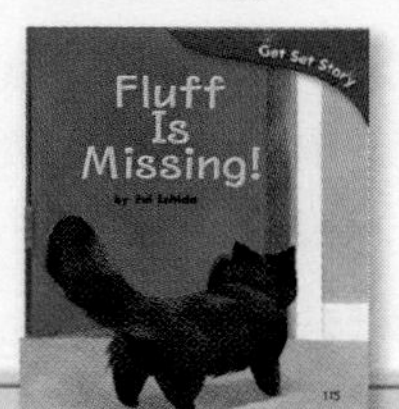

Comprehension Skill Instruction

Teach Drawing Conclusions, TE T50

Words to Know

children	picture
come	your
family	black
father	block
loves	Fluff
mother	plan
people	

Word Work

25-40 minutes

Phonemic Awareness

Teach Blending and Segmenting Phonemes, TE T45

High-Frequency Words Instruction

Teach TE T46–T47, Tr 4-1; **Practice** PB 171, 173.

Spelling: Practice

Teach The Short *o* Sound, TE T52

Vocabulary: Review

Practice High-Frequency Words, TE T52

High-Frequency Words

children	mother
come	people
family	picture
father	your
loves	

Options for Guided Reading

80-100 minutes

Extra Support

Before Reading Preview VR *Grandpa's Visit.* See VR Guide, p. 15.

During Reading Read the book together; coach reading. Help children apply Summarize Strategy.

After Reading Discuss the book and Responding questions. **Fluency Practice:** Have children reread VR with a partner. Assign *Tom's Plan,* PL Theme 4, pp. 9–12, for partner reading.

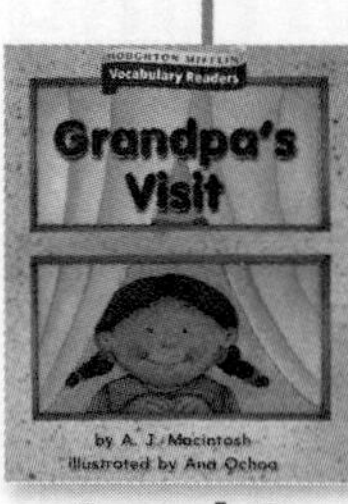

Level C

✓ = opportunity for ongoing assessment; adjust groups accordingly

▲ On Level

Before Reading Discuss PL *Hot Dog,* TE T39–T41. Preview LR *My Family,* TE T89.

During Reading Coach reading as children begin story. **Fluency Modeling:** Model fluent reading, then have children model it.

After Reading Discuss the sequence of events in the story. Then have children write answers to Responding questions. ✓ Assign *Tom's Plan,* PL Theme 4, pp. 9–12, for partner reading.

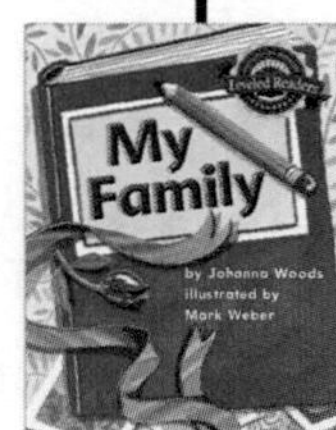

Level D

■ Above Level

Before Reading Have children model the Summarize Strategy and discuss Responding questions for LR *Shopping,* TE T90.

During Reading **Fluency Check:** Monitor children's oral reading. ✓

After Reading Have children summarize for a partner, telling story events in order. Assign *Tom's Plan,* PL Theme 4, pp. 9–12, for partner reading.

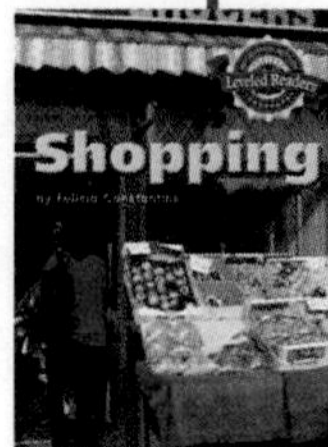

Level J

◆ English Language Learners

Before Reading To review VR vocabulary, have children demonstrate or give examples. See VR Guide, p. 15.

During Reading **Fluency Practice:** Have children reread book. Option: Preview and coach reading of *Hot Dog,* PL Theme 4, pp. 5–8, TE T39–T41.

After Reading Help children summarize VR. Have partners discuss, draw, or write facts they learned. ✓

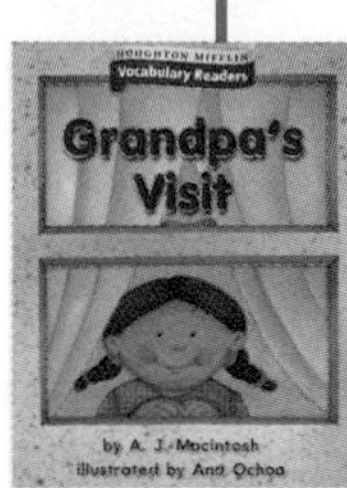

Level C

4 WHOLE GROUP Writing and Language

25-40 minutes

Writing

Teach Interactive Writing: A Class Album, TE T53

Practice Assign Writing Prompt, TE T45.

Optional Resources

Teacher Read Aloud

Reread Big Book: *An Egg Is An Egg,* TE T32–T35.

Independent Work

Self-Selected Reading

Choose from
- classroom/school library
- Leveled Bibliography, TE T6–T7
- *I Love Reading,* Theme 4, take-home book 32
- Little Readers for Guided Reading

Centers
- Classroom Management Kit
- Classroom Management activities, TE T28–T29

Differentiated Instruction

- High-Frequency Words
  - Word Wall, TE T44
  - Reteaching or Extension, TE R28–R29

TE = Teacher Edition; PB = Practice Book; Tr = Transparency; LR = Leveled Reader; PL = Phonics Library; VR = Vocabulary Reader; VR Guide = Vocabulary Readers Teacher's Manual; LBB = Little Big Book; TP = Theme Paperback

Day 3 Balanced Literacy Plan

Teacher Notes

1 Reading and Comprehension

20-30 minutes

▼ Anthology Selection

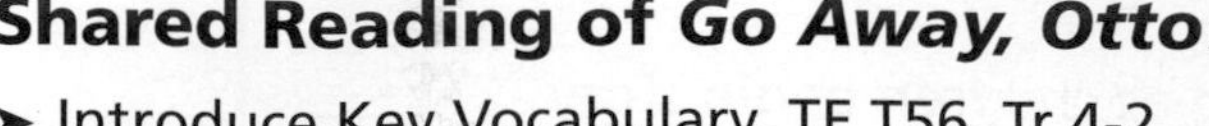

Shared Reading of *Go Away, Otto!*

- Introduce Key Vocabulary, TE T56, Tr 4-2

  clean sorry pillows visit
- Set Purpose; Review Comprehension Strategy and Skill, TE T56–T57
- Read Anthology Selection pp. 124–141 (independent, partner, or audio CD).
- Discuss questions; retell the story, TE T67.

Words to Know

New This Week

children	pictures
come	your
family	black
father	blocks
love	fluff
mother	plan
people	

Kindergarten Review

play

Comprehension Skill Instruction

Teach Drawing Conclusions, TE T68–T69

Practice Assign PB 176.

2 Word Work

25-40 minutes

Phonemic Awareness Instruction

Teach Blending and Segmenting Phonemes, TE T55

Spelling and Phonics

Teach The Short *o* Sound, TE T70

Vocabulary Instruction

Teach Family Words, TE T70

3 Options for Guided Reading

SMALL GROUP

80-100 minutes

● Extra Support

Before Reading Review Responding questions from VR *Grandpa's Visit.* Preview LR *Jobs,* TE T88. Have children model Summarize.

During Reading Coach as children read story. **Fluency Modeling:** Model fluent reading; have children model.

After Reading **Fluency Practice:** Have partners reread story. Have children answer Responding questions. ✓

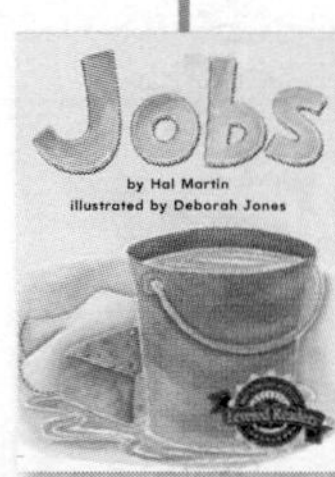

Level C

✓ = opportunity for ongoing assessment; adjust groups accordingly

▲ On Level

Before Reading Discuss Responding questions for LR *My Family,* TE T89.

During Reading **Fluency Check:** Ask individuals to read story aloud. ✓

After Reading Have children summarize story for a partner, telling events in order.

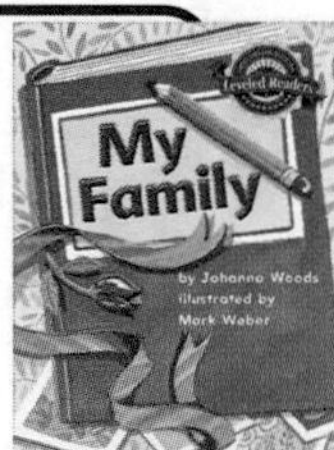

Level D

■ Above Level

Before Reading Review LBB *An Egg Is An Egg.* See TE T32–T35, R4–R5.

During Reading **Fluency Modeling:** Model fluent reading, then have children model it. Have them read first half of story independently.

After Reading Ask questions; have children cite text to support answers. Have partners summarize story events in order.

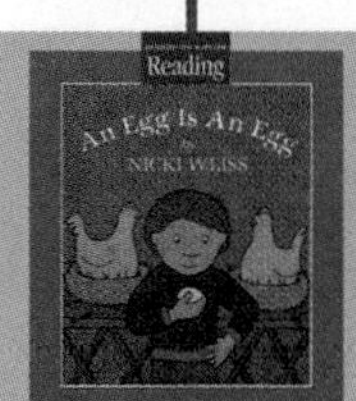

Level G

◆ English Language Learners

Before Reading Preview *Tom's Plan*, PL Theme 4, pp. 9–12. Model Phonics/Decoding Strategy.

During Reading **Fluency Modeling:** Read aloud each page; have children do echo reading.

After Reading Discuss story; help children find/read words with *l,* short *o.* Have children use illustrations to retell story to partners.

4 WHOLE GROUP

Writing and Language

30-40 minutes

Writing

Practice Assign Write a Sentence, Anthology p. 143.

Grammar

Teach Is It a Sentence?, TE T71

Optional Resources

Teacher Read Aloud

Choose a book from your class/school library or from the Leveled Bibliography, TE T6–T7.

Suggestion: *Good-bye Curtis* by Kevin Henkes

Independent Work

Self-Selected Reading

Choose from

- classroom/school library
- Leveled Bibliography, TE T6–T7
- *I Love Reading,* Theme 4, take-home book 32
- Little Readers for Guided Reading

Centers

- Classroom Management Kit
- Classroom Management activities, TE T28–T29
- Responding activities, TE T67

Differentiated Instruction

- Comprehension Reteaching and Extension, Drawing Conclusions, TE R34–R35
- High-Frequency Word Review: Word Wall, TE T54

TE = Teacher Edition; PB = Practice Book; Tr = Transparency; LR = Leveled Reader; PL = Phonics Library; VR = Vocabulary Reader; VR Guide = Vocabulary Readers Teacher's Manual; LBB = Little Big Book; TP = Theme Paperback

Day 4 Balanced Literacy Plan

Teacher Notes

Reading and Comprehension

20-30 minutes

Shared Reading of Social Studies Link

- "Helping at Home," Anthology pp. 144–147, TE T74–T75 (independent, partner, or group)
- Skill: How to Read a Social Studies Article, TE T74
- Introduce Concept Vocabulary, TE T74.

Concept Vocabulary

make your bed
set the table

Word Work

25-40 minutes

Phonemic Awareness/Phonics Instruction

Teach Blending and Segmenting Phonemes, TE T73

Review Clusters with *r,* TE T76; Contractions with *'s,* TE T77

Spelling and Phonics

Practice The Short *o* Sound, TE T78

Vocabulary Instruction

Teach Exclamatory Words, TE T78

3
SMALL GROUP

Options for Guided Reading

80-100 minutes

Extra Support

Before Reading Review Responding questions for LR *Jobs,* TE T88.

During Reading Have children reread story. **Fluency Check:** Have individuals read aloud. ✓

After Reading Model using the words *first, next,* and *last* to summarize story events. Have children retell the story to a partner.

Level C

✓ = opportunity for ongoing assessment; adjust groups accordingly

▲ On Level

Before Reading Have children summarize LR *My Family,* telling story events in sequence. ✓ Preview a teacher-selected book or TP *Biscuit Finds a Friend,* TE R3. Have children make predictions about the story.

During Reading Have children begin story and model Phonics/Decoding Strategy.

After Reading Discuss the story so far. Have children finish story.

Level G

■ Above Level

Before Reading Review first half of LBB *An Egg Is An Egg,* TE T32–T35.

During Reading Have children finish book.

After Reading Discuss how book connects to theme. Have children write journal entries to connect it to personal experience or other reading.

Level G

English Language Learners

Before Reading Build background and preview LR *Jobs at Home,* TE T91. Have children make predictions about the story.

During Reading Read story. **Fluency Modeling:** Reread each page; have children do echo reading. Reinforce Phonics/Decoding Strategy.

After Reading Discuss Responding questions, TE T91. **Fluency Practice:** Have children reread with partners or audio CD.

Level C

Writing and Language

30-40 minutes

Writing

Practice Independent Writing: Writing Answers to Questions; assign PB 180.

Optional Resources

Teacher Read Aloud

Continue selected Read Aloud book from Day 3 or choose a new one from your class or school library.

Independent Work

Self-Selected Reading

Choose from

- classroom/school library
- Leveled Bibliography, TE T6–T7
- children's magazines
- *I Love Reading,* Theme 4, take-home book 32
- Little Readers for Guided Reading

Centers

- Classroom Management Kit
- Classroom Management activities, TE T28–T29
- Responding activities, TE T67

Differentiated Instruction

- High-Frequency Words: Word Wall, TE T72
- Study Skills: Reading a Picture Map, TE R40

TE = Teacher Edition; PB = Practice Book; Tr = Transparency; LR = Leveled Reader; PL = Phonics Library; VR = Vocabulary Reader; VR Guide = Vocabulary Readers Teacher's Manual; LBB = Little Big Book; TP = Theme Paperback

Day 5 Balanced Literacy Plan

Teacher Notes

Reading and Comprehension

20-30 minutes

Book Share

- Ask children to explain how they applied the comprehension skill and strategy to books they have read this week.
- Help children use genre and text features to compare and contrast what they have read.
- As a class, discuss one *how, why,* or *what if* question. See examples on Blackline Master 1 to use as a guide.

Word Work

25-40 minutes

Phonemic Awareness Instruction

Teach Blending and Segmenting Phonemes, TE T81

High-Frequency Words

Practice Word Wall/Vocabulary Speed Drill, TE T80

Spelling and Phonics

Practice The Short *o* Sound, TE T86

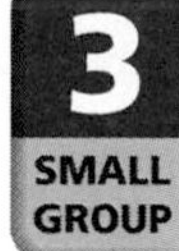

Options for Guided Reading

80-100 minutes

Extra Support

Before Reading Preview *Jock's Hut,* PL Theme 4, pp. 13–16. Have children find/read words with *l,* short *o.* See TE T83–T85.

During Reading Have children read and model Phonics/Decoding Strategy. **Fluency Check:** Have individuals reread aloud. ✓

After Reading Have partners make connections between the story and LR *Grandpa's Visit.* Assign On My Way Practice Reader *Family Day* for partner reading.

Jock's Hut
by Denise Zimmer
illustrated by Alexi Natchev

Jock gets big flags, glass clocks, and brass jugs in his hut.

13

✓ = opportunity for ongoing assessment; adjust groups accordingly

◆ English Language Learners

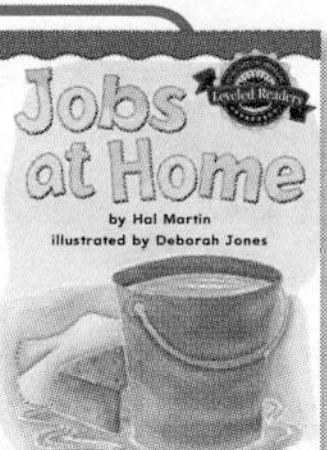

Level C

Before Reading Review LR *Jobs at Home,* TE T91.

During Reading Coach rereading of book. **Fluency Check:** Have individuals reread aloud. ✓

After Reading Help children summarize LR story events in sequence. Have children draw/caption a picture about a book they read this week.✓

Mixed Ability Levels

Literature Circles Form small, mixed-ability groups. Ask groups to discuss the main Anthology selection, Link, Leveled Readers, and other books they have read this week. Pose questions or topics for each group, and circulate among groups to offer support. Suggested group activities:

- Respond to specific Literature Discussion questions on Blackline Master 1.
- Discuss story or text elements, authors' choice of language, and/or illustrations.
- Connect book topics or themes to personal experiences or other reading.

Writing and Language

30-40 minutes

Writing

Practice Assign Writing Prompt, TE T81.

Grammar

Review Is It a Sentence?, TE T87

Listening and Speaking

Practice Conversation, TE T87

Optional Resources

Teacher Read Aloud

Choose a nonfiction book related to Social Studies or Science unit.

Independent Work

Self-Selected Reading

Choose from

- classroom/school library
- Leveled Bibliography, TE T6–T7
- children's magazines
- consumer text such as books about cooking, cleaning, etc.
- *I Love Reading,* Theme 4, take-home book 32
- Little Readers for Guided Reading

Centers

- Classroom Management Kit
- Classroom Management activities, TE T28–T29
- Responding activities, TE T67

Differentiated Instruction

- Vocabulary: Speed Drill, TE T80
- Comprehension Review: Drawing Conclusions, TE T82

End-of-Week Assessment

- Weekly Skills Tests for Theme 4, Week 1
- Fluency Assessment, *Jock's Hut,* PL Theme 4, pp. 13–16, TE T83–T85
- Alternative Assessment, Teacher's Resource Blackline Master 52

TE = Teacher Edition; PB = Practice Book; Tr = Transparency; LR = Leveled Reader; PL = Phonics Library; VR = Vocabulary Reader; VR Guide = Vocabulary Readers Teacher's Manual; LBB = Little Big Book; TP = Theme Paperback

Day 1 Balanced Literacy Plan

Teacher Notes

Reading and Comprehension

20-30 minutes

Shared Reading of Daily Message, TE T102

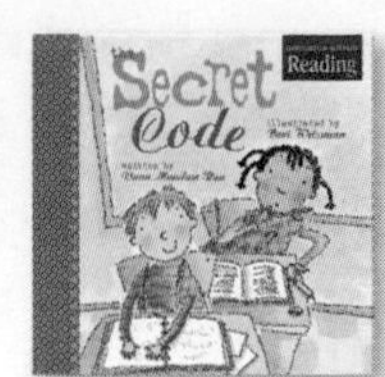

Shared Reading of Big Book

- Introduce Comprehension Strategy and Skill
  Evaluate, TE T104
  Compare and Contrast, TE T105
- Read aloud *The Secret Code,* TE T104–T107.

Word Work

25-40 minutes

Phonemic Awareness/Phonics Instruction

Teach Blending Segmenting Phonemes, TE T103

Teach Clusters with *s*, TE T108; Blending More Short *e* Words, TE T109

Practice Assign PB 181–182, 183–184, 185.

Teach Silent Letters in *kn, wr, gn*, TE T110

Teach TE T108, T109, T110

Spelling/Phonics

Teach The Short *e* Sound, TE T114

Practice Assign PB 231.

Vocabulary

Teach Word Wall: *play, is, see, a, to, she, and, the, said, are, my,* TE T102

Options for Guided Reading

80-100 minutes

Extra Support

Before Reading Preview *Knock, Knock,* PL Theme 4, pp. 17–20. Model Phonics/Decoding Strategy. See TE T111–T113.

During Reading Coach as children read story.

After Reading Discuss story; have children find/read words with *s*, short *e*, *kn, wr, gn.* **Fluency Modeling:** Model fluent reading. Have partners reread story.

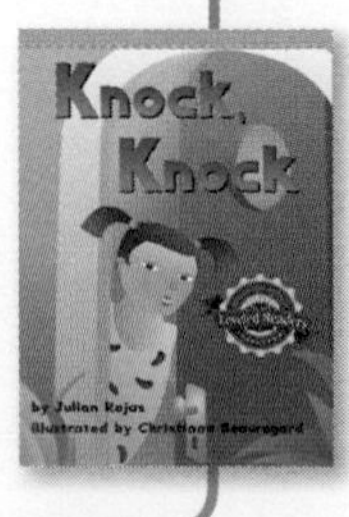

✓ = opportunity for ongoing assessment; adjust groups accordingly

▲ On Level

Before Reading Preview *Knock, Knock,* PL Theme 4, pp. 17–20. Model Phonics/Decoding Strategy. See TE T111–T113.

During Reading Have children begin story. **Fluency Modeling:** Model Phonics/Decoding Strategy and fluent reading.

After Reading Have children retell story so far and find/read words with *s,* short *e, kn, wr, gn.* **Fluency Practice:** Have partners finish story and reread for fluency.

■ Above Level

Before Reading Preview LR *Happy Birthday, Sam!,* TE T162. Have students model the Summarize Strategy.

During Reading Have children read first half of story. **Fluency Modeling:** Model fluent reading.

After Reading Have children finish reading and write answers to Responding questions. 

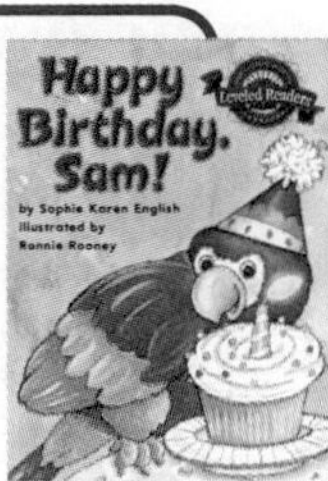

Level I

◆ English Language Learners

Before Reading Preview VR *A New School.* See VR Guide, p. 16.

During Reading **Fluency Modeling:** Read aloud each page; have children do echo reading.

After Reading Discuss Responding pages. Have children reread with partners or audio CD.

Level B

Writing and Language  25-40 minutes

Writing

Teach Shared Writing: A Class Message, TE T115

Practice Assign Writing Prompt, TE T103.

Viewing

Teach Retelling/Summarizing, TE T115

Optional Resources

Teacher Read Aloud

Reread Big Book: *The Secret Code,* TE T104–T107.

Read *Too Much Noise!,* TE T18–T19.

Independent Work

Self-Selected Reading

Choose from

- classroom/school library
- Leveled Bibliography, TE T6–T7
- *I Love Reading,* Theme 4, take-home book 33
- Little Readers for Guided Reading

Centers

- Classroom Management Kit
- Classroom Management activities, TE T100–T101

Differentiated Instruction

- Phonics Reteaching or Extension:
  –Clusters with *s,* TE R18–R19
  –Blending More Short *e* Words, TE R20–R21
- High-Frequency Words Review: Word Wall, TE T102

TE = Teacher Edition; PB = Practice Book; Tr = Transparency; LR = Leveled Reader; PL = Phonics Library; VR = Vocabulary Reader; VR Guide = Vocabulary Readers Teacher's Manual; LBB = Little Big Book; TP = Theme Paperback

Day 2 Balanced Literacy Plan

Teacher Notes

Reading and Comprehension

20-30 minutes

▼ Anthology Selection

Shared Reading of Get Set Story

➤ Build Background and Vocabulary, TE T120

➤ Read *Zack and His Friends,* Anthology pp. 149–155.

Comprehension Skill Instruction

Teach Compare and Contrast, TE T122

Words to Know

friends	today
girl	write
know	best
play	knelt
read	rest
she	sign
sing	snack

Word Work

25-40 minutes

Phonemic Awareness

Teach Blending and Segmenting Phonemes, TE T117

High-Frequency Words Instruction

Teach TE T118–T119, Tr 4-3, **Practice** Assign PB 186, 187.

Spelling and Phonics

Teach The Short e Sound, TE T124

Vocabulary

Practice High-Frequency Words, TE T124

High-Frequency Words

friends	she
girl	sing
know	today
play	write
read	

Options for Guided Reading

80-100 minutes

● Extra Support

Before Reading Preview VR *A New School.* See VR Guide, p. 16.

During Reading Read the book together; coach reading. Help children apply Evaluate Strategy.

After Reading Discuss the book and Responding questions. **Fluency Practice:** Have children reread VR with a partner. Assign *Miss Nell,* PL Theme 4, pp. 21–24, for partner reading.

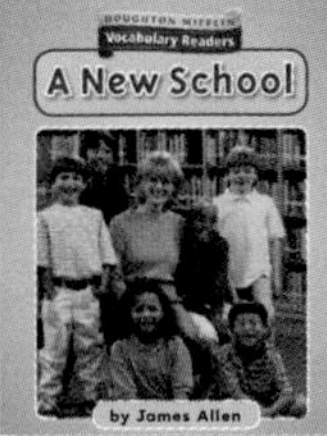

Level B

✓ = opportunity for ongoing assessment; adjust groups accordingly

▲ On Level

Before Reading Discuss PL *Knock, Knock,* TE T111–T113. Preview LR *Pets for the Twins,* TE T161.

During Reading Coach reading as children begin story. **Fluency Modeling:** Model fluent reading, then have children model it.

After Reading Discuss the sequence of events in the story. Then have children write answers to Responding questions. ✓ Assign *Miss Nell,* PL Theme 4, pp. 21–24, for partner reading.

Level E

 Above Level

Before Reading Have children model the Evaluate Strategy and discuss Responding questions for LR *Happy Birthday, Sam!,* TE T162.

During Reading **Fluency Check:** Monitor children's oral reading. ✓

After Reading Have children summarize for a partner, telling story events in order. Assign *Miss Nell,* PL Theme 4, pp. 21–24, for partner reading.

Level I

 English Language Learners

Before Reading To review VR vocabulary, have children demonstrate or give examples. See VR Guide, p. 16.

During Reading **Fluency Practice:** Have children reread book. Option: Preview and coach reading of *Knock, Knock,* PL Theme 4, pp. 17–20, TE T111–T113.

After Reading Help children summarize VR. Have partners discuss, draw, or write facts they learned. ✓

Level B

Writing and Language  25-40 minutes

Writing

Teach Interactive Writing: A Class Message, TE T125

Practice Assign Writing Prompt, TE T117.

Optional Resources

Teacher Read Aloud

Reread Big Book: *The Secret Code,* TE T104–T107.

Independent Work

Self-Selected Reading

Choose from

- classroom/school library
- Leveled Bibliography, TE T6–T7
- *I Love Reading,* Theme 4, take-home book 33
- Little Readers for Guided Reading

Centers

- Classroom Management Kit
- Classroom Management activities, TE T100–T101

Differentiated Instruction

- High-Frequency Words
  –Word Wall, TE T102
  –Reteaching or Extension, TE R30–R31

TE = Teacher Edition; PB = Practice Book; Tr = Transparency; LR = Leveled Reader; PL = Phonics Library; VR = Vocabulary Reader; VR Guide = Vocabulary Readers Teacher's Manual; LBB = Little Big Book; TP = Theme Paperback

Day 3 Balanced Literacy Plan

Teacher Notes

Reading and Comprehension
20-30 minutes

Shared Reading of *Two Best Friends*

▼ Anthology Selection

- Introduce Key Vocabulary, TE T128, Tr 4-4
  books new smile Dear sign
- Set Purpose; Review Comprehension Strategy and Skill, TE T128–T129
- Read Anthology Selection pp. 158–175 (independent, partner, or audio CD).
- Discuss questions; retell the story, TE T139.

Words to Know
New This Week

friends	today
girls	write
know	best
play	knelt
read	rest
she	sign
sing	snack

Comprehension Skill Instruction

Teach Compare and Contrast, TE T140–T141

Practice Assign PB 191.

Word Work

25-40 minutes

Phonemic Awareness Instruction

Teach Blending and Segmenting Phonemes, TE T127

Spelling and Phonics Instruction

Teach The Short *e* Sound, TE T142

Vocabulary Instruction

Teach Sensory Words, TE T142

Options for Guided Reading

80-100 minutes

Extra Support

Before Reading Review Responding questions from VR *A New School.* Preview LR *Sit, Ned!,* TE T160. Have children model Evaluate.

During Reading Coach as children read story. **Fluency Modeling:** Model fluent reading; have children model.

After Reading **Fluency Practice:** Have partners reread story. Have children answer Responding questions. ✓

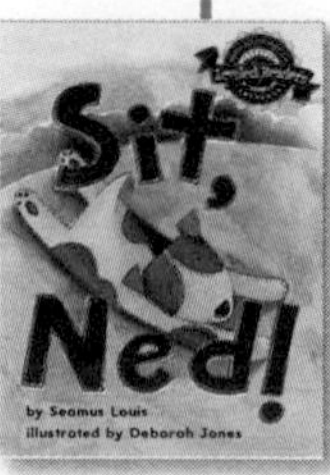

Level D

✓ = opportunity for ongoing assessment; adjust groups accordingly

▲ On Level

Level E

Before Reading Discuss Responding questions for LR *Pets for the Twins,* TE T161.

During Reading **Fluency Check:** Ask individuals to read story aloud. ✓

After Reading Have children summarize story for a partner, telling events in order.

■ Above Level

Before Reading Review LBB *The Secret Code.* See TE T104–T107, R8–R9.

During Reading **Fluency Modeling:** Model fluent reading, then have children model it. Have them read first half of story independently.

After Reading Ask questions; have children cite text to support answers. Have partners summarize story events in order.

Level G

English Language Learners

Before Reading Preview *Miss Nell,* PL Theme 4, pp. 21–24. Model Phonics/Decoding Strategy.

During Reading **Fluency Modeling:** Read aloud each page; have children do echo reading.

After Reading Discuss story; help children find/read words with *s,* short *e, kn, wr, gn.* Have children use illustrations to retell story to partners.

Writing and Language

30-40 minutes

Writing

Practice Assign Write a Card, Anthology p. 177.

Grammar

Teach Telling Sentences, TE T143

Optional Resources

Teacher Read Aloud

Choose a book from your class/school library or from the Leveled Bibliography, TE T6–T7.

Suggestion: *The Ugly Vegetables* by Grace Lin

Independent Work

Self-Selected Reading

Choose from

- classroom/school library
- Leveled Bibliography, TE T6–T7
- *I Love Reading,* Theme 4, take-home book 33
- Little Readers for Guided Reading

Centers

- Classroom Management Kit
- Classroom Management activities, TE T100–T101
- Responding activities, TE T139

Differentiated Instruction

- Comprehension Reteaching and Extension, Compare and Contrast, TE R36–R37
- High-Frequency Word Review: Word Wall, TE T126

TE = Teacher Edition; PB = Practice Book; Tr = Transparency; LR = Leveled Reader; PL = Phonics Library; VR = Vocabulary Reader; VR Guide = Vocabulary Readers Teacher's Manual; LBB = Little Big Book; TP = Theme Paperback

Day 4 Balanced Literacy Plan

Teacher Notes

1 WHOLE GROUP

Reading and Comprehension

20-30 minutes

Shared Reading of Social Studies Link

- "How Mail Gets to You," Anthology pp. 178–181, TE T146–T147 (independent, partner, or group)
- Skill: How to Read a Social Studies Article, TE T146
- Introduce Concept Vocabulary, TE T146.

Concept Vocabulary

mail carriers
zip code
address
post offices
deliver

2 WHOLE GROUP

Word Work

25-40 minutes

Phonemic Awareness/Phonics Instruction

Teach Blending and Segmenting Phonemes, TE T145

Review Clusters with *l*, TE T148; More Short *o* Words, TE T149

Spelling and Phonics

Practice The Short *e* Sound, TE T150

Vocabulary Instruction

Teach Words and Symbols on Signs, TE T150

3 SMALL GROUP

Options for Guided Reading

80-100 minutes

Extra Support

Before Reading Review Responding questions for LR *Sit, Ned!*, TE T160.

During Reading Have children reread story. **Fluency Check:** Have individuals read aloud. ✓

After Reading Model using the words *first, next,* and *last* to summarize story events. Have children retell the story to a partner.

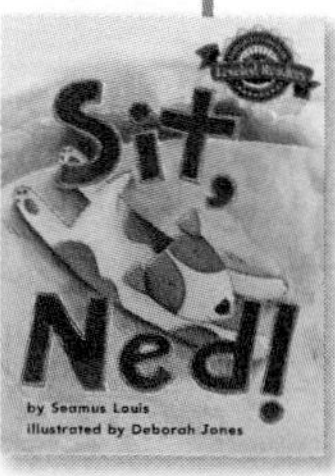

Level D

✓ = opportunity for ongoing assessment; adjust groups accordingly

▲ On Level

Before Reading Have children summarize LR *Pets for the Twins,* telling story events in sequence. ✓ Preview a teacher-selected book or TP *Come! Sit! Speak!,* TE R7. Have children make predictions about the story.

During Reading Have children begin story and model Phonics/Decoding Strategy.

After Reading Discuss the story so far. Have children finish story.

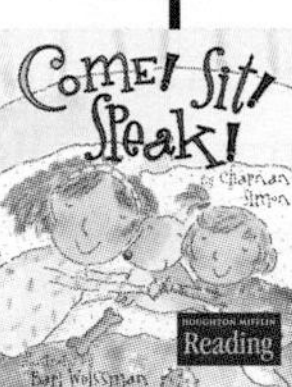

Level H

■ Above Level

Before Reading Review first half of LBB *The Secret Code,* TE T104–T107.

During Reading Have children finish book.

After Reading Discuss how book connects to theme. Have children write journal entries to connect it to personal experience or other reading.

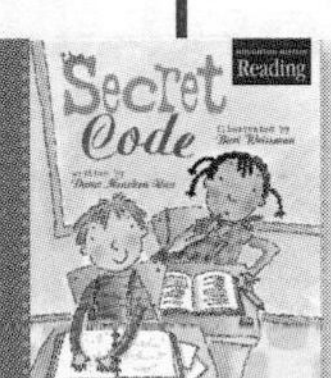

Level G

◆ English Language Learners

Before Reading Build background and preview LR *Ned,* TE T163. Have children make predictions about the story.

During Reading Read story. **Fluency Modeling:** Reread each page; have children do echo reading. Reinforce Phonics/Decoding Strategy.

After Reading Discuss Responding questions, TE T163. **Fluency Practice:** Have children reread with partners or audio CD.

Level C

Writing and Language

30-40 minutes

Writing

Practice Independent Writing: Writing Sentences on a Topic; assign PB 195.

Optional Resources

Teacher Read Aloud

Continue selected Read Aloud book from Day 3 or choose a new one from your class or school library.

Independent Work

Self-Selected Reading

Choose from

- classroom/school library
- Leveled Bibliography, TE T6–T7
- children's magazines
- *I Love Reading,* Theme 4, take-home book 33
- Little Readers for Guided Reading

Centers

- Classroom Management Kit
- Classroom Management activities, TE T100–T101
- Responding activities, TE T139

Differentiated Instruction

- Visual Literacy: Using Photographs, TE T147
- High-Frequency Words: Word Wall, TE T144
- Study Skills: Reading a Picture Map, TE R40

TE = Teacher Edition; PB = Practice Book; Tr = Transparency; LR = Leveled Reader; PL = Phonics Library; VR = Vocabulary Reader; VR Guide = Vocabulary Readers Teacher's Manual; LBB = Little Big Book; TP = Theme Paperback

Day 5 Balanced Literacy Plan

Teacher Notes

Reading and Comprehension

Book Share

- Ask children to explain how they applied the comprehension skill and strategy to books they have read this week.
- Help children use genre and text features to compare and contrast what they have read.
- As a class, discuss one *how, why,* or *what if* question. See examples on Blackline Master 1 to use as a guide.

Word Work

Phonemic Awareness Instruction

Teach Blending and Segmenting Phonemes, TE T153

High-Frequency Words

Practice Word Wall/Vocabulary Speed Drill, TE T152

Spelling and Phonics

Practice The Short *e* Sound, TE T158

Options for Guided Reading

80-100 minutes

Extra Support

Before Reading Preview *Deb and Bess,* PL Theme 4, pp. 25–28. Have children find/read words with *s,* short *e, kn, wr, gn.* See TE T155–T157.

During Reading Have children read and model Phonics/Decoding Strategy. **Fluency Check:** Have individuals reread aloud. ✓

After Reading Have partners make connections between the story and LR *Sit, Ned!* Assign On My Way Practice Reader *Best Friends* for partner reading.

✓ = opportunity for ongoing assessment; adjust groups accordingly

◆ English Language Learners

Level C

Before Reading Review LR *Ned,* TE T163.

During Reading Coach rereading of book. **Fluency Check:** Have individuals reread aloud. ✓

After Reading Help children summarize LR story events in sequence. Have children draw/caption a picture about a book they read this week. ✓

●▲■◆ Mixed Ability Levels

Literature Circles Form small, mixed-ability groups. Ask groups to discuss the main Anthology selection, Link, Leveled Readers, and other books they have read this week. Pose questions or topics for each group, and circulate among groups to offer support. Suggested group activities:

- Respond to specific Literature Discussion questions on Blackline Master 1.
- Discuss story or text elements, authors' choice of language, and/or illustrations.
- Connect book topics or themes to personal experiences or other reading.

Writing and Language

30-40 minutes

Writing

Practice Assign Writing Prompt, TE T153.

Grammar

Review Telling Sentences, TE T159

Listening and Speaking

Practice Readers' Theater, TE T159

Optional Resources

Teacher Read Aloud

Choose a nonfiction book related to Social Studies or Science unit.

Independent Work

Self-Selected Reading

Choose from

- classroom/school library
- Leveled Bibliography, TE T6–T7
- children's magazines
- consumer text such as books about mail delivery, stamps, etc.
- *I Love Reading,* Theme 4, take-home book 33
- Little Readers for Guided Reading

Centers

- Classroom Management Kit
- Classroom Management activities, TE T100–T101
- Responding activities, TE T139

Differentiated Instruction

- Vocabulary: Speed Drill, TE T152
- Comprehension Review: Compare and Contrast, TE T154

End-of-Week Assessment

- Weekly Skills Tests for Theme 4, Week 2
- Fluency Assessment, *Deb and Bess,* PL Theme 4, pp. 25–28, TE T155–T157
- Alternative Assessment, Teacher's Resource Blackline Master 54

TE = Teacher Edition; PB = Practice Book; Tr = Transparency; LR = Leveled Reader; PL = Phonics Library; VR = Vocabulary Reader; VR Guide = Vocabulary Readers Teacher's Manual; LBB = Little Big Book; TP = Theme Paperback

Day 1 Balanced Literacy Plan

Teacher Notes

Reading and Comprehension

20-30 minutes

Shared Reading of Daily Message, TE T174

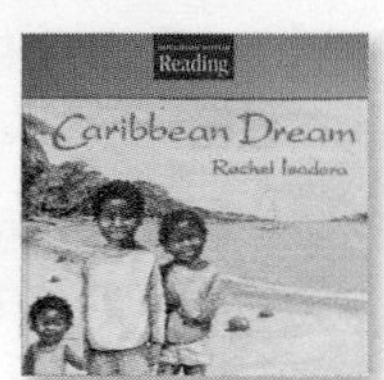

Shared Reading of Big Book

- Introduce Comprehension Strategy and Skill:
  Monitor/Clarify, TE T176
  Sequence of Events, TE T177
- Read aloud *Caribbean Dream*, TE T176–T179.

Word Work

25-40 minutes

Phonemic Awareness/Phonics Instruction

Teach Blending and Segmenting Phonemes, TE T175

Teach Triple Clusters, TE T180

Practice Assign PB 196.

Teach Blending More Short *u* Words, TE T181–T182

Practice Assign PB 197–198.

Spelling/Phonics

Teach The Short *u* Sound, TE T186

Practice Assign PB 231.

Vocabulary

Teach Word Wall: *here, and, to, like, is, my, are, the, I, said,* TE T174

Options for Guided Reading

80-100 minutes

Extra Support

Before Reading Preview *Buzzing Bug,* PL Theme 4, pp. 29–32. Model Phonics/Decoding Strategy. See TE T183–T185.

During Reading Coach as children read story.

After Reading Discuss story; have children find/read words with triple clusters and short *u*. **Fluency Modeling:** Model fluent reading. Have partners reread story.

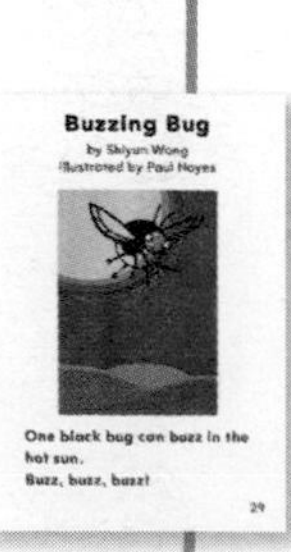

✓ = opportunity for ongoing assessment; adjust groups accordingly

 **On Level**

Before Reading Preview *Buzzing Bug,* PL Theme 4, pp. 29–32. Model Phonics/Decoding Strategy. See TE T183–T185.

During Reading Have children begin story. **Fluency Modeling:** Model Phonics/Decoding Strategy and fluent reading.

After Reading Have children retell story so far and find/read words with triple clusters and short *u.* **Fluency Practice:** Have partners finish story and reread for fluency.

■ **Above Level**

Before Reading Preview LR *Scruffy,* TE T234. Have students model the Monitor/Clarify Strategy.

During Reading Have children read first half of story. **Fluency Modeling:** Model fluent reading.

After Reading Have children finish reading and write answers to Responding questions. ✓

Level I

 **English Language Learners**

Before Reading Preview VR *Dogs Learn Every Day.* See VR Guide, p. 17.

During Reading **Fluency Modeling:** Read aloud each page; have children do echo reading.

After Reading Discuss Responding pages. Have children reread with partners or audio CD.

Level C

Writing and Language

25-40 minutes

Writing

Teach Shared Writing: A Class Letter, TE T187

Practice Assign Writing Prompt, TE T175.

Viewing

Teach Looking at Fine Art, TE T187

Optional Resources

Teacher Read Aloud

Reread Big Book: *Caribbean Dream,* TE T176–T179.

Read *Too Much Noise!,* TE T18–T19.

Independent Work

Self-Selected Reading

Choose from

- classroom/school library
- Leveled Bibliography, TE T6–T7
- *I Love Reading,* Theme 4, take-home book 37
- Little Readers for Guided Reading

Centers

- Classroom Management Kit
- Classroom Management activities, TE T172–T173

Differentiated Instruction

- Phonics Reteaching or Extension:
  –Triple Clusters, TE R24–R25
  –Blending More Short *u* Words, TE R26–R27
- High-Frequency Words Review: Word Wall, TE T174

TE = Teacher Edition; PB = Practice Book; Tr = Transparency; LR = Leveled Reader; PL = Phonics Library; VR = Vocabulary Reader; VR Guide = Vocabulary Readers Teacher's Manual; LBB = Little Big Book; TP = Theme Paperback

Day 2 Balanced Literacy Plan

Teacher Notes

Reading and Comprehension

20-30 minutes

Shared Reading of Get Set Story

➤ Build Background and Vocabulary, TE T192

➤ Read *Dad's Big Plan,* Anthology pp. 183–189.

Comprehension Skill Instruction

Teach Sequence of Events, TE T194

▼ Anthology Selection

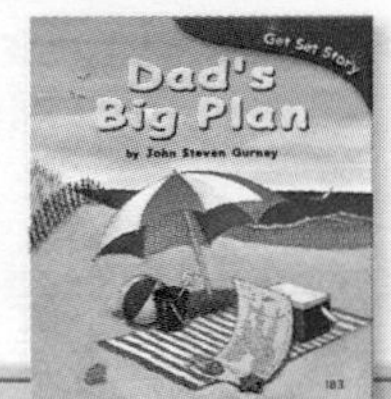

Words to Know

car	their
down	walk
hear	would
hold	just
hurt	must
learn	scrub

Word Work

25-40 minutes

Phonemic Awareness

Teach Blending and Segmenting Phonemes, TE T189

High-Frequency Words Instruction

Teach TE T190–T191, Tr 4-5; **Practice** PB 199, 200.

High-Frequency Words

car	learn
down	their
hear	walk
hold	would
hurt	

Spelling and Phonics

Teach The Short *u* Sound, TE T196

Vocabulary

Practice High-Frequency Words, TE T196

Options for Guided Reading

80-100 minutes

Extra Support

Before Reading Preview VR *Dogs Learn Every Day.* See VR Guide, p. 17.

During Reading Read the book together; coach reading. Help children apply Monitor/Clarify Strategy.

After Reading Discuss the book and Responding questions. **Fluency Practice:** Have children reread VR with a partner. Assign *Duff in the Mud,* PL Theme 4, pp. 33–36, for partner reading.

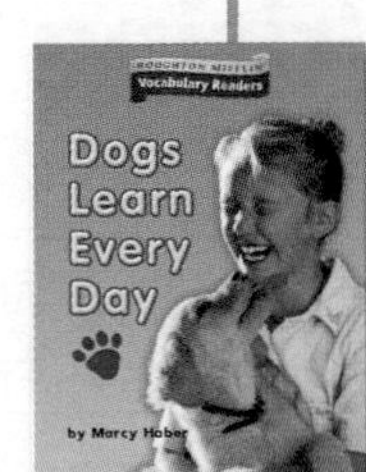

Level C

✓ = opportunity for ongoing assessment; adjust groups accordingly

▲ On Level

Before Reading Discuss PL *Buzzing Bug,* TE T183–T185. Preview LR *A Bird on the Bus,* TE T233.

During Reading Coach reading as children begin story. **Fluency Modeling:** Model fluent reading, then have children model it.

After Reading Discuss the sequence of events in the story. Then have children write answers to Responding questions. ✓ Assign *Duff in the Mud,* PL Theme 4, pp. 33–36, for partner reading.

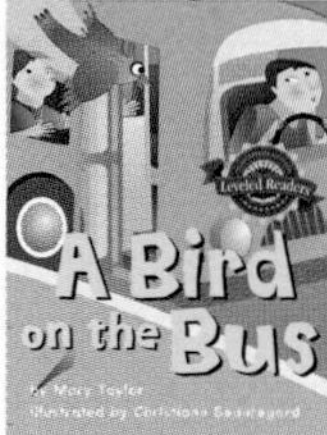

Level E

■ Above Level

Before Reading Have children model the Monitor/Clarify Strategy and discuss Responding questions for LR *Scruffy,* TE T234.

During Reading **Fluency Check:** Monitor children's oral reading. ✓

After Reading Have children summarize for a partner, telling story events in order. Assign *Duff in the Mud,* PL Theme 4, pp. 33–36, for partner reading.

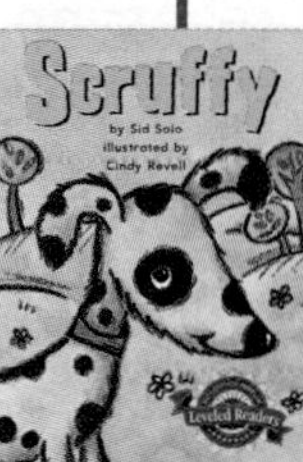

Level I

◆ English Language Learners

Before Reading To review VR vocabulary, have children demonstrate or give examples. See VR Guide, p. 17.

During Reading **Fluency Practice:** Have children reread book. Option: Preview and coach reading of *Buzzing Bug,* PL Theme 4, pp. 29–32, TE T183–T185.

After Reading Help children summarize VR. Have partners discuss, draw, or write facts they learned. ✓

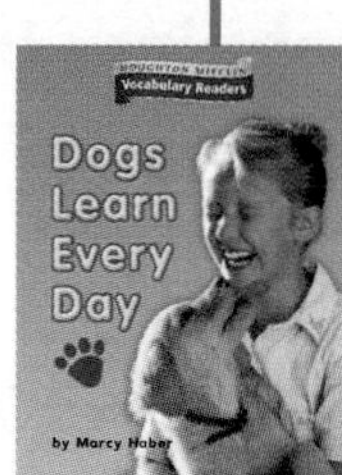

Level C

4 WHOLE GROUP Writing and Language

25-40 minutes

Writing

Teach Interactive Writing: A Class Letter, TE T197

Practice Assign Writing Prompt, TE T189.

Optional Resources

Teacher Read Aloud

Reread Big Book: *Caribbean Dream,* TE T176–T179.

Independent Work

Self-Selected Reading

Choose from

- classroom/school library
- Leveled Bibliography, TE T6–T7
- *I Love Reading,* Theme 4, take-home book 37
- Little Readers for Guided Reading

Centers

- Classroom Management Kit
- Classroom Management activities, TE T172–T173

Differentiated Instruction

- High-Frequency Words
  –Word Wall, TE T188
  –Reteaching or Extension, TE R32–R33

TE = Teacher Edition; PB = Practice Book; Tr = Transparency; LR = Leveled Reader; PL = Phonics Library; VR = Vocabulary Reader; VR Guide = Vocabulary Readers Teacher's Manual; LBB = Little Big Book; TP = Theme Paperback

Day 3 Balanced Literacy Plan

Teacher Notes

Reading and Comprehension

20-30 minutes

▼ Anthology Selection

Shared Reading of *Dog School*

- Introduce Story Vocabulary, TE T200, Tr 4-6

chase	face	school	street
day	leash	stay	

- Set Purpose; Review Comprehension Strategy and Skill, TE T200–T201
- Read Anthology Selection pp. 192–209 (independent, partner, or audio CD).
- Discuss questions; retell the story, TE T211.

Comprehension Skill Instruction

Teach Sequence of Events, TE T212–T213, Tr 4-7

Practice Assign PB 203.

Words to Know
New This Week

car	their
down	walk
hear	would
hold	just
hurt	must
learn	scrub

Word Work

25-40 minutes

Phonemic Awareness Instruction

Teach Blending and Segmenting Phonemes, TE T199

Spelling and Phonics Instruction

Teach The Short *u* Sound, TE T214

Vocabulary Instruction

Teach Question Words, TE T214

Options for Guided Reading

80-100 minutes

● Extra Support

Before Reading Review Responding questions from VR *Dogs Learn Every Day.* Preview LR *My Pup,* TE T232. Have children model Monitor/Clarify.

During Reading Coach as children read story. **Fluency Modeling:** Model fluent reading; have children model.

After Reading **Fluency Practice:** Have partners reread story. Have children answer Responding questions. ✓

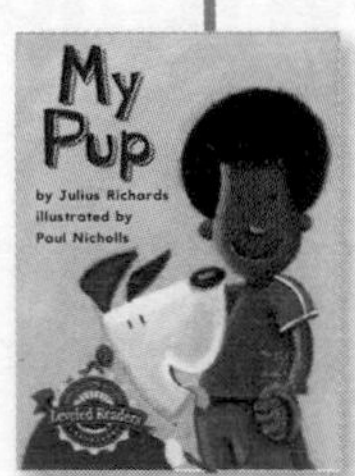

Level C

✓ = opportunity for ongoing assessment; adjust groups accordingly

▲ On Level

Level E

Before Reading Discuss Responding questions for LR *A Bird on the Bus,* TE T233.

During Reading **Fluency Check:** Ask individuals to read story aloud. ✓

After Reading Have children summarize story for a partner, telling events in order.

■ Above Level

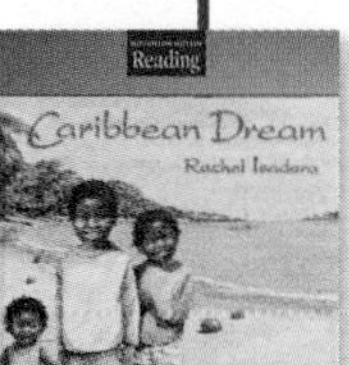

Level F

Before Reading Review LBB *Caribbean Dream.* See TE T176–T179, R12–R13.

During Reading **Fluency Modeling:** Model fluent reading, then have children model it. Have them read first half of story independently.

After Reading Ask questions; have children cite text to support answers. Have partners summarize story events in order.

 English Language Learners

Before Reading Preview *Duff in the Mud* PL Theme 4, pp. 33–36. Model Phonics/Decoding Strategy.

During Reading **Fluency Modeling:** Read aloud each page; have children do echo reading.

After Reading Discuss story; help children find/read words with triple clusters and short *u.* Have children use illustrations to retell story to partners.

4 WHOLE GROUP

Writing and Language

 30-40 minutes

Writing

Practice Assign Make a Poster, Anthology p. 211.

Grammar

Teach Asking Sentences, TE T215

Optional Resources

Teacher Read Aloud

Choose a book from your class/school library or from the Leveled Bibliography, TE T6–T7.

Suggestion: *Four Friends in Summer* by Tomie dePaola

Independent Work

Self-Selected Reading

Choose from
- classroom/school library
- Leveled Bibliography, TE T6–T7
- *I Love Reading,* Theme 4, take-home book 37
- Little Readers for Guided Reading

Centers
- Classroom Management Kit
- Classroom Management activities, TE T172–T173
- Responding activities, TE T211

Differentiated Instruction
- Comprehension Reteaching and Extension, Sequence of Events, TE R38–R39
- High-Frequency Word Review: Word Wall, TE T198

TE = Teacher Edition; PB = Practice Book; Tr = Transparency; LR = Leveled Reader; PL = Phonics Library; VR = Vocabulary Reader; VR Guide = Vocabulary Readers Teacher's Manual; LBB = Little Big Book; TP = Theme Paperback

Day 4 Balanced Literacy Plan

Teacher Notes

Reading and Comprehension

20-30 minutes

Shared Reading of Social Studies Link

- "Daycare for Dogs," Anthology pp. 212–215, TE T218–T219 (independent, partner, or group)
- Skill: How to Read a Social Studies Article, TE T218
- Introduce Concept Vocabulary, TE T218.

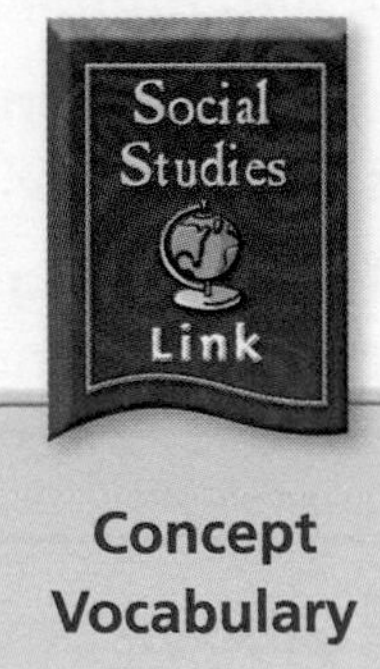

Concept Vocabulary

daycare
busy
groomed

Word Work

25-40 minutes

Phonemic Awareness/Phonics Instruction

Teach Blending and Segmenting Phonemes, TE T217

Review Clusters with *s;* Silent Letters in *kn, wr, gn,* TE T220; More Short *e* Words, TE T221

Spelling and Phonics

Practice The Short *u* Sound, TE T222

Vocabulary Instruction

Teach Noise Words, TE T222

Options for Guided Reading

80-100 minutes

Extra Support

Before Reading Review Responding questions for LR *My Pup,* TE T232.

During Reading Have children reread story. **Fluency Check:** Have individuals read aloud. ✓

After Reading Model using the words *first, next,* and *last* to summarize story events. Have children retell the story to a partner.

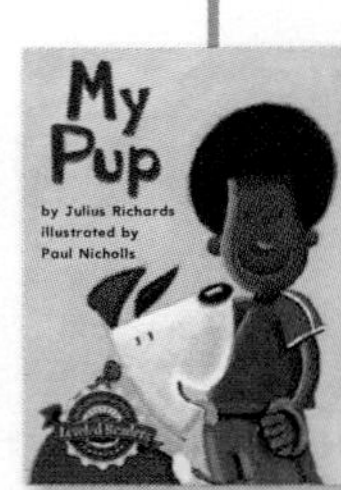

Level C

✓ = opportunity for ongoing assessment; adjust groups accordingly

On Level

Before Reading Have children summarize LR *A Bird on the Bus,* telling story events in sequence. ✓ Preview a teacher-selected book or TP *The Day the Sheep Showed Up,* TE R11. Have children make predictions about the story.

During Reading Have children begin story and model Phonics/Decoding Strategy.

After Reading Discuss the story so far. Have children finish story.

Level E

Above Level

Before Reading Review first half of LBB *Caribbean Dream,* TE T176–T179.

During Reading Have children finish book.

After Reading Discuss how book connects to theme. Have children write journal entries to connect it to personal experience or other reading.

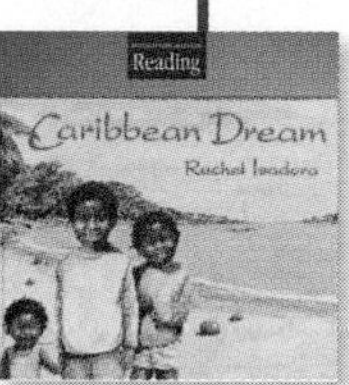

Level F

◆ English Language Learners

Before Reading Build background and preview LR *Me and My Pup,* TE T235. Have children make predictions about the story.

During Reading Read story. **Fluency Modeling:** Reread each page; have children do echo reading. Reinforce Phonics/Decoding Strategy.

After Reading Discuss Responding questions, TE T235. **Fluency Practice:** Have children reread with partners or audio CD.

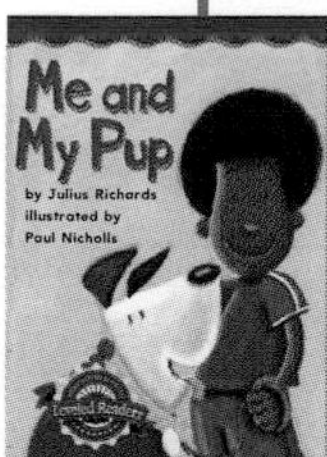

Level C

Writing and Language

30-40 minutes

Writing

Practice Independent Writing: Writing Questions; assign PB 208.

Optional Resources

Teacher Read Aloud

Continue selected Read Aloud book from Day 3 or choose a new one from your class or school library.

Independent Work

Self-Selected Reading

Choose from

- classroom/school library
- Leveled Bibliography, TE T6–T7
- children's magazines
- *I Love Reading,* Theme 4, take-home book 37
- Little Readers for Guided Reading

Centers

- Classroom Management Kit
- Classroom Management activities, TE T172–T173
- Responding activities, TE T211

Differentiated Instruction

- Visual Literacy: Using Photographs, TE T219
- High-Frequency Words: Word Wall, TE T216
- Study Skills: Reading a Picture Map, TE R40

TE = Teacher Edition; PB = Practice Book; Tr = Transparency; LR = Leveled Reader; PL = Phonics Library; VR = Vocabulary Reader; VR Guide = Vocabulary Readers Teacher's Manual; LBB = Little Big Book; TP = Theme Paperback

Day 5 Balanced Literacy Plan

Teacher Notes

Reading and Comprehension

20-30 minutes

Book Share

- Ask children to explain how they applied the comprehension skill and strategy to books they have read this week.
- Help children use genre and text features to compare and contrast what they have read.
- As a class, discuss one *how, why,* or *what if* question. See examples on Blackline Master 1 to use as a guide.

Word Work

25-40 minutes

Phonemic Awareness Instruction

Teach Blending and Segmenting Phonemes, TE T225

Vocabulary

Practice Wordwall/Vocabulary Speed Drill, TE T224

Spelling and Phonics

Practice The Short *u* Sound, TE T230

3 SMALL GROUP

Options for Guided Reading

80-100 minutes

Extra Support

Before Reading Preview *Jess and Mom,* PL Theme 4, pp. 37–40. Have children find/read words with triple clusters and short *u.* See TE T227–T229.

During Reading Have children read and model Phonics/Decoding Strategy. **Fluency Check:** Have individuals reread aloud. ✓

After Reading Have partners make connections between the story and LR *My Pup.* Assign On My Way Practice Reader *The Bug Jug Band* for partner reading.

✓ = opportunity for ongoing assessment; adjust groups accordingly

 English Language Learners

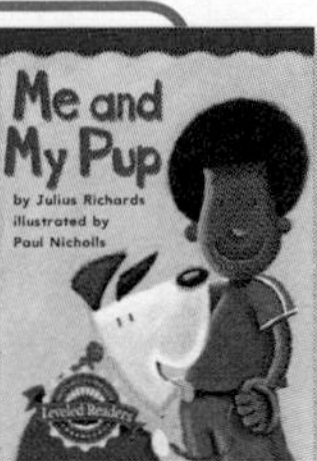

Level C

Before Reading Review LR *Me and My Pup,* TE T235.

During Reading Coach rereading of book. **Fluency Check:** Have individuals reread aloud. ✓

After Reading Help children summarize LR story events in sequence. Have children draw/caption a picture about a book they read this week. ✓

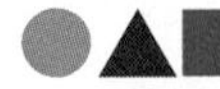 Mixed Ability Levels

Literature Circles Form small, mixed-ability groups. Ask groups to discuss the main Anthology selection, Link, Leveled Readers, and other books they have read this week. Pose questions or topics for each group, and circulate among groups to offer support. Suggested group activities:

- Respond to specific Literature Discussion questions on Blackline Master 1.
- Discuss story or text elements, authors' choice of language, and/or illustrations.
- Connect book topics or themes to personal experiences or other reading.

Optional Resources

Teacher Read Aloud

Choose a nonfiction book related to Social Studies or Science unit.

Independent Work

Self-Selected Reading

Choose from

- classroom/school library
- Leveled Bibliography, TE T6–T7
- children's magazines
- consumer text such as books about dogs, animals, etc.
- Little Readers for Guided Reading

Centers

- Classroom Management Kit
- Classroom Management activities, TE T172–T173
- Responding activities, TE T211

Differentiated Instruction

- Vocabulary: Speed Drill, TE T224
- Comprehension Review: Sequence of Events, TE T226

Writing and Language

30-40 minutes

Writing

Practice Assign Writing Prompt, TE T225.

Grammar

Review Asking Sentences, TE T231

Viewing

Practice Environmental Print, TE T231

End-of-Week Assessment

End-of-Week Assessment

- Weekly Skills Tests for Theme 4, Week 3
- Fluency Assessment, *Jess and Mom,* PL Theme 4, pp. 37–40, TE T227–T229
- Alternative Assessment, Teacher's Resource Blackline Master 57

End-of-Theme Assessment

- Integrated Theme Tests for Theme 4

TE = Teacher Edition; PB = Practice Book; Tr = Transparency; LR = Leveled Reader; PL = Phonics Library; VR = Vocabulary Reader; VR Guide = Vocabulary Readers Teacher's Manual; LBB = Little Big Book; TP = Theme Paperback

Theme 5 Overview

	Week 1
Reading and Comprehension	**Shared Reading** Main Selection: *Moving Day* Science Link: "Hermit Crabs" Book Share **Comprehension** Strategy: Question Skill: Compare and Contrast Content Skill: How to Read a Science Article
Word Work	**Phonemic Awareness:** Segmenting Phonemes; Count Sounds in Words **Phonics:** Digraphs *sh, th, wh* **Phonics:** Digraphs *ch, tch* **Phonics Review:** Short *u;* Triple Clusters **Vocabulary:** Antonyms; Size Words **High-Frequency Words:** *grow, light, long, more, other, right, room, small, these* **Spelling:** Words Spelled with *sh* or *ch*
Options for Guided Reading	**Vocabulary Reader** *Where Is the Crab?* **Leveled Readers:** Extra Support: *Just Right!* On Level: *Chad and the Big Egg* Above Level: *Miss Hen's Feast* ELL: *Big, Small, or Just Right?* **Phonics Library** *The Shed* *Champ* *Hen's Chicks* **Theme Paperbacks** **Literature Circles**
Writing and Oral Language	**Shared Writing:** An Alternate Ending **Interactive Writing:** An Alternate Ending **Independent Writing:** Writing Complete Sentences **Grammar:** Exclamations **Listening and Speaking:** Visualizing **Listening and Speaking:** Conversation
Assessment Options	• Weekly Skills Test for Theme 5, Week 1 • Fluency Assessment: Phonics Library

- Use **Launching the Theme** on pages T16–T17 of the Teacher's Edition to introduce the theme.
- Use the **Focus on Genre** section to help children explore the unique characteristics of poetry.

Week 2

Shared Reading
Main Selection: *Me on the Map*
Social Studies Link: "Children of the World"
Book Share

Comprehension
Strategy: Summarize
Skill: Making Generalizations
Content Skill: How to Read a Map

Phonemic Awareness: Segmenting Phonemes; Count Sounds in Words
Phonics: Blending Long *a* Words (CVCe); Soft *c* and *g*
Phonics: Final *nd, ng, nk*
Phonics Review: Digraphs *sh, th, wh;* Digraphs *ch, tch*
Vocabulary: Social Studies Words; State and Country Words
High-Frequency Words: *could, house, how, over, own, so, world*
Spelling: The Long *a* Sound (*a*- consonant -e)

Vocabulary Reader
Where We Live

Leveled Readers:
Extra Support: *Jake Makes a Map*
On Level: *Places in the United States*
Above Level: *My Neighborhood*
ELL: *Jake's Map*

Phonics Library
Pets in a Tank
Gram's Trip
Stuck in the House

Literature Circles

Shared Writing: A Class Letter
Interactive Writing: A Class Letter
Independent Writing: Writing a Journal Entry
Grammar: Which Kind of Sentence?
Listening and Speaking: Compare and Contrast
Viewing: Gathering Information

- Weekly Skills Test for Theme 5, Week 2
- Fluency Assessment: Phonics Library

Week 3

Shared Reading
Main Selection: *The Kite*
Art Link: "How to Make a Kite"
Book Share

Comprehension
Strategy: Monitor/Clarify
Skill: Cause and Effect
Content Skill: How to Read Directions

Phonemic Awareness: Segment Phonemes; Count Sounds in Words
Phonics: Long *i* (CVCe)
Phonics: Contractions
Phonics Review: Blending Long *a* Words (CVCe); Soft *c* and *g;* Final *nd, ng, nk*
Vocabulary: Base Words with *-ing;* Weather Words
High-Frequency Words: *fly, give, good, her, little, our, try, was*
Spelling: The Long *i* Sound (*i*- consonant -e)

Vocabulary Reader
Perfect Kite Weather

Leveled Readers:
Extra Support: *The Best Place*
On Level: *The Just-Right House*
Above Level: *The Surprise Snow*
ELL: *A Good Home*

Phonics Library
Pine Lake
Fun Rides
Jim and Sal

Literature Circles

Shared Writing: A Class Paragraph
Interactive Writing: A Class Paragraph
Independent Writing: Writing a Paragraph
Grammar: Using *I* or *me* in Sentences
Listening: Compare and Contrast
Speaking and Listening: Discussion

- Weekly Skills Test, Theme 5, Week 3
- Fluency Assessment: Phonics Library

Day 1 Balanced Literacy Plan

Teacher Notes

Reading and Comprehension

20-30 minutes

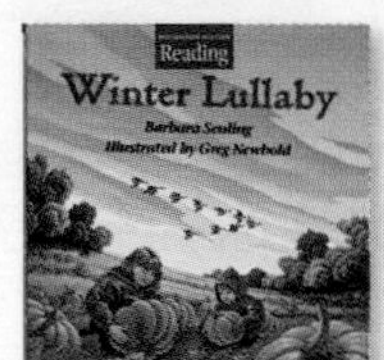

Shared Reading of Daily Message, TE T28

Shared Reading of Big Book

- Read aloud *Winter Lullaby,* TE T17, R2.
- Model fluent reading; discuss the story.

Word Work

25-40 minutes

Phonemic Awareness/Phonics Instruction

Teach Segmenting, Counting Phonemes, TE T29, T32

Teach Digraphs *sh, th, wh,* TE T32–T34

Practice Assign PB 1–2.

Spelling Instruction: Words Spelled with *sh* or *ch*

Pretest and Teach Spelling Principle, TE T38

Assign Take-Home Spelling Word List, PB 303

she fish much chin shell chop

Challenge: shoe, chair

Vocabulary Instruction

Teach Spelling Patterns *-ash, -ush,* TE T38

Options for Guided Reading

80-100 minutes

Extra Support

Before Reading Preview *The Shed,* PL Theme 5, pp. 5–8. Model Phonics/Decoding Strategy. See TE T35–T37.

During Reading Coach as children read story.

After Reading Discuss story; have children find/read words with *sh, th, wh.* **Fluency Modeling:** Model fluent reading. Have partners reread story.

✓ = opportunity for ongoing assessment; adjust groups accordingly

▲ On Level

Before Reading Preview *The Shed,* PL Theme 5, pp. 5–8, and review TE T35–T37.

During Reading Have children begin story. **Fluency Modeling:** Model Phonics/Decoding Strategy and fluent reading.

After Reading Have children retell story so far and find/read words with *sh, th, wh.* **Fluency Practice:** Have partners finish story and reread for fluency.

■ Above Level

Before Reading Preview LR *Miss Hen's Feast,* TE T92.

During Reading Have children read first half of story. **Fluency Modeling:** Model fluent reading.

After Reading Have children finish reading and write answers to Responding questions. ✓

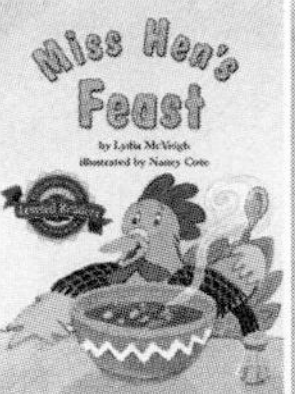

Level I

◆ English Language Learners

Before Reading Preview VR *Where Is the Crab?* See VR Guide, p. 18.

During Reading **Fluency Modeling:** Read aloud each page; have children do echo reading.

After Reading Discuss Responding pages. Have children reread with partners or audio CD.

Level C

Writing and Language

25-40 minutes

Writing

Teach Shared Writing: An Alternate Ending, TE T39

Practice Assign Writing Prompt, TE T29.

Listening and Speaking

Teach Visualizing, TE T39

Optional Resources

Teacher Read Aloud

Reread the Big Book: *Winter Lullaby,* TE T17, R2.

Read *The Two Japanese Frogs,* TE T30–T31.

Independent Work

Self-Selected Reading

Choose from

- classroom/school library
- Leveled Bibliography, TE T6–T7
- *I Love Reading,* Theme 5, take-home books 38–40
- Little Readers for Guided Reading

Centers

- Classroom Management Kit
- Classroom Management activities, TE T26–T27

Differentiated Instruction

- Phonics Reteaching or Extension: Digraphs *sh, th, wh,* TE R12–R13
- High-Frequency Words Review: Word Wall, TE T28

TE = Teacher Edition; PB = Practice Book; Tr = Transparency; LR = Leveled Reader; PL = Phonics Library; VR = Vocabulary Reader; VR Guide = Vocabulary Readers Teacher's Manual; LBB = Little Big Book; TP = Theme Paperback

Day 2 Balanced Literacy Plan

Teacher Notes

Reading and Comprehension

20-30 minutes

▼ Anthology Selection

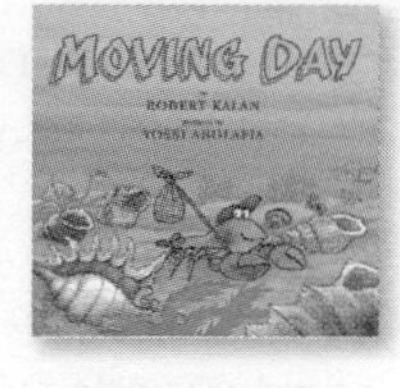

Shared Reading of *Moving Day* (Part 1)

- Build Background and Vocabulary; Introduce Story Vocabulary, TE T46–T47, Tr 5-2

fancy	hide	plain	smooth
heavy	inside	rough	wait

- Introduce Comprehension Strategy and Skill:
  Question, TE T48
  Compare and Contrast, TE T48, TE T56
- Set Purpose, TE T49
- Read Anthology Selection pp. 17–37 (independent, partner, or audio CD).

Words to Know

grow	small
light	these
long	shell
more	this
other	that's
right	smooth
room	why

Word Work

25-40 minutes

Phonemic Awareness/Phonics Instruction

Teach Segmenting, Counting Phonemes, TE T41, T42

Teach Digraphs *ch, tch,* TE T42–T43; Practice PB 3–4.

High-Frequency Words Instruction

Teach TE T44–T45, Tr 5-1; Practice PB 5–6.

Spelling Instruction

Teach Words Spelled with *sh* or *ch,* TE T64

High-Frequency Words

grow	right
light	room
long	small
more	these
other	

Options for Guided Reading

80-100 minutes

Extra Support

Before Reading Preview VR *Where Is the Crab?* See VR Guide, p. 18.

During Reading Read the book together; coach reading. Help children apply Question Strategy.

After Reading Help children compare this book to *Moving Day.* **Fluency Practice:** Have children reread VR. Assign *Champ,* PL Theme 5, pp. 9–12, for partner reading.

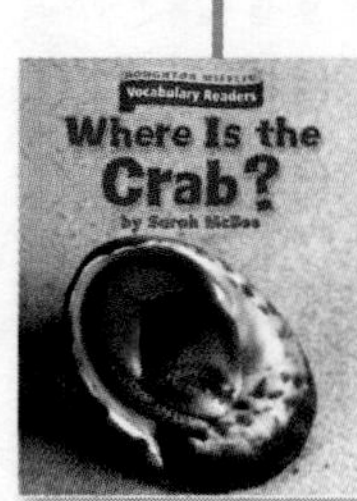

Level C

✓ = opportunity for ongoing assessment; adjust groups accordingly

▲ On Level

Before Reading Discuss PL *The Shed,* TE T36. Preview LR *Chad and the Big Egg,* TE T91.

During Reading Coach reading as children begin story. Have children model the Question Strategy. **Fluency Modeling:** Model fluent reading, then have children model it.

After Reading Children finish reading and write answers to Responding questions. ✓ Assign *Champ,* PL Theme 5, pp. 9–12, for partner reading.

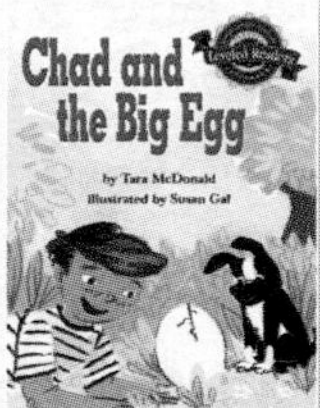

Level F

■ Above Level

Before Reading Have children model the Question Strategy and discuss Responding questions for LR *Miss Hen's Feast,* TE T92.

During Reading **Fluency Check:** Monitor children's oral reading. ✓

After Reading Have children discuss the story with a partner. Assign *Champ,* PL Theme 5, pp. 9–12, for partner reading.

Level I

 English Language Learners

Before Reading To review VR vocabulary, have children demonstrate or give examples. See VR Guide, p. 18.

During Reading Model Question Strategy. Help children apply the Question Strategy. **Fluency Practice:** Have children reread book.
Option: Preview and coach reading of *The Shed,* PL Theme 5, pp. 5–8, TE T35–T37.

After Reading Help children summarize VR. Have partners discuss, draw, or write facts they learned. ✓

Level C

Writing and Language

25-40 minutes

Writing

Teach Interactive Writing: An Alternate Ending, TE T65

Practice Assign Writing Prompt, TE T41.

Optional Resources

Teacher Read Aloud

Reread Big Book: *Winter Lullaby.* See TE T17, R2.

Independent Work

Self-Selected Reading

Choose from

- classroom/school library
- Leveled Bibliography, TE T6–T7
- *I Love Reading,* Theme 5, take-home books 38–42
- Little Readers for Guided Reading

Centers

- Classroom Management Kit
- Classroom Management activities, TE T26–T27

Differentiated Instruction

- Phonics Reteaching or Extension: Digraphs *ch, tch,* TE R14–R15
- High-Frequency Words
  –Word Wall, TE T40
  –Review, TE T64
  –Reteaching or Extension, TE R24–R25

TE = Teacher Edition; PB = Practice Book; Tr = Transparency; LR = Leveled Reader; PL = Phonics Library; VR = Vocabulary Reader; VR Guide = Vocabulary Readers Teacher's Manual; LBB = Little Big Book; TP = Theme Paperback

Day 3 Balanced Literacy Plan

Teacher Notes

Reading and Comprehension

20-30 minutes

▼ Anthology Selection

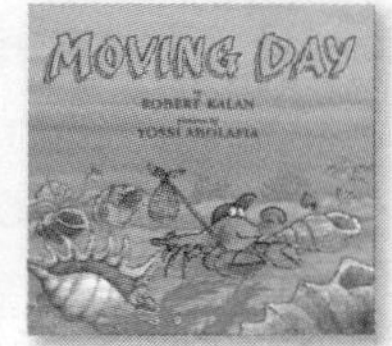

Shared Reading of *Moving Day* (Part 2)

- ➤ Read Anthology Selection pp. 38–42 (independent, partner, or audio CD).
- ➤ Discuss Responding questions, TE T68; have children cite text to support answers.

Comprehension Skill Instruction

Teach Compare and Contrast, TE T70–T71, Tr 5-3

Practice Assign PB 11 or retelling of story.

Word Work

25-40 minutes

Phonemic Awareness Instruction

Teach Segmenting, Counting Phonemes, TE T67

Spelling: Words Spelled with *sh* or *ch*

Practice Assign PB 12 or activity, TE T72.

Vocabulary Instruction

Teach Antonyms, TE T72

Practice Assign PB 13.

Options for Guided Reading

80-100 minutes

● Extra Support

Before Reading Discuss Responding questions from VR *Where Is the Crab?* See VR Guide, p. 18. Preview LR *Just Right!*, TE T90.

During Reading Coach as children read story. **Fluency Modeling:** Model fluent reading, then have children model it.

After Reading **Fluency Practice:** Have partners reread story. Have children write answers to Responding questions. ✓

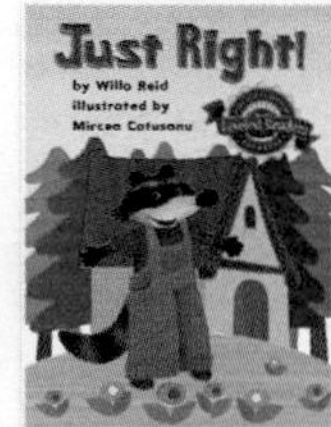

Level C

✓ = opportunity for ongoing assessment; adjust groups accordingly

▲ On Level

Before Reading Discuss Responding questions for LR *Chad and the Big Egg,* TE T91.

During Reading **Fluency Check:** Ask individuals to read story aloud. ✓

After Reading Create a Venn Diagram; see TE T70, Tr 5-3 for format. Have children compare/contrast story elements in the LR. Complete the diagram together.

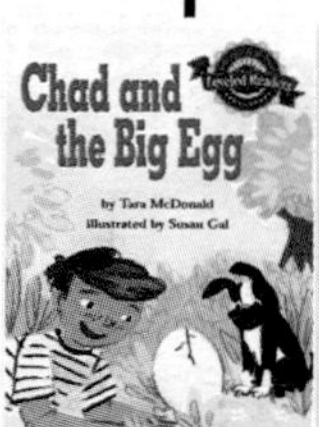

Level F

■ Above Level

Before Reading Preview TP *The Leaving Morning.* See TE R5.

During Reading **Fluency Modeling:** Model fluent reading, then have children model it. Have them read first half of story independently.

After Reading Ask questions; have children cite text to support answers. Create a Venn Diagram; see TE T70, Tr 5-3 for format. Have children compare/contrast story elements in the TP. Complete the diagram together.

Level F

 English Language Learners

Before Reading Preview *Champ,* PL Theme 5, pp. 9–12. Model Phonics/Decoding Strategy.

During Reading **Fluency Modeling:** Read aloud each page; have children do echo reading.

After Reading Discuss story; help children find/read words with *th, wh, ch, tch.* Have children use illustrations to retell story to partners.

4 WHOLE GROUP Writing and Language

30-40 minutes

Writing

Teach Assign Write the Answer to a Question, Anthology p. 45.

Grammar

Teach Exclamations, TE T73

Practice Assign PB 14.

Optional Resources

Teacher Read Aloud

Choose a book from your class/school library or from the Leveled Bibliography, TE T6–T7.

Suggestion: *The Little House* by Virginia Lee Burton

Independent Work

Self-Selected Reading

Choose from

- classroom/school library
- Leveled Bibliography, TE T6–T7
- *I Love Reading,* Theme 5, take-home books 38–42
- Little Readers for Guided Reading

Centers

- Classroom Management Kit
- Classroom Management activities, TE T26–T27
- Responding activities, TE T68–T69

Differentiated Instruction

- Comprehension Reteaching or Extension, Compare and Contrast, TE R30–R31
- High-Frequency Word Review: Word Wall, TE T66

TE = Teacher Edition; PB = Practice Book; Tr = Transparency; LR = Leveled Reader; PL = Phonics Library; VR = Vocabulary Reader; VR Guide = Vocabulary Readers Teacher's Manual; LBB = Little Big Book; TP = Theme Paperback

Day 4 Balanced Literacy Plan

Teacher Notes

Reading and Comprehension

20-30 minutes

Shared Reading of Science Link

- "Hermit Crabs," Anthology pp. 46–49, TE T76–T77 (independent, partner, or group)
- Skill: How to Read a Science Article, Anthology p. 46, TE T76
- Introduce Concept Vocabulary, TE T76.

Concept Vocabulary

pulls
ducks
hides
switch

Word Work

25-40 minutes

Phonemic Awareness/Phonics Instruction

Teach Segmenting, Counting Phonemes, TE T75

Review Short *u,* TE T78; Triple Clusters, TE T79

Spelling: Words Spelled with *sh* or *ch*

Practice Assign PB 15 or activity, TE T80.

Vocabulary Instruction

Teach Size Words, TE T80

3 SMALL GROUP

Options for Guided Reading

80-100 minutes

Extra Support

Before Reading Review Responding questions for LR *Just Right!,* TE T90. Begin a Venn Diagram; see TE T70, Tr 5-3 for format. Help children compare/contrast story elements in the LR.

During Reading Have children reread story. **Fluency Check:** Have individuals read aloud. ✓

After Reading Work with students to complete the Venn Diagram. Have partners compare/contrast other story elements.

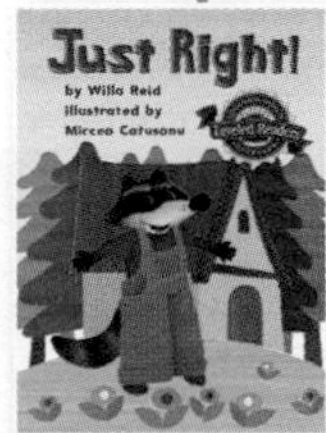

Level C

✓ = opportunity for ongoing assessment; adjust groups accordingly

▲ On Level

Before Reading Have children summarize LR *Chad and the Big Egg.* ✓ Preview a teacher-selected book or TP *Greetings, Sun,* TE R4.

During Reading Have children begin story and model Phonics/Decoding Strategy.

After Reading Discuss the story so far. Have children finish story.

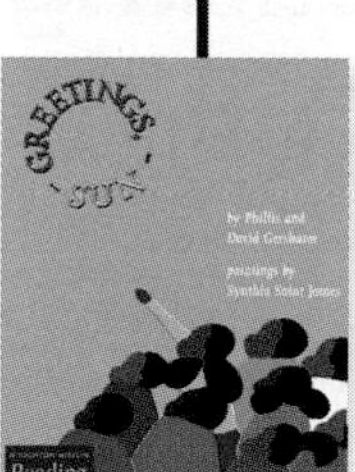
Level E

■ Above Level

Before Reading Review first half of TP *The Leaving Morning,* TE R5. Have children make predictions about second half.

During Reading Have children finish book.

After Reading Discuss how book connects to theme. Have children write journal entries to connect it to personal experience or other reading.

Level F

◆ English Language Learners

Before Reading Build background and preview LR *Big, Small, or Just Right?,* TE T93.

During Reading Read story. **Fluency Modeling:** Reread each page; have children do echo reading. Reinforce Phonics/Decoding Strategy.

After Reading Discuss Responding questions, TE T93. **Fluency Practice:** Have children reread with partners or audio CD.

Level C

4 WHOLE GROUP

Writing and Language

30-40 minutes

Writing

Teach Writing Complete Sentences, TE T81

Practice Assign PB 16.

Optional Resources

Teacher Read Aloud

Continue selected Read Aloud book from Day 3 or choose a new one from your class or school library.

Independent Work

Self-Selected Reading

Choose from

- classroom/school library
- Leveled Bibliography, TE T6–T7
- children's magazines
- *I Love Reading,* Theme 5, take-home books 38–42
- Little Readers for Guided Reading

Centers

- Classroom Management Kit
- Classroom Management activities, TE T26–T27
- Responding activities, TE T68–T69

Differentiated Instruction

- Visual Literacy: Sequence of Photographs, TE T77
- High-Frequency Words: Word Wall, TE T74
- Study Skills
  - Glossary, TE R36
  - Reading a Map, TE R37

TE = Teacher Edition; PB = Practice Book; Tr = Transparency; LR = Leveled Reader; PL = Phonics Library; VR = Vocabulary Reader; VR Guide = Vocabulary Readers Teacher's Manual; LBB = Little Big Book; TP = Theme Paperback

Day 5 Balanced Literacy Plan

Teacher Notes

Reading and Comprehension

20-30 minutes

Book Share

- Ask children to give examples of how they applied the comprehension skill and strategy to books they have read this week.
- Help children use genre and text features to compare and contrast what they have read.
- As a class, discuss one *how, why,* or *what if* question. See examples on Blackline Master 1 to use as a guide.

Word Work

25-40 minutes

Phonemic Awareness Instruction

Teach Segmenting, Counting Phonemes, TE T83

High-Frequency Words

Cumulative Review Word Wall, TE T82

Spelling

Test See TE T88.

Options for Guided Reading

80-100 minutes

● Extra Support

Before Reading Preview *Hen's Chicks,* PL Theme 5, pp. 13–16. Have children find/read words with *sh, th, wh, ch, tch.* See TE T85–T87.

During Reading Have children read and model Phonics/Decoding Strategy. **Fluency Check:** Have individuals reread aloud. ✓

After Reading Have partners make connections between the story and LR *Just Right!* Assign On My Way Practice Reader *The Chip Chop Ship* for partner reading.

✓ = opportunity for ongoing assessment; adjust groups accordingly

◆ English Language Learners

Before Reading Review LR *Big, Small, or Just Right?*, TE T93.

During Reading Coach rereading of book. **Fluency Check:** Have individuals reread aloud. ✓

After Reading Help children summarize LR. Have children draw/caption a picture about a book they read this week. ✓

Level C

●▲■◆ Mixed Ability Levels

Literature Circles Form small, mixed-ability groups. Ask groups to discuss the main Anthology selection, Link, Leveled Readers, and other books they have read this week. Pose questions or topics for each group, and circulate among groups to offer support. Suggested group activities:

- Respond to specific Literature Discussion questions on Blackline Master 1.
- Discuss story or text elements, authors' choice of language, and/or illustrations.
- Connect book topics or themes to personal experiences or other reading.

Writing and Language

30-40 minutes

Writing

Practice Assign Writing Prompt, TE T83.

Grammar

Review Exclamations, TE T89

Listening and Speaking

Teach Conversation, TE T89

Optional Resources

Teacher Read Aloud

Choose a nonfiction book related to Social Studies or Science unit.

Independent Work

Self-Selected Reading

Choose from

- classroom/school library
- Leveled Bibliography, TE T6–T7
- children's magazines
- consumer text such as maps, recipes, charts
- *I Love Reading,* Theme 5, take-home books 38–42
- Little Readers for Guided Reading

Centers

- Classroom Management Kit
- Classroom Management activities, TE T26–T27
- Responding activities, TE T68–T69

Differentiated Instruction

- High-Frequency Word Review, TE T88
- Comprehension Review: Compare and Contrast, TE T84

End-of-Week Assessment

- Weekly Skills Tests for Theme 5, Week 1
- Fluency Assessment, *Hen's Chicks,* PL Theme 5, pp. 13–16, TE T85–T87
- Alternative Assessment, Teacher's Resource Blackline Master 64

TE = Teacher Edition; PB = Practice Book; Tr = Transparency; LR = Leveled Reader; PL = Phonics Library; VR = Vocabulary Reader; VR Guide = Vocabulary Readers Teacher's Manual; LBB = Little Big Book; TP = Theme Paperback

Day 1 Balanced Literacy Plan

Teacher Notes

Reading and Comprehension

20-30 minutes

Shared Reading of Daily Message, TE T116

Listening Comprehension

- Read aloud *The City Mouse and the Country Mouse,* TE T118–T119.
- Model fluent reading; discuss the story.

Word Work

25-40 minutes

Phonemic Awareness/Phonics Instruction

Teach Segmenting, Counting Phonemes, TE T117, T120

Teach Blending Long *a* Words; Soft *c* and *g,* TE T120–T121

Practice Assign PB 19–20.

Teach Final *nd, ng, nk,* TE T122

Practice Assign PB 21.

Spelling Instruction: The Long *a* Sound

Pretest and Teach Spelling Principle, TE T126

Assign Take-Home Spelling Word List, PB 303

make came take name gave game

Challenge: place, skate

Vocabulary Instruction

Teach Spelling Patterns *-ate, -ake,* TE T126

Options for Guided Reading

80-100 minutes

Extra Support

Before Reading Preview *Pets in a Tank,* PL Theme 5, pp. 17–20. Model Phonics/Decoding Strategy. See TE T123–T125.

During Reading Coach as children read story.

After Reading Discuss story; have children find/read words with long *a* and final *nd, ng, nk.* **Fluency Modeling:** Model fluent reading. Have partners reread story.

✓ = opportunity for ongoing assessment; adjust groups accordingly

▲ On Level

Before Reading Preview *Pets in a Tank,* PL Theme 5, pp. 17–20, and review TE T123–T125.

During Reading Have children begin story. **Fluency Modeling:** Model Phonics/Decoding Strategy and fluent reading.

After Reading Have children retell story so far and find/read words with *long a* and final *nd, ng, nk.* **Fluency Practice:** Have partners finish story and reread for fluency.

■ Above Level

Before Reading Preview LR *My Neighborhood,* TE 176.

During Reading Have children read first half of story. **Fluency Modeling:** Model fluent reading.

After Reading Have children finish reading and write answers to Responding questions. ✓

Level J

◆ English Language Learners

Before Reading Preview VR *Where We Live.* See VR Guide, p. 19.

During Reading **Fluency Modeling:** Read aloud each page; have children do echo reading.

After Reading Discuss Responding pages. Have children reread with partners or audio CD.

Level C

4 Writing and Language  25-40 minutes

WHOLE GROUP

Writing

Teach Shared Writing: A Class Letter, TE T127

Practice Assign Writing Prompt, TE T117.

Listening and Speaking

Teach Compare and Contrast, TE T127

Optional Resources

Teacher Read Aloud

Reread *The City Mouse and the Country Mouse,* TE T118–T119

Independent Work

Self-Selected Reading

Choose from

- classroom/school library
- Leveled Bibliography, TE T6–T7
- *I Love Reading,* Theme 5, take-home books 43–48
- Little Readers for Guided Reading

Centers

- Classroom Management Kit
- Classroom Management activities, TE T114–T115

Differentiated Instruction

- Phonics Reteaching or Extension: Long *a* (CVC*e*), TE R16–R17
- Phonics Reteaching or Extension: Final *nd, nk, ng,* TE R18–R19
- High-Frequency Word Review: Word Wall, TE T116

TE = Teacher Edition; PB = Practice Book; Tr = Transparency; LR = Leveled Reader; PL = Phonics Library; VR = Vocabulary Reader; VR Guide = Vocabulary Readers Teacher's Manual; LBB = Little Big Book; TP = Theme Paperback

Day 2 Balanced Literacy Plan

Teacher Notes

Reading and Comprehension

20-30 minutes

▼ Anthology Selection

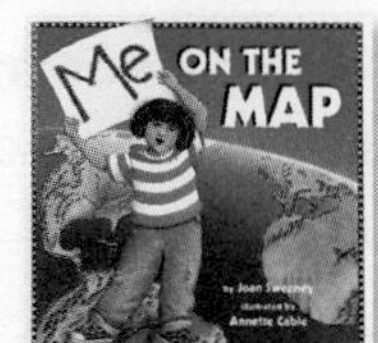

Shared Reading of *Me on the Map* (Part 1)

- Build Background and Vocabulary; Introduce Story Vocabulary, TE T132, T133, T135, Tr 5-6

ball	Earth	special	town/s
giant	street/s	country/countries	

- Introduce Comprehension Strategy and Skill:
  Summarize, TE T134
  Making Generalizations, TE T134, T144
- Set Purpose, TE T135
- Read Anthology Selection pp. 56–69 (independent, partner, or audio CD).

Words to Know

could	world
house	find
how	giant
over	place
own	state
so	think

Word Work

25-40 minutes

Phonemic Awareness/Phonics Instruction

Teach Segmenting, Counting Phonemes, TE T129

High-Frequency Words Instruction

Teach TE T130–T131, Tr 5-5; Practice PB 22–23.

Spelling Instruction

Review The Long *a* Sound, TE T148

High-Frequency Words

could	own
house	so
how	world
over	

Options for Guided Reading

80-100 minutes

Extra Support

Before Reading Preview VR *Where We Live.* See VR Guide, p. 19.

During Reading Read the book together; coach reading. Help children apply Summarize Strategy.

After Reading Help children compare this book to *Me on the Map.* **Fluency Practice:** Have children reread VR. Assign *Gram's Trip,* PL Theme 5, pp. 21–24, for partners.

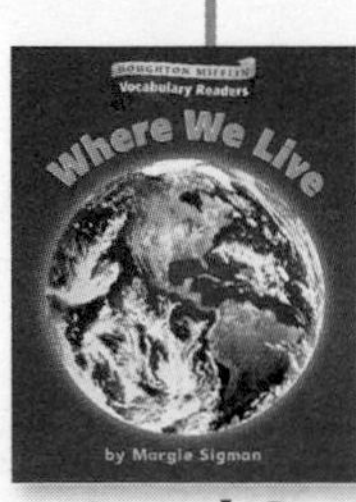

Level C

✓ = opportunity for ongoing assessment; adjust groups accordingly

▲ On Level

Before Reading Discuss PL *Pets in a Tank,* TE T124. Preview LR *Places in the United States,* TE T175.

During Reading Coach reading as children begin story. Have children model the Summarize Strategy. **Fluency Modeling:** Model fluent reading, then have children model it.

After Reading Children finish reading and write answers to Responding questions. ✓ Assign *Gram's Trip,* PL Theme 5, pp. 21–24, for partner reading.

Level J

■ Above Level

Before Reading Have children model the Summarize Strategy and discuss Responding questions for LR *My Neighborhood,* TE 176.

During Reading **Fluency Check:** Monitor children's oral reading. ✓

After Reading Have children discuss the story with a partner. Assign *Gram's Trip,* PL Theme 5, pp. 21–24, for partner reading.

Level J

◆ English Language Learners

Before Reading To review VR vocabulary, have children demonstrate or give examples. See VR Guide, p. 19.

During Reading Model Summarize Strategy. Help children apply the Summarize Strategy. **Fluency Practice:** Have children reread book. Option: Preview and coach reading of *Pets in a Tank,* PL Theme 5, pp. 17–20, TE T123–T125.

After Reading Help children summarize VR. Have partners discuss, draw, or write facts they learned. ✓

Level C

4 WHOLE GROUP Writing and Language

25-40 minutes

Writing

Teach Interactive Writing: A Class Letter, TE T149

Practice Assign Writing Prompt, TE T129.

Optional Resources

Teacher Read Aloud

Choose a book from your class/school library or from the Leveled Bibliography, TE T6–T7.

Suggestion: *A House Is a House for Me* by Mary Ann Hoberman

Independent Work

Self-Selected Reading

Choose from

- classroom/school library
- Leveled Bibliography, TE T6–T7
- *I Love Reading,* Theme 5, take-home books 43–48
- Little Readers for Guided Reading

Centers

- Classroom Management Kit
- Classroom Management activities, TE T114–T115

Differentiated Instruction

- High-Frequency Words
  - –Word Wall, TE T128
  - –Review, TE T148
  - –Reteaching or Extension, TE R26–R27

TE = Teacher Edition; PB = Practice Book; Tr = Transparency; LR = Leveled Reader; PL = Phonics Library; VR = Vocabulary Reader; VR Guide = Vocabulary Readers Teacher's Manual; LBB = Little Big Book; TP = Theme Paperback

Day 3 Balanced Literacy Plan

Teacher Notes

Reading and Comprehension

20-30 minutes

▼ Anthology Selection

Shared Reading of *Me on the Map* (Part 2)

➤ Read Anthology Selection pp. 70–79 (independent, partner, or audio CD).

➤ Discuss Responding questions, TE T152; have children cite text to support answers.

Comprehension Skill Instruction

Teach Making Generalizations, TE T154–T155, Tr 5-7

Practice Assign PB 27 or retelling of story.

Word Work

25-40 minutes

Phonemic Awareness Instruction

Teach Segmenting, Counting Phonemes, TE T151

Spelling: The Long *a* Sound

Practice Assign PB 28 or activity, TE T156.

Vocabulary Instruction

Teach Social Studies Words, TE T156

Practice Assign PB 29.

Options for Guided Reading

80-100 minutes

● Extra Support

Before Reading Discuss Responding questions from VR *Where We Live.* See VR Guide, p. 19. Preview LR *Jake Makes a Map,* TE T174.

During Reading Coach as children read story. **Fluency Modeling:** Model fluent reading, then have children model it.

After Reading **Fluency Practice:** Have partners reread story. Have children write answers to Responding questions. ✓

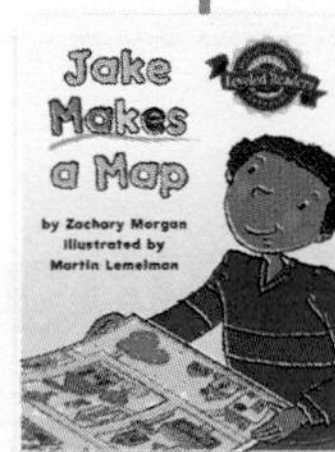

Level D

✓ = opportunity for ongoing assessment; adjust groups accordingly

▲ On Level

Before Reading Discuss Responding questions for LR *Places in the United States,* TE T175.

During Reading **Fluency Check:** Ask individuals to read story aloud. ✓

After Reading Create a Generalizations Chart; see TE T154, Tr 5-7 for format. Help children make generalizations about the LR. Complete the chart.

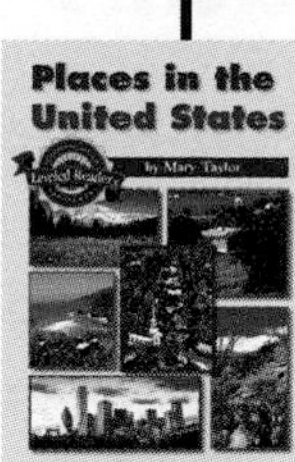

Level J

■ Above Level

Before Reading Preview a teacher-selected book, such as *Annabell Again.* See TE R8.

During Reading **Fluency Modeling:** Model fluent reading, then have children model it. Have them read first half of story independently.

After Reading Ask questions; have children cite text to support answers. Create a Generalizations Chart; see TE T154, Tr 5-7 for format. Help children make generalizations about the teacher-selected book. Complete the chart together.

◆ English Language Learners

Before Reading Preview *Gram's Trip,* PL Theme 5, pp. 21–24. Model Phonics/Decoding Strategy.

During Reading **Fluency Modeling:** Read aloud each page; have children do echo reading.

After Reading Discuss story; help children find/read words with long *a* and final *nd, ng, nk.* Have children use illustrations to retell story to partners.

4 WHOLE GROUP Writing and Language

30-40 minutes

Writing

Teach Assign Write a Postcard, Anthology p. 81.

Grammar

Teach Which Kind of Sentence?, TE T157

Practice Assign PB 30.

Optional Resources

Teacher Read Aloud

Continue selected Read Aloud book from Day 2 or choose a new one from your class or school library.

Independent Work

Self-Selected Reading

Choose from

- classroom/school library
- Leveled Bibliography, TE T6–T7
- *I Love Reading,* Theme 5, take-home books 43–48
- Little Readers for Guided Reading

Centers

- Classroom Management Kit
- Classroom Management activities, TE T114–T115
- Responding activities, TE T152–T153

Differentiated Instruction

- Comprehension Reteaching or Extension, Making Generalizations, TE R32–R33
- High-Frequency Word Review: Word Wall, TE T116

TE = Teacher Edition; PB = Practice Book; Tr = Transparency; LR = Leveled Reader; PL = Phonics Library; VR = Vocabulary Reader; VR Guide = Vocabulary Readers Teacher's Manual; LBB = Little Big Book; TP = Theme Paperback

Day 4 Balanced Literacy Plan

Teacher Notes

1 Reading and Comprehension

20-30 minutes

WHOLE GROUP

Shared Reading of Social Studies Link

- "Children of the World," Anthology pp. 82–85, TE T160–T161 (independent, partner, or group)
- Skill: How to Read a Map, Anthology p. 82, TE T160
- Introduce Concept Vocabulary, TE T160.

Concept Vocabulary

wood
adobe
apartment

2 Word Work

25-40 minutes

WHOLE GROUP

Phonemic Awareness/Phonics Instruction

Teach Segmenting, Counting Phonemes, TE T159

Review Digraphs *sh, th, wh*, TE T162; Digraphs *ch, tch*, TE T163

Spelling: The Long *a* Sound

Practice Assign PB 31 or activity, TE T164.

Vocabulary Instruction

Teach State and Country Names, TE T164

3 Options for Guided Reading

80-100 minutes

SMALL GROUP

Extra Support

Before Reading Review Responding questions for LR *Jake Makes a Map,* TE T174. Begin a Generalizations Chart; see TE T154, Tr 5-7 for format. Help children make generalizations about the LR.

During Reading Have children reread story. **Fluency Check:** Have individuals read aloud. ✓

After Reading Work with students to complete the Generalizations Chart. Have partners make other generalizations.

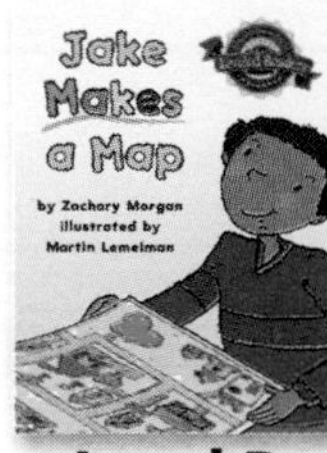

Level D

✓ = opportunity for ongoing assessment; adjust groups accordingly

▲ On Level

Before Reading Have children summarize LR *Places in the United States.* ✓ Preview a teacher-selected book, such as *Moving Day,* TE R7.

During Reading Have children begin story and model Phonics/Decoding Strategy.

After Reading Discuss the story so far. Have children finish story.

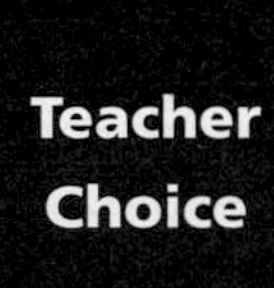

■ Above Level

Before Reading Review first half of selected book. Have children make predictions about second half.

During Reading Have children finish book.

After Reading Discuss how book connects to theme. Have children write journal entries to connect it to personal experience or other reading.

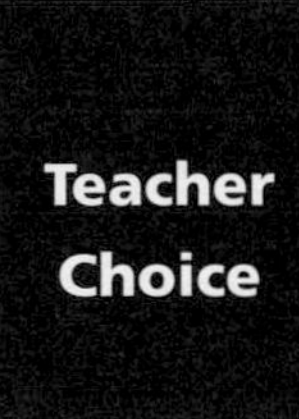

 English Language Learners

Before Reading Build background and preview LR *Jake's Map,* TE T177.

During Reading Read story. **Fluency Modeling:** Reread each page; have children do echo reading. Reinforce Phonics/Decoding Strategy.

After Reading Discuss Responding questions, TE T177. **Fluency Practice:** Have children reread with partners or audio CD.

Level C

Writing and Language

30-40 minutes

Writing

Teach Journal Entry, TE T165

Practice Assign PB 32.

Optional Resources

Teacher Read Aloud

Choose a new book from your class library or school library.

Independent Work

Self-Selected Reading

Choose from

- classroom/school library
- Leveled Bibliography, TE T6–T7
- children's magazines
- *I Love Reading,* Theme 5, take-home books 43–48
- Little Readers for Guided Reading

Centers

- Classroom Management Kit
- Classroom Management activities, TE T114–T115
- Responding activities, TE T152–T153

Differentiated Instruction

- Writer's Craft: Communicating Information, TE T161
- High-Frequency Words: Word Wall, TE T158
- Study Skills
  - Glossary, TE R36
  - Reading a Map, TE R37

TE = Teacher Edition; PB = Practice Book; Tr = Transparency; LR = Leveled Reader; PL = Phonics Library; VR = Vocabulary Reader; VR Guide = Vocabulary Readers Teacher's Manual; LBB = Little Big Book; TP = Theme Paperback

Day 5 Balanced Literacy Plan

Teacher Notes

Reading and Comprehension

20-30 minutes

Book Share

Book Share

- ➤ Ask children to give examples of how they applied the comprehension skill and strategy to books they have read this week.
- ➤ Help children use genre and text features to compare and contrast what they have read.
- ➤ As a class, discuss one *how, why,* or *what if* question. See examples on Blackline Master 1 to use as a guide.

Word Work

25-40 minutes

Phonemic Awareness Instruction

Teach Segmenting, Counting Phonemes, TE T167

High-Frequency Words

Cumulative Review Word Wall, TE T166

Spelling

Test See TE T172.

Options for Guided Reading

80-100 minutes

● Extra Support

Before Reading Preview *Stuck in the House,* PL Theme 5, pp. 25–28. Have children find/read words with long *a* and final *nd, ng, nk.* See TE T169–T171.

During Reading Have children read and model Phonics/Decoding Strategy. **Fluency Check:** Have individuals reread aloud. ✓

After Reading Have partners make connections between the story and LR *Jake Makes a Map.* Assign On My Way Practice Reader *What Can You See at a Lake?* for partner reading.

✓ = opportunity for ongoing assessment; adjust groups accordingly

◆ English Language Learners

Before Reading Review LR *Jake's Map,* TE T177.

During Reading Coach rereading of book. **Fluency Check:** Have individuals reread aloud. ✓

After Reading Help children summarize LR. Have children draw/caption a picture about a book they read this week. ✓

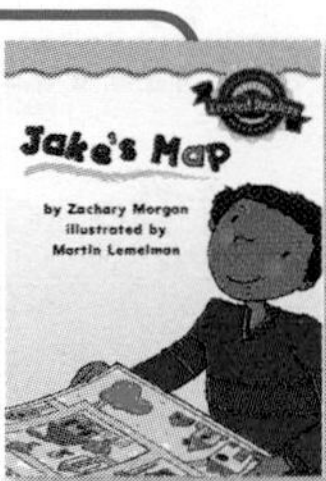

Level C

●▲■◆ Mixed Ability Levels

Literature Circles Form small, mixed-ability groups. Ask groups to discuss the main Anthology selection, Link, Leveled Readers, and other books they have read this week. Pose questions or topics for each group, and circulate among groups to offer support. Suggested group activities:

- Respond to specific Literature Discussion questions on Blackline Master 1.
- Discuss story or text elements, authors' choice of language, and/or illustrations.
- Connect book topics or themes to personal experiences or other reading.

Writing and Language

30-40 minutes

Writing

Practice Assign Writing Prompt, TE T167.

Grammar

Review Which Kind of Sentence?, TE T173

Viewing

Teach Gathering Information, TE T173

Optional Resources

Teacher Read Aloud

Choose a nonfiction book related to Social Studies or Science unit.

Independent Work

Self-Selected Reading

Choose from

- classroom/school library
- Leveled Bibliography, TE T6–T7
- children's magazines
- consumer text such as maps, recipes, charts
- *I Love Reading,* Theme 5, take-home books 43–48
- Little Readers for Guided Reading

Centers

- Classroom Management Kit
- Classroom Management activities, TE T114–T115
- Responding activities, TE T152–T153

Differentiated Instruction

- High-Frequency Words Review, TE T172
- Comprehension Review: Making Generalizations, TE T168

End-of-Week Assessment

- Weekly Skills Tests for Theme 5, Week 2
- Fluency Assessment, *Stuck in the House,* PL Theme 5, pp. 25–28, TE T169–T171
- Alternative Assessment, Teacher's Resource Blackline Master 69

TE = Teacher Edition; PB = Practice Book; Tr = Transparency; LR = Leveled Reader; PL = Phonics Library; VR = Vocabulary Reader; VR Guide = Vocabulary Readers Teacher's Manual; LBB = Little Big Book; TP = Theme Paperback

Day 1 Balanced Literacy Plan

Teacher Notes

Reading and Comprehension

20-30 minutes

Shared Reading of Daily Message, TE T188

Listening Comprehension:

- Read aloud *The Mouse's House,* TE T190–T191.
- Model fluent reading; discuss the story.

Word Work

25-40 minutes

Phonemic Awareness/Phonics Instruction

Teach Segmenting, Counting Phonemes, TE T189, T192

Teach Blending Long *i* Words (CVCe), TE T192–T193

Practice Assign PB 33–34.

Teach Contractions, TE T194

Practice Assign PB 35.

Spelling Instruction: The Long *i* Sound

Pretest and Teach Spelling Principle, TE T198

Assign Take-Home Spelling Word List, PB 305

five nine kite ride like time

Challenge: prize, smile

Vocabulary Instruction

Teach Spelling Patterns *-ite, -ide,* TE T198

Options for Guided Reading

80-100 minutes

Extra Support

Before Reading Preview *Pine Lake,* PL Theme 5, pp. 29–32. Model Phonics/Decoding Strategy. See TE T195–T197.

During Reading Coach as children read story.

After Reading Discuss story; have children find/read words with long *i* (CVCe) and contractions. **Fluency Modeling:** Model fluent reading. Have partners reread story.

✓ = opportunity for ongoing assessment; adjust groups accordingly

▲ On Level

Before Reading Preview *Pine Lake,* PL Theme 5, pp. 29–32, and review TE T195–T197.

During Reading Have children begin story. **Fluency Modeling:** Model Phonics/Decoding Strategy and fluent reading.

After Reading Have children retell story so far and find/read words with long *i* (CVCe) and contractions. **Fluency Practice:** Have partners finish story and reread for fluency.

■ Above Level

Before Reading Preview LR *The Surprise Snow,* TE T242.

During Reading Have children read first half of story. **Fluency Modeling:** Model fluent reading.

After Reading Have children finish reading and write answers to Responding questions. ✓

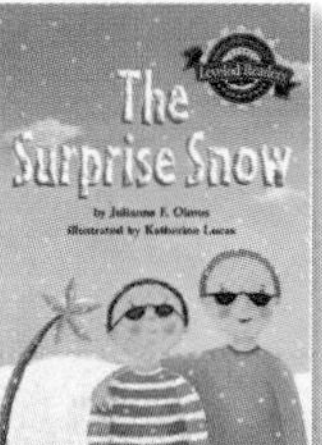

Level K

◆ English Language Learners

Before Reading Preview VR *Perfect Kite Weather.* See VR Guide, p. 20.

During Reading **Fluency Modeling:** Read aloud each page; have children do echo reading.

After Reading Discuss Responding pages. Have children reread with partners or audio CD.

Level C

4 WHOLE GROUP Writing and Language

 25-40 minutes

Writing

Teach Shared Writing: A Class Paragraph, TE T199

Practice Assign Writing Prompt, TE T189.

Listening

Teach Compare and Contrast, TE T199

Optional Resources

Teacher Read Aloud

Reread *The Mouse's House,* TE T190–T191.

Independent Work

Self-Selected Reading

Choose from

- classroom/school library
- Leveled Bibliography, TE T6–T7
- *I Love Reading,* Theme 5, take-home book 49
- Little Readers for Guided Reading

Centers

- Classroom Management Kit
- Classroom Management activities, TE T186–T187

Differentiated Instruction

- Phonics Reteaching or Extension: Long *i* (CVCe), TE R20–R21
- Phonics Reteaching or Extension: Contractions, TE R22–R23
- High-Frequency Words Review: Word Wall, TE T188

TE = Teacher Edition; PB = Practice Book; Tr = Transparency; LR = Leveled Reader; PL = Phonics Library; VR = Vocabulary Reader; VR Guide = Vocabulary Readers Teacher's Manual; LBB = Little Big Book; TP = Theme Paperback

Day 2 Balanced Literacy Plan

Teacher Notes

Reading and Comprehension

20-30 minutes

▼ Anthology Selection

Shared Reading of *The Kite* (Part 1)

- Build Background and Vocabulary; Introduce Story Vocabulary, TE T204–T205, Tr 5-11

anywhere	convinced	news	raining
beautiful	easy	perfect	weather

- Introduce Comprehension Strategy and Skill: Monitor/Clarify, TE T206
  Cause and Effect, TE T206, TE T211
- Set Purpose, TE T207
- Read Anthology Selection pp. 89–94 (independent, partner, or audio CD).

Words to Know

give	like
good	she'll
her	can't
little	isn't
try	doesn't
was	didn't
fly	it's
our	we've
kite	

Word Work

25-40 minutes

Phonemic Awareness/Phonics Instruction

Teach Segmenting, Counting Phonemes, TE T201

High-Frequency Words Instruction

Teach TE T202–T203, Tr 5-10; Practice PB 36–37.

Spelling Instruction

Review The Long *i* Sound, TE T214

High-Frequency Words

give	try
good	was
her	fly
little	our

Options for Guided Reading

80-100 minutes

Extra Support

Before Reading Preview VR *Perfect Kite Weather.* See VR Guide, p. 20.

During Reading Read the book together; coach reading. Help children apply Monitor/Clarify Strategy.

After Reading Help children compare this book to *The Kite.* **Fluency Practice:** Have children reread VR. Assign *Fun Rides,* PL Theme 5, pp. 33–36, for partner reading.

Level C

✓ = opportunity for ongoing assessment; adjust groups accordingly

 **On Level**

Before Reading Discuss PL *Pine Lake,* TE T196. Preview LR *The Just-Right House,* TE T241.

During Reading Coach reading as children begin story. Have children model the Monitor/Clarify Strategy. **Fluency Modeling:** Model fluent reading, then have children model it.

After Reading Children finish reading and write answers to Responding questions. ✓ Assign *Fun Rides,* PL Theme 5, pp. 33–36, for partner reading.

Level F

 **Above Level**

Before Reading Have children model the Monitor/Clarify Strategy and discuss Responding questions for LR *The Surprise Snow,* TE T242.

During Reading **Fluency Check:** Monitor children's oral reading. ✓

After Reading Have children discuss the story with a partner. Assign *Fun Rides,* PL Theme 5, pp. 33–36, for partner reading.

Level K

 **English Language Learners**

Before Reading To review VR vocabulary, have children demonstrate or give examples. See VR Guide, p. 20.

During Reading Model Monitor/Clarify Strategy. Help children apply the Monitor/Clarify Strategy. **Fluency Practice:** Have children reread book.

After Reading Help children summarize VR. Have partners discuss, draw, or write facts they learned. ✓

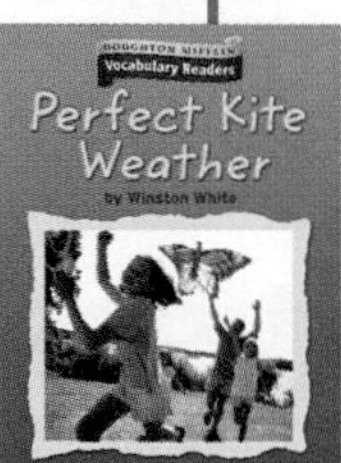

Level C

Writing and Language

 25-40 minutes

Writing

Teach Interactive Writing: A Class Paragraph, TE T215

Practice Assign Writing Prompt, TE T201.

Optional Resources

Teacher Read Aloud

Choose a book from your class/school library or from the Leveled Bibliography, TE T6–T7.

Suggestion: *Wake Up House!* by Dee Lillegard

Independent Work

Self-Selected Reading

Choose from

- classroom/school library
- Leveled Bibliography, TE T6–T7
- *I Love Reading,* Theme 5, take-home book 49
- Little Readers for Guided Reading

Centers

- Classroom Management Kit
- Classroom Management activities, T186–T187

Differentiated Instruction

- High-Frequency Words
  - Word Wall, TE T200
  - Review, TE T214
  - Reteaching or Extension, TE R28–R29

TE = Teacher Edition; PB = Practice Book; Tr = Transparency; LR = Leveled Reader; PL = Phonics Library; VR = Vocabulary Reader; VR Guide = Vocabulary Readers Teacher's Manual; LBB = Little Big Book; TP = Theme Paperback

Day 3 Balanced Literacy Plan

Teacher Notes

Reading and Comprehension

20-30 minutes

▼ Anthology Selection

Shared Reading of *The Kite* (Part 2)

- Read Anthology Selection pp. 95–101 (independent, partner, or audio CD).
- Discuss Responding questions, TE T218; have children cite text to support answers.

Comprehension Skill Instruction

Teach Cause and Effect, TE T220–T221, Tr 5-12

Practice Assign PB 41 or retelling of story.

Word Work

25-40 minutes

Phonemic Awareness Instruction

Teach Segmenting, Counting Phonemes, TE T217

Spelling: The Long *i* Sound

Practice Assign PB 43 or activity, TE T222.

Vocabulary Instruction

Teach Base Words with *-ing,* TE T222

Practice Assign PB 44.

Options for Guided Reading

80-100 minutes

Extra Support

Before Reading Discuss Responding questions from VR *Perfect Kite Weather.* See VR Guide, p. 20. Preview LR *The Best Place,* TE T240.

During Reading Coach as children read story. **Fluency Modeling:** Model fluent reading, then have children model it.

After Reading **Fluency Practice:** Have partners reread story. Have children write answers to Responding questions. ✓

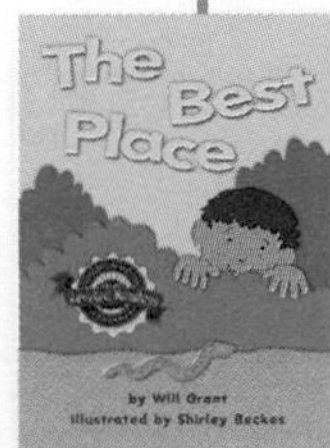

Level C

✓ = opportunity for ongoing assessment; adjust groups accordingly

 **On Level**

Before Reading Discuss Responding questions for LR *The Just-Right House,* TE T241.

During Reading **Fluency Check:** Ask individuals to read story aloud. ✓

After Reading Create a Cause and Effect Chart; see TE T220, Tr 5-12 for format. Help children list cause/effect elements in the LR. Complete the chart together.

Level F

 **Above Level**

Before Reading Preview teacher-selected book, such as *Another Fine Mess.* See TE R11.

During Reading **Fluency Modeling:** Model fluent reading, then have children model it. Have them read first half of story independently.

After Reading Ask questions; have children cite text to support answers. Create a Cause and Effect Chart; see TE T220, Tr 5-12 for format. Help children list cause/effect elements in the teacher-selected book. Complete the chart together.

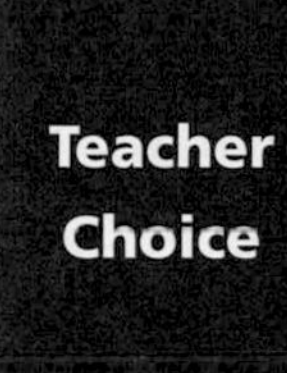

 **English Language Learners**

Before Reading Preview *Fun Rides,* PL Theme 5, pp. 33–36. Model Phonics/Decoding Strategy.

During Reading **Fluency Modeling:** Read aloud each page; have children do echo reading.

After Reading Discuss story; help children find/read words with long *i* (CVCe) and contractions. Have children use illustrations to retell story to partners.

Writing and Language

 30-40 minutes

Writing

Practice Assign Write Sentences, Anthology p. 105.

Grammar

Teach Using *I* or *me* in Sentences, TE T223

Practice Assign PB 45.

Optional Resources

Teacher Read Aloud

Continue selected Read Aloud book from Day 2 or choose a new one from your class or school library.

Independent Work

Self-Selected Reading

Choose from

- classroom/school library
- Leveled Bibliography, TE T6–T7
- *I Love Reading,* Theme 5, take-home book 49
- Little Readers for Guided Reading

Centers

- Classroom Management Kit
- Classroom Management activities, TE T186–T187
- Responding activities, TE T218–T219

Differentiated Instruction

- Comprehension Reteaching or Extension, Cause and Effect, TE R34–R35
- High-Frequency Word Review: Word Wall, TE T216

TE = Teacher Edition; PB = Practice Book; Tr = Transparency; LR = Leveled Reader; PL = Phonics Library; VR = Vocabulary Reader; VR Guide = Vocabulary Readers Teacher's Manual; LBB = Little Big Book; TP = Theme Paperback

Day 4 Balanced Literacy Plan

Teacher Notes

Reading and Comprehension

20-30 minutes

Shared Reading of Art Link

- "How to Make a Kite," Anthology pp. 106–109, TE T226–T227 (independent, partner, or group)
- Skill: How to Read Directions, Anthology p. 106, TE T226
- Introduce Concept Vocabulary, TE T226.

Concept Vocabulary

trace
lace
loop

Word Work

25-40 minutes

Phonemic Awareness/Phonics Instruction

Teach Segmenting, Counting Phonemes, TE T225

Review Long *a;* Soft *c* and *g,* TE T228; Final *nd, ng, nk,* TE T229

Spelling: The Long *i* Sound

Practice Assign PB 46 or activity, TE T230.

Vocabulary Instruction

Teach Weather Words, TE T230

3 SMALL GROUP

Options for Guided Reading

80-100 minutes

Extra Support

Before Reading Review Responding questions for LR *The Best Place,* TE T240. Begin a Cause and Effect Chart; see TE T220, Tr 5-12 for format. Help children list cause/effect elements in the LR.

During Reading Have children reread story. **Fluency Check:** Have individuals read aloud. ✓

After Reading Work with students to complete the Cause and Effect Chart. Have partners list other cause/effect elements.

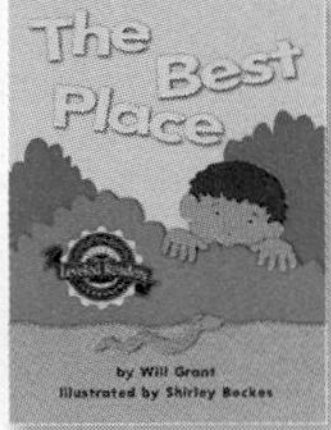

Level C

✓ = opportunity for ongoing assessment; adjust groups accordingly

▲ On Level

Before Reading Have children summarize LR *The Just-Right House.* ✓ Preview a teacher-selected book such as *From Here to There,* TE R10.

During Reading Have children begin story and model Phonics/Decoding Strategy.

After Reading Discuss the story so far. Have children finish story.

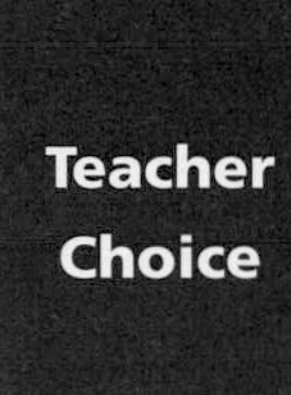

■ Above Level

Before Reading Review first half of teacher-selected book. Have children make predictions about second half.

During Reading Have children finish book.

After Reading Discuss how book connects to theme. Have children write journal entries to connect it to personal experience or other reading.

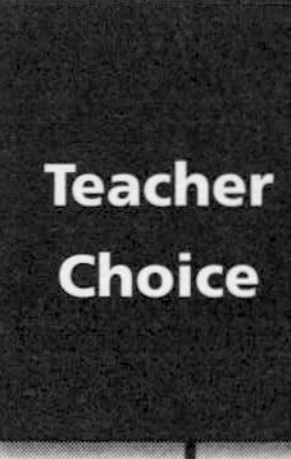

◆ English Language Learners

Before Reading Build background and preview LR *A Good Home,* TE T243.

During Reading Read story. **Fluency Modeling:** Reread each page; have children do echo reading. Reinforce Phonics/Decoding Strategy.

After Reading Discuss Responding questions, TE T243. **Fluency Practice:** Have children reread with partners or audio CD.

Level C

Optional Resources

Teacher Read Aloud

Choose a new book from your class or school library.

Independent Work

Self-Selected Reading

Choose from

- classroom/school library
- Leveled Bibliography, TE T6–T7
- children's magazines
- *I Love Reading,* Theme 5, take-home book 49
- Little Readers for Guided Reading

Centers

- Classroom Management Kit
- Classroom Management activities, TE T186–T187
- Responding activities, TE T218–T219

Differentiated Instruction

- Visual Literacy: Picture Key, TE T227
- High-Frequency Words: Word Wall, TE T224
- Study Skills
  - Glossary, TE R36
  - Reading a Map, TE R37

4 WHOLE GROUP

Writing and Language

30-40 minutes

Writing

Teach Writing a Paragraph, TE T231

Practice Assign PB 47.

TE = Teacher Edition; PB = Practice Book; Tr = Transparency; LR = Leveled Reader; PL = Phonics Library; VR = Vocabulary Reader; VR Guide = Vocabulary Readers Teacher's Manual; LBB = Little Big Book; TP = Theme Paperback

Day 5 Balanced Literacy Plan

Teacher Notes

Reading and Comprehension

Book Share

- Ask children to give examples of how they applied the comprehension skill and strategy to books they have read this week.
- Help children use genre and text features to compare and contrast what they have read.
- As a class, discuss one *how, why,* or *what if* question. See examples on Blackline Master 1 to use as a guide.

Word Work

Phonemic Awareness Instruction

Teach Segmenting, Counting Phonemes, TE T233

High-Frequency Words

Cumulative Review Word Wall, TE T232

Spelling

Test See TE T238.

Options for Guided Reading

Extra Support

Before Reading Preview *Jim and Sal,* PL Theme 5, pp. 37–40. Have children find/read words with long *i* and contractions. See TE T235–T237.

During Reading Have children read and model Phonics/ Decoding Strategy. **Fluency Check:** Have individuals reread aloud. ✓

After Reading Have partners make connections between the story and LR *The Best Place.* Assign On My Way Practice Reader *Stripe and the Nice Mice* for partner reading.

✓ = opportunity for ongoing assessment; adjust groups accordingly

◆ English Language Learners

Before Reading Review LR *A Good Home*, TE T243.

During Reading Coach rereading of book. **Fluency Check:** Have individuals reread aloud. ✔

After Reading Help children summarize LR. Have children draw/caption a picture about a book they read this week. ✔

Level C

●▲■◆ Mixed Ability Levels

Literature Circles Form small, mixed-ability groups. Ask groups to discuss the main Anthology selection, Link, Leveled Readers, and other books they have read this week. Pose questions or topics for each group, and circulate among groups to offer support. Suggested group activities:

- Respond to specific Literature Discussion questions on Blackline Master 1.
- Discuss story or text elements, authors' choice of language, and/or illustrations.
- Connect book topics or themes to personal experiences or other reading.

Writing and Language

30-40 minutes

Writing

Practice Assign Writing Prompt, TE T233.

Grammar

Review Using *I* or *me* in Sentences, TE T239

Speaking and Listening

Teach Discussion, TE T239

Optional Resources

Teacher Read Aloud

Choose a nonfiction book related to Social Studies or Science unit.

Independent Work

Self-Selected Reading

Choose from

- classroom/school library
- Leveled Bibliography, TE T6–T7
- children's magazines
- consumer texts such as craft books, maps, etc.

Centers

- Classroom Management Kit
- Classroom Management activities, TE T186–T187
- Responding activities, TE T218–T219

Differentiated Instruction

- High-Frequency Words Review, TE T238
- Comprehension Review: Cause and Effect, TE T234,

Assessment

End-of-Week Assessment

- Weekly Skills Tests for Theme 5, Week 3
- Fluency Assessment, *Jim and Sal,* PL Theme 5, pp. 37–40, TE T235–237.
- Alternative Assessment, Teacher's Resource Blackline Master 73

End-of-Theme Assessment

- Integrated Theme Tests for Theme 5

TE = Teacher Edition; PB = Practice Book; Tr = Transparency; LR = Leveled Reader; PL = Phonics Library; VR = Vocabulary Reader; VR Guide = Vocabulary Readers Teacher's Manual; LBB = Little Big Book; TP = Theme Paperback

Theme 6 Overview

	Week 1
Reading and Comprehension	**Shared Reading** Main Selection: *The Sleeping Pig* Social Studies Link: "What Is a Desert?" Book Share **Comprehension** Strategy: Summarize Skill: Story Structure Content Skill: How to Read a Social Studies Article
Word Work	**Phonemic Awareness:** Segment Phonemes; Count Sounds in Words **Phonics:** Long *o* (CV, CVCe) and Long *u* (CVCe) **Phonics:** Final Clusters *ft, lk, nt* **Phonics Review:** Long *i* (CVCe); Contractions **Vocabulary:** Alphabetical Order; Fruits and Vegetables **High-Frequency Words:** *by, climb, found, morning, out, shout, show* **Spelling:** Words with Long *o*
Options for Guided Reading	**Vocabulary Reader** *What Can You See?* **Leveled Readers:** Extra Support: *The Huge Carrot* On Level: *Watermelon for Lunch* Above Level: *Hide-and-Seek* ELL: *The Carrot* **Phonics Library** *Duke's Gift* *Legs Gets His Lunch* *The Nest* **Theme Paperbacks** **Literature Circles**
Writing and Oral Language	**Shared Writing:** A Letter of Persuasion **Interactive Writing:** A Letter of Persuasion **Independent Writing:** Writing to Persuade **Grammar:** Naming Words for People and Animals **Listening:** For Enjoyment **Speaking and Listening:** Compare and Contrast
Assessment Options	• Weekly Skills Test for Theme 6, Week 1 • Fluency Assessment: Phonics Library

Use **Launching the Theme** on pages T16–T17 of the Teacher's Edition to introduce the theme.

Week 2	Week 3
Shared Reading Main Selection: *EEK! There's a Mouse in the House* Math Link: "Animals Big and Small" Book Share **Comprehension** Strategy: Question Skill: Noting Details Content Skill: How to Read a Pictograph	**Shared Reading** Main Selection: *Red-Eyed Tree Frog* Poetry Link: "The Snake; The Toucan" Book Share **Comprehension** Strategy: Predict/Infer Skill: Making Predictions Content Skill: How to Read a Poem
Phonemic Awareness: Segment Phonemes; Count Sounds in Words **Phonics:** Long *e* (CV, CVCe) **Phonics:** Vowel Pairs *ee, ea* **Phonics Review:** Long *o* (CV, CVCe) and Long *u* (CVCe); Final Clusters *ft, lk, nt* **Vocabulary:** Rhyming Words; Expressions of Surprise **High-Frequency Words:** *cow, door, horse, now, table, there, through, wall* **Spelling:** Words with Long *e* (*e, ee, ea*)	**Phonemic Awareness:** Segment Phonemes; Count Sounds in Words **Phonics:** Vowel Pairs *ai, ay* **Phonics Review:** Long *e* (CV, CVCe); Vowel Pairs *ee, ea* **Vocabulary:** Parts of the Body; Animal Action Words **High-Frequency Words:** *been, evening, far, forest, goes, hungry, near, soon* **Spelling:** Words with *ay*
Vocabulary Reader *In the Barn* **Leveled Readers:** Extra Support: *The Feast* On Level: *Going Fishing* Above Level: *Zeke Takes a Bath* ELL: *Fun and Food to Eat* **Phonics Library** *Seal Beach* *Pete and Peach* *Gram's Huge Meal* **Literature Circles**	**Vocabulary Reader** *Animals in the Rain Forest* **Leveled Readers:** Extra Support: *Looking for Frogs* On Level: *The Mouse in the Forest* Above Level: *Animals at Night* ELL: *How Many Frogs?* **Phonics Library** *Rain Day* *Cub's Long Day* *Jay's Trip* **Literature Circles**
Shared Writing: A Class Story **Interactive Writing:** A Class Story **Independent Writing:** Answering a Comprehension Question **Grammar:** Naming Words for Things and Places **Listening and Speaking:** Compare and Contrast **Viewing:** Retelling	**Shared Writing:** A Class Summary **Interactive Writing:** A Class Summary **Independent Writing:** Writing a Summary **Grammar:** Naming Words for One or More **Listening:** To Retell **Listening and Speaking:** Listening for Information
• Weekly Skills Test for Theme 6, Week 2 • Fluency Assessment: Phonics Library	• Weekly Skills Test, Theme 6, Week 3 • Fluency Assessment: Phonics Library

Day 1 Balanced Literacy Plan

Teacher Notes

Reading and Comprehension

20-30 minutes

Shared Reading of Daily Message, TE T28

Shared Reading of Big Book

- Read aloud *Two's Company,* TE T17, R2.
- Model fluent reading; discuss the story.

Word Work

25-40 minutes

Phonemic Awareness/Phonics Instruction

Teach Segmenting, Counting Phonemes, TE T29, T32

Teach Blending Long *o* Words and Long *u* Words (CV, CVCe); Final Clusters *ft, lk, nt,* TE T32–T33, T34

Practice Assign PB 53–56, 57.

Spelling Instruction: The Long *o* Sound

Pretest and Teach Spelling Principle, TE T38

Assign Take-Home Spelling Word List, PB 307

go bone so nose home no

Challenge: also, woke

Vocabulary Instruction

Teach Spelling Pattern *-oke,* TE T38

Options for Guided Reading

80-100 minutes

Extra Support

Before Reading Preview *Duke's Gift,* PL Theme 6, pp. 5–8. Model Phonics/Decoding Strategy. See TE T35–T37.

During Reading Coach as children read story.

After Reading Discuss story; have children find/read words with long *o,* long *u,* and final *ft, lk, nt.* **Fluency Modeling:** Model fluent reading. Have partners reread story.

✓ = opportunity for ongoing assessment; adjust groups accordingly

▲ On Level

Before Reading Preview *Duke's Gift,* PL Theme 6, pp. 5–8, and review TE T35–T37.

During Reading Have children begin story. **Fluency Modeling:** Model Phonics/Decoding Strategy and fluent reading.

After Reading Have children retell story so far and find/read words with long *o,* long *u,* and final *ft, lk, nt.* **Fluency Practice:** Have partners finish story and reread for fluency.

■ Above Level

Before Reading Preview LR *Hide-and-Seek,* TE T86.

During Reading Have children read first half of story. **Fluency Modeling:** Model fluent reading.

After Reading Have children finish reading and write answers to Responding questions. ✓

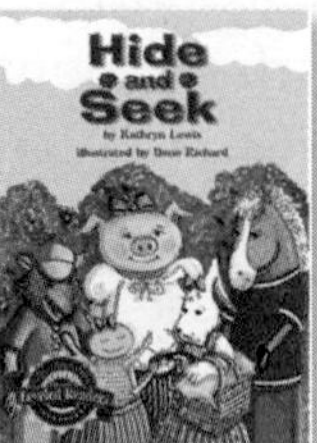

Level H

◆ English Language Learners

Before Reading Preview VR *What Can You See?* See VR Guide, p. 21.

During Reading **Fluency Modeling:** Read aloud each page; have children do echo reading.

After Reading Discuss Responding pages. Have children reread with partners or audio CD.

Level C

Writing and Language

25-40 minutes

Writing

Teach Shared Writing: A Letter of Persuasion, TE T39

Practice Assign Writing Prompt, TE T29.

Listening

Teach For Enjoyment, TE T39

Optional Resources

Teacher Read Aloud

Reread the Big Book: *Two's Company,* TE T17, R2.

Read *Fox, Alligator, and Rabbit,* TE T30–T31.

Independent Work

Self-Selected Reading

Choose from

- classroom/school library
- Leveled Bibliography, TE T6–T7
- *I Love Reading,* Theme 6, take-home books 51–57
- Little Readers for Guided Reading

Centers

- Classroom Management Kit
- Classroom Management activities, TE T26–T27

Differentiated Instruction

- Phonics Reteaching or Extension: Long *o* (CVC*e*), and Long *u* (CVC*e*), TE R12–R13
- Phonics Reteaching or Extension: Final Clusters *ft, lk, nt,* TE R14–R15
- High-Frequency Words Review: Word Wall, TE T28

TE = Teacher Edition; PB = Practice Book; Tr = Transparency; LR = Leveled Reader; PL = Phonics Library; VR = Vocabulary Reader; VR Guide = Vocabulary Readers Teacher's Manual; LBB = Little Big Book; TP = Theme Paperback

Day 2 Balanced Literacy Plan

Teacher Notes

Reading and Comprehension

20-30 minutes

Shared Reading of *The Sleeping Pig* (Part 1)

▼ Anthology Selection

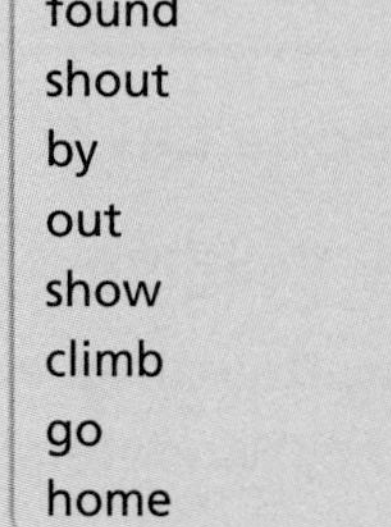

- Build Background and Vocabulary; Introduce Story Vocabulary, TE T44–T45, Tr 6-2

began	coyote	howl	tail
celebrate	cricket	rabbit	watermelon

- Introduce Comprehension Strategy and Skill: Summarize, TE T46
  Story Structure, TE T46, TE T55
- Set Purpose, TE T47
- Read Anthology Selection pp. 134–140 (independent, partner, or audio CD).

Words to Know

morning	woke
found	nose
shout	whole
by	huge
out	use
show	tune
climb	went
go	lift
home	

Word Work

25-40 minutes

Phonemic Awareness/Phonics Instruction

Teach Segmenting, Counting Phonemes, TE T41

High-Frequency Words Instruction

Teach TE T42–T43, Tr 6-1; **Practice** PB 58–59.

High-Frequency Words

by	out
climb	shout
found	show
morning	

Spelling Instruction

Review The Long *o* Sound, TE T58

Options for Guided Reading

80-100 minutes

● Extra Support

Before Reading Preview VR *What Can You See?,* VR Guide, p. 21.

During Reading Read the book together; coach reading. Help children apply Summarize Strategy.

After Reading Help children compare this book to *The Sleeping Pig.* **Fluency Practice:** Have children reread VR. Assign *Legs Gets His Lunch,* PL Theme 6, pp. 9–12, for partner reading.

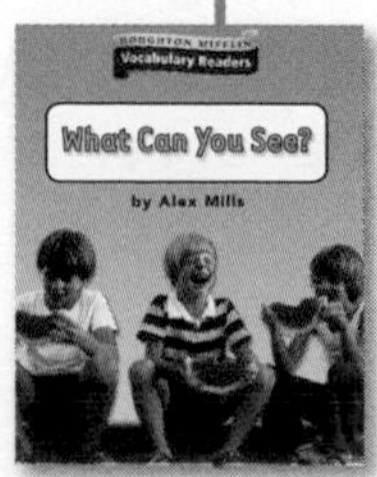

Level C

✓ = opportunity for ongoing assessment; adjust groups accordingly

▲ On Level

Before Reading Discuss PL *Duke's Gift,* TE T36. Preview LR *Watermelon for Lunch,* TE T85.

During Reading Coach reading as children begin story. Have children model the Summarize Strategy. **Fluency Modeling:** Model fluent reading, then have children model it.

After Reading Children finish reading and write answers to Responding questions. ✓ Assign *Legs Gets His Lunch,* PL Theme 6, pp. 9–12, for partner reading.

Level G

■ Above Level

Before Reading Have children model the Summarize Strategy and discuss Responding questions for LR *Hide-and-Seek,* TE T86.

During Reading **Fluency Check:** Monitor children's oral reading. ✓

After Reading Have children discuss the story with a partner. Assign *Legs Gets His Lunch,* PL Theme 6, pp. 9–12, for partner reading.

Level H

◆ English Language Learners

Before Reading To review VR vocabulary, have children demonstrate or give examples. See VR Guide, p. 21.

During Reading Model Summarize Strategy. Help children apply the Summarize Strategy. **Fluency Practice:** Have children reread book.

After Reading Help children summarize VR. Have partners discuss, draw, or write facts they learned. ✓

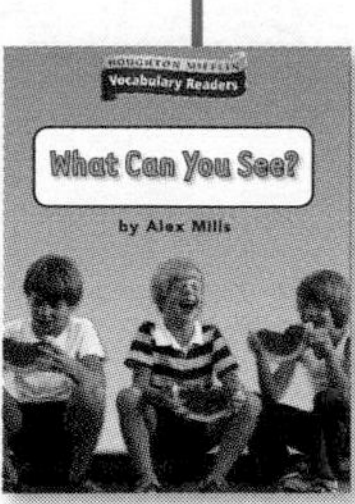

Level C

4 WHOLE GROUP Writing and Language

25-40 minutes

Writing

Teach Interactive Writing: A Letter of Persuasion, TE T59

Practice Assign Writing Prompt, TE T41.

Optional Resources

Teacher Read Aloud

Reread Big Book: *Two's Company.* See TE T17, R2.

Independent Work

Self-Selected Reading

Choose from

- classroom/school library
- Leveled Bibliography, TE T6–T7
- *I Love Reading,* Theme 6, take-home books 51–57
- Little Readers for Guided Reading

Centers

- Classroom Management Kit
- Classroom Management activities, TE T26–T27

Differentiated Instruction

- High-Frequency Words
  - Word Wall, TE T40
  - Review, TE T42–T43
  - Reteaching or Extension, TE R20–R21

TE = Teacher Edition; PB = Practice Book; Tr = Transparency; LR = Leveled Reader; PL = Phonics Library; VR = Vocabulary Reader; VR Guide = Vocabulary Readers Teacher's Manual; LBB = Little Big Book; TP = Theme Paperback

Day 3 Balanced Literacy Plan

Teacher Notes

Reading and Comprehension

20-30 minutes

Shared Reading of *The Sleeping Pig* (Part 2)

▼ Anthology Selection

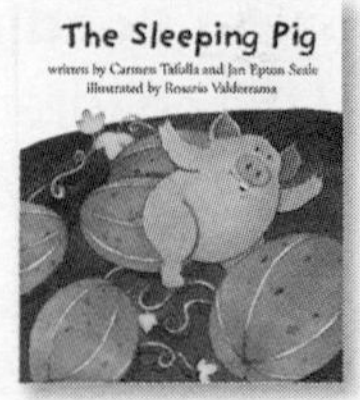

- Read Anthology Selection pp. 141–152 (independent, partner, or audio CD).
- Discuss questions, TE T62; have children cite text to support answers.

Comprehension Skill Instruction

Teach Story Structure, TE T64–T65, Tr 6-3

Practice Assign PB 62 or retelling of story.

Word Work

25-40 minutes

Phonemic Awareness Instruction

Teach Segmenting, Counting Phonemes, TE T61

Spelling: Words with Long *o*

Practice Assign PB 63 or activity, TE T66.

Vocabulary Instruction

Teach Alphabetical Order, TE T66

Practice Assign PB 65.

Options for Guided Reading

80-100 minutes

● Extra Support

Before Reading Discuss Responding questions from VR *What Can You See?* See VR Guide, p. 21. Preview LR *The Huge Carrot,* TE T84.

During Reading Coach as children read story. **Fluency Modeling:** Model fluent reading; have children model.

After Reading **Fluency Practice:** Have partners reread story. Have children answer Responding questions. ✓

Level D

✓ = opportunity for ongoing assessment; adjust groups accordingly

▲ On Level

Before Reading Discuss Responding questions for LR *Watermelon for Lunch,* TE T85.

During Reading **Fluency Check:** Ask individuals to read story aloud. ✓

After Reading Create a Story Map; see TE T64, Tr 6-3 for format. Have children identify the important parts of the LR. Complete the Story Map together.

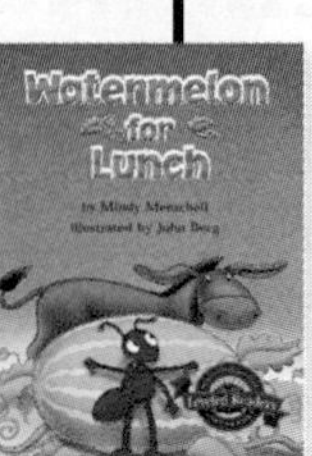

Level G

■ Above Level

Before Reading Preview TP *Fishing Bears.* See TE R5.

During Reading **Fluency Modeling:** Model fluent reading, then have children model it. Have them read first half of story independently.

After Reading Ask questions; have children cite text to support answers. Create a Story Map; see TE T64, Tr 6-3 for format. Have children identify the important parts of the TP. Complete the Story Map together.

Level F

◆ English Language Learners

Before Reading Preview *Legs Gets His Lunch,* PL Theme 6, pp. 9–12. Model Phonics/Decoding Strategy.

During Reading **Fluency Modeling:** Read aloud each page; have children do echo reading.

After Reading Discuss story; help children find/read words with long *o,* long *u,* and final *ft, lk, nt.* Have children use illustrations to retell story to partners.

Optional Resources

Teacher Read Aloud

Choose a book from your class/school library or from the Leveled Bibliography, TE T6–T7.

Suggestion: *Harry the Dirty Dog* by Gene Zion

Independent Work

Self-Selected Reading

Choose from

- classroom/school library
- Leveled Bibliography, TE T6–T7
- *I Love Reading,* Theme 6, take-home books 51–57
- Little Readers for Guided Reading

Centers

- Classroom Management Kit
- Classroom Management activities, TE T26–T27
- Responding activities, TE T62–T63

Differentiated Instruction

- Comprehension Reteaching or Extension: Story Structure, TE R26–R27
- High-Frequency Word Review: Word Wall, TE T60

Writing and Language

30-40 minutes

Writing

Practice Assign Write a Poster, Anthology p. 155.

Grammar

Teach Naming Words for People and Animals, TE T67

Practice Assign PB 67.

TE = Teacher Edition; PB = Practice Book; Tr = Transparency; LR = Leveled Reader; PL = Phonics Library; VR = Vocabulary Reader; VR Guide = Vocabulary Readers Teacher's Manual; LBB = Little Big Book; TP = Theme Paperback

Day 4 Balanced Literacy Plan

Teacher Notes

Reading and Comprehension

20-30 minutes

Shared Reading of Social Studies Link

- "What Is a Desert?" Anthology pp. 156–159, TE T70–T71 (independent, partner, or group)
- Skill: How to Read a Social Studies Article, Anthology p. 156, TE T70
- Introduce Concept Vocabulary, TE T70.

Concept Vocabulary
desert
scorpions
cactus
camels

Word Work

25-40 minutes

Phonemic Awareness/Phonics Instruction

Teach Segmenting, Counting Phonemes, TE T69

Review Long *i* (CVCe), TE T72; Contractions, TE T73

Spelling: Words with Long *o*

Practice Assign PB 68 or activity, TE T74.

Vocabulary Instruction

Teach Words That Name Fruits and Vegetables, TE T74

3 SMALL GROUP

Options for Guided Reading

80-100 minutes

Extra Support

Before Reading Review Responding questions for LR *The Huge Carrot,* TE T84. Begin a Story Map; see TE T64, Tr 6-3 for format. Have children identify the important parts of the LR.

During Reading Have children reread story. **Fluency Check:** Have individuals read aloud. ✓

After Reading Work with students to complete the Story Map. Have partners identify other story elements.

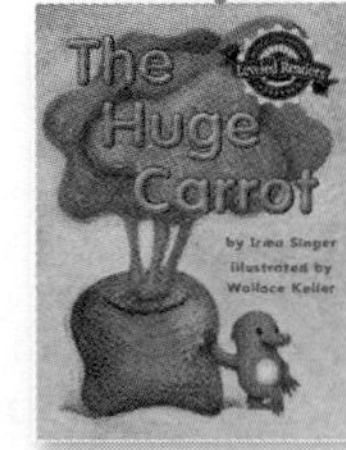

Level D

✓ = opportunity for ongoing assessment; adjust groups accordingly

▲ On Level

Before Reading Have children summarize LR *Watermelon for Lunch.* ✓ Preview a teacher-selected book or TP *The Little Red Hen,* TE R4.

During Reading Have children begin story and model Phonics/Decoding Strategy.

After Reading Discuss the story so far. Have children finish story.

Level F

■ Above Level

Before Reading Review first half of TP *Fishing Bears,* TE R5. Have children make predictions about second half.

During Reading Have children finish book.

After Reading Discuss how book connects to theme. Have children write journal entries to connect it to personal experience or other reading.

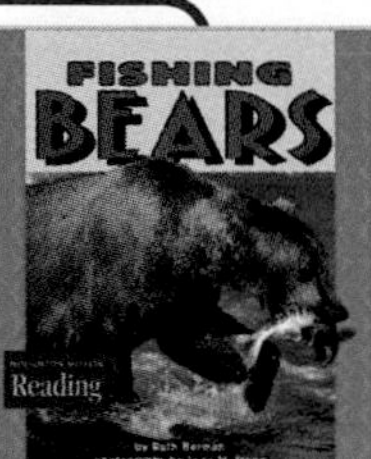

Level F

◆ English Language Learners

Before Reading Build background and preview LR *The Carrot,* TE T87.

During Reading Read story. **Fluency Modeling:** Reread each page; have children do echo reading. Reinforce Phonics/Decoding Strategy.

After Reading Discuss Responding questions, TE T87. **Fluency Practice:** Have children reread with partners or audio CD.

Level C

Optional Resources

Teacher Read Aloud

Continue selected Read Aloud book from Day 3 or choose a new one from your class or school library.

Independent Work

Self-Selected Reading

Choose from

- classroom/school library
- Leveled Bibliography, TE T6–T7
- children's magazines
- *I Love Reading,* Theme 6, take-home books 51–57
- Little Readers for Guided Reading

Centers

- Classroom Management Kit
- Classroom Management activities, TE T26–T27
- Responding activities, TE T62–T63

Differentiated Instruction

- High-Frequency Words: Word Wall, TE T68
- Study Skills
  – Parts of a Book, TE R32

4 WHOLE GROUP

Writing and Language

30-40 minutes

Writing

Teach Writing to Persuade, TE T75

Practice Assign PB 69.

TE = Teacher Edition; PB = Practice Book; Tr = Transparency; LR = Leveled Reader; PL = Phonics Library; VR = Vocabulary Reader; VR Guide = Vocabulary Readers Teacher's Manual; LBB = Little Big Book; TP = Theme Paperback

Day 5 Balanced Literacy Plan

Teacher Notes

Reading and Comprehension

20-30 minutes

Book Share

- Ask children to explain how they applied the comprehension skill and strategy to books they have read this week.
- Help children use genre and text features to compare and contrast what they have read.
- As a class, discuss one *how, why,* or *what if* question. See examples on Blackline Master 1 to use as a guide.

Word Work

25-40 minutes

Phonemic Awareness Instruction

Teach Segmenting, Counting Phonemes, TE T77

High-Frequency Words

Cumulative Review Word Wall, TE T76

Spelling

Test See TE T82.

Options for Guided Reading

80-100 minutes

Extra Support

Before Reading Preview *The Nest,* PL Theme 6, pp. 13–16. Have children find/read words with long *o,* long *u,* and final *ft, lk, nt.* See TE T79.

During Reading Have children read and model Phonics/Decoding Strategy. **Fluency Check:** Have individuals reread aloud. ✓

After Reading Have partners make connections between the story and LR *The Huge Carrot.* Assign On My Way Practice Reader *Fox and Mule* for partner reading.

✓ = opportunity for ongoing assessment; adjust groups accordingly

◆ English Language Learners

Before Reading Review LR *The Carrot,* TE T87.

During Reading Coach rereading of book. **Fluency Check:** Have individuals reread aloud. ✔

After Reading Help children summarize LR. Have children draw/caption a picture about a book they read this week. ✔

Level C

●▲■◆ Mixed Ability Levels

Literature Circles Form small, mixed-ability groups. Ask groups to discuss the main Anthology selection, Link, Leveled Readers, and other books they have read this week. Pose questions or topics for each group, and circulate among groups to offer support. Suggested group activities:

- Respond to specific Literature Discussion questions on Blackline Master 1.
- Discuss story or text elements, authors' choice of language, and/or illustrations.
- Connect book topics or themes to personal experiences or other reading.

Literature Circle

4 WHOLE GROUP Writing and Language

30-40 minutes

Writing

Practice Assign Writing Prompt, TE T77.

Grammar

Review Naming Words for People and Animals, TE T83

Listening and Speaking

Teach Compare and Contrast, TE T83

Optional Resources

Teacher Read Aloud

Choose a nonfiction book related to Social Studies or Science unit.

Independent Work

Self-Selected Reading

Choose from
- classroom/school library
- Leveled Bibliography, TE T6–T7
- children's magazines
- consumer texts such as books about the desert, maps, etc.

Centers
- Classroom Management Kit
- Classroom Management activities, TE T26–T27
- Responding activities, TE T62–T63

Differentiated Instruction
- High-Frequency Words Review, TE T82
- Comprehension Review: Story Structure, TE T78

End-of-Week Assessment
- Weekly Skills Tests for Theme 6, Week 1
- Fluency Assessment, *The Nest,* PL Theme 6, pp. 13–16, TE T79–T81
- Alternative Assessment, Teacher's Resource Blackline Master 79

TE = Teacher Edition; PB = Practice Book; Tr = Transparency; LR = Leveled Reader; PL = Phonics Library; VR = Vocabulary Reader; VR Guide = Vocabulary Readers Teacher's Manual; LBB = Little Big Book; TP = Theme Paperback

Day 1 Balanced Literacy Plan

Teacher Notes

Reading and Comprehension

20-30 minutes

Shared Reading of Daily Message, TE T110

Listening Comprehension

- Read aloud *Tiger and Anansi,* TE T112–T113.
- Model fluent reading; discuss the story.

Word Work

25-40 minutes

Phonemic Awareness/Phonics Instruction

Teach Blending, Segmenting Phonemes, TE T111, T114

Teach Blending Long *e* Words (CV, CVCe); Vowel Pairs *ee, ea,* TE T114–T115, T116

Practice Assign PB 72–73, 74–75.

Spelling Instruction: Words with Long *e (e, ee, ea)*

Pretest and Teach Spelling Principle, TE T120

Assign Take-Home Spelling Word List, PB 307

eat feet he me mean see

Challenge: maybe, sheep

Vocabulary Instruction

Teach Spelling Pattern *-eat,* TE T120

Options for Guided Reading

80-100 minutes

Extra Support

Before Reading Preview *Seal Beach,* PL Theme 6, pp. 17–20. Model Phonics/Decoding Strategy. See TE T117–T119.

During Reading Coach as children read story.

After Reading Discuss story; have children find/read words with long e and vowel pairs *ee, ea.* **Fluency Modeling:** Model fluent reading. Have partners reread story.

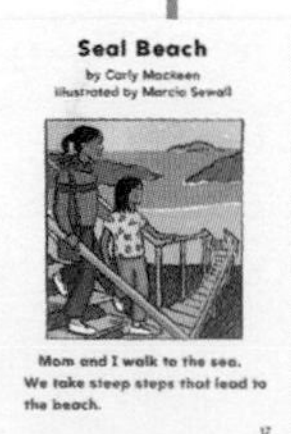

✓ = opportunity for ongoing assessment; adjust groups accordingly

▲ On Level

Before Reading Preview *Seal Beach,* PL Theme 6, pp. 17–20, and review TE T117–T119.

During Reading Have children begin story. **Fluency Modeling:** Model Phonics/Decoding Strategy and fluent reading.

After Reading Have children retell story so far and find/read words with long *e* and vowel pairs *ee, ea.* **Fluency Practice:** Have partners finish story and reread for fluency.

■ Above Level

Before Reading Preview LR *Zeke Takes a Bath,* TE T168.

During Reading Have children read first half of story. **Fluency Modeling:** Model fluent reading.

After Reading Have children finish reading and write answers to Responding questions. ✓

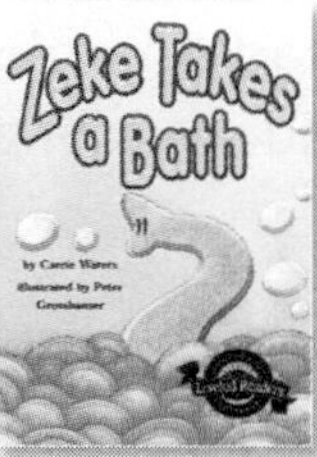

Level J

◆ English Language Learners

Before Reading Preview VR *In the Barn.* See VR Guide, p. 22.

During Reading **Fluency Modeling:** Read aloud each page; have children do echo reading.

After Reading Discuss Responding pages. Have children reread with partners or audio CD.

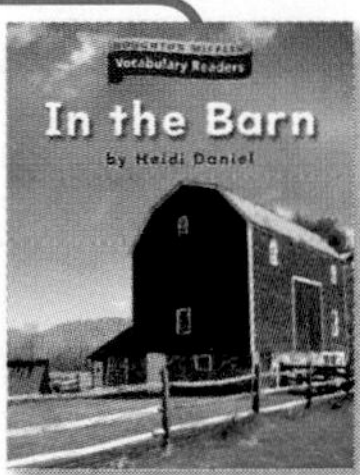

Level D

Optional Resources

Teacher Read Aloud

Reread *Tiger and Anansi,* TE T112–T113.

Independent Work

Self-Selected Reading

Choose from

- classroom/school library
- Leveled Bibliography, TE T6–T7
- *I Love Reading,* Theme 6, take-home books 58–61
- Little Readers for Guided Reading

Centers

- Classroom Management Kit
- Classroom Management activities, TE T108–T109

Differentiated Instruction

- Phonics Reteaching or Extension: Long *e* and Vowel Pairs *ee, ea,* TE R16–R17
- High-Frequency Words Review: Word Wall, TE T110

4 WHOLE GROUP

Writing and Language

25-40 minutes

Writing

Teach Shared Writing: A Class Story, TE T121

Practice Assign Writing Prompt, TE T111.

Listening and Speaking

Teach Compare and Contrast, TE T121

TE = Teacher Edition; PB = Practice Book; Tr = Transparency; LR = Leveled Reader; PL = Phonics Library; VR = Vocabulary Reader; VR Guide = Vocabulary Readers Teacher's Manual; LBB = Little Big Book; TP = Theme Paperback

Day 2 Balanced Literacy Plan

Teacher Notes

Reading and Comprehension

20-30 minutes

Shared Reading of *EEK! There's a Mouse in the House* (Part 1)

➤ Build Background and Vocabulary; Introduce Story Vocabulary, TE T126–T127, Tr 6-6

barn	elephant	marched	mouse
dancing	laying	mercy	tangled

➤ Introduce Comprehension Strategy and Skill:
Question, TE T128
Noting Details, TE T128, TE T136

➤ Set Purpose, TE T129

➤ Read Anthology Selection pp. 165–172 (independent, partner, or audio CD).

▼ **Anthology Selection**

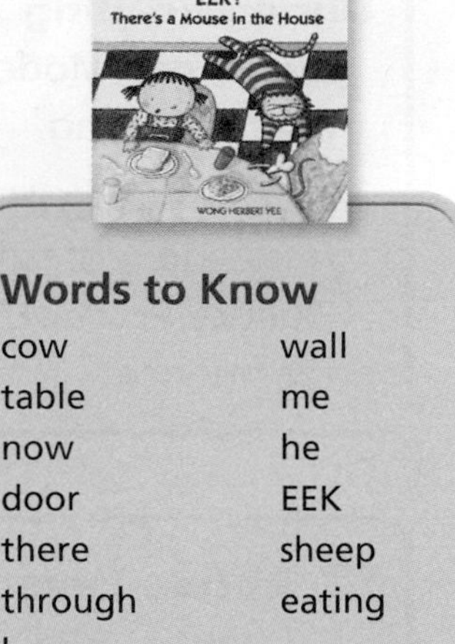

Words to Know

cow	wall
table	me
now	he
door	EEK
there	sheep
through	eating
horse	

Word Work

25-40 minutes

Phonemic Awareness/Phonics Instruction

Teach Segmenting, Counting Phonemes, TE T123

High-Frequency Words Instruction

Teach TE T124–T125, Tr 6-5; Practice PB 76–77.

Spelling Instruction

Review Words with Long *e (e, ee, ea),* TE T140

High-Frequency Words

cow	table
door	there
horse	through
now	wall

3
SMALL GROUP

Options for Guided Reading

80-100 minutes

● **Extra Support**

Before Reading Preview VR *In the Barn,* VR Guide, p. 22.

During Reading Read the book together; coach reading. Help children apply Question Strategy.

After Reading Help children compare this book to *EEK! There's a Mouse in the House.* **Fluency Practice:** Have children reread VR. Assign *Pete and Peach,* PL Theme 6, pp. 21–24, for partner reading.

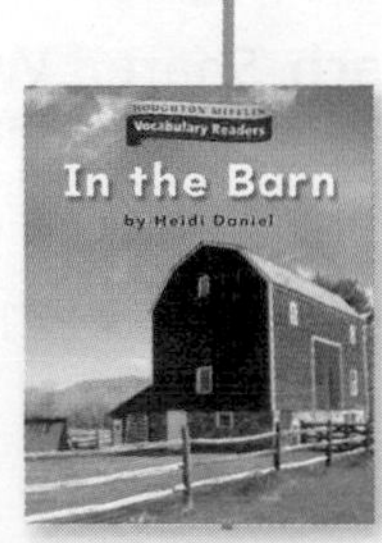

Level D

✓ = opportunity for ongoing assessment; adjust groups accordingly

▲ On Level

Before Reading Discuss PL *Seal Beach,* TE T118. Preview LR *Going Fishing,* TE T167.

During Reading Coach reading as children begin story. Have children model the Question Strategy. **Fluency Modeling:** Model fluent reading, then have children model it.

After Reading Children finish reading and write answers to Responding questions. ✓ Assign *Pete and Peach,* PL Theme 6, pp. 21–24, for partner reading.

Level F

■ Above Level

Before Reading Have children model the Question Strategy and discuss Responding questions for LR *Zeke Takes a Bath,* TE T168.

During Reading **Fluency Check:** Monitor children's oral reading. ✓

After Reading Have children discuss the story with a partner. Assign *Pete and Peach,* PL Theme 6, pp. 21–24, for partner reading.

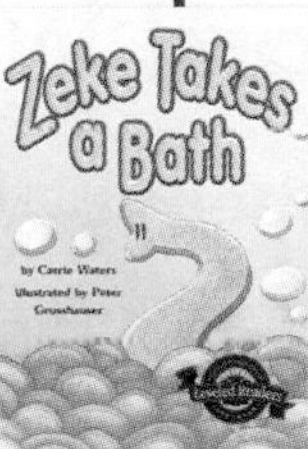

Level J

◆ English Language Learners

Before Reading To review VR vocabulary, have children demonstrate or give examples. See VR Guide, p. 22.

During Reading Model Question Strategy. Help children apply the Question Strategy. **Fluency Practice:** Have children reread book. Option: Preview and coach reading of *Seal Beach,* PL Theme 6, pp. 17–20, TE T117–119.

After Reading Help children summarize VR. Have partners discuss, draw, or write facts they learned. ✓

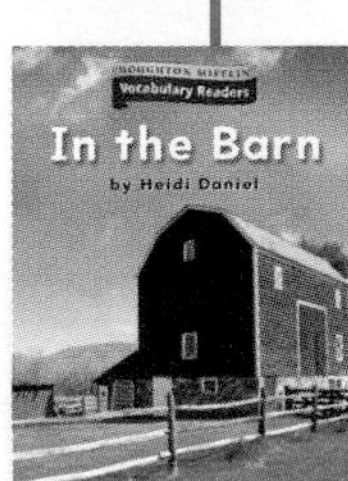

Level D

4 WHOLE GROUP Writing and Language

25-40 minutes

Writing

Teach Interactive Writing: A Class Story, TE T141

Practice Assign Writing Prompt, TE T123.

Optional Resources

Teacher Read Aloud

Choose a book from your class/school library or from the Leveled Bibliography, TE T6–T7.

Suggestion: *Tops and Bottoms* by Janet Stevens

Independent Work

Self-Selected Reading

Choose from

- classroom/school library
- Leveled Bibliography, TE T6–T7
- *I Love Reading,* Theme 6, take-home books 58–61
- Little Readers for Guided Reading

Centers

- Classroom Management Kit
- Classroom Management activities, T108–T109

Differentiated Instruction

- High-Frequency Words
  - –Word Wall, TE T122
  - – Review, TE T140
  - – Reteaching or Extension, TE R22–R23

TE = Teacher Edition; PB = Practice Book; Tr = Transparency; LR = Leveled Reader; PL = Phonics Library; VR = Vocabulary Reader; VR Guide = Vocabulary Readers Teacher's Manual; LBB = Little Big Book; TP = Theme Paperback

Day 3 Balanced Literacy Plan

Teacher Notes

Reading and Comprehension

20-30 minutes

Shared Reading of *EEK! There's a Mouse in the House* (Part 2)

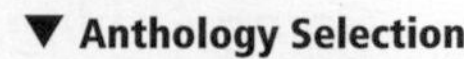

▼ Anthology Selection

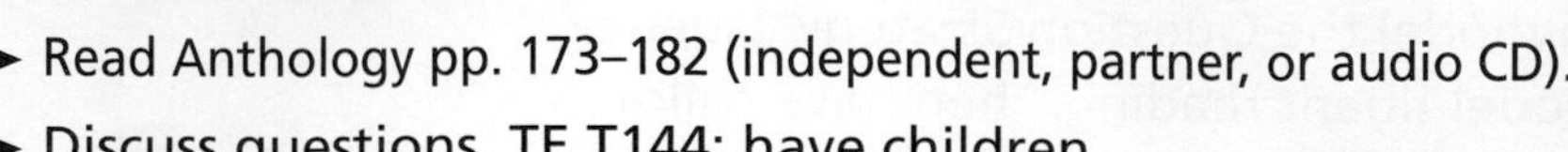

- Read Anthology pp. 173–182 (independent, partner, or audio CD).
- Discuss questions, TE T144; have children cite text to support answers.

Comprehension Skill Instruction

Teach Noting Details, TE T146–T147

Practice Assign PB 80 or retelling of story.

Word Work

25-40 minutes

Phonemic Awareness Instruction

Teach Segmenting, Counting Phonemes, TE T143

Spelling: Words with Long e *(e, ee, ea)*

Practice Assign PB 81 or activity, TE T148.

Vocabulary Instruction

Teach Rhyming Words, TE T148; **Practice** Assign PB 82.

Options for Guided Reading

80-100 minutes

● Extra Support

Before Reading Discuss Responding questions from VR *In the Barn.* See VR Guide, p. 22. Preview LR *The Feast,* TE T166.

During Reading Coach as children read story. **Fluency Modeling:** Model fluent reading; have children model.

After Reading **Fluency Practice:** Have partners reread story. Have children answer Responding questions. ✓

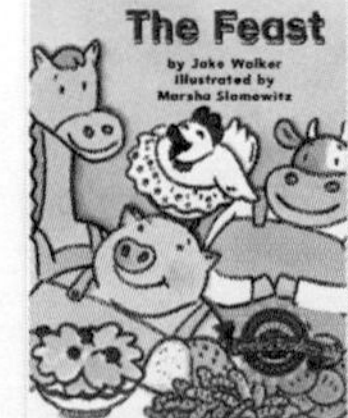

Level E

✓ = opportunity for ongoing assessment; adjust groups accordingly

▲ On Level

Before Reading Discuss Responding questions for LR *Going Fishing,* TE T167.

During Reading **Fluency Check:** Ask individuals to read story aloud. ✓

After Reading Use a Word Web or chart to list details about events, characters, ideas, or topics in the LR. Complete the list together.

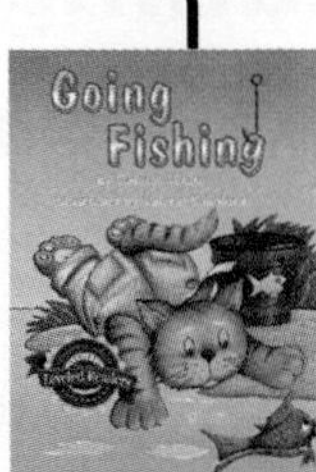

Level F

■ Above Level

Before Reading Preview a teacher-selected book, such as *Henry and Mudge and Annie's Perfect Pet,* see TE R8.

During Reading **Fluency Modeling:** Model fluent reading, then have children model it. Have them read first half of story independently.

After Reading Ask questions; have children cite text to support answers. Use a Word Web or chart to list details about events, characters, ideas, or topics in the teacher-selected book. Complete the list together.

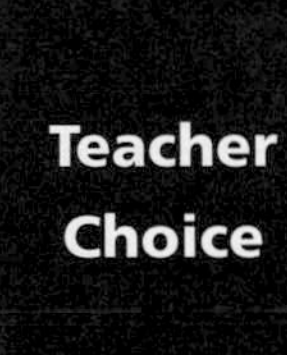

◆ English Language Learners

Before Reading Preview *Pete and Peach,* PL Theme 6, pp. 21–24. Model Phonics/Decoding Strategy.

During Reading **Fluency Modeling:** Read aloud each page; have children do echo reading.

After Reading Discuss story; help children find/read words with long *e* and vowel pairs *ee, ea.* Have children use illustrations to retell story to partners.

Optional Resources

Teacher Read Aloud

Continue selected Read Aloud book from Day 2 or choose a new one from your class or school library.

Independent Work

Self-Selected Reading

Choose from

- classroom/school library
- Leveled Bibliography, TE T6–T7
- *I Love Reading,* Theme 6, take-home books 58–61
- Little Readers for Guided Reading

Centers

- Classroom Management Kit
- Classroom Management activities, TE T108–T109
- Responding activities, TE T144–T145

Differentiated Instruction

- Comprehension Reteaching or Extension: Noting Details, TE R28–R29
- High-Frequency Word Review: Word Wall, TE T142

4 WHOLE GROUP Writing and Language

30-40 minutes

Writing

Practice Assign Write a List, Anthology p. 185.

Grammar

Teach Naming Words for Places and Things, TE T149

Practice Assign PB 83.

TE = Teacher Edition; PB = Practice Book; Tr = Transparency; LR = Leveled Reader; PL = Phonics Library; VR = Vocabulary Reader; VR Guide = Vocabulary Readers Teacher's Manual; LBB = Little Big Book; TP = Theme Paperback

Day 4 Balanced Literacy Plan

Teacher Notes

Reading and Comprehension

20-30 minutes

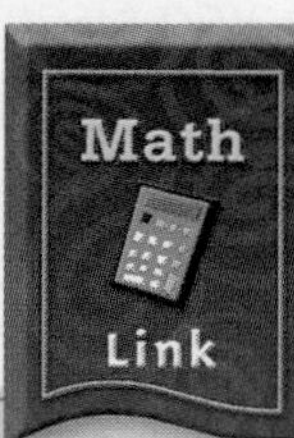

Concept Vocabulary
pictograph
feet
inches
harvest
Cubs

Shared Reading of Math Link

- "Animals Big and Small," Anthology pp. 186–189, TE T152–T153 (independent, partner, or group)
- Skill: How to Read a Pictograph, Anthology p. 186, TE T152
- Introduce Concept Vocabulary, TE T152.

Word Work

Phonemic Awareness/Phonics Instruction

Teach Segmenting, Counting Phonemes, TE T151

Review Long *o* (CV, CVCe) and Long *u* (CVCe), TE T154; Final Clusters *ft, lk, nt,* TE T155

Spelling: Words with Long e *(e, ee, ea)*

Practice Assign PB 84 or activity, TE T156.

Vocabulary Instruction

Teach Expressions of Surprise, TE T156

3 SMALL GROUP

Options for Guided Reading

80-100 minutes

Extra Support

Before Reading Review Responding questions for LR *The Feast,* TE T166. Use a Word Web or chart to list details about events, characters, ideas, or topics in the LR.

During Reading Have children reread story. **Fluency Check:** Have individuals read aloud. ✓

After Reading Have partners complete a list of details about the LR.

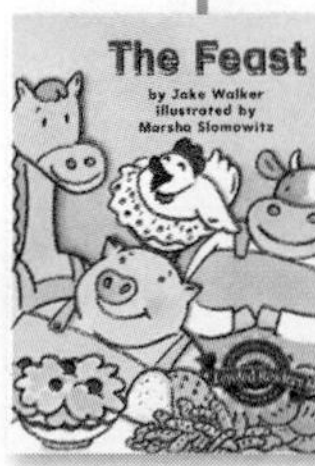

Level E

✓ = opportunity for ongoing assessment; adjust groups accordingly

▲ On Level

Before Reading Have children summarize LR *Going Fishing.* ✓ Preview a teacher-selected book such as *Every Autumn Comes the Bear,* TE R7.

During Reading Have children begin story and model Phonics/Decoding Strategy.

After Reading Discuss the story so far. Have children finish story.

■ Above Level

Before Reading Review first half of selected book. Have children make predictions about second half.

During Reading Have children finish book.

After Reading Discuss how book connects to theme. Have children write journal entries to connect it to personal experience or other reading.

◆ English Language Learners

Before Reading Build background and preview LR *Fun and Food to Eat,* TE T169.

During Reading Read story. **Fluency Modeling:** Reread each page; have children do echo reading. Reinforce Phonics/Decoding Strategy.

After Reading Discuss Responding questions, TE T169. **Fluency Practice:** Have children reread with partners or audio CD.

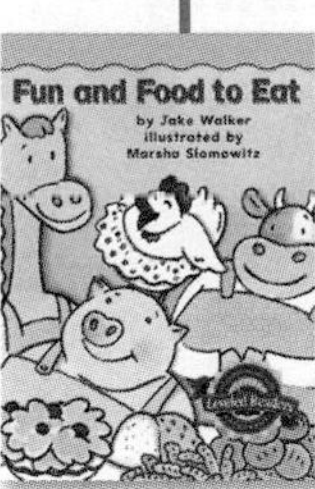

Level D

4 WHOLE GROUP Writing and Language

30-40 minutes

Writing

Teach Answering a Comprehension Question, TE T157

Practice Assign PB 85.

Optional Resources

Teacher Read Aloud

Choose a new book from your class or school library.

Independent Work

Self-Selected Reading

Choose from

- classroom/school library
- Leveled Bibliography, TE T6–T7
- children's magazines
- *I Love Reading,* Theme 6, take-home books 58–61
- Little Readers for Guided Reading

Centers

- Classroom Management Kit
- Classroom Management activities, TE T108–T109
- Responding activities, TE T144–T145

Differentiated Instruction

- Visual Literacy: Showing with Words, TE T153
- High-Frequency Words: Word Wall, TE T150
- Study Skills
  – Parts of a Book, TE R32

TE = Teacher Edition; PB = Practice Book; Tr = Transparency; LR = Leveled Reader; PL = Phonics Library; VR = Vocabulary Reader; VR Guide = Vocabulary Readers Teacher's Manual; LBB = Little Big Book; TP = Theme Paperback

Day 5 Balanced Literacy Plan

Teacher Notes

Reading and Comprehension

20-30 minutes

Book Share

- Ask children to explain how they applied the comprehension skill and strategy to books they have read this week.
- Help children use genre and text features to compare and contrast what they have read.
- As a class, discuss one *how, why,* or *what if* question. See examples on Blackline Master 1 to use as a guide.

Word Work

25-40 minutes

Phonemic Awareness Instruction

Teach Segmenting, Counting Phonemes, TE T159

High-Frequency Words

Cumulative Review Word Wall, TE T158

Spelling

Test See TE T164.

Options for Guided Reading

80-100 minutes

Extra Support

Before Reading Preview *Gram's Huge Meal,* PL Theme 6, pp. 25–28. Have children find/read words with long *e* and vowel pairs *ee, ea.* See TE T161–T163.

During Reading Have children read and model Phonics/ Decoding Strategy. **Fluency Check:** Have individuals reread aloud. ✓

After Reading Have partners make connections between the story and LR *The Feast.* Assign On My Way Practice Reader *What Animal Is It?* for partner reading.

✓ = opportunity for ongoing assessment; adjust groups accordingly

◆ English Language Learners

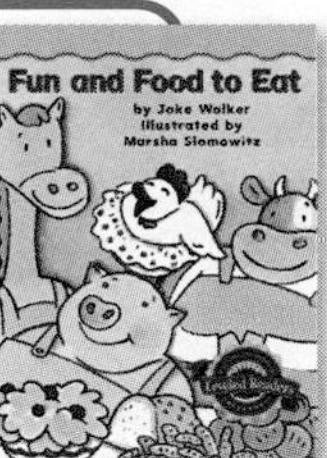

Level D

Before Reading Review LR *Fun and Food to Eat,* TE T169.

During Reading Coach rereading of book. **Fluency Check:** Have individuals reread aloud. ✔

After Reading Help children summarize LR. Have children draw/caption a picture about a book they read this week. ✔

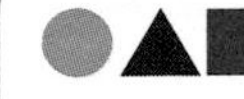 Mixed Ability Levels

Literature Circles Form small, mixed-ability groups. Ask groups to discuss the main Anthology selection, Link, Leveled Readers, and other books they have read this week. Pose questions or topics for each group, and circulate among groups to offer support. Suggested group activities:

- Respond to specific Literature Discussion questions on Blackline Master 1.
- Discuss story or text elements, authors' choice of language, and/or illustrations.
- Connect book topics or themes to personal experiences or other reading.

Writing and Language

30-40 minutes

Writing

Practice Assign Writing Prompt, TE T159.

Grammar

Review Naming Words for Places and Things, TE T165

Viewing

Teach Retelling, TE T165

Optional Resources

Teacher Read Aloud

Choose a nonfiction book related to Social Studies or Science unit.

Independent Work

Self-Selected Reading

Choose from

- classroom/school library
- Leveled Bibliography, TE T6–T7
- children's magazines
- consumer texts such as charts, graphs, etc.

Centers

- Classroom Management Kit
- Classroom Management activities, TE T108–T109
- Responding activities, TE T144–T145

Differentiated Instruction

- High-Frequency Words Review, TE T164
- Comprehension Review: Noting Details, TE T160

End-of-Week Assessment

- Weekly Skills Tests for Theme 6, Week 2
- Fluency Assessment, *Gram's Huge Meal,* PL Theme 6, pp. 25–28, TE T161–T163
- Alternative Assessment, Teacher's Resource Blackline Master 8

TE = Teacher Edition; PB = Practice Book; Tr = Transparency; LR = Leveled Reader; PL = Phonics Library; VR = Vocabulary Reader; VR Guide = Vocabulary Readers Teacher's Manual; LBB = Little Big Book; TP = Theme Paperback

Day 1 Balanced Literacy Plan

Teacher Notes

Reading and Comprehension

Shared Reading of Daily Message, TE T180

Listening Comprehension

- Read aloud *Life in a Rain Forest,* TE T182–T183.
- Model fluent reading; discuss the story.

Word Work

Phonemic Awareness/Phonics Instruction

Teach Segmenting, Counting Phonemes, TE T181, T184

Teach Vowel Pairs *ai, ay,* TE T184–T186

Practice Assign PB 86–87.

Spelling Instruction: Words with *ay*

Pretest and Teach Spelling Principle, TE T190

Assign Take-Home Spelling Word List, PB 309

day may play say stay way

Challenge: away, holiday

Vocabulary Instruction

Teach Spelling Pattern *-ay,* TE T190

Options for Guided Reading

Extra Support

Before Reading Preview *Rain Day,* PL Theme 6, pp. 29–32. Model Phonics/Decoding Strategy. See TE T187–T189.

During Reading Coach as children read story.

After Reading Discuss story; have children find/read words with *ai, ay.* **Fluency Modeling:** Model fluent reading. Have partners reread story.

✓ = opportunity for ongoing assessment; adjust groups accordingly

▲ On Level

Before Reading Preview *Rain Day,* PL Theme 6, pp. 29–32, and review TE T187–T189.

During Reading Have children begin story. **Fluency Modeling:** Model Phonics/Decoding Strategy and fluent reading.

After Reading Have children retell story so far and find/read words with *ai, ay.* **Fluency Practice:** Have partners finish story and reread for fluency.

■ Above Level

Before Reading Preview LR *Animals at Night,* TE T240.

During Reading Have children read first half of story. **Fluency Modeling:** Model fluent reading.

After Reading Have children finish reading and write answers to Responding questions. ✓

Level L

◆ English Language Learners

Before Reading Preview VR *Animals in the Rain Forest.* See VR Guide, p. 23.

During Reading **Fluency Modeling:** Read aloud each page; have children do echo reading.

After Reading Discuss Responding pages. Have children reread with partners or audio CD.

Level C

4 WHOLE GROUP

Writing and Language

25-40 minutes

Writing

Teach Shared Writing: A Class Summary, TE T191

Practice Assign Writing Prompt, TE T181.

Listening

Teach To Retell, TE T191

Optional Resources

Teacher Read Aloud

Reread *Life in a Rain Forest,* TE T182–T183.

Independent Work

Self-Selected Reading

Choose from

- classroom/school library
- Leveled Bibliography, TE T6–T7
- *I Love Reading,* Theme 6, take-home book 62–63
- Little Readers for Guided Reading

Centers

- Classroom Management Kit
- Classroom Management activities, TE T178–T179

Differentiated Instruction

- Phonics Reteaching or Extension: Vowel Pairs *ai, ay,* TE R18–R19
- High-Frequency Words Review: Word Wall, TE T180

TE = Teacher Edition; PB = Practice Book; Tr = Transparency; LR = Leveled Reader; PL = Phonics Library; VR = Vocabulary Reader; VR Guide = Vocabulary Readers Teacher's Manual; LBB = Little Big Book; TP = Theme Paperback

Day 2 Balanced Literacy Plan

Teacher Notes

Reading and Comprehension

20-30 minutes

Shared Reading of *Red-Eyed Tree Frog* (Part 1)

▼ Anthology Selection

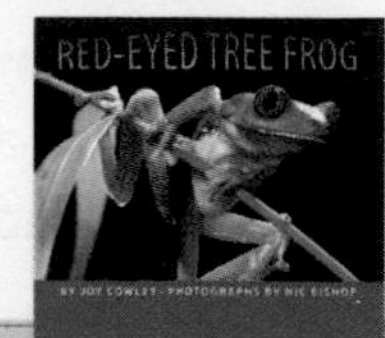

- Build Background and Vocabulary; Introduce Story Vocabulary, TE T196–T197, Tr 6-9

boa	eyes	macaw	tongue
caterpillar	iguana/s	moves	toucan
eyed	katydid	poisonous	

- Introduce Comprehension Strategy and Skill: Predict/Infer, TE T198
  Making Predictions, TE T198, TE T207
- Set Purpose, TE T199
- Read Anthology Selection pp. 193–206 (independent, partner, or audio CD).

Words to Know

been	evening
far	near
forest	rain
goes	wait
hungry	day
soon	away

High-Frequency Words

been	goes
evening	hungry
far	near
forest	soon

Word Work

25-40 minutes

Phonemic Awareness/Phonics Instruction

Teach Segmenting, Counting Phonemes, TE T193

High-Frequency Words Instruction

Teach TE T194–T195, Tr 6-8; Practice PB 88–89.

Spelling Instruction

Review Words with *ay*, TE T212

3 SMALL GROUP

Options for Guided Reading

80-100 minutes

Extra Support

Before Reading Preview VR *Animals in the Rain Forest.* See VR Guide, p. 23.

During Reading Read the book together; coach reading. Help children apply Predict/Infer Strategy.

After Reading Help children compare this book to *Red-Eyed Tree Frog.* **Fluency Practice:** Have children reread VR. Assign *Cub's Long Day,* PL Theme 6, pp. 33–36, for partner reading.

Level C

✓ = opportunity for ongoing assessment; adjust groups accordingly

▲ On Level

Before Reading Discuss PL *Rain Day,* TE T188. Preview LR *The Mouse in the Forest,* TE T239.

During Reading Coach reading as children begin story. Have children model the Predict/Infer Strategy. **Fluency Modeling:** Model fluent reading, then have children model it.

After Reading Children finish reading and write answers to Responding questions. ✓ Assign *Cub's Long Day,* PL Theme 6, pp. 33–36, for partner reading.

Level I

■ Above Level

Before Reading Have children model the Predict/Infer Strategy and discuss Responding questions for LR *Animals at Night,* TE T240.

During Reading **Fluency Check:** Monitor children's oral reading. ✓

After Reading Have children discuss the story with a partner. Assign *Cub's Long Day,* PL Theme 6, pp. 33–36, for partner reading.

Level L

◆ English Language Learners

Before Reading To review VR vocabulary, have children demonstrate or give examples. See VR Guide, p. 23.

During Reading Predict/Infer Strategy. Help children apply the Predict/Infer Strategy. **Fluency Practice:** Have children reread book. Option: Preview and coach reading of *Rain Day,* PL Theme 6, pp. 29–32, TE T187–T189.

After Reading Help children summarize VR. Have partners discuss, draw, or write facts they learned. ✓

Level C

Writing and Language

25-40 minutes

Writing

Teach Interactive Writing: A Class Summary, TE T213

Practice Assign Writing Prompt, TE T193.

Optional Resources

Teacher Read Aloud

Choose a book from your class/school library or from the Leveled Bibliography, TE T6–T7.

Suggestion: *Young Mouse and Elephant* by Pamela J. Farris

Independent Work

Self-Selected Reading

Choose from

- classroom/school library
- Leveled Bibliography, TE T6–T7
- *I Love Reading,* Theme 6, take-home books 62–63
- Little Readers for Guided Reading

Centers

- Classroom Management Kit
- Classroom Management activities, TE T178–T179

Differentiated Instruction

- High-Frequency Words
  - Word Wall, TE T192
  - Review, TE T212
  - Reteaching or Extension, TE R24–R25

TE = Teacher Edition; PB = Practice Book; Tr = Transparency; LR = Leveled Reader; PL = Phonics Library; VR = Vocabulary Reader; VR Guide = Vocabulary Readers Teacher's Manual; LBB = Little Big Book; TP = Theme Paperback

Day 3 Balanced Literacy Plan

Teacher Notes

Reading and Comprehension

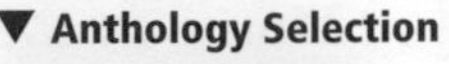

20-30 minutes

Shared Reading of *Red-Eyed Tree Frog* (Part 2)

▼ Anthology Selection

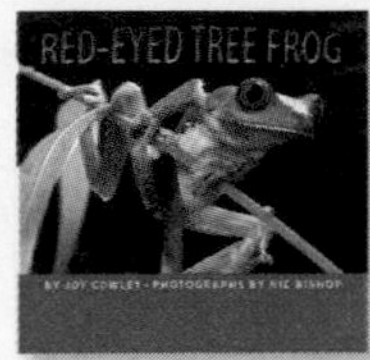

- Read Anthology Selection pp. 207–214 (independent, partner, or audio CD).
- Discuss questions, TE T216; have children cite text to support answers.

Comprehension Skill Instruction

Teach Making Predictions, TE T218–T219

Practice Assign PB 92 or retelling of story.

Word Work

25-40 minutes

Phonemic Awareness Instruction

Teach Segmenting, Counting Phonemes, TE T215

Spelling: Words with *ay*

Practice Assign PB 93 or activity, TE T220.

Vocabulary Instruction

Teach Parts of the Body, TE T220

Practice Assign PB 94.

Options for Guided Reading

80-100 minutes

Extra Support

Before Reading Discuss Responding questions from VR *Animals in the Rain Forest.* See VR Guide, p. 23. Preview LR *Looking for Frogs,* TE T238.

During Reading Coach as children read story. **Fluency Modeling:** Model fluent reading; have children model.

After Reading **Fluency Practice:** Have partners reread story. Have children answer Responding questions. ✓

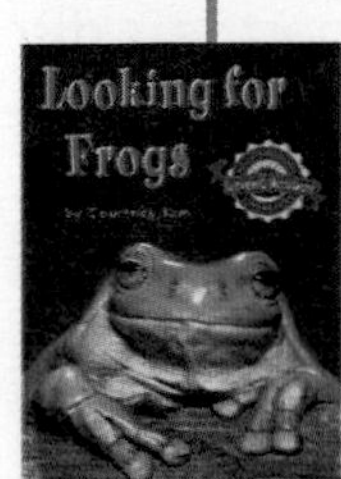

Level D

✓ = opportunity for ongoing assessment; adjust groups accordingly

 **On Level**

Before Reading Discuss Responding questions for LR *The Mouse in the Forest,* TE T239.

During Reading **Fluency Check:** Ask individuals to read story aloud. ✓

After Reading Have children predict what might happen if the author continued the LR story or the same characters were in new situations. Complete the list of predictions together.

Level I

 **Above Level**

Before Reading Preview teacher-selected book, such as *Annie and the Wild Animals,* see TE R11.

During Reading **Fluency Modeling:** Model fluent reading, then have children model it. Have them read first half of story independently.

After Reading Ask questions; have children cite text to support answers. Have children predict what might happen if the author continued the teacher-selected story. Complete the list of predictions together.

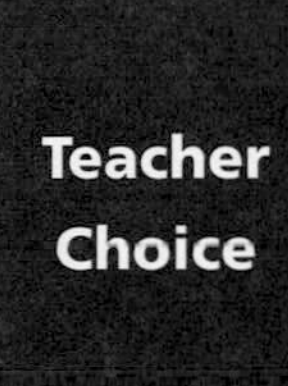

◆ **English Language Learners**

Before Reading Preview *Cub's Long Day,* PL Theme 6, pp. 33–36. Model Phonics/Decoding Strategy.

During Reading **Fluency Modeling:** Read aloud each page; have children do echo reading.

After Reading Discuss story; help children find/read words with *ai, ay.* Have children use illustrations to retell story to partners.

Writing and Language

30-40 minutes

Writing

Practice Assign Write a Riddle, Anthology p. 217.

Grammar

Teach Naming Words for One or More, TE T221

Practice Assign PB 95.

Optional Resources

Teacher Read Aloud

Continue selected Read Aloud book from Day 3 or choose a new one from your class or school library.

Independent Work

Self-Selected Reading

Choose from

- classroom/school library
- Leveled Bibliography, TE T6–T7
- *I Love Reading,* Theme 6, take-home books 62–63
- Little Readers for Guided Reading

Centers

- Classroom Management Kit
- Classroom Management activities, TE T178–T179
- Responding activities, TE T216–T217

Differentiated Instruction

- Comprehension Reteaching or Extension: Making Predictions, TE R30–R31
- High-Frequency Word Review: Word Wall, TE T214

TE = Teacher Edition; PB = Practice Book; Tr = Transparency; LR = Leveled Reader; PL = Phonics Library; VR = Vocabulary Reader; VR Guide = Vocabulary Readers Teacher's Manual; LBB = Little Big Book; TP = Theme Paperback

Day 4 Balanced Literacy Plan

Teacher Notes

Reading and Comprehension

20-30 minutes

Shared Reading of Poetry Link

- Poems, Anthology pp. 218–219, TE T224–T225 (independent, partner, or group)
- Skill: How to Read a Poem, Anthology p. 218, TE T224
- Introduce Concept Vocabulary, TE T224.

Poetry Link

Concept Vocabulary

jaws
few
boast
bill
while

Word Work

25-40 minutes

Phonemic Awareness/Phonics Instruction

Teach Segmenting, Counting Phonemes, TE T223

Review Long *e* (CV, CVCe), TE T226; Vowel Pairs *ee, ea,* TE T227

Spelling: Words with *ay*

Practice Assign PB 96 or activity, TE T228.

Vocabulary Instruction

Teach Animal Action Words, TE T228

Options for Guided Reading

80-100 minutes

Extra Support

Before Reading Review Responding questions for LR *Looking for Frogs,* TE T238. Have children predict what might happen if the author continued the LR story or the same characters were in new situations.

During Reading Have children reread story. **Fluency Check:** Have individuals read aloud. ✓

After Reading Have partners make a list of predictions about the LR.

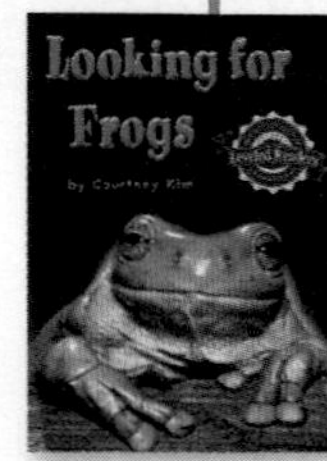

Level D

✓ = opportunity for ongoing assessment; adjust groups accordingly

▲ On Level

Before Reading Have children summarize LR *The Mouse in the Forest.* ✓ Preview a teacher-selected book such as *Tiny's Bath,* TE R10.

During Reading Have children begin story and model Phonics/Decoding Strategy.

After Reading Discuss the story so far. Have children finish story.

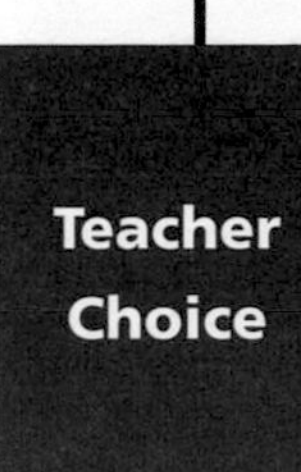

 Above Level

Before Reading Review first half of selected book. Have children make predictions about second half.

During Reading Have children finish book.

After Reading Discuss how book connects to theme. Have children write journal entries to connect it to personal experience or other reading.

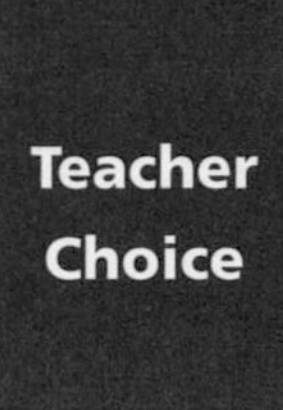

◆ English Language Learners

Before Reading Build background and preview LR *How Many Frogs?,* TE T241.

During Reading Read story. **Fluency Modeling:** Reread each page; have children do echo reading. Reinforce Phonics/Decoding Strategy.

After Reading Discuss Responding questions, TE T241. **Fluency Practice:** Have children reread with partners or audio CD.

Level C

Writing and Language

30-40 minutes

Writing

Teach Writing a Summary, TE T229

Practice Assign PB 97.

Optional Resources

Teacher Read Aloud

Choose a new book from your class or school library.

Independent Work

Self-Selected Reading

Choose from

- classroom/school library
- Leveled Bibliography, TE T6–T7
- children's magazines
- *I Love Reading,* Theme 6, take-home books 62–63
- Little Readers for Guided Reading

Centers

- Classroom Management Kit
- Classroom Management activities, TE T178–T179
- Responding activities, TE T216–T217

Differentiated Instruction

- High-Frequency Words: Word Wall, TE T222
- Study Skills
  – Parts of a Book, TE R32

TE = Teacher Edition; PB = Practice Book; Tr = Transparency; LR = Leveled Reader; PL = Phonics Library; VR = Vocabulary Reader; VR Guide = Vocabulary Readers Teacher's Manual; LBB = Little Big Book; TP = Theme Paperback

Day 5 Balanced Literacy Plan

Teacher Notes

Reading and Comprehension

20-30 minutes

Book Share

- Ask children to give examples of how they applied the comprehension skill and strategy to books they have read this week.
- Help children use genre and text features to compare and contrast what they have read.
- As a class, discuss one *how, why,* or *what if* question. See examples on Blackline Master 1 to use as a guide.

Word Work

25-40 minutes

Phonemic Awareness Instruction

Teach Segmenting, Counting Phonemes, TE T231

High-Frequency Words:

Cumulative Review Word Wall, TE T230

Spelling

Test See TE T236.

Options for Guided Reading

80-100 minutes

Extra Support

Before Reading Preview *Jay's Trip,* PL Theme 6, pp. 37–40. Have children find/read words with *ai, ay.* See TE T233–T235.

During Reading Have children read and model Phonics/Decoding Strategy. **Fluency Check:** Have individuals reread aloud. ✓

After Reading Have partners make connections between the story and LR *Looking for Frogs.* Assign On My Way Practice Reader *The Real Wolf* for partner reading.

✓ = opportunity for ongoing assessment; adjust groups accordingly

◆ English Language Learners

Level C

Before Reading Review LR *How Many Frogs?*, TE T241.

During Reading Coach rereading of book. **Fluency Check:** Have individuals reread aloud. ✓

After Reading Help children summarize LR. Have children draw/caption a picture about a book they read this week. ✓

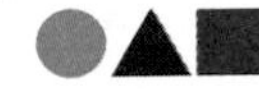 Mixed Ability Levels

Literature Circles Form small, mixed-ability groups. Ask groups to discuss the main Anthology selection, Link, Leveled Readers, and other books they have read this week. Pose questions or topics for each group, and circulate among groups to offer support. Suggested group activities:

- Respond to specific Literature Discussion questions on Blackline Master 1.
- Discuss story or text elements, authors' choice of language, and/or illustrations.
- Connect book topics or themes to personal experiences or other reading.

Writing and Language

 30-40 minutes

Writing

Practice Assign Writing Prompt, TE T231

Grammar

Review Naming Words for One or More, TE T237

Listening and Speaking

Teach Listening for Information, TE T237

Optional Resources

Teacher Read Aloud

Choose a nonfiction book related to Social Studies or Science unit.

Independent Work

Self-Selected Reading

Choose from

- classroom/school library
- Leveled Bibliography, TE T6–T7
- children's magazines
- consumer texts such as poetry books, articles about rain forest wildlife, etc.

Centers

- Classroom Management Kit
- Classroom Management activities, TE T178–T179
- Responding activities, TE T216–T217

Differentiated Instruction

- High-Frequency Words Review, TE T236
- Comprehension Review: Making Predictions, TE T232

Assessment

End-of-Week Assessment

- Weekly Skills Tests for Theme 6, Week 3
- Fluency Assessment, *Jay's Trip,* PL Theme 6, pp. 37–40, TE T233–T235
- Alternative Assessment, Teacher's Resource Blackline Master 84

End-of-Theme Assessment

- Integrated Theme Tests for Theme 6

TE = Teacher Edition; PB = Practice Book; Tr = Transparency; LR = Leveled Reader; PL = Phonics Library; VR = Vocabulary Reader; VR Guide = Vocabulary Readers Teacher's Manual; LBB = Little Big Book; TP = Theme Paperback

Theme 7 Overview

	Week 1
Reading and Comprehension	**Shared Reading** Main Selection: *That Toad Is Mine!* Poetry Link: Poems Book Share **Comprehension** Strategy: Summarize Skill: Problem Solving Content Skill: How to Read Poetry
Word Work	**Phonemic Awareness:** Segment Phonemes **Phonics:** Vowel Pairs *oa* and *ow* **Phonics Review:** Vowel Pairs *ai, ay* **Vocabulary:** Categorizing; Friendship Words **High-Frequency Words:** *again, both, gone, hard, or, turn, want* **Spelling:** More Long *o* Spellings
Options for Guided Reading	**Vocabulary Reader** *Friends Share* **Leveled Readers:** Extra Support: *The Bike Trip* On Level: *The Best Class Trip* Above Level: *The Endless Puzzle* ELL: *The Bike Ride* **Phonics Library** *Pet Show* *Nick Is Sick* *Don's Boat* **Theme Paperbacks** **Literature Circles**
Writing and Oral Language	**Shared Writing:** An Opinion **Interactive Writing:** An Opinion **Independent Writing:** Writing Clearly with Naming Words **Grammar:** Proper Nouns for People and Animals **Listening and Speaking:** Conflict Resolution
Assessment Options	• Weekly Skills Test for Theme 7, Week 1 • Fluency Assessment: Phonics Library

- Use **Launching the Theme** on pages T16–T17 of the Teacher's Edition to introduce the theme.
- Use the **Focus on Genre** section to help children explore the unique characteristics of plays.

Week 2

Shared Reading
Main Selection: *Lost!*
Social Studies Link: "On the Move"
Book Share

Comprehension
Strategy: Monitor/Clarify
Skill: Sequence of Events
Content Skill: How to Read a Diagram

Phonemic Awareness: Segment Phonemes
Phonics: The /o͝o/ Sound for *oo*
Phonics: Compound Words
Phonics Review: Vowel Pairs *oa* and *ow*
Vocabulary: Multiple-Meaning Words; City Words
High-Frequency Words: *afraid, any, bear, follow, idea, most, tall, water*
Spelling Instruction: The Vowel Sound in *book*

Vocabulary Reader
A Visit to the City

Leveled Readers:
Extra Support: *Cupcakes*
On Level: *A Walk in the Woods*
Above Level: *Breakfast for Bears*
ELL: *Pig's Tall Hat*

Phonics Library
Chan's Gift
Ann Can't Sleep
Rick and Dad Go Camping

Literature Circles

Shared Writing: A Description
Interactive Writing: A Description
Independent Writing: Writing a Message
Grammar: Proper Nouns for Places and Things
Viewing: Environmental Print

- Weekly Skills Test for Theme 7, Week 2
- Fluency Assessment: Phonics Library

Week 3

Shared Reading
Main Selection: *If You Give a Pig a Pancake*
Health Link: "Blueberry Pancakes"
Book Share

Comprehension
Strategy: Question
Skill: Fantasy and Realism
Content Skill: How to Read a Recipe

Phonemic Awareness: Segment Phonemes
Phonics: Vowel Pairs *oo, ew, ue, ou, u, u_e* (/o͞o/)
Phonics: Long *i* (*ie, igh*)
Phonics Review: The /o͝o/ Sound for *oo*
Vocabulary: Syllabication; House Words
High-Frequency Words: *build, old, piece, shoe, start, under, very, wear*
Spelling: The Vowel Sound in *moon*

Vocabulary Reader
My Dog

Leveled Readers:
Extra Support: *Under a Full Moon*
On Level: *If You Miss Your Bus*
Above Level: *The Blue Kangaroo*
ELL: *Good Night!*

Phonics Library
Clues from Boots
Lou's Tooth
A Clean Room

Literature Circles

Shared Writing: A Class Poem
Interactive Writing: A Class Poem
Independent Writing: Writing an Invitation
Grammar: Pronouns
Listening and Speaking: Conversation

- Weekly Skills Test, Theme 7, Week 3
- Fluency Assessment: Phonics Library

Day 1 Balanced Literacy Plan

Teacher Notes

Reading and Comprehension

20-30 minutes

Shared Reading of Daily Message, TE T28

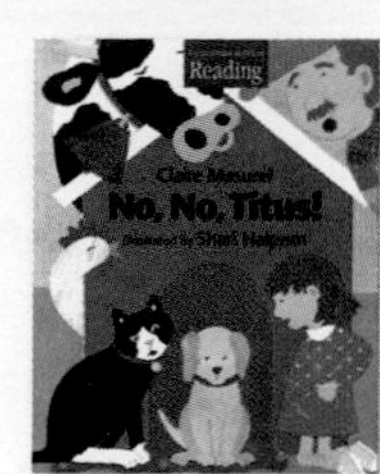

Shared Reading of Big Book

- Read aloud *No, No, Titus!*, TE T17, R2.
- Model fluent reading; discuss the story.

Word Work

25-40 minutes

Phonemic Awareness/Phonics Instruction

Teach Substituting Phonemes, TE T29, T32

Teach Vowel Pairs *oa* and *ow*, TE T32–T34

Practice Assign PB 103–104.

Spelling Instruction: More Long *o* Spellings (*oa, ow*)

Pretest and Teach Spelling Principle, TE T38

Practice Take-Home Spelling Word List, PB 311

boat slow coat grow show toad

Challenge: coast, know

Vocabulary Instruction

Teach Words with Long *o* Spelled *ow*, TE T38

Options for Guided Reading

80-100 minutes

Extra Support

Before Reading Preview *Pet Show*, PL Theme 7, pp. 5–11. Model Phonics/Decoding Strategy. See TE T35–T37.

During Reading Coach as children read story.

After Reading Discuss story; have children find/read words with *oa, ow.* **Fluency Modeling:** Model fluent reading. Have partners reread story.

✓ = opportunity for ongoing assessment; adjust groups accordingly

 **On Level**

Before Reading Preview *Pet Show,* PL Theme 7 pp. 5–11, and review TE T35–T37.

During Reading Have children begin story. **Fluency Modeling:** Model Phonics/Decoding Strategy and fluent reading.

After Reading Have children retell story so far and find/read words with *oa, ow.* **Fluency Practice:** Have partners finish story and reread for fluency.

Level J

 **Above Level**

Before Reading Preview LR *The Endless Puzzle,* TE T86.

During Reading Have children read first half of story. **Fluency Modeling:** Model fluent reading.

After Reading Have children finish reading and write answers to Responding questions. ✓

◆ **English Language Learners**

Before Reading Preview VR *Friends Share.* See VR Guide, p. 24.

During Reading **Fluency Modeling:** Read aloud each page; have children do echo reading.

After Reading Discuss Responding pages. Have children reread with partners or audio CD.

Level C

Writing and Language

25-40 minutes

Writing

Teach Shared Writing: An Opinion, TE T39

Practice Assign Writing Prompt, TE T29.

Listening and Speaking

Teach Group Discussion, TE T39

Optional Resources

Teacher Read Aloud

Reread the *Big Book: No, No, Titus!,* TE T17, R2.

Read *Tops and Bottoms,* TE T30–T31.

Independent Work

Self-Selected Reading

Choose from

- classroom/school library
- Leveled Bibliography, TE T6–T7
- *I Love Reading,* Theme 7, take-home books 64–65
- Little Readers for Guided Reading

Centers

- Classroom Management Kit
- Classroom Management activities, TE T26–T27

Differentiated Instruction

- Phonics Reteaching or Extension: Vowel Pairs *oa, ow,* TE R12–R13
- High-Frequency Words Review: Word Wall, TE T28

TE = Teacher Edition; PB = Practice Book; Tr = Transparency; LR = Leveled Reader; PL = Phonics Library; VR = Vocabulary Reader; VR Guide = Vocabulary Readers Teacher's Manual; LBB = Little Big Book; TP = Theme Paperback

Day 2 Balanced Literacy Plan

Teacher Notes

Reading and Comprehension

20-30 minutes

Shared Reading of *That Toad Is Mine!* (Part 1)

▼ Anthology Selection

- Build Background and Vocabulary; Introduce Story Vocabulary, TE T44–T45, Tr 7-2

agree	crayons	hoptoad	toys	food
book/s	fault	lemonade	candy bars	share

- Introduce Comprehension Strategy and Skill:
  Summarize, TE T46
  Problem Solving, TE T46, T54
- Set Purpose, TE T47
- Read Anthology Selection pp. 18–26 (independent, partner, or audio CD).

Words to Know

again	hard
both	toad
gone	road
or	hoptoad
want	know
turn	

Word Work

25-40 minutes

Phonemic Awareness/Phonics Instruction

Teach Substituting Phonemes, TE T41

High-Frequency Words Instruction

Teach TE T42–T43, Tr 7-1; **Practice** PB 105, 107.

Spelling Instruction

Review More Long *o* Spellings (*oa, ow*), TE T58

High-Frequency Words

again	gone
or	want
both	hard
turn	

Options for Guided Reading

80-100 minutes

● **Extra Support**

Before Reading Preview VR *Friends Share,* VR Guide, p. 24.

During Reading Read the book together; coach reading. Help children apply Summarize Strategy.

After Reading Help children compare this book to *That Toad Is Mine!* **Fluency Practice:** Have children reread VR. Assign *Nick Is Sick,* PL Theme 7, pp. 13–20, for partner reading.

Level C

✓ = opportunity for ongoing assessment; adjust groups accordingly

On Level

Before Reading Discuss PL *Pet Show,* TE T36. Preview LR *The Best Class Trip,* TE T85.

During Reading Coach reading as children begin story. Have children model the Question Strategy. **Fluency Modeling:** Model fluent reading, then have children model it. ✓

After Reading Have children write answers to Responding questions. ✓ Assign *Nick Is Sick,* PL Theme 7, pp. 13–20, for partner reading.

Level F

Above Level

Before Reading Have children model the Summarize Strategy and discuss Responding questions for LR *The Endless Puzzle,* TE T86.

During Reading **Fluency Check:** Monitor children's oral reading. ✓

After Reading Have children discuss the story with a partner. Assign *Nick Is Sick,* PL Theme 7, pp. 13–20, for partner reading.

Level J

◆ English Language Learners

Before Reading To review VR vocabulary, have children demonstrate or give examples. See VR Guide, p. 24.

During Reading Model Summarize Strategy. Help children apply the Summarize Strategy. **Fluency Practice:** Have children reread book. Option: Preview and coach reading of *Pet Show,* PL Theme 7, pp. 5–11, TE T35–T37.

After Reading Help children summarize VR. Have partners discuss, draw, or write facts they learned. ✓

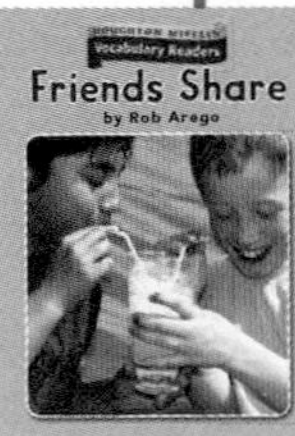

Level C

Optional Resources

Teacher Read Aloud

Reread Big Book: *No, No, Titus!* See TE T17, R2.

Independent Work

Self-Selected Reading

Choose from

- classroom/school library
- Leveled Bibliography, TE T6–T7
- *I Love Reading,* Theme 7, take-home books 64–65
- Little Readers for Guided Reading

Centers

- Classroom Management Kit
- Classroom Management activities, TE T26–T27

Differentiated Instruction

- Phonics Reteaching or Extension: Vowel Pairs *oa, ow,* TE R12–R13
- High-Frequency Words
  - Word Wall, TE T40
  - Review, TE T58
  - Reteaching or Extension, TE R22–R23

Writing and Language

25-40 minutes

Writing

Teach Interactive Writing: An Opinion, TE T59

Practice Assign Writing Prompt, TE T41.

TE = Teacher Edition; PB = Practice Book; Tr = Transparency; LR = Leveled Reader; PL = Phonics Library; VR = Vocabulary Reader; VR Guide = Vocabulary Readers Teacher's Manual; LBB = Little Big Book; TP = Theme Paperback

Day 3 Balanced Literacy Plan

Teacher Notes

Reading and Comprehension

20-30 minutes

Shared Reading of *That Toad Is Mine!* (Part 2)

▼ Anthology Selection

- Read Anthology Selection pp. 27–37 (independent, partner, or audio CD).
- Discuss Responding questions, TE T62; have children cite text to support answers.

Comprehension Skill Instruction

Teach Problem Solving, TE T64–T65, Tr 7-3

Practice Assign PB 111 or retelling of story.

Word Work

25-40 minutes

Phonemic Awareness Instruction

Teach Substituting Phonemes, TE T61

Spelling: More Long *o* Spellings (*oa, ow*)

Practice Assign PB 112 or activity, TE T66.

Vocabulary Instruction

Teach Categorizing, TE T66

Practice Assign PB 113.

Options for Guided Reading

80-100 minutes

● Extra Support

Before Reading Discuss Responding questions from VR *Friends Share.* See VR Guide, p. 24. Preview LR *The Bike Trip,* TE T84.

During Reading Coach as children read story. **Fluency Modeling:** Model fluent reading, then have children model it.

After Reading **Fluency Practice:** Have partners reread story. Have children write answers to Responding questions. ✓

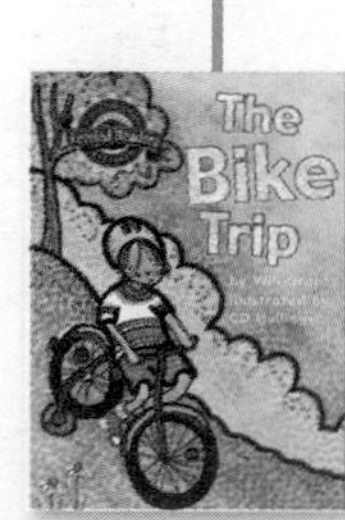

Level D

✓ = opportunity for ongoing assessment; adjust groups accordingly

▲ On Level

Before Reading Discuss Responding questions for LR *The Best Class Trip!*, TE T85.

During Reading **Fluency Check:** Ask individuals to read story aloud. ✓

After Reading Help children list the problem and solutions suggested in the LR. Complete list together.

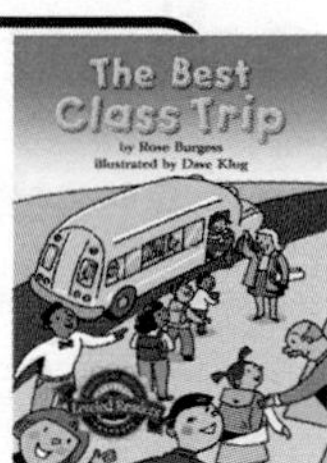

Level F

■ Above Level

Before Reading Preview TP *Busy Bea.* See TE R5.

During Reading **Fluency Modeling:** Model fluent reading, then have children model it. Have them read first half of story independently.

After Reading Ask questions; have children cite text to support answers. Help children list the problem and solutions suggested in the TP. Complete list together.

Level G

 English Language Learners

Before Reading Preview *Nick Is Sick,* PL Theme 7, pp. 13–20. Model Phonics/Decoding Strategy.

During Reading **Fluency Modeling:** Read aloud each page; have children do echo reading.

After Reading Discuss story; help children find/read words with *oa, ow.* Have children use illustrations to retell story to partners.

4 WHOLE GROUP Writing and Language

30-40 minutes

Writing

Practice Assign Write a Sign, Anthology p. 39.

Grammar

Teach Proper Nouns for People and Animals, TE T67

Practice Assign PB 114.

Optional Resources

Teacher Read Aloud

Choose a book from your class/school library or from the Leveled Bibliography, TE T6–T7.

Suggestion: *The Birthday Letters* by Charlotte Pomerantz

Independent Work

Self-Selected Reading

Choose from

- classroom/school library
- Leveled Bibliography, TE T6–T7
- *I Love Reading,* Theme 7, take-home books 64–65
- Little Readers for Guided Reading

Centers

- Classroom Management Kit
- Classroom Management activities, TE T26–T27
- Responding activities, TE T62–T63

Differentiated Instruction

- Comprehension Reteaching or Extension: Problem Solving, TE R28–R29
- High-Frequency Word Review: Word Wall, TE T60

TE = Teacher Edition; PB = Practice Book; Tr = Transparency; LR = Leveled Reader; PL = Phonics Library; VR = Vocabulary Reader; VR Guide = Vocabulary Readers Teacher's Manual; LBB = Little Big Book; TP = Theme Paperback

Day 4 Balanced Literacy Plan

Teacher Notes

1 WHOLE GROUP Reading and Comprehension 20-30 minutes

Shared Reading of Poetry Link

- Poems, Anthology pp. 40–41, TE T70–T71 (independent, partner, or group)
- Skill: How to Read Poetry, Anthology p. 40, TE T70
- Introduce Concept Vocabulary, TE T70.

Concept Vocabulary
tug
grins
giggles

2 WHOLE GROUP Word Work 25-40 minutes

Phonemic Awareness/Phonics Instruction

Teach Substituting Phonemes, TE T69

Review Vowel Pairs *ai* and *ay*, TE T72

Spelling: More Long *o* Spellings (*oa, ow*)

Practice Assign PB 115 or activity, TE T74.

Vocabulary Instruction

Teach Friendship Words, TE T74

3 SMALL GROUP Options for Guided Reading 80-100 minutes

Extra Support

Before Reading Review Responding questions for LR *The Bike Trip,* TE T84. Help children list the problem and solutions suggested in the LR.

During Reading Have children reread story. **Fluency Check:** Have individuals read aloud. ✓

After Reading Have partners complete a numbered list of problems and solutions in the LR.

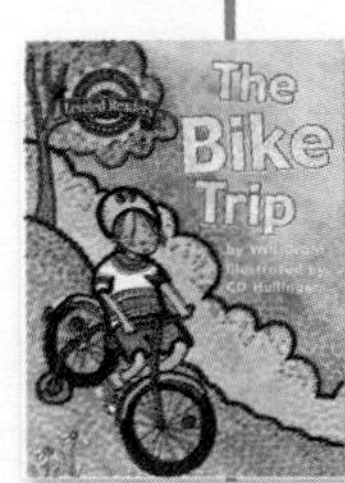

Level D

✓ = opportunity for ongoing assessment; adjust groups accordingly

 **On Level**

Before Reading Have children summarize LR *The Best Class Trip.* ✓ Preview a teacher-selected book or TP *The Puddle,* TE R4.

During Reading Have children begin story and model Phonics/Decoding Strategy.

After Reading Discuss the story so far. Have children finish story.

Level G

 **Above Level**

Before Reading Review first half of TP *Busy Bea,* TE R5. Have children make predictions about second half.

During Reading Have children finish book.

After Reading Discuss how book connects to theme. Have children write journal entries to connect it to personal experience or other reading.

Level G

 **English Language Learners**

Before Reading Build background and preview LR *The Bike Ride,* TE T87.

During Reading Read story. **Fluency Modeling:** Reread each page; have children do echo reading. Reinforce Phonics/Decoding Strategy.

After Reading Discuss Responding questions, TE T87. **Fluency Practice:** Have children reread with partners or audio CD.

Level D

Writing and Language

30-40 minutes

Writing

Teach Writing Clearly with Naming Words, TE T75

Practice Assign PB 116.

Optional Resources

Teacher Read Aloud

Continue selected Read Aloud book from Day 3 or choose a new one from your class or school library.

Independent Work

Self-Selected Reading

Choose from

- classroom/school library
- Leveled Bibliography, TE T6–T7
- children's magazines
- *I Love Reading,* Theme 7, take-home books 64–65
- Little Readers for Guided Reading

Centers

- Classroom Management Kit
- Classroom Management activities, TE T26–T27
- Responding activities, TE T62–T63

Differentiated Instruction

- Writer's Craft: Using Rhyme, TE T71
- High-Frequency Words: Word Wall, TE T68
- Study Skills: Reading a Diagram, TE R34

TE = Teacher Edition; PB = Practice Book; Tr = Transparency; LR = Leveled Reader; PL = Phonics Library; VR = Vocabulary Reader; VR Guide = Vocabulary Readers Teacher's Manual; LBB = Little Big Book; TP = Theme Paperback

Day 5 Balanced Literacy Plan

Teacher Notes

Reading and Comprehension

20-30 minutes

Book Share

Book Share

- ➤ Ask children to give examples of how they applied the comprehension skill and strategy to books they have read this week.
- ➤ Help children use genre and text features to compare and contrast what they have read.
- ➤ As a class, discuss one *how, why,* or *what if* question. See examples on Blackline Master 1 to use as a guide.

Word Work

25-40 minutes

Phonemic Awareness Instruction

Teach Substituting Phonemes, TE T77

High-Frequency Words

Cumulative Review Word Wall, TE T76

Spelling

Test See TE T82.

Options for Guided Reading

80-100 minutes

● Extra Support

Before Reading Preview *Don's Boat,* PL Theme 7, pp. 21–27. Have children find/read words with *oa, ow.* See TE T79–T81.

During Reading Have children read and model Phonics/Decoding Strategy. **Fluency Check:** Have individuals reread aloud. ✓

After Reading Have partners make connections between the story and LR *The Bike Trip.* Assign On My Way Practice Reader *Joan and Coach Snow* for partner reading.

✓ = opportunity for ongoing assessment; adjust groups accordingly

English Language Learners

Before Reading Review LR *The Bike Ride,* TE T87.

During Reading Coach rereading of book. **Fluency Check:** Have individuals reread aloud. ✓

After Reading Help children summarize LR. Have children draw/caption a picture about a book they read this week. ✓

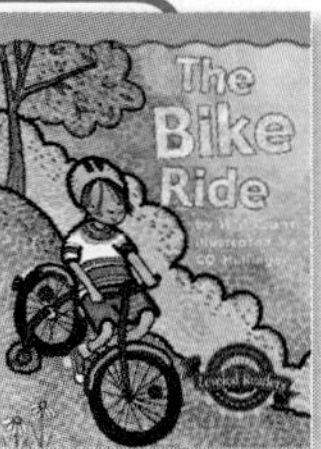

Level D

Mixed Ability Levels

Literature Circles Form small, mixed-ability groups. Ask groups to discuss the main Anthology selection, Link, Leveled Readers, and other books they have read this week. Pose questions or topics for each group, and circulate among groups to offer support. Suggested group activities:

- Respond to specific Literature Discussion questions on Blackline Master 1.
- Discuss story or text elements, authors' choice of language, and/or illustrations.
- Connect book topics or themes to personal experiences or other reading.

Writing and Language

30-40 minutes

Writing

Practice Assign Writing Prompt, TE T77.

Grammar

Review Proper Nouns for People and Animals, TE T83

Speaking and Listening

Teach Conflict Resolution, TE T83

Optional Resources

Teacher Read Aloud

Choose a nonfiction book related to Social Studies or Science unit.

Independent Work

Self-Selected Reading

Choose from

- classroom/school library
- Leveled Bibliography, TE T6–T7
- children's magazines
- consumer text such as poem anthologies or biographies about poets
- *I Love Reading,* Theme 7, take-home books 64–65
- Little Readers for Guided Reading

Centers

- Classroom Management Kit
- Classroom Management activities, TE T26–T27
- Responding activities, TE T62–T63

Differentiated Instruction

- High-Frequency Words Review: TE T82
- Comprehension Review: Problem Solving, TE T78

End-of-Week Assessment

- Weekly Skills Tests for Theme 7, Week 1
- Fluency Assessment, *Don's Boat,* PL Theme 7, pp. 21–27, TE T79–T81
- Alternative Assessment, Teacher's Resource Blackline Master 91

TE = Teacher Edition; PB = Practice Book; Tr = Transparency; LR = Leveled Reader; PL = Phonics Library; VR = Vocabulary Reader; VR Guide = Vocabulary Readers Teacher's Manual; LBB = Little Big Book; TP = Theme Paperback

Day 1 Balanced Literacy Plan

Teacher Notes

Reading and Comprehension

20-30 minutes

Shared Reading of Daily Message, TE T110

Listening Comprehension

- Read aloud *The Crow and the Pitcher,* TE T112–T113.
- Model fluent reading; discuss the story.

Word Work

25-40 minutes

Phonemic Awareness/Phonics Instruction

Teach Segmenting, Counting Phonemes, TE T111, T114

Teach The /ŏŏ/ Sound for *oo*; Compound Words, TE T114–T115, T116

Practice Assign PB 119–120, 121.

Spelling Instruction: The Vowel Sound in *book*

Pretest and Teach Spelling Principle, TE T120

Assign Take-Home Spelling Word List, PB 311

book cook foot good look took

Challenge: crook, hoof

Vocabulary Instruction

Teach Words with /ŏŏ/, TE T120

Options for Guided Reading

80-100 minutes

Extra Support

Before Reading Preview *Chan's Gift,* PL Theme 7, pp. 29–35. Model Phonics/Decoding Strategy. See TE T117–T119.

During Reading Coach as children read story.

After Reading Discuss story; have children find/read words with /ŏŏ/. **Fluency Modeling:** Model fluent reading. Have partners reread story.

✓ = opportunity for ongoing assessment; adjust groups accordingly

▲ On Level

Before Reading Preview *Chan's Gift,* PL Theme 7, pp. 29–35, and review TE T117–T119.

During Reading Have children begin story. **Fluency Modeling:** Model Phonics/Decoding Strategy and fluent reading.

After Reading Have children retell story so far and find/read words with /o͞o/. **Fluency Practice:** Have partners finish story and reread for fluency.

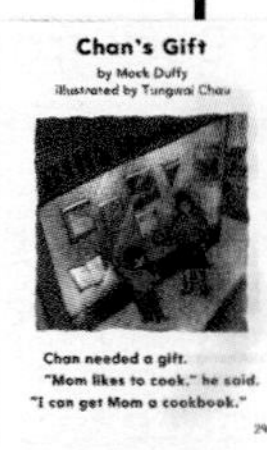

■ Above Level

Before Reading Preview LR *Breakfast for Bears,* TE T170.

During Reading Have children read first half of story. **Fluency Modeling:** Model fluent reading.

After Reading Have children finish reading and write answers to Responding questions. ✓

Level I

◆ English Language Learners

Before Reading Preview VR *A Visit to the City.* See VR Guide, p. 25.

During Reading **Fluency Modeling:** Read aloud each page; have children do echo reading.

After Reading Discuss Responding pages. Have children reread with partners or audio CD.

Level D

4 WHOLE GROUP

Writing and Language

25-40 minutes

Writing

Teach Shared Writing: A Description, TE T121

Practice Assign Writing Prompt, TE T111.

Listening and Speaking

Teach Reader's Theater, TE T121

Optional Resources

Teacher Read Aloud

Reread *The Crow and the Pitcher,* TE T112–T113.

Independent Work

Self-Selected Reading

Choose from
- classroom/school library
- Leveled Bibliography, TE T6–T7
- *I Love Reading,* Theme 7, take-home book 66
- Little Readers for Guided Reading

Centers
- Classroom Management Kit
- Classroom Management activities, TE T108–T109

Differentiated Instruction

- Phonics Reteaching or Extension: The Sound /o͞o/ for *oo*, TE R14–R15
- Phonics Reteaching or Extension: Compound Words, TE R16–R17
- High-Frequency Words Review: Word Wall, TE T110

TE = Teacher Edition; PB = Practice Book; Tr = Transparency; LR = Leveled Reader; PL = Phonics Library; VR = Vocabulary Reader; VR Guide = Vocabulary Readers Teacher's Manual; LBB = Little Big Book; TP = Theme Paperback

Day 2 Balanced Literacy Plan

Teacher Notes

Reading and Comprehension

20-30 minutes

Shared Reading of *Lost!* (Part 1)

- Build Background and Vocabulary; Introduce Story Vocabulary, TE T126–T127, Tr 7-6

building/s	disappears	friendly	park	worry
city	elevator	library	scare	

- Introduce Comprehension Strategy and Skill: Monitor/Clarify, TE T128
  Sequence of Events, TE T128, T134
- Set Purpose, TE T129
- Read Anthology Selection pp. 48–62 (independent, partner, or audio CD).

▼ Anthology Selection

Lost! David McPhail

Words to Know

afraid	inside
idea	someone
any	books
most	look/s
bear	good
tall	outside
follow	good-bye
water	playground
anything	

Word Work

25-40 minutes

Phonemic Awareness/Phonics Instruction

Teach Substituting Phonemes, TE T123

High-Frequency Words Instruction

Teach TE T124–T125, Tr 7-5

Practice Assign PB 122–123.

Spelling Instruction

Review The Vowel Sound in *book*, TE T142

High-Frequency Words

afraid	bear
idea	tall
any	follow
most	water

Options for Guided Reading

80-100 minutes

Extra Support

Before Reading Preview VR *A Visit to the City.* See VR Guide, p. 25.

During Reading Read the book together; coach reading. Help children apply Monitor/Clarify Strategy.

After Reading Help children compare this book to *Lost!* **Fluency Practice:** Have children reread VR. Assign *Ann Can't Sleep,* PL Theme 7, pp. 37–44, for partner reading.

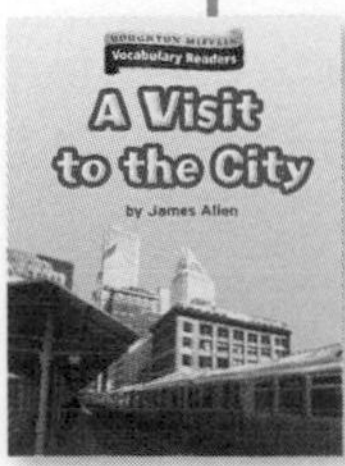

Level D

✓ = opportunity for ongoing assessment; adjust groups accordingly

▲ On Level

Before Reading Discuss PL *Chan's Gift,* TE T118. Preview LR *A Walk in the Woods,* TE T169.

During Reading Coach reading as children begin story. Have children model the Monitor/Clarify Strategy. **Fluency Modeling:** Model fluent reading, then have children model it. ✓

After Reading Have children finish reading and write answers to Responding questions. ✓ Assign *Ann Can't Sleep,* PL Theme 7, pp. 37–43, for partner reading.

Level F

■ Above Level

Before Reading Have children model the Monitor/Clarify Strategy and discuss Responding questions for LR *Breakfast for Bears,* TE T170.

During Reading **Fluency Check:** Monitor children's oral reading. ✓

After Reading Have children discuss the story with a partner. Assign *Ann Can't Sleep,* PL Theme 7, pp. 37–43, for partner reading.

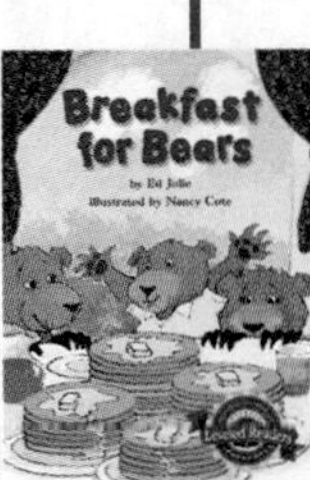

Level I

◆ English Language Learners

Before Reading To review VR vocabulary, have children demonstrate or give examples. See VR Guide, p. 25.

During Reading Model Monitor/Clarify Strategy. Help children apply the Monitor/Clarify Strategy. **Fluency Practice:** Have children reread book. Option: Preview and coach reading of *Chan's Gift,* PL Theme 7, pp. 29–35, TE T117–T119.

After Reading Help children summarize VR. Have partners discuss, draw, or write facts they learned. ✓

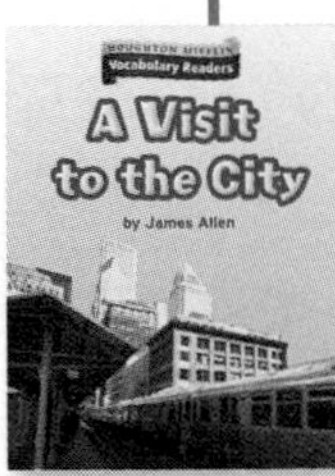

Level D

4 WHOLE GROUP Writing and Language

25-40 minutes

Writing

Teach Interactive Writing: A Description, TE T143

Practice Assign Writing Prompt, TE T123.

Optional Resources

Teacher Read Aloud

Suggestion: *Snail Started It!* by Katja Reider

Independent Work

Self-Selected Reading

Choose from

- classroom/school library
- Leveled Bibliography, TE T6–T7
- *I Love Reading,* Theme 7, take-home book 66
- Little Readers for Guided Reading

Centers

- Classroom Management Kit
- Classroom Management activities, TE T108–T109

Differentiated Instruction

- High-Frequency Words
  - Word Wall, TE T122
  - Review, TE T142
  - Reteaching or Extension, TE R24–R25

TE = Teacher Edition; PB = Practice Book; Tr = Transparency; LR = Leveled Reader; PL = Phonics Library; VR = Vocabulary Reader; VR Guide = Vocabulary Readers Teacher's Manual; LBB = Little Big Book; TP = Theme Paperback

Day 3 Balanced Literacy Plan

Teacher Notes

Reading and Comprehension

20-30 minutes

Shared Reading of *Lost!* (Part 2)

- Read Anthology Selection pp. 63–69 (independent, partner, or audio CD).
- Discuss Responding questions, TE T146; have children cite text to support answers.

▼ Anthology Selection

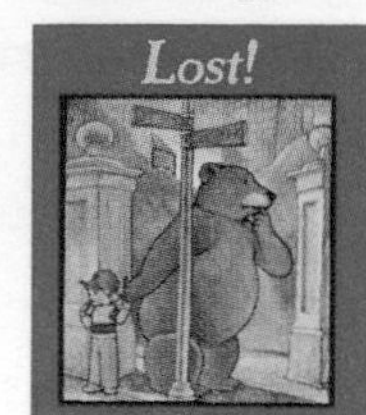

Comprehension Skill Instruction

Teach Sequence of Events, TE T148–T149, Tr 7-7

Practice Assign PB 126 or retelling of story.

Word Work

25-40 minutes

Phonemic Awareness Instruction

Teach Substituting Phonemes, TE T145

Spelling: The Vowel Sound in *book*

Practice Assign PB 127 or activity, TE T150.

Vocabulary Instruction

Teach Multiple-Meaning Words, TE T150

Practice Assign PB 128.

Options for Guided Reading

80-100 minutes

Extra Support

Before Reading Discuss Responding questions from VR *A Visit to the City.* See VR Guide, p. 25. Preview LR *Cupcakes,* TE T168.

During Reading Coach as children read story. **Fluency Modeling:** Model fluent reading, then have children model it.

After Reading **Fluency Practice:** Have partners reread story. Have children write answers to Responding questions. ✓

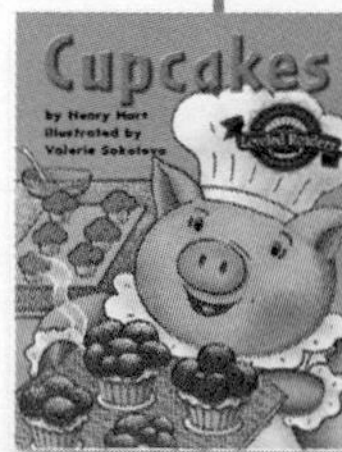

Level E

✓ = opportunity for ongoing assessment; adjust groups accordingly

▲ On Level

Before Reading Discuss Responding questions for LR *A Walk in the Woods,* TE T169.

During Reading **Fluency Check:** Ask individuals to read story aloud. ✓

After Reading Create a Sequence of Events Chart; see TE T148 or Tr 7-7 for format. Help children describe the sequence of events in their LR. Complete the chart together.

Level F

■ Above Level

Before Reading Preview teacher-selected book such as *The Stubborn Pumpkin,* TE R8.

During Reading **Fluency Modeling:** Model fluent reading, then have children model it. Have them read first half of story independently.

After Reading Ask questions; have children cite text to support answers. Create a Sequence of Events Chart; see TE T148 or Tr 7-7 for format. Help children describe the sequence of events in the selected book. Complete the chart together.

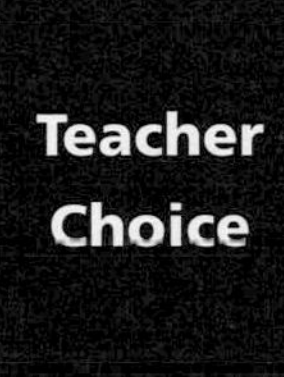

◆ English Language Learners

Before Reading Preview *Ann Can't Sleep,* PL Theme 7, pp. 37–44. Model Phonics/Decoding Strategy.

During Reading **Fluency Modeling:** Read aloud each page; have children do echo reading.

After Reading Discuss story; help children find/read words with /o͞o/. Have children use illustrations to retell story to partners.

4 WHOLE GROUP

Writing and Language

30-40 minutes

Writing

Practice Assign Write a Journal Entry, Anthology p. 71.

Grammar

Teach Proper Nouns for Places and Things, TE T151

Practice Assign PB 129.

Optional Resources

Teacher Read Aloud

Continue selected Read Aloud book from Day 2 or choose a new one from your class or school library.

Independent Work

Self-Selected Reading

Choose from

- classroom/school library
- Leveled Bibliography, TE T6–T7
- *I Love Reading,* Theme 7, take-home book 66
- Little Readers for Guided Reading

Centers

- Classroom Management Kit
- Classroom Management activities, TE T108–T109
- Responding activities, TE T146–T147

Differentiated Instruction

- High-Frequency Word Review: Word Wall, TE T144

TE = Teacher Edition; PB = Practice Book; Tr = Transparency; LR = Leveled Reader; PL = Phonics Library; VR = Vocabulary Reader; VR Guide = Vocabulary Readers Teacher's Manual; LBB = Little Big Book; TP = Theme Paperback

Day 4 Balanced Literacy Plan

Teacher Notes

Reading and Comprehension

20-30 minutes

Shared Reading of Social Studies Link

- "On the Move," Anthology pp. 72–75, TE T154–T155 (independent, partner, or group)
- Skill: How to Read a Diagram, Anthology p. 72, TE T154
- Introduce Concept Vocabulary, TE T154.

Concept Vocabulary

space shuttle
airplane
bicycle
train

Word Work

25-40 minutes

Phonemic Awareness/Phonics Instruction

Teach Substituting Phonemes, TE T153

Review Vowel Pairs *oa* and *ow,* TE T156–T157

Spelling: The Vowel Sound in *book*

Practice Assign PB 130 or activity, TE T158.

Vocabulary Instruction

Teach City Words, TE T158

3
SMALL
GROUP

Options for Guided Reading

80-100 minutes

Extra Support

Before Reading Review Responding questions for LR *Cupcakes,* TE T168. Begin a Sequence of Events Chart; see TE T148 or Tr 7-7. Help children describe the sequence of events in the LR.

During Reading Have children reread story. **Fluency Check:** Have individuals read aloud. ✓

After Reading Work with children to complete the Sequence of Events Chart. Have partners discuss the sequence of events.

Level E

✓ = opportunity for ongoing assessment; adjust groups accordingly

▲ On Level

Before Reading Have children summarize LR *A Walk in the Woods.* ✓ Preview a teacher-selected book such as *Inch by Inch,* TE R7.

During Reading Have children begin story and model Phonics/Decoding Strategy.

After Reading Discuss the story so far. Have children finish story.

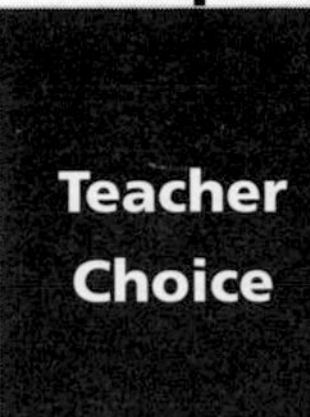

■ Above Level

Before Reading Review first half of TP *The Stubborn Pumpkin,* TE R8. Have children make predictions about second half.

During Reading Have children finish book.

After Reading Discuss how book connects to theme. Have children write journal entries to connect it to personal experience or other reading.

 English Language Learners

Before Reading Build background and preview LR *Pig's Tall Hat,* TE T171.

During Reading Read story. **Fluency Modeling:** Reread each page; have children do echo reading. Reinforce Phonics/Decoding Strategy.

After Reading Discuss Responding questions, TE T171. **Fluency Practice:** Have children reread with partners or audio CD.

Level E

Writing and Language

30-40 minutes

Writing

Teach Writing a Message, TE T159 **Practice** Assign PB 131.

Optional Resources

Teacher Read Aloud

Choose a new book from your class or school library.

Independent Work

Self-Selected Reading

Choose from
- classroom/school library
- Leveled Bibliography, TE T6–T7
- children's magazines
- *I Love Reading,* Theme 7, take-home book 66
- Little Readers for Guided Reading

Centers
- Classroom Management Kit
- Classroom Management activities, TE T108–T109
- Responding activities, TE T146–T147

Differentiated Instruction
- Visual Literacy: Recognizing Signs, TE T155
- High-Frequency Words: Word Wall, TE T152
- Study Skills: Reading a Diagram, TE R34

TE = Teacher Edition; PB = Practice Book; Tr = Transparency; LR = Leveled Reader; PL = Phonics Library; VR = Vocabulary Reader; VR Guide = Vocabulary Readers Teacher's Manual; LBB = Little Big Book; TP = Theme Paperback

Day 5 Balanced Literacy Plan

Teacher Notes

Reading and Comprehension

20-30 minutes

Book Share

Book Share

- Ask children to give examples of how they applied the comprehension skill and strategy to books they have read this week.
- Help children use genre and text features to compare and contrast what they have read.
- As a class, discuss one *how, why,* or *what if* question. See examples on Blackline Master 1 to use as a guide.

Word Work

25-40 minutes

Phonemic Awareness Instruction

Teach Phoneme Substitution, TE T161

High-Frequency Words

Cumulative Review Word Wall, TE T160

Spelling

Test See TE T166.

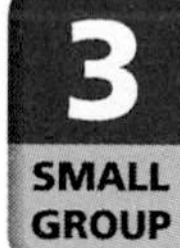

Options for Guided Reading

80-100 minutes

Extra Support

Before Reading Preview *Rick and Dad Go Camping,* PL Theme 7, pp. 45–51. Have children find/read words with /o͞o/, compound words. See TE T163–T165.

During Reading Have children read and model Phonics/Decoding Strategy. **Fluency Check:** Have individuals reread aloud. ✓

After Reading Have partners make connections between the story and LR *Cupcakes.* Assign On My Way Practice Reader *Nell's First Day Kit* for partner reading.

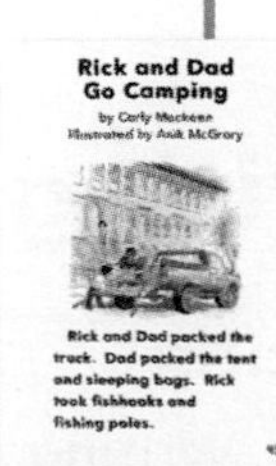

✓ = opportunity for ongoing assessment; adjust groups accordingly

◆ English Language Learners

Before Reading Review LR *Pig's Tall Hat,* TE T171.

During Reading Coach rereading of book. **Fluency Check:** Have individuals reread aloud. ✓

After Reading Help children summarize LR. Have children draw/caption a picture about a book they read this week. ✓

Level E

●▲■◆ Mixed Ability Levels

Literature Circles Form small, mixed-ability groups. Ask groups to discuss the main Anthology selection, Link, Leveled Readers, and other books they have read this week. Pose questions or topics for each group, and circulate among groups to offer support. Suggested group activities:

- Respond to specific Literature Discussion questions on Blackline Master 1.
- Discuss story or text elements, authors' choice of language, and/or illustrations.
- Connect book topics or themes to personal experiences or other reading.

Writing and Language

30-40 minutes

Writing

Practice Assign Writing Prompt, TE T161.

Grammar

Review Proper Nouns for Places and Things, TE T167

Viewing

Teach Environmental Print, TE T167

Optional Resources

Teacher Read Aloud

Choose a nonfiction book related to Social Studies or Science unit.

Independent Work

Self-Selected Reading

Choose from

- classroom/school library
- Leveled Bibliography, TE T6–T7
- children's magazines
- consumer text such as books about transportation, books about technology, etc.
- *I Love Reading,* Theme 7, take-home book 66
- Little Readers for Guided Reading

Centers

- Classroom Management Kit
- Classroom Management activities, TE T108–T109
- Responding activities, TE T146–T147

Differentiated Instruction

- High-Frequency Words Review, TE T166
- Comprehension Review: Sequence of Events, TE T162

End-of-Week Assessment

- Weekly Skills Tests for Theme 7, Week 2
- Fluency Assessment, *Rick and Dad Go Camping,* PL Theme 7, pp. 45–51, TE T163–T165
- Alternative Assessment, Teacher's Resource Blackline Master 94

TE = Teacher Edition; PB = Practice Book; Tr = Transparency; LR = Leveled Reader; PL = Phonics Library; VR = Vocabulary Reader; VR Guide = Vocabulary Readers Teacher's Manual; LBB = Little Big Book; TP = Theme Paperback

Day 1 Balanced Literacy Plan

Teacher Notes

Reading and Comprehension

Shared Reading of Daily Message, TE T182

Listening Comprehension

- Read aloud *The Grasshopper and the Ant,* TE T184–T185.
- Model fluent reading; discuss the story.

Word Work

Phonemic Awareness/Phonics Instruction

Teach Phoneme Substitution, TE T183, T186

Teach Vowels *oo, ew, ue, ou, u, u_e* (/o͞o/); Long *i (ie, igh),* TE T186–T187, T188

Practice Assign PB 132–133, 134.

Spelling Instruction: The Vowel Sound in *moon*

Pretest and Teach Spelling Principle, TE T192

Practice Take-Home Spelling Word List, PB 313

food moon room soon too zoo

Challenge: balloon, moose

Vocabulary Instruction

Teach Words with *igh,* TE T192

Options for Guided Reading

80-100 minutes

Extra Support

Before Reading Preview *Clues from Boots,* PL Theme 7, pp. 53–59. Model Phonics/Decoding Strategy. See TE T189–T191.

During Reading Coach as children read story.

After Reading Discuss story; have children find/read words with /o͞o/ *(oo, ew, ue, ou)* and long *i (ie, igh).*
Fluency Modeling: Model fluent reading. Have partners reread story.

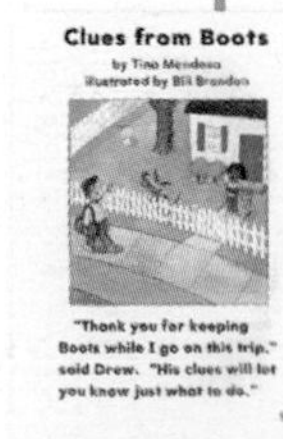

✓ = opportunity for ongoing assessment; adjust groups accordingly

▲ On Level

Before Reading Preview *Clues from Boots,* PL Theme 7, pp. 53–59, and review TE T189–T191.

During Reading Have children begin story. **Fluency Modeling:** Model Phonics/Decoding Strategy and fluent reading.

After Reading Have children retell story so far and find/read words with /o͞o/ *(oo, ew, ue, ou)* and long *i (ie, igh)*. **Fluency Practice:** Have partners finish story and reread for fluency.

■ Above Level

Before Reading Preview LR *The Blue Kangaroo,* TE T242.

During Reading Have children read first half of story. **Fluency Modeling:** Model fluent reading.

After Reading Have children finish reading and write answers to Responding questions. ✓

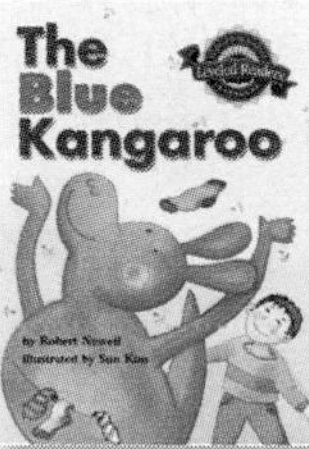

Level H

◆ English Language Learners

Before Reading Preview VR *My Dog.* See VR Guide, p. 26.

During Reading **Fluency Modeling:** Read aloud each page; have children do echo reading.

After Reading Discuss Responding pages. Have children reread with partners or audio CD.

Level C

4 WHOLE GROUP Writing and Language

25-40 minutes

Writing

Teach Shared Writing: A Class Poem, TE T193

Practice Assign Writing Prompt, TE T183.

Listening and Speaking

Teach Retell a Story, TE T193

Optional Resources

Teacher Read Aloud

Reread *The Grasshopper and the Ant,* TE T184–T185.

Independent Work

Self-Selected Reading

Choose from

- classroom/school library
- Leveled Bibliography, TE T6–T7
- *I Love Reading,* Theme 7, take-home books 53, 67–70, 71–72
- Little Readers for Guided Reading

Centers

- Classroom Management Kit
- Classroom Management activities, TE T180–T181

Differentiated Instruction

- Phonics Reteaching or Extension: Vowel Pairs *oo, ew, ue, ou, u, u_e* (/o͞o/), TE R18–R19
- Phonics Reteaching or Extension: Long *i (igh, ie),* TE R20–R21
- High-Frequency Words Review: Word Wall, TE T182

TE = Teacher Edition; PB = Practice Book; Tr = Transparency; LR = Leveled Reader; PL = Phonics Library; VR = Vocabulary Reader; VR Guide = Vocabulary Readers Teacher's Manual; LBB = Little Big Book; TP = Theme Paperback

Day 2 Balanced Literacy Plan

Teacher Notes

Reading and Comprehension

20-30 minutes

Shared Reading of *If You Give a Pig a Pancake* (Part 1)

➤ Build Background and Vocabulary; Introduce Story Vocabulary, TE T198–T199, Tr 7-10

born	closet	maple syrup	piano	remind
bubbles	favorite	music	probably	

➤ Introduce Comprehension Strategy and Skill:
Question, TE T200
Fantasy and Realism, TE T200, T206

➤ Set Purpose, TE T201

➤ Read Anthology Selection pp. 80–94 (independent, partner, or audio CD).

▼ Anthology Selection

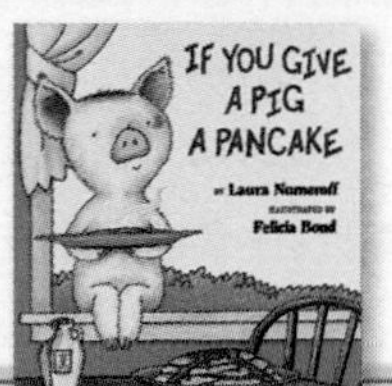

Words to Know

old	build
piece	you
shoes	too
start	through
under	glue
very	might
wear	

Word Work

25-40 minutes

Phonemic Awareness/Phonics Instruction

Teach Phoneme Substitution, TE T195

High-Frequency Words Instruction

Teach TE T196–T197, Tr 7-9; **Practice** PB 135, 137.

High-Frequency Words

build	piece
start	very
old	shoes
under	wear

Spelling Instruction

Review The Vowel Sound in *moon*, TE T214

Options for Guided Reading

80-100 minutes

SMALL GROUP

Extra Support

Before Reading Preview VR *My Dog.* See VR Guide, p. 26.

During Reading Read the book together; coach reading. Help children apply Question Strategy.

After Reading Help children compare this book to *If You Give a Pig a Pancake.* **Fluency Practice:** Have children reread VR. Assign *Lou's Tooth,* PL Theme 7, pp. 61–68, for partner reading.

Level C

✓ = opportunity for ongoing assessment; adjust groups accordingly

▲ On Level

Before Reading Discuss PL *Clues from Boots,* TE T190. Preview LR *If You Miss Your Bus,* TE T241.

During Reading Coach reading as children begin story. Have children model the Question Strategy. **Fluency Modeling:** Model fluent reading; have children model.

After Reading Have children finish reading and write answers to Responding questions. ✓ Assign *Lou's Tooth,* PL Theme 7, pp. 61–68, for partner reading.

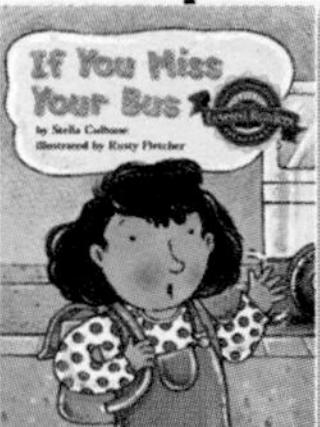

Level F

■ Above Level

Before Reading Have children model the Question Strategy and discuss Responding questions for LR *The Blue Kangaroo,* TE T242.

During Reading **Fluency Check:** Monitor children's oral reading. ✓

After Reading Have children discuss the story with a partner. Assign *Lou's Tooth,* PL Theme 7, pp. 61–68, for partner reading.

Level H

 English Language Learners

Before Reading To review VR vocabulary, have children demonstrate or give examples. See VR Guide, p. 26.

During Reading Model Question Strategy. Help children apply the Question Strategy. **Fluency Practice:** Have children reread book. Option: Preview and coach reading of *Clues from Boots,* PL Theme 7, pp. 53–59, TE T189–T191.

After Reading Help children summarize VR. Have partners discuss, draw, or write facts they learned. ✓

Level C

Writing and Language

 25-40 minutes

Writing

Teach Interactive Writing: A Class Poem, TE T215

Practice Assign Writing Prompt, TE T195.

Optional Resources

Teacher Read Aloud

Choose a book from your class/school library or from the Leveled Bibliography, TE T6–T7.

Suggestion: *One Fine Day* by Nonny Hogrogian

Independent Work

Self-Selected Reading

Choose from

- classroom/school library
- Leveled Bibliography, TE T6–T7
- *I Love Reading,* Theme 7, take-home books 53, 67–70, 71–72
- Little Readers for Guided Reading

Centers

- Classroom Management Kit
- Classroom Management activities, TE T180–T181

Differentiated Instruction

- Phonics Reteaching or Extension: Vowel Pairs *oo, ew, ue, ou, u, u_e* (/o͞o/), TE R18–R19
- Phonics Reteaching or Extension: Long *i (igh, ie)*, TE R20–R21
- High-Frequency Words
  - Word Wall, TE T194
  - Review, TE T214
  - Reteaching or Extension, TE R26–R27

TE = Teacher Edition; PB = Practice Book; Tr = Transparency; LR = Leveled Reader; PL = Phonics Library; VR = Vocabulary Reader; VR Guide = Vocabulary Readers Teacher's Manual; LBB = Little Big Book; TP = Theme Paperback

Day 3 Balanced Literacy Plan

Teacher Notes

Reading and Comprehension

20-30 minutes

▼ Anthology Selection

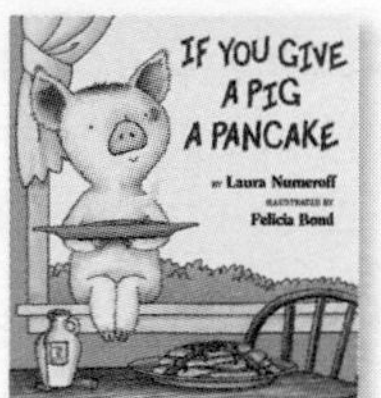

Shared Reading of *If You Give a Pig a Pancake* (Part 2)

- Read Anthology Selection pp. 95–103 (independent, partner, or audio CD).
- Discuss Responding questions, TE T218; have children cite text to support answers.

Comprehension Skill Instruction

Teach Fantasy and Realism, TE T220–T221

Practice Assign PB 140 or retelling of story.

Word Work

25-40 minutes

Phonemic Awareness Instruction

Teach Phoneme Substitution, TE T217

Spelling: The Vowel Sound in *moon*

Practice Assign PB 141 or activity, TE T222.

Vocabulary Instruction

Teach Syllabication, TE T222

Practice Assign PB 142.

Options for Guided Reading

80-100 minutes

Extra Support

Before Reading Discuss Responding questions from VR *My Dog.* See VR Guide, p. 26. Preview LR *Under a Full Moon,* TE T240.

During Reading Coach as children read story. **Fluency Modeling:** Model fluent reading, then have children model it.

After Reading **Fluency Practice:** Have partners reread story. Have children write answers to Responding questions. ✓

Level D

✓ = opportunity for ongoing assessment; adjust groups accordingly

 On Level

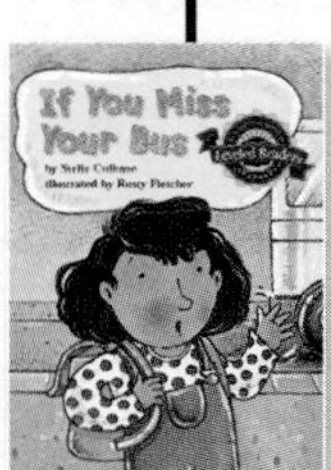

Level F

Before Reading Discuss Responding questions for LR *If You Miss Your Bus,* TE T241.

During Reading **Fluency Check:** Ask individuals to read story aloud. ✓

After Reading Make a two-column chart and have children suggest events that are real and make-believe in the LR. Complete chart together.

 Above Level

Before Reading Preview a teacher-selected book such as *Yoko,* TE R11.

During Reading **Fluency Modeling:** Model fluent reading, then have children model it. Have them read first half of story independently.

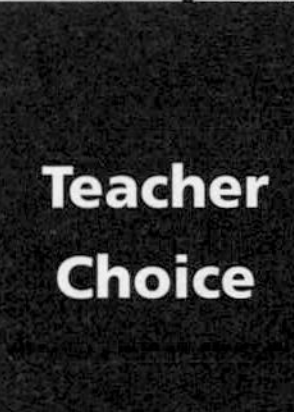

After Reading Ask questions; have children cite text to support answers. Make a two-column chart and have children suggest events that are real and make-believe in the LR. Complete chart together.

 English Language Learners

Before Reading Preview *Lou's Tooth,* PL Theme 7, pp. 61–68. Model Phonics/Decoding Strategy.

During Reading **Fluency Modeling:** Read aloud each page; have children do echo reading.

After Reading Discuss story; help children find/read words with /o͞o/ *(oo, ew, ue, ou)* and long *i (ie, igh).* Have children use illustrations to retell story to partners.

Writing and Language  30-40 minutes

Writing

Practice Assign Write a Story, Anthology p. 105.

Grammar

Teach Pronouns, TE T223

Practice Assign PB 143.

Optional Resources

Teacher Read Aloud

Continue selected Read Aloud from Day 2 or choose a new one from your class or school library.

Independent Work

Self-Selected Reading

Choose from

- classroom/school library
- Leveled Bibliography, TE T6–T7
- *I Love Reading,* Theme 7, take-home books 53, 67–70, 71–72
- Little Readers for Guided Reading

Centers

- Classroom Management Kit
- Classroom Management activities, TE T180–T181
- Responding activities, TE T218–T219

Differentiated Instruction

- Comprehension Reteaching or Extension: Vowel Pairs *oo, ew, ue, ou, u, u_e* (/o͞o/), TE R18–R19
- Comprehension Reteaching or Extension: Long *i (igh, ie),* TE R20–R21
- High-Frequency Word Review: Word Wall, TE T216

TE = Teacher Edition; PB = Practice Book; Tr = Transparency; LR = Leveled Reader; PL = Phonics Library; VR = Vocabulary Reader; VR Guide = Vocabulary Readers Teacher's Manual; LBB = Little Big Book; TP = Theme Paperback

Day 4 Balanced Literacy Plan

Teacher Notes

Reading and Comprehension

20-30 minutes

Shared Reading of Health Link

- "Blueberry Pancakes," Anthology pp. 106–109, TE T226–T227 (independent, partner, or group)
- Skill: How to Read a Recipe, Anthology p. 106, TE T226
- Introduce Concept Vocabulary, TE T226.

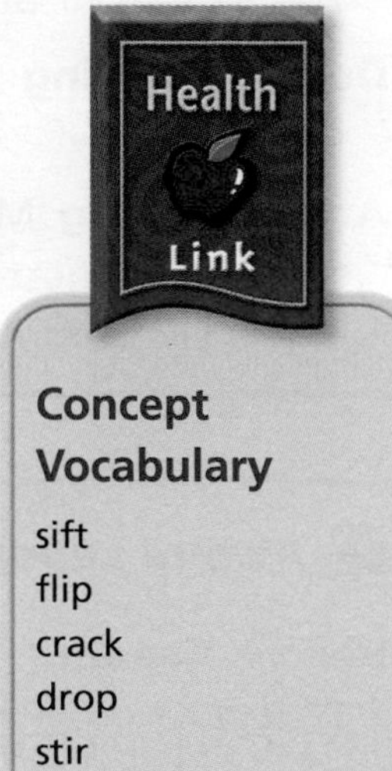

Concept Vocabulary

sift
flip
crack
drop
stir

Word Work

25-40 minutes

Phonemic Awareness/Phonics Instruction

Teach Phoneme Substitution, TE T225

Review The /o͞o/ Sound for *oo*, TE T228; Compound Words, TE T229

Spelling: The Vowel Sound in *moon*

Practice Assign PB 144 or activity, TE T230.

Vocabulary Instruction

Teach House Words, TE T230

Options for Guided Reading

80-100 minutes

Extra Support

Before Reading Review Responding questions for LR *Under a Full Moon,* TE T240. Help children start a two-column chart and have children suggest events that are real and make-believe in the LR.

During Reading Have children reread story. **Fluency Check:** Have individuals read aloud. ✓

After Reading Have partners complete two-column chart for the LR.

Level D

✓ = opportunity for ongoing assessment; adjust groups accordingly

▲ On Level

Before Reading Have children summarize LR *If You Miss Your Bus.* ✓ Preview a teacher-selected book such as *Rabbit and Hare Divide an Apple,* TE R10.

During Reading Have children begin story and model Phonics/Decoding Strategy.

After Reading Discuss the story so far. Have children finish story.

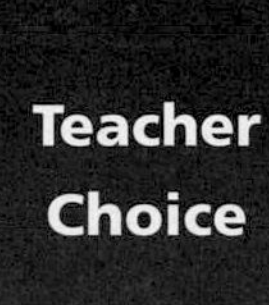

■ Above Level

Before Reading Review first half of selected book. Have children make predictions about second half.

During Reading Have children finish book.

After Reading Discuss how book connects to theme. Have children write journal entries to connect it to personal experience or other reading.

 English Language Learners

Before Reading Build background and preview LR *Good Night!,* TE T243.

During Reading Read story. **Fluency Modeling:** Reread each page; have children do echo reading. Reinforce Phonics/Decoding Strategy.

After Reading Discuss Responding questions, TE T243. **Fluency Practice:** Have children reread with partners or audio CD.

Level D

Writing and Language

30-40 minutes

Writing

Teach Writing an Invitation, TE T231

Practice Assign PB 145.

Optional Resources

Teacher Read Aloud

Choose a new book from your class or school library.

Independent Work

Self-Selected Reading

Choose from

- classroom/school library
- Leveled Bibliography, TE T6–T7
- children's magazines
- *I Love Reading,* Theme 7, take-home books 53, 67–70, 71–72
- Little Readers for Guided Reading

Centers

- Classroom Management Kit
- Classroom Management activities, TE T180–T181
- Responding activities, TE T218–T219

Differentiated Instruction

- Visual Literacy: Viewing Categories, TE T227
- High-Frequency Words: Word Wall, TE T224
- Study Skills: Reading a Diagram, TE R34

TE = Teacher Edition; PB = Practice Book; Tr = Transparency; LR = Leveled Reader; PL = Phonics Library; VR = Vocabulary Reader; VR Guide = Vocabulary Readers Teacher's Manual; LBB = Little Big Book; TP = Theme Paperback

Day 5 Balanced Literacy Plan

Teacher Notes

Reading and Comprehension

20-30 minutes

Book Share

- Ask children to give examples of how they applied the comprehension skill and strategy to books they have read this week.
- Help children use genre and text features to compare and contrast what they have read.
- As a class, discuss one *how, why,* or *what if* question. See examples on Blackline Master 1 to use as a guide.

Book Share

Word Work

25-40 minutes

Phonemic Awareness Instruction

Teach Phoneme Substitution, TE T233

High-Frequency Words

Cumulative Review Word Wall, TE T232

Spelling

Test See TE T238.

Options for Guided Reading

80-100 minutes

Extra Support

Before Reading Preview *A Clean Room,* PL Theme 7, pp. 69–75. Have children find/read words with /o͞o/ *(oo, ew, ue, ou)* and long *i (ie, igh)*. See TE T235–T237.

During Reading Have children read and model Phonics/Decoding Strategy. **Fluency Check:** Have individuals reread aloud. ✓

After Reading Have partners make connections between the story and LR *Under a Full Moon.* Assign On My Way Practice Reader *What Can You Do?* for partner reading.

✓ = opportunity for ongoing assessment; adjust groups accordingly

 English Language Learners

Level D

Before Reading Review LR *Good Night!*, TE T243.

During Reading Coach rereading of book. **Fluency Check:** Have individuals reread aloud. ✓

After Reading Help children summarize LR. Have children draw/caption a picture about a book they read this week. ✓

 Mixed Ability Levels

Literature Circles Form small, mixed-ability groups. Ask groups to discuss the main Anthology selection, Link, Leveled Readers, and other books they have read this week. Pose questions or topics for each group, and circulate among groups to offer support. Suggested group activities:

- Respond to specific Literature Discussion questions on Blackline Master 1.
- Discuss story or text elements, authors' choice of language, and/or illustrations.
- Connect book topics or themes to personal experiences or other reading.

Writing and Language

30-40 minutes

Writing

Practice Assign Writing Prompt, TE T233.

Grammar

Review Pronouns, TE T239

Speaking

Teach Conversation, TE T239

Optional Resources

Teacher Read Aloud

Choose a nonfiction book related to Social Studies or Science unit.

Independent Work

Self-Selected Reading

Choose from

- classroom/school library
- Leveled Bibliography, TE T6–T7
- children's magazines
- consumer text such as books about food, books about nutrition, etc.

Centers

- Classroom Management Kit
- Classroom Management activities, TE T180–T181
- Responding activities, TE T226–T227

Differentiated Instruction

- High-Frequency Words Review, TE T238
- Comprehension Review: Fantasy and Realism, TE T234

End-of-Week Assessment

- Weekly Skills Tests for Theme 7, Week 3
- Fluency Assessment, *A Clean Room,* PL Theme 7, pp. 69–75, TE T235–T237
- Alternative Assessment, Teacher's Resource Blackline Master 97

End-of-Theme Assessment

- Integrated Theme Tests for Theme 7

TE = Teacher Edition; PB = Practice Book; Tr = Transparency; LR = Leveled Reader; PL = Phonics Library; VR = Vocabulary Reader; VR Guide = Vocabulary Readers Teacher's Manual; LBB = Little Big Book; TP = Theme Paperback

Theme 8 Overview

	Week 1
Reading and Comprehension	**Shared Reading** Main Selection: *The Forest* Science Link: "Saving the Earth" Book Share **Comprehension** Strategy: Summarize Skill: Categorize and Classify Content Skill: How to Read a Pamphlet
Word Work	**Phonemic Awareness:** Segment Phonemes **Phonics:** Base Words and Endings *-s, -ed, -ing* **Phonics Review:** Vowel Pairs *oo, ew, ue, ou, u, u_e* (/o͞o/); Long *i (ie, igh)* **Vocabulary:** Compound Words; Nature Words **High-Frequency Words:** *about, because, draw, happy, part, teacher, tiny* **Spelling:** Adding *-s* to Naming Words
Options for Guided Reading	**Vocabulary Reader** *Types of Trees* **Leveled Readers:** Extra Support: *Planting Beans and Beets* On Level: *Many Kinds of Birds* Above Level: *In the Forest* ELL: *Planting a Garden* **Phonics Library** *A Fine Spring Day* *Sunset Beach* *Mom's Spring Jobs* **Theme Paperbacks** **Literature Circles**
Writing and Oral Language	**Shared Writing:** A Class Summary **Interactive Writing:** A Class Summary **Independent Writing:** Writing in a Learning Log **Grammar:** Action Words **Listening and Speaking:** Listening to Summarize
Assessment Options	• Weekly Skills Test for Theme 8, Week 1 • Fluency Assessment: Phonics Library

Use **Launching the Theme** on pages T16–T17 of the Teacher's Edition to introduce the theme.

Week 2

Shared Reading
Main Selection: *Butterfly*
Art Link: "Earth"
Book Share

Comprehension
Strategy: Evaluate
Skill: Topic, Main Idea, Details/Summarizing
Content Skill: How to Look at Fine Art

Phonemic Awareness: Segment Phonemes
Phonics: Vowel Pairs *oi, ow* (/ou/)
Phonics: Syllabication
Phonics Review: Base Words and Endings *-s, -ed, -ing*
Vocabulary: Science Words; Color and Pattern Words
High-Frequency Words: *always, arms, body, eight, ready, seven, warm*
Spelling: The Vowel Sound in *cow*

Vocabulary Reader
The Life of a Butterfly

Leveled Readers:
Extra Support: *Hello, Little Chick!*
On Level: *The Penguin Family*
Above Level: *Sea Turtles*
ELL: *Hello, Chick!*

Phonics Library
Hound Dog and Round Dog
Allen Camps Out
Scout the Grouch

Literature Circles

Shared Writing: An Informational Paragraph
Interactive Writing: An Informational Paragraph
Independent Writing: An Informational Paragraph
Grammar: Present Tense
Viewing: Monitor Understanding

- Weekly Skills Test for Theme 8, Week 2
- Fluency Assessment: Phonics Library

Week 3

Shared Reading
Main Selection: *Johnny Appleseed*
Science Link: "Life Cycle of an Apple"
Book Share

Comprehension
Strategy: Predict/Infer
Skill: Drawing Conclusions
Content Skill: How to Read a Time Line

Phonemic Awareness: Segment Phonemes
Phonics: Base Words and Endings *-ed, -ing*
Phonics Review: Vowel Pairs *ou, ow* (/ou/); Syllabication
Vocabulary: Homophones; Words That Describe Apple Products
High-Frequency Words: *butter, carry, kind, person, put, saw, were, work*
Spelling: Words That End with *-ed* or *-ing*

Vocabulary Reader
Mom's Stories

Leveled Readers:
Extra Support: *Juan Bobo*
On Level: *Rachel Carson*
Above Level: *George Washington Carver*
ELL: *The Story of Juan Bobo*

Phonics Library
Hen's Big Show
Writing Home
Sam Sundown's Problem

Literature Circles

Shared Writing: A Character Sketch
Interactive Writing: A Character Sketch
Independent Writing: Writing Clearly with Action Words
Grammar: Action Words with *-ed*
Speaking: Giving a Report

- Weekly Skills Test, Theme 8, Week 3
- Fluency Assessment: Phonics Library

Day 1 Balanced Literacy Plan

Teacher Notes

Reading and Comprehension

20-30 minutes

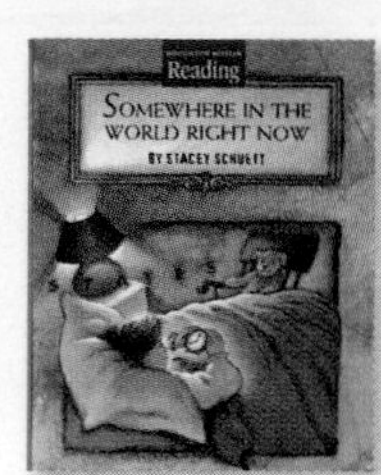

Shared Reading of Daily Message, TE T28

Shared Reading of Big Book

- ➤ Read aloud *Somewhere in the World Right Now,* TE T17, R2.
- ➤ Model fluent reading; discuss the story.

Word Work

25-40 minutes

Phonemic Awareness/Phonics Instruction

Teach Deleting, Substituting Phonemes, TE T29, T32

Teach Base Words and Endings *-s, -ed, -ing*, TE T32–T34

Practice Assign PB 151.

Spelling Instruction: Adding *-s* to Naming Words

Pretest and Teach Spelling Principle, TE T38

Assign Take-Home Spelling Word List, PB 315

cup cups frog frogs tree trees

Challenge: gloves, birds

Vocabulary Instruction

Teach Words with *-s, -ed, -ing,* TE T38

Options for Guided Reading

80-100 minutes

● Extra Support

Before Reading Preview *A Fine Spring Day,* PL Theme 8, pp. 5–11. Model Phonics/Decoding Strategy. See TE T35–T37.

During Reading Coach as children read story.

After Reading Discuss story; have children find/read words with *-s, -ed, -ing.* **Fluency Modeling:** Model fluent reading. Have partners reread story.

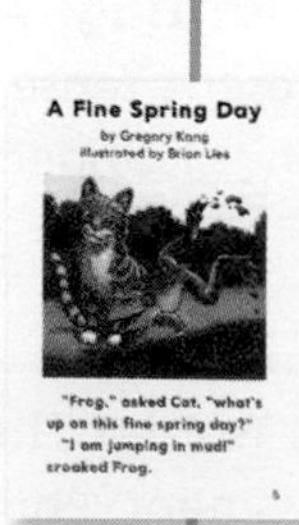

✓ = opportunity for ongoing assessment; adjust groups accordingly

▲ On Level

Before Reading Preview *A Fine Spring Day,* PL Theme 8, pp. 5–11, and review TE T35–T37.

During Reading Have children begin story. **Fluency Modeling:** Model Phonics/Decoding Strategy and fluent reading.

After Reading Have children retell story so far and find/read words with *-s, -ed, -ing.* **Fluency Practice:** Have partners finish story and reread for fluency.

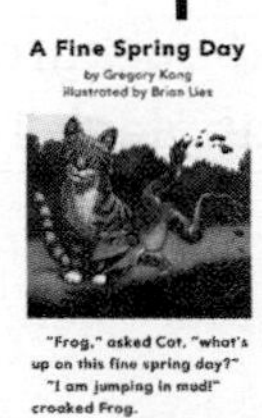

■ Above Level

Before Reading Preview LR *In the Forest,* TE T84.

During Reading Have children read first half of story. **Fluency Modeling:** Model fluent reading.

After Reading Have children finish reading and write answers to Responding questions. ✓

Level L

◆ English Language Learners

Before Reading Preview VR *Types of Trees.* See VR Guide, p. 27.

During Reading **Fluency Modeling:** Read aloud each page; have children do echo reading.

After Reading Discuss Responding pages. Have children reread with partners or audio CD.

Level D

4 WHOLE GROUP

Writing and Language

25-40 minutes

Writing

Teach Shared Writing: A Class Summary, TE T39

Practice Assign Writing Prompt, TE T29.

Listening and Speaking

Teach Assessing and Evaluating, TE T39

Optional Resources

Teacher Read Aloud

Reread the Big Book: *Somewhere in the World Right Now,* TE T17, R2.

Read *Eight Years Old and Going Strong,* TE T30–T31.

Independent Work

Self-Selected Reading

Choose from

- classroom/school library
- Leveled Bibliography, TE T6–T7
- *I Love Reading,* Theme 8, take-home books 73–75
- Little Readers for Guided Reading

Centers

- Classroom Management Kit
- Classroom Management activities, TE T26–T27

Differentiated Instruction

- Phonics Reteaching or Extension: Base Words and Endings *-s, -ed, -ing,* TE R12–R13
- High-Frequency Words Review: Word Wall, TE T28

TE = Teacher Edition; PB = Practice Book; Tr = Transparency; LR = Leveled Reader; PL = Phonics Library; VR = Vocabulary Reader; VR Guide = Vocabulary Readers Teacher's Manual; LBB = Little Big Book; TP = Theme Paperback

Day 2 Balanced Literacy Plan

Teacher Notes

1 WHOLE GROUP Reading and Comprehension

20-30 minutes

▼ Anthology Selection

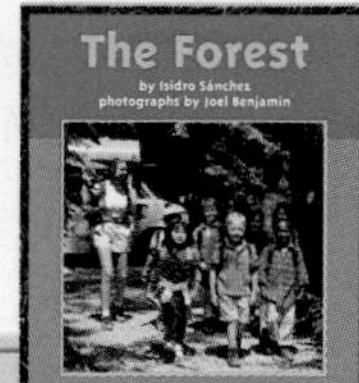

Shared Reading of *The Forest* (Part 1)

- Build Background and Vocabulary; Introduce Story Vocabulary, TE T44–T45, Tr 8-3

acorns	branches	different	poisonous
beautiful	careful	interesting	types

- Introduce Comprehension Strategy and Skill: Summarize, TE T46
  Categorize and Classify, TE T46, TE T49
- Set Purpose, TE T47
- Read Anthology Selection pp. 136–142 (independent, partner, or audio CD).

Words to Know

about	tiny
because	tells
draw	loves
happy	planted
teacher	added
part	

2 WHOLE GROUP Word Work

25-40 minutes

Phonemic Awareness/Phonics Instruction

Teach Deleting, Substituting Phonemes, TE T41

High-Frequency Words Instruction

Teach TE T42–T43, Tr 8-2, **Practice** Assign PB 152–153.

Spelling Instruction

Review Adding *-s* to Naming Words, TE T56

High-Frequency Words

about	part
because	teacher
draw	tiny
happy	

3 SMALL GROUP Options for Guided Reading

80-100 minutes

Extra Support

Before Reading Preview VR *Types of Trees.* See VR Guide, p. 27.

During Reading Read the book together; coach reading. Help children apply Summarize Strategy.

After Reading Help children compare this book to *The Forest.* **Fluency Practice:** Have children reread VR. Assign *Sunset Beach,* PL Theme 8, pp. 12–20, for partner reading.

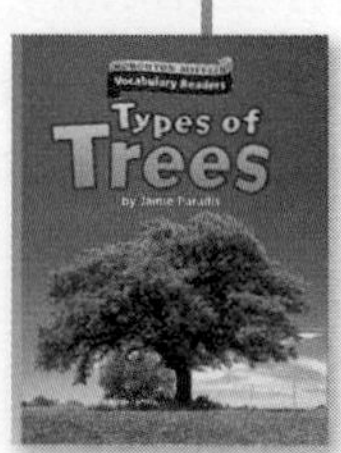

Level D

✓ = opportunity for ongoing assessment; adjust groups accordingly

▲ On Level

Before Reading Discuss PL *A Fine Spring Day,* TE T36. Preview LR *Many Kinds of Birds,* TE T83.

During Reading Coach reading as children begin story. Have children model the Summarize Strategy. **Fluency Modeling:** Model fluent reading, then have children model it.

After Reading Children finish reading and write answers to Responding questions. ✓ Assign *Sunset Beach,* PL Theme 8, pp. 12–20, for partner reading.

Level I

■ Above Level

Before Reading Have children model the Summarize Strategy and discuss Responding questions for LR *In the Forest,* TE T84.

During Reading **Fluency Check:** Monitor children's oral reading. ✓

After Reading Have children discuss the story with a partner. Assign *Sunset Beach,* PL Theme 8, pp. 12–20, for partner reading.

Level L

◆ English Language Learners

Before Reading To review VR vocabulary, have children demonstrate or give examples. See VR Guide, p. 27.

During Reading Model Summarize Strategy. Help children apply the Summarize Strategy. **Fluency Practice:** Have children reread book. Option: Preview and coach reading of *A Fine Spring Day,* PL Theme 8, pp. 5–11, TE T35–T37.

After Reading Help children summarize VR. Have partners discuss, draw, or write facts they learned. ✓

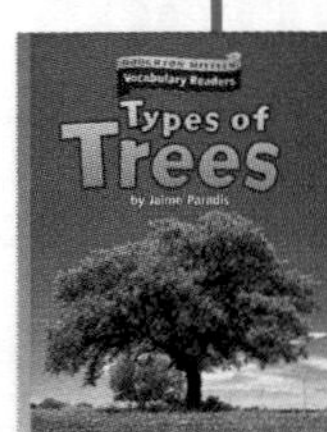

Level D

4 WHOLE GROUP Writing and Language

25-40 minutes

Writing

Teach Interactive Writing: A Class Summary, TE T57

Practice Assign Writing Prompt, TE T41.

Optional Resources

Teacher Read Aloud

Reread Big Book: *Somewhere in the World Right Now.* See TE T17, R2.

Independent Work

Self-Selected Reading

Choose from

- classroom/school library
- Leveled Bibliography, TE T6–T7
- *I Love Reading,* Theme 8, take-home books 73–75
- Little Readers for Guided Reading

Centers

- Classroom Management Kit
- Classroom Management activities, T26–T27

Differentiated Instruction

- High-Frequency Words
  - Word Walls, TE T40
  - Review TE T56
  - Reteaching or Extension, TE R20–R21

TE = Teacher Edition; PB = Practice Book; Tr = Transparency; LR = Leveled Reader; PL = Phonics Library; VR = Vocabulary Reader; VR Guide = Vocabulary Readers Teacher's Manual; LBB = Little Big Book; TP = Theme Paperback

Day 3 Balanced Literacy Plan

Teacher Notes

Reading and Comprehension

20-30 minutes

▼ Anthology Selection

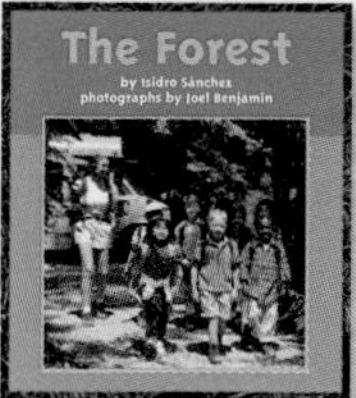

Shared Reading of *The Forest* (Part 2)

- Read Anthology Selection pp. 143–149 (independent, partner, or audio CD).
- Discuss questions, TE T60; have children cite text to support answers.

Comprehension Skill Instruction

Teach Categorize and Classify, TE T62–T63, Tr 8-4

Practice Assign PB 156 or retelling of story.

Word Work

25-40 minutes

Phonemic Awareness Instruction

Teach Deleting, Substituting Phonemes, TE T59

Spelling: Adding *-s* to Naming Words

Practice Assign PB 157 or activity, TE T64.

Vocabulary Instruction

Teach Compound Words, TE T64

Practice Assign PB 159.

Options for Guided Reading

80-100 minutes

Extra Support

Before Reading Discuss Responding questions from VR *Types of Trees.* See VR Guide, p. 27. Preview LR *Planting Beans and Beets,* TE T82.

During Reading Coach as children read story. **Fluency Modeling:** Model fluent reading; have children model.

After Reading **Fluency Practice:** Have partners reread story. Have children answer Responding questions. ✓

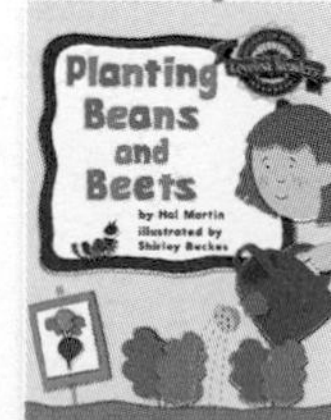

Level D

✓ = opportunity for ongoing assessment; adjust groups accordingly

On Level

Before Reading Discuss Responding questions for LR *Many Kinds of Birds,* TE T83.

During Reading **Fluency Check:** Ask individuals to read story aloud. ✓

After Reading Create a Categorize and Classify Chart; see TE T62, Tr 8-4 for format. Have children suggest categories and classify elements in the LR. Complete the chart together.

Level I

Above Level

Before Reading Preview TP *This Is Our Earth.* See TE R5.

During Reading **Fluency Modeling:** Model fluent reading, then have children model it. Have them read first half of story independently.

After Reading Ask questions; have children cite text to support answers. Create a Categorize and Classify Chart; see TE T62, Tr 8-4 for format. Have children suggest categories and classify elements in the TP. Complete the chart together.

Level I

English Language Learners

Before Reading Preview *Sunset Beach,* PL Theme 8, pp. 12–20. Model Phonics/Decoding Strategy.

During Reading **Fluency Modeling:** Read aloud each page; have children do echo reading.

After Reading Discuss story; help children find/read words with *-s, -ed, -ing.* Have children use illustrations to retell story to partners.

Optional Resources

Teacher Read Aloud

Choose a book from your class/school library or from the Leveled Bibliography, TE T6–T7.

Suggestion: *A Tree Is Nice* by Janet May Udry

Independent Work

Self-Selected Reading

Choose from

- classroom/school library
- Leveled Bibliography, TE T6–T7
- *I Love Reading,* Theme 8, take-home books 73–75
- Little Readers for Guided Reading

Centers

- Classroom Management Kit
- Classroom Management activities, T26–T27
- Responding activities, TE T60–T61

Differentiated Instruction

- Comprehension Reteaching or Extension: Categorize and Classify, TE R26–R27
- High-Frequency Word Review: Word Wall, TE T58

Writing and Language

30-40 minutes

Writing

Practice Assign Write a Forest Guide, Anthology p. 151.

Grammar

Teach Action Words, TE T65

Practice Assign PB 161.

TE = Teacher Edition; PB = Practice Book; Tr = Transparency; LR = Leveled Reader; PL = Phonics Library; VR = Vocabulary Reader; VR Guide = Vocabulary Readers Teacher's Manual; LBB = Little Big Book; TP = Theme Paperback

Day 4 Balanced Literacy Plan

Teacher Notes

Reading and Comprehension

20-30 minutes

Shared Reading of Social Studies Link

- "Saving the Earth," Anthology pp. 152–155, TE T68–T69 (independent, partner, or group)
- Skill: How to Read a Pamphlet, Anthology p. 152, TE T68
- Introduce Concept Vocabulary, TE T68.

Concept Vocabulary

litter
electricity
gas
gallons
recycle

Word Work

25-40 minutes

Phonemic Awareness/Phonics Instruction

Teach Deleting, Substituting Phonemes, TE T67

Review Vowel Pairs *oo, ew, ue, ou; u, u_e* (/o͞o/), TE T70; Long *i (ie, igh)*, TE T71

Spelling: Adding *-s* to Naming Words

Practice Assign PB 162 or activity, TE T72.

Vocabulary Instruction

Teach Nature Words, TE T72

3 SMALL GROUP

Options for Guided Reading

80-100 minutes

Extra Support

Before Reading Review Responding questions for LR *Planting Beans and Beets,* TE T82. Begin a Categorize and Classify Chart; see TE T62, Tr 8-4 for format. Have children suggest categories and classify elements in the LR.

During Reading Have children reread story. **Fluency Check:** Have individuals read aloud. ✓

After Reading Work with students to complete the Categorize and Classify Chart. Have partners categorize and classify other story elements.

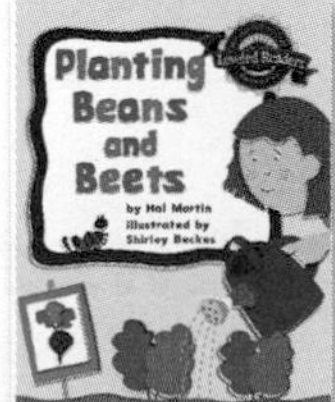

Level D

✓ = opportunity for ongoing assessment; adjust groups accordingly

▲ On Level

Before Reading Have children summarize LR *Many Kind of Birds.* ✓ Preview a teacher-selected book or TP *How Do You Know It's Spring?,* TE R4.

During Reading Have children begin story and model Phonics/Decoding Strategy.

After Reading Discuss the story so far. Have children finish story.

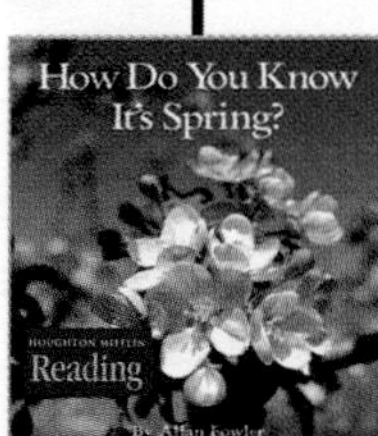

Level I

■ Above Level

Before Reading Review first half of TP *This Is Our Earth,* TE R5. Have children make predictions about second half.

During Reading Have children finish book.

After Reading Discuss how book connects to theme. Have children write journal entries to connect it to personal experience or other reading.

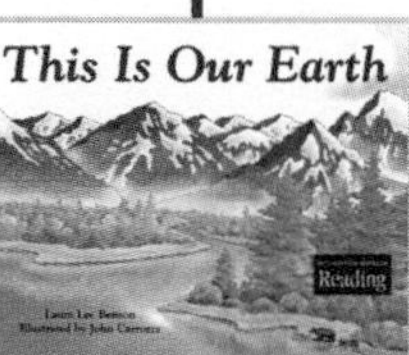

Level I

◆ English Language Learners

Before Reading Build background and preview LR *Planting a Garden,* TE T85.

During Reading Read story. **Fluency Modeling:** Reread each page; have children do echo reading. Reinforce Phonics/Decoding Strategy.

After Reading Discuss Responding questions, TE T85. **Fluency Practice:** Have children reread with partners or audio CD.

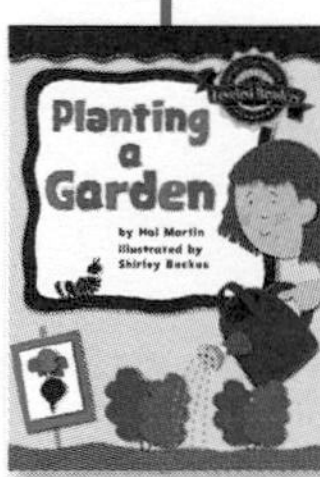

Level D

4 WHOLE GROUP

Writing and Language

30-40 minutes

Writing

Teach Writing in a Learning Log, TE T73

Practice Assign PB 163.

Optional Resources

Teacher Read Aloud

Continue selected Read Aloud book from Day 3 or choose a new one from your class or school library.

Independent Work

Self-Selected Reading

Choose from

- classroom/school library
- Leveled Bibliography, TE T6–T7
- children's magazines
- *I Love Reading,* Theme 8, take-home books 73–75
- Little Readers for Guided Reading

Centers

- Classroom Management Kit
- Classroom Management activities, TE T26–T27
- Responding activities, TE T60–T61

Differentiated Instruction

- Writer's Craft: Writing Lists, TE T69
- High-Frequency Words: Word Wall, TE T66
- Study Skills
  - – Using Reference Resources, TE R32
  - – Locating Information, TE R33
  - – Organizing Information, TE R34

TE = Teacher Edition; PB = Practice Book; Tr = Transparency; LR = Leveled Reader; PL = Phonics Library; VR = Vocabulary Reader; VR Guide = Vocabulary Readers Teacher's Manual; LBB = Little Big Book; TP = Theme Paperback

Day 5 Balanced Literacy Plan

Teacher Notes

Reading and Comprehension

20-30 minutes

Book Share

- Ask children to explain how they applied the comprehension skill and strategy to books they have read this week.
- Help children use genre and text features to compare and contrast what they have read.
- As a class, discuss one *how, why,* or *what if* question. See examples on Blackline Master 1 to use as a guide.

Word Work

25-40 minutes

Phonemic Awareness Instruction

Teach Deleting, Substituting Phonemes, TE T75

High-Frequency Words

Cumulative Review Word Wall, TE T74

Spelling

Test See TE T80.

Options for Guided Reading

80-100 minutes

Extra Support

Before Reading Preview *Mom's Spring Jobs,* PL Theme 8, pp. 21–27. Have children find/read words with *-s, -ed, -ing.* See TE T77–T79.

During Reading Have children read and model Phonics/Decoding Strategy. **Fluency Check:** Have individuals reread aloud. ✓

After Reading Have partners make connections between the story and LR *Planting Beans and Beets.* Assign On My Way Practice Reader *How Raven Played a Trick* for partner reading.

✓ = opportunity for ongoing assessment; adjust groups accordingly

◆ English Language Learners

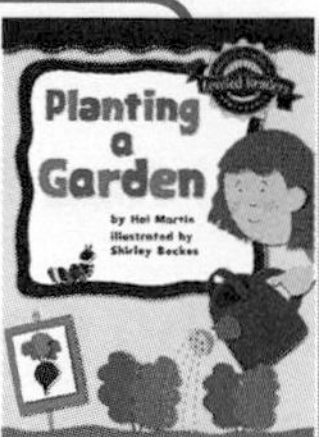

Level D

Before Reading Review LR *Planting a Garden,* TE T85.

During Reading Coach rereading of book. **Fluency Check:** Have individuals reread aloud. ✓

After Reading Help children summarize LR. Have children draw/caption a picture about a book they read this week. ✓

Mixed Ability Levels

Literature Circles Form small, mixed-ability groups. Ask groups to discuss the main Anthology selection, Link, Leveled Readers, and other books they have read this week. Pose questions or topics for each group, and circulate among groups to offer support. Suggested group activities:

- Respond to specific Literature Discussion questions on Blackline Master 1.
- Discuss story or text elements, authors' choice of language, and/or illustrations.
- Connect book topics or themes to personal experiences or other reading.

Writing and Language

30-40 minutes

Writing

Practice Assign Writing Prompt, TE T75.

Grammar

Review Action Words, TE T81

Listening and Speaking

Teach Listening to Summarize, TE T81

Optional Resources

Teacher Read Aloud

Choose a nonfiction book related to Social Studies or Science unit.

Independent Work

Self-Selected Reading

Choose from

- classroom/school library
- Leveled Bibliography, TE T6–T7
- children's magazines
- consumer texts such as informational pamphlets, travel brochures, etc.
- *I Love Reading,* Theme 8, take-home books 73–75
- Little Readers for Guided Reading

Centers

- Classroom Management Kit
- Classroom Management activities, TE T26–T27
- Responding activities, TE T60–T61

Differentiated Instruction

- High-Frequency Word Review, TE T80
- Comprehension Review: Categorize and Classify TE T76

End-of-Week Assessment

- Weekly Skills Tests for Theme 8, Week 1
- Fluency Assessment, *Mom's Spring Jobs,* PL Theme 8, pp. 21–27, TE T77–T79
- Alternative Assessment, Teacher's Resource Blackline Master 105

TE = Teacher Edition; PB = Practice Book; Tr = Transparency; LR = Leveled Reader; PL = Phonics Library; VR = Vocabulary Reader; VR Guide = Vocabulary Readers Teacher's Manual; LBB = Little Big Book; TP = Theme Paperback

Day 1 Balanced Literacy Plan

Teacher Notes

Reading and Comprehension

20-30 minutes

Shared Reading of Daily Message, TE T108

Listening Comprehension

- Read aloud *The Ant and the Chrysalis,* TE T110–T111.
- Model fluent reading; discuss the story.

Word Work

25-40 minutes

Phonemic Awareness/Phonics Instruction

Teach Deleting, Substituting Phonemes, TE T109, T112

Teach Vowel Pairs *ow, ou* (/ou/), TE T112–T113

Practice Assign PB 166–167.

Teach Syllabication (VCCV Pattern), TE T114

Practice Assign PB 168.

Spelling Instruction: The Vowel Sound in *cow*

Pretest and Teach Spelling Principle, TE T118

Practice Take-Home Spelling Word List, PB 315

cow house down now found out

Challenge: pouch, crowded

Vocabulary Instruction

Teach Words That Rhyme with *out* and *down,* TE T118

Options for Guided Reading

80-100 minutes

Extra Support

Before Reading Preview *Hound Dog and Round Dog,* PL Theme 8, pp. 29–35. Model Phonics/Decoding Strategy. See TE T115–T117.

During Reading Coach as children read story.

After Reading Discuss story; have children find/read words with *ow, ou* (/ou/). **Fluency Modeling:** Model fluent reading. Have partners reread story.

✓ = opportunity for ongoing assessment; adjust groups accordingly

▲ On Level

Before Reading Preview *Hound Dog and Round Dog,* PL Theme 8, pp. 29–35, and review TE T115–T117.

During Reading Have children begin story. **Fluency Modeling:** Model Phonics/Decoding Strategy and fluent reading.

After Reading Have children retell story so far and find/read words with *ow, ou* (/ou/). **Fluency Practice:** Have partners finish story and reread for fluency.

■ Above Level

Before Reading Preview LR *Sea Turtles,* TE T164.

During Reading Have children read first half of story. **Fluency Modeling:** Model fluent reading.

After Reading Have children finish reading and write answers to Responding questions. ✓

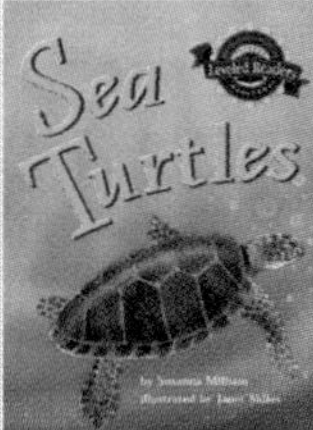

Level L

◆ English Language Learners

Before Reading Preview VR *The Life of a Butterfly.* See VR Guide, p. 28.

During Reading **Fluency Modeling:** Read aloud each page; have children do echo reading.

After Reading Discuss Responding pages. Have children reread with partners or audio CD.

Level E

4 WHOLE GROUP Writing and Language

25-40 minutes

Writing

Teach Shared Writing: An Informational Paragraph, TE T119

Practice Assign Writing Prompt, TE T109.

Listening and Speaking

Teach Dramatizing a Story, TE T119

Optional Resources

Teacher Read Aloud

Reread Big Book: *The Ant and the Chrysalis,* TE T110–T111.

Independent Work

Self-Selected Reading

Choose from

- classroom/school library
- Leveled Bibliography, TE T6–T7
- *I Love Reading,* Theme 8, take-home books 76–77
- Little Readers for Guided Reading

Centers

- Classroom Management Kit
- Classroom Management activities, TE T106–T107

Differentiated Instruction

- Phonics Reteaching or Extension: Vowel Pairs *ou, ow,* TE R14–R15
- Phonics Reteaching or Extension: Syllabication, TE R16–R17
- High-Frequency Words Review: Word Wall, TE T108

TE = Teacher Edition; PB = Practice Book; Tr = Transparency; LR = Leveled Reader; PL = Phonics Library; VR = Vocabulary Reader; VR Guide = Vocabulary Readers Teacher's Manual; LBB = Little Big Book; TP = Theme Paperback

Day 2 Balanced Literacy Plan

Teacher Notes

Reading and Comprehension

20-30 minutes

Shared Reading of *Butterfly* (Part 1)

▼ Anthology Selection

- Build Background and Vocabulary; Introduce Story Vocabulary, TE T124–T125, Tr 8-8

butterfly	changing	danger	nectar	suit/s
caterpillar/s	chrysalis	enemies	orange	

- Introduce Comprehension Strategy and Skill: Evaluate, TE T126
  Topic, Main Idea, Details/Summarizing, TE T126, TE T129
- Set Purpose, TE T127
- Read Anthology Selection pp. 162–169 (independent, partner, or audio CD).

Words to Know

always	yellow
eight	now
arms	how
seven	flowers
warm	pouch
ready	out
body	about

Word Work

25-40 minutes

Phonemic Awareness/Phonics Instruction

Teach Deleting, Substituting Phonemes, TE T121

High-Frequency Words Instruction

Teach TE T122–T123, Tr 8-7, **Practice** Assign PB 169 and 171.

Spelling Instruction

Review The Vowel Sound in *cow*, TE T136

High-Frequency Words

always	ready
arms	seven
body	warm
eight	

Options for Guided Reading

80-100 minutes

Extra Support

Before Reading Preview VR *The Life of a Butterfly.* See VR Guide, p. 28.

During Reading Read the book together; coach reading. Help children apply Evaluate Strategy.

After Reading Help children compare this book to *Butterfly.* **Fluency Practice:** Have children reread VR. Assign *Allen Camps Out,* PL Theme 8, pp. 36–44, for partner reading.

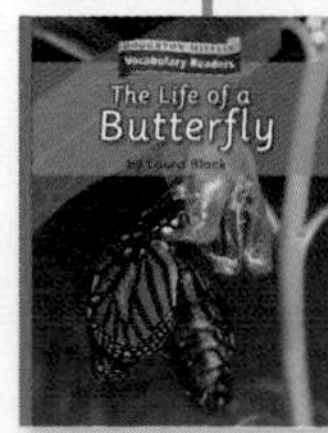

Level E

✓ = opportunity for ongoing assessment; adjust groups accordingly

▲ On Level

Before Reading Discuss PL *Hound Dog and Round Dog,* TE T116. Preview LR *The Penguin Family,* TE T163.

During Reading Coach reading as children begin story. Have children model the Evaluate Strategy. **Fluency Modeling:** Model fluent reading, then have children model it.

After Reading Children finish reading and write answers to Responding questions. ✓ Assign *Allen Camps Out,* PL Theme 8, pp. 36–44, for partner reading.

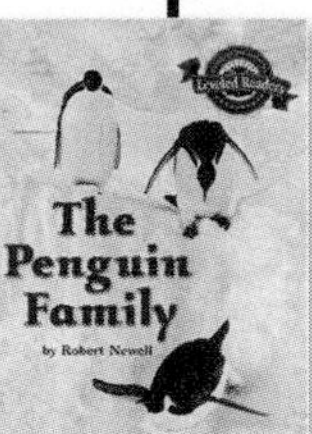

Level J

■ Above Level

Before Reading Have children model the Evaluate Strategy and discuss Responding questions for LR *Sea Turtles,* TE T164.

During Reading **Fluency Check:** Monitor children's oral reading. ✓

After Reading Have children discuss the story with a partner. Assign *Allen Camps Out,* PL Theme 8, pp. 36–44, for partner reading.

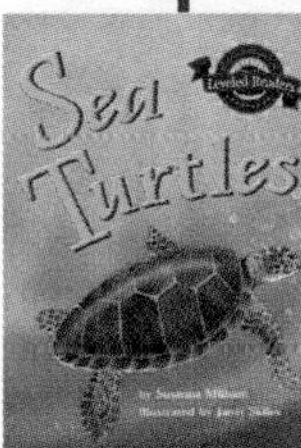

Level L

◆ English Language Learners

Before Reading To review VR vocabulary, have children demonstrate or give examples. See VR Guide, p. 28.

During Reading Model Evaluate Strategy. Help children apply the Evaluate Strategy. **Fluency Practice:** Have children reread book.
Option: Preview and coach reading of *Hound Dog and Round Dog.* PL Theme 8, pp. 29–35, TE T115–T117.

After Reading Help children summarize VR. Have partners discuss, draw, or write facts they learned. ✓

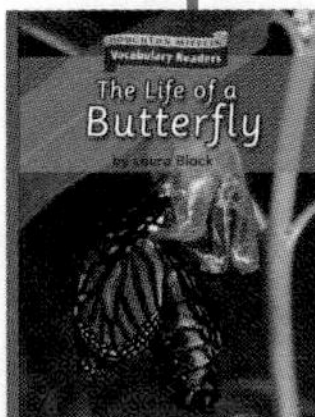

Level E

Optional Resources

Teacher Read Aloud

Choose a book from your class/school library or from the Leveled Bibliography, TE T6–T7.

Suggestion: *Time of Wonder* by Robert McCloskey

Independent Work

Self-Selected Reading

Choose from

- classroom/school library
- Leveled Bibliography, TE T6–T7
- *I Love Reading,* Theme 8, take-home books 76–77
- Little Readers for Guided Reading

Centers

- Classroom Management Kit
- Classroom Management activities, TE T106–T107

Differentiated Instruction

- High-Frequency Words
  - Word Wall, TE T120
  - Review, TE T136
  - Reteaching or Extension, TE R22–R23

4 WHOLE GROUP

Writing and Language

25-40 minutes

Writing

Teach Interactive Writing: An Informational Paragraph, TE T137

Practice Assign Writing Prompt, TE T121.

TE = Teacher Edition; PB = Practice Book; Tr = Transparency; LR = Leveled Reader; PL = Phonics Library; VR = Vocabulary Reader; VR Guide = Vocabulary Readers Teacher's Manual; LBB = Little Big Book; TP = Theme Paperback

Day 3 Balanced Literacy Plan

Teacher Notes

Reading and Comprehension

20-30 minutes

Shared Reading of *Butterfly* (Part 2)

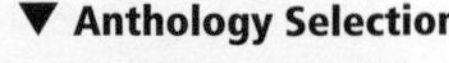

▼ Anthology Selection

- ➤ Read Anthology Selection pp. 170–177 (independent, partner, or audio CD).
- ➤ Discuss questions, TE T140; have children cite text to support answers.

Comprehension Skill Instruction

Teach Topic, Main Idea, Details/Summarizing, TE T142–T143, Tr 8-9

Practice Assign PB 174 or retelling of story.

Word Work

25-40 minutes

Phonemic Awareness Instruction

Teach Deleting, Substituting Phonemes, TE T139

Spelling: The Vowel Sound in *cow*

Practice Assign PB 175 or activity, TE T144.

Vocabulary Instruction

Teach Science Words, TE T144

Practice Assign PB 176.

Options for Guided Reading

80-100 minutes

● Extra Support

Before Reading Discuss Responding questions from VR *The Life of a Butterfly.* See VR Guide, p. 28. Preview LR *Hello, Little Chick!,* TE T162.

During Reading Coach as children read story.
Fluency Modeling: Model fluent reading; have children model.

After Reading **Fluency Practice:** Have partners reread story. Have children answer Responding questions. ✓

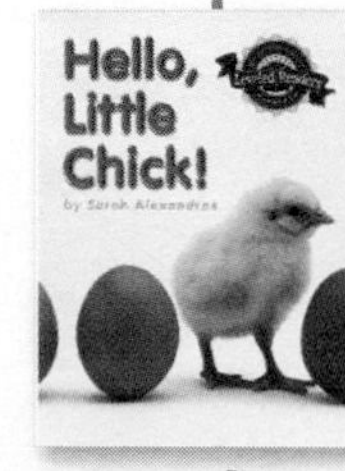

Level D

✓ = opportunity for ongoing assessment; adjust groups accordingly

▲ On Level

Before Reading Discuss Responding questions for LR *The Penguin Family,* TE T163.

During Reading **Fluency Check:** Ask individuals to read story aloud. ✓

After Reading Create a Topic, Main Idea, and Details Chart; see TE T142, Tr 8-9 for format. Have children suggest the topic, main idea, and details in the LR. Complete the chart together.

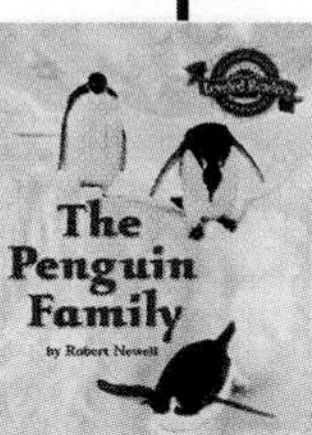

Level J

■ Above Level

Before Reading Preview a teacher-selected book such as *The Top and Bottom of the World,* see TE R8.

During Reading **Fluency Modeling:** Model fluent reading, then have children model it. Have them read first half of story independently.

After Reading Ask questions; have children cite text to support answers. Create a Topic, Main Idea, and Details Chart; see TE T142, Tr 8-9 for format. Have children suggest the topic, main idea, and details in the teacher-selected book. Complete the chart together.

◆ English Language Learners

Before Reading Preview *Allen Camps Out,* PL Theme 8, pp. 36–44. Model Phonics/Decoding Strategy.

During Reading **Fluency Modeling:** Read aloud each page; have children do echo reading.

After Reading Discuss story; help children find/read words with *ow, ou* (/ou/). Have children use illustrations to retell story to partners.

Optional Resources

Teacher Read Aloud

Continue selected Read Aloud book from Day 3 or choose a new one from your class or school library.

Independent Work

Self-Selected Reading

Choose from

- classroom/school library
- Leveled Bibliography, TE T6–T7
- *I Love Reading,* Theme 8, take-home books 76–77
- Little Readers for Guided Reading

Centers

- Classroom Management Kit
- Classroom Management activities, TE T106–T107
- Responding activities, TE T140–T141

Differentiated Instruction

- Comprehension Reteaching and Extension: Topic, Main Idea, Details/Summarizing, TE R28–R29
- High-Frequency Word Review: Word Wall, TE T138

4 WHOLE GROUP Writing and Language

30-40 minutes

Writing

Practice Assign Write a Description, Anthology p. 179.

Grammar

Teach Present Tense, TE T145

Practice Assign PB 177.

TE = Teacher Edition; PB = Practice Book; Tr = Transparency; LR = Leveled Reader; PL = Phonics Library; VR = Vocabulary Reader; VR Guide = Vocabulary Readers Teacher's Manual; LBB = Little Big Book; TP = Theme Paperback

Day 4 Balanced Literacy Plan

Teacher Notes

Reading and Comprehension

20-30 minutes

Shared Reading of Art Link

- "Earth," Anthology pp. 180–181, TE T148–T149 (independent, partner, or group)
- Skill: How to Look at Fine Art, Anthology p. 180, TE T148
- Introduce Concept Vocabulary, TE T148.

Concept Vocabulary

art
landscape
Earth
respect

Word Work

25-40 minutes

Phonemic Awareness/Phonics Instruction

Teach Deleting, Substituting Phonemes, TE T147

Review Base Words and Endings *-s, -ed, -ing,* TE T150–T151

Spelling: The Vowel Sound in *cow*

Practice Assign PB 178 or activity, TE T152.

Vocabulary Instruction

Teach Color and Pattern Words, TE T152

Options for Guided Reading

80-100 minutes

Extra Support

Before Reading Review Responding questions for LR *Hello, Little Chick!*, TE T162. Begin a Topic, Main Idea, and Details Chart; see TE T142, Tr 8-9 for format. Have children suggest the topic, main idea, and details in the LR.

During Reading Have children reread story. **Fluency Check:** Have individuals read aloud. ✓

After Reading Work with students to complete the Topic, Main Idea, and Details Chart. Have partners list other details from the story.

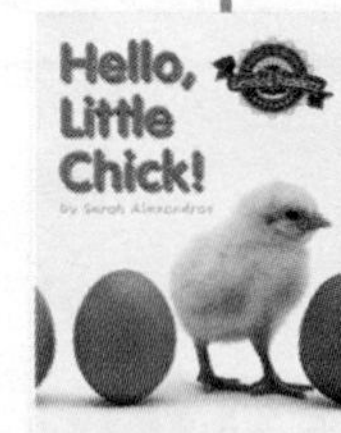

Level D

✓ = opportunity for ongoing assessment; adjust groups accordingly

▲ On Level

Before Reading Have children summarize LR *The Penguin Family.* ✓ Preview a teacher-selected book such as *Tale of a Tadpole,* TE R7.

During Reading Have children begin story and model Phonics/Decoding Strategy.

After Reading Discuss the story so far. Have children finish story.

■ Above Level

Before Reading Review first half of selected book. Have children make predictions about second half.

During Reading Have children finish book.

After Reading Discuss how book connects to theme. Have children write journal entries to connect it to personal experience or other reading.

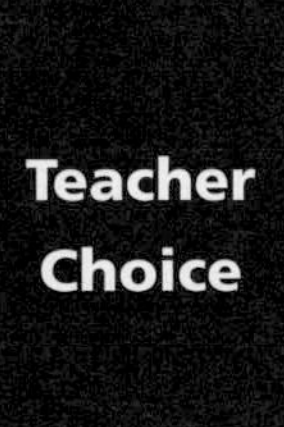

◆ English Language Learners

Before Reading Build background and preview LR *Hello, Chick!,* TE T165.

During Reading Read story. **Fluency Modeling:** Reread each page; have children do echo reading. Reinforce Phonics/Decoding Strategy.

After Reading Discuss Responding questions, TE T165. **Fluency Practice:** Have children reread with partners or audio CD.

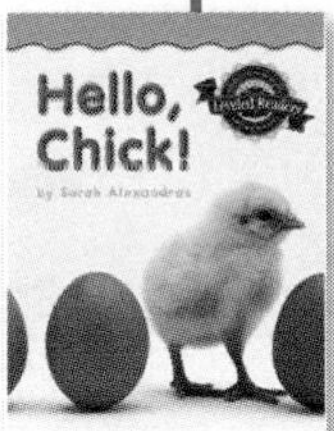

Level D

4 WHOLE GROUP Writing and Language

30-40 minutes

Writing

Teach An Informational Paragraph, TE T153

Practice Assign PB 179.

Optional Resources

Teacher Read Aloud

Choose a new book from your class or school library.

Independent Work

Self-Selected Reading

Choose from

- classroom/school library
- Leveled Bibliography, TE T6–T7
- children's magazines
- *I Love Reading,* Theme 8, take-home books 76–77
- Little Readers for Guided Reading

Centers

- Classroom Management Kit
- Classroom Management activities, TE T106–T107
- Responding activities, TE T140–T141

Differentiated Instruction

- Writer's Craft: Writing an Acrostic, TE T149
- High-Frequency Words: Word Wall, TE T146
- Study Skills
  - Using Reference Resources, TE R32
  - Locating Information, TE R33
  - Organizing Information, TE R34

TE = Teacher Edition; PB = Practice Book; Tr = Transparency; LR = Leveled Reader; PL = Phonics Library; VR = Vocabulary Reader; VR Guide = Vocabulary Readers Teacher's Manual; LBB = Little Big Book; TP = Theme Paperback

Day 5 Balanced Literacy Plan

Teacher Notes

Reading and Comprehension

20-30 minutes

Book Share

- Ask children to explain how they applied the comprehension skill and strategy to books they have read this week.
- Help children use genre and text features to compare and contrast what they have read.
- As a class, discuss one *how, why,* or *what if* question. See examples on Blackline Master 1 to use as a guide.

Word Work

25-40 minutes

Phonemic Awareness Instruction

Teach Deleting, Substituting Phonemes, TE T155

High-Frequency Words

Cumulative Review Word Wall, TE T154

Spelling

Test See TE T160.

Options for Guided Reading

80-100 minutes

Extra Support

Before Reading Preview *Scout the Grouch,* PL Theme 8, pp. 45–51. Have children find/read words with *ou, ow* (/ou/). See TE T157–T159.

During Reading Have children read and model Phonics/ Decoding Strategy. **Fluency Check:** Have individuals reread aloud. ✓

After Reading Have partners make connections between the story and LR *Hello, Little Chick!* Assign On My Way Practice Reader *All About the Weather* for partner reading.

✓ = opportunity for ongoing assessment; adjust groups accordingly

◆ English Language Learners

Before Reading Review LR *Hello, Chick!,* TE T165.

During Reading Coach rereading of book. **Fluency Modeling:** Have individuals reread aloud. ✓

After Reading Help children summarize LR. Have children draw/caption a picture about a book they read this week. ✓

Level D

●▲■◆ Mixed Ability Levels

Literature Circles Form small, mixed-ability groups. Ask groups to discuss the main Anthology selection, Link, Leveled Readers, and other books they have read this week. Pose questions or topics for each group, and circulate among groups to offer support. Suggested group activities:

- Respond to specific Literature Discussion questions on Blackline Master 1.
- Discuss story or text elements, authors' choice of language, and/or illustrations.
- Connect book topics or themes to personal experiences or other reading.

Writing and Language

30-40 minutes

Writing

Practice Assign Writing Prompt, TE T155.

Grammar

Review Present Tense, TE T161

Viewing

Teach Monitor Understanding, TE T161

Optional Resources

Teacher Read Aloud

Choose a nonfiction book related to Social Studies or Science unit.

Independent Work

Self-Selected Reading

Choose from

- classroom/school library
- Leveled Bibliography, TE T6–T7
- children's magazines
- consumer texts such as books of paintings, landscape photographs, etc.

Centers

- Classroom Management Kit
- Classroom Management activities, TE T106–T107
- Responding activities, TE T140–T141

Differentiated Instruction

- High Frequency Word Review, TE T160
- Comprehension Review: Topic, Main Idea, Details-Summarizing, TE T156

End-of-Week Assessment

- Weekly Skills Tests for Theme 8, Week 2
- Fluency Assessment, *Scout the Grouch,* PL Theme 8, pp. 45–51, TE T157–T159
- Alternative Assessment, Teacher's Resource Blackline Master 109

TE = Teacher Edition; PB = Practice Book; Tr = Transparency; LR = Leveled Reader; PL = Phonics Library; VR = Vocabulary Reader; VR Guide = Vocabulary Readers Teacher's Manual; LBB = Little Big Book; TP = Theme Paperback

Day 1 Balanced Literacy Plan

Teacher Notes

Reading and Comprehension

20-30 minutes

Shared Reading of Daily Message, TE T176

Listening Comprehension

- Read aloud *Paul Bunyan,* TE T178–T179.
- Model fluent reading; discuss the story.

Word Work

25-40 minutes

Phonemic Awareness/Phonics Instruction

Teach Deleting, Substituting Phonemes, TE T177, T180

Teach Base Words and Endings *-ed, -ing,* TE T180–T182

Practice Assign PB 180.

Spelling Instruction: Words That End with *-ed or -ing*

Pretest and Teach Spelling Principle, TE T186

Assign Take-Home Spelling Word List, PB 317

checking missed filled sleeping landed telling

Challenge: bluffing, planted

Vocabulary Instruction

Teach Adding *-ed* and *-ing* to Words, TE T186

Options for Guided Reading

80-100 minutes

Extra Support

Before Reading Preview *Hen's Big Show,* PL Theme 8, pp. 53–59. Model Phonics/Decoding Strategy. See TE T183–T185.

During Reading Coach as children read story.

After Reading Discuss story; have children find/read words with *-s, -ed, -ing*. **Fluency Modeling:** Model fluent reading. Have partners reread story.

✓ = opportunity for ongoing assessment; adjust groups accordingly

▲ On Level

Before Reading Preview *Hen's Big Show,* PL Theme 8, pp. 53–59, and review TE T183–T185.

During Reading Have children begin story. **Fluency Modeling:** Model Phonics/Decoding Strategy and fluent reading.

After Reading Have children retell story so far and find/read words with *-s, -ed, -ing.* **Fluency Practice:** Have partners finish story and reread for fluency.

■ Above Level

Before Reading Preview LR *George Washington Carver,* TE T236.

During Reading Have children read first half of story. **Fluency Modeling:** Model fluent reading.

After Reading Have children finish reading and write answers to Responding questions. ✓

Level M

◆ English Language Learners

Before Reading Preview VR *Mom's Stories.* See VR Guide, p. 29.

During Reading **Fluency Modeling:** Read aloud each page; have children do echo reading.

After Reading Discuss Responding pages. Have children reread with partners or audio CD.

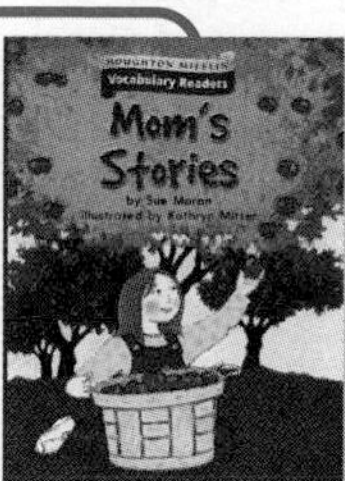

Level D

4 WHOLE GROUP

Writing and Language

25-40 minutes

Writing

Teach Shared Writing: A Character Sketch, TE T187

Practice Assign Writing Prompt, TE T177.

Listening and Speaking

Teach Retelling a Story, TE T187

Optional Resources

Teacher Read Aloud

Reread *Paul Bunyan,* TE T178–T179.

Independent Work

Self-Selected Reading

Choose from

- classroom/school library
- Leveled Bibliography, TE T6–T7
- *I Love Reading,* Theme 8, take-home books 78–79
- Little Readers for Guided Reading

Centers

- Classroom Management Kit
- Classroom Management activities, TE T174–T175

Differentiated Instruction

- Phonics Reteaching or Extension: Base Words and Endings *-ed, -ing,* TE R18–R19
- High-Frequency Words Review: Word Wall, TE T176

TE = Teacher Edition; PB = Practice Book; Tr = Transparency; LR = Leveled Reader; PL = Phonics Library; VR = Vocabulary Reader; VR Guide = Vocabulary Readers Teacher's Manual; LBB = Little Big Book; TP = Theme Paperback

Day 2 Balanced Literacy Plan

Teacher Notes

1 Reading and Comprehension

20-30 minutes

WHOLE GROUP

Shared Reading of *Johnny Appleseed* (Part 1)

▼ Anthology Selection

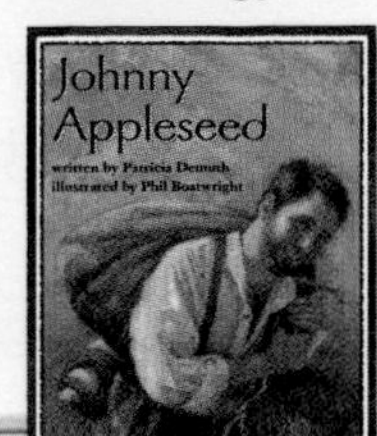

- Build Background and Vocabulary; Introduce Story Vocabulary, TE T192–T193, Tr 8-13

apple	cider	river	years
bread	clothes	stories	young

- Introduce Comprehension Strategy and Skill:
  Predict/Infer, TE T194
  Drawing Conclusions, TE T194, TE T199
- Set Purpose, TE T195
- Read Anthology Selection pp. 185–199 (independent, partner, or audio CD).

Words to Know

carry	work
kind	person
put	liked
saw	stopped
butter	moving
were	

2 Word Work

25-40 minutes

WHOLE GROUP

Phonemic Awareness/Phonics Instruction

Teach Deleting, Substituting Phonemes, TE T189

High-Frequency Words Instruction

Teach TE T190–T191, Tr 8-12, **Practice** PB 181–182.

Spelling Instruction

Review Words That End with *-ed* or *-ing*, TE T208

High-Frequency Words

butter	put
carry	saw
kind	were
person	work

3 Options for Guided Reading

80-100 minutes

SMALL GROUP

● Extra Support

Before Reading Preview VR *Mom's Stories.* See VR Guide, p. 29.

During Reading Read the book together; coach reading. Help children apply Predict/Infer Strategy.

After Reading Help children compare this book to *Johnny Appleseed.* **Fluency Practice:** Have children reread VR. Assign *Writing Home,* PL Theme 8, pp. 60–68, for partner reading.

Level D

✓ = opportunity for ongoing assessment; adjust groups accordingly

▲ On Level

Before Reading Discuss PL *Hen's Big Show,* TE T184. Preview LR *Rachel Carson,* TE T235.

During Reading Coach reading as children begin story. Have children model the Predict/Infer Strategy. **Fluency Modeling:** Model fluent reading, then have children model it.

After Reading Children finish reading and write answers to Responding questions. ✓ Assign *Writing Home,* PL Theme 8, pp. 60–68, for partner reading.

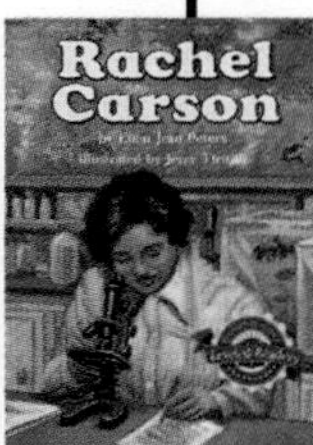

Level J

■ Above Level

Before Reading Have children model the Predict/Infer Strategy and discuss Responding questions for LR *George Washington Carver,* TE T236.

During Reading **Fluency Check:** Monitor children's oral reading. ✓

After Reading Have children discuss the story with a partner. Assign *Writing Home,* PL Theme 8, pp. 60–68, for partner reading.

Level M

◆ English Language Learners

Before Reading To review VR vocabulary, have children demonstrate or give examples. See VR Guide, p. 29.

During Reading Model Predict/Infer Strategy. Help children apply the Predict/Infer Strategy. **Fluency Practice:** Have children reread book.
Option: Preview and coach reading of *Hen's Big Show,* PL Theme 8, pp. 53–59, TE T183–T185.

After Reading Help children summarize VR. Have partners discuss, draw, or write facts they learned. ✓

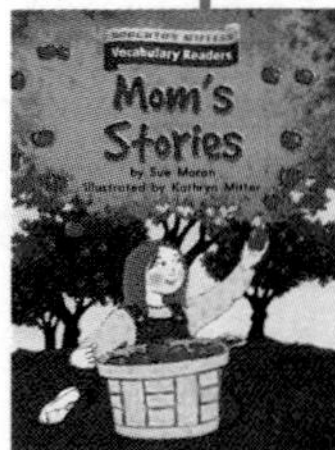

Level D

4 WHOLE GROUP Writing and Language

25-40 minutes

Writing

Teach Interactive Writing: A Character Sketch, TE T209

Practice Assign Writing Prompt, TE T189.

Optional Resources

Teacher Read Aloud

Choose a book from your class/school library or from the Leveled Bibliography, TE T6–T7.

Suggestion: *Crab Moon* by Ruth Horowitz

Independent Work

Self-Selected Reading

Choose from

- classroom/school library
- Leveled Bibliography, TE T6–T7
- *I Love Reading,* Theme 8, take-home books 78–79
- Little Readers for Guided Reading

Centers

- Classroom Management Kit
- Classroom Management activities, TE T174–T175

Differentiated Instruction

- High-Frequency Words
  –Word Wall, TE T188
  –Review, TE T208
  –Reteaching or Extension, TE R24–R25

TE = Teacher Edition; PB = Practice Book; Tr = Transparency; LR = Leveled Reader; PL = Phonics Library; VR = Vocabulary Reader; VR Guide = Vocabulary Readers Teacher's Manual; LBB = Little Big Book; TP = Theme Paperback

Day 3 Balanced Literacy Plan

Teacher Notes

Reading and Comprehension

20-30 minutes

▼ Anthology Selection

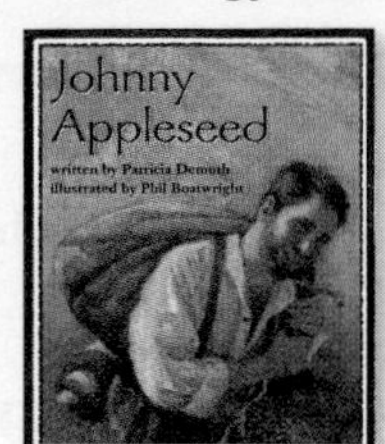

Shared Reading of *Johnny Appleseed* (Part 2)

- Read Anthology Selection pp. 200–206 (independent, partner, or audio CD).
- Discuss questions, TE T212; have children cite text to support answers.

Comprehension Skill Instruction

Teach Drawing Conclusions, TE T214–T215

Practice Assign PB 185 or retelling of story.

Word Work

25-40 minutes

Phonemic Awareness Instruction

Teach Deleting, Substituting Phonemes, TE T211

Spelling: Words That End with *-ed* or *-ing*

Practice Assign PB 186 or activity, TE T216.

Vocabulary Instruction

Teach Homophones, TE T216

Practice Assign PB 187.

Options for Guided Reading

80-100 minutes

● Extra Support

Before Reading Discuss Responding questions from VR *Mom's Stories.* See VR Guide, p. 29. Preview LR *Juan Bobo,* TE T234.

During Reading Coach as children read story. **Fluency Modeling:** Model fluent reading; then have children model.

After Reading **Fluency Practice:** Have partners reread story. Have children answer Responding questions. ✓

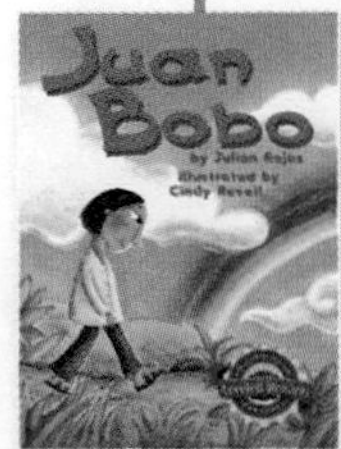

Level E

✓ = opportunity for ongoing assessment; adjust groups accordingly

 **On Level**

Before Reading Discuss Responding questions for LR *Rachel Carson,* TE T235.

During Reading **Fluency Check:** Ask individuals to read story aloud. ✓

After Reading Help children draw conclusions about what happens in their LR. Complete the list of conclusions together.

Level J

 **Above Level**

Before Reading Preview a teacher-selected book, such as *Our Earth,* see TE R11.

During Reading **Fluency Modeling:** Model fluent reading, then have children model it. Have them read first half of story independently.

After Reading Ask questions; have children cite text to support answers. Help children draw conclusions about what happens in the teacher-selected book. Complete the list of conclusions together.

◆ **English Language Learners**

Before Reading Preview *Writing Home,* PL Theme 8, pp. 60–68. Model Phonics/Decoding Strategy.

During Reading **Fluency Modeling:** Read aloud each page; have children do echo reading.

After Reading Discuss story; help children find/read words with *-s, -ed, -ing.* Have children use illustrations to retell story to partners.

Optional Resources

Teacher Read Aloud

Continue selected Read Aloud book from Day 3 or choose a new one from your class or school library.

Independent Work

Self-Selected Reading

Choose from

- classroom/school library
- Leveled Bibliography, TE T6–T7
- *I Love Reading,* Theme 8, take-home books 78–79
- Little Readers for Guided Reading

Centers

- Classroom Management Kit
- Classroom Management activities, TE T174–T175
- Responding activities, TE T212–T213

Differentiated Instruction

- Comprehension Reteaching or Extension: Drawing Conclusions, TE R30–R31
- High-Frequency Word Review: Word Wall, TE T210

Writing and Language

30-40 minutes

Writing

Practice Assign Write a Journal Entry, Anthology p. 209.

Grammar

Teach Action Words with *-ed,* TE T217

Practice Assign PB 188.

TE = Teacher Edition; PB = Practice Book; Tr = Transparency; LR = Leveled Reader; PL = Phonics Library; VR = Vocabulary Reader; VR Guide = Vocabulary Readers Teacher's Manual; LBB = Little Big Book; TP = Theme Paperback

Day 4 Balanced Literacy Plan

Teacher Notes

Reading and Comprehension

20-30 minutes

Shared Reading of Science Link

- "Life Cycle of an Apple," Anthology pp. 210–213, TE T220–T221 (independent, partner, or group)
- Skill: How to Read a Time Line, Anthology p. 210, TE T220
- Introduce Concept Vocabulary, TE T220.

Concept Vocabulary

time line
blossoms
bud
life cycle
pollen
ripe

Word Work

25-40 minutes

Phonemic Awareness/Phonics Instruction

Teach Deleting, Substituting Phonemes, TE T219

Review Vowel Pairs *ou, ow* (/ou/), TE T222–T223

Spelling: Words That End with *-ed* or *-ing*

Practice Assign PB 189 or activity, TE T224.

Vocabulary Instruction

Teach Words That Name Apple Products, TE T224

Options for Guided Reading

80-100 minutes

Extra Support

Before Reading Review Responding questions for LR *Juan Bobo,* TE T234. Help children draw conclusions about what happens in their LR.

During Reading Have children reread story. **Fluency Check:** Have individuals read aloud. ✓

After Reading Have partners complete a list of conclusions about the LR.

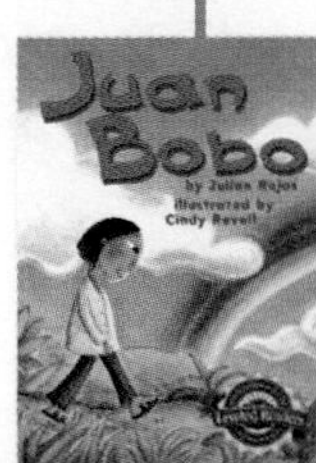

Level E

✓ = opportunity for ongoing assessment; adjust groups accordingly

▲ **On Level**

Before Reading Have children summarize LR *Rachel Carson.* ✓ Preview a teacher-selected book such as *Elephants Swim,* TE R10.

During Reading Have children begin story and model Phonics/Decoding Strategy.

After Reading Discuss the story so far. Have children finish story.

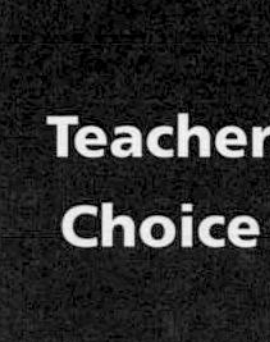

Teacher Choice

■ **Above Level**

Before Reading Review first half of selected book. Have children make predictions about second half.

During Reading Have children finish book.

After Reading Discuss how book connects to theme. Have children write journal entries to connect it to personal experience or other reading.

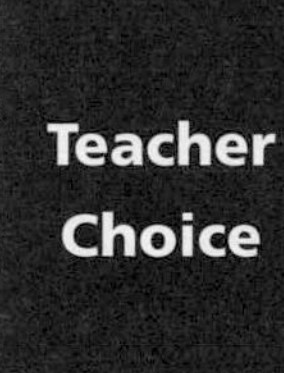

Teacher Choice

◆ **English Language Learners**

Before Reading Build background and preview LR *The Story of Juan Bobo,* TE T237.

During Reading Read story. **Fluency Modeling:** Reread each page; have children do echo reading. Reinforce Phonics/Decoding Strategy.

After Reading Discuss Responding questions, TE T237. **Fluency Practice:** Have children reread with partners or audio CD.

Level D

4 WHOLE GROUP

Writing and Language

30-40 minutes

Writing

Teach Writing Clearly with Action Words, TE T225

Practice Assign PB 190.

Optional Resources

Teacher Read Aloud

Choose a new book from your class or school library.

Independent Work

Self-Selected Reading

Choose from

- classroom/school library
- Leveled Bibliography, TE T6–T7
- children's magazines
- *I Love Reading,* Theme 8, take-home books 78–79
- Little Readers for Guided Reading

Centers

- Classroom Management Kit
- Classroom Management activities, TE T174–T175
- Responding activities, TE T212–T213

Differentiated Instruction

- Visual Literacy: Viewing Photographs, TE T221
- High-Frequency Words: Word Wall, TE T218
- Study Skills
  - –Using Reference Resources, TE R32
  - –Locating Information, TE R33
  - –Organizing Information, TE R34

TE = Teacher Edition; PB = Practice Book; Tr = Transparency; LR = Leveled Reader; PL = Phonics Library; VR = Vocabulary Reader; VR Guide = Vocabulary Readers Teacher's Manual; LBB = Little Big Book; TP = Theme Paperback

Day 5 Balanced Literacy Plan

Teacher Notes

Reading and Comprehension

20-30 minutes

Book Share

- Ask children to give examples of how they applied the comprehension skill and strategy to books they have read this week.
- Help children use genre and text features to compare and contrast what they have read.
- As a class, discuss one *how, why,* or *what if* question. See examples on Blackline Master 1 to use as a guide.

Word Work

25-40 minutes

Phonemic Awareness Instruction

Teach Deleting, Substituting Phonemes, TE T227

High-Frequency Words

Cumulative Review Word Wall, TE T226

Spelling

Test See TE T232.

Options for Guided Reading

80-100 minutes

Extra Support

Before Reading Preview *Sam Sundown's Problem,* PL Theme 8, pp. 69–75. Have children find/read words with *-ed, -ing.* See TE T229–T231.

During Reading Have children read and model Phonics/Decoding Strategy. **Fluency Check:** Have individuals reread aloud. ✓

After Reading Have partners make connections between the story and LR *Juan Bobo.* Assign On My Way Practice Reader *Hiking at Pound Beach* for partner reading.

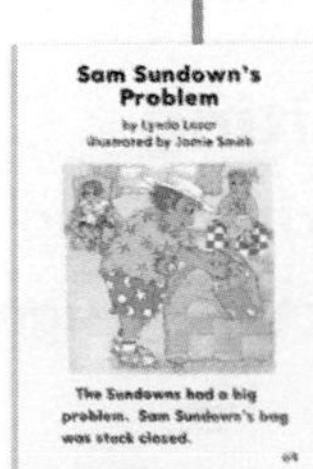

✓ = opportunity for ongoing assessment; adjust groups accordingly

◆ English Language Learners

Before Reading Review LR *The Story of Juan Bobo,* TE T237.

During Reading Coach rereading of book. **Fluency Check:** Have individuals reread aloud. ✓

After Reading Help children summarize LR. Have children draw/caption a picture about a book they read this week. ✓

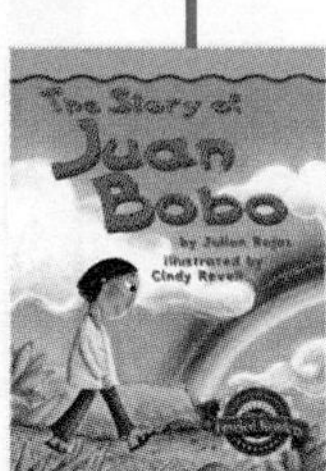

Level D

●▲■◆ Mixed Ability Levels

Literature Circles Form small, mixed-ability groups. Ask groups to discuss the main Anthology selection, Link, Leveled Readers, and other books they have read this week. Pose questions or topics for each group, and circulate among groups to offer support. Suggested group activities:

- Respond to specific Literature Discussion questions on Blackline Master 1.
- Discuss story or text elements, authors' choice of language, and/or illustrations.
- Connect book topics or themes to personal experiences or other reading.

Writing and Language

30-40 minutes

Writing

Practice Assign Writing Prompt, TE T227.

Grammar

Review Action Words with *-ed,* TE T233

Speaking

Teach Giving a Report, TE T233

Optional Resources

Teacher Read Aloud

Choose a nonfiction book related to Social Studies or Science unit.

Independent Work

Self-Selected Reading

Choose from

- classroom/school library
- Leveled Bibliography, TE T6–T7
- children's magazines
- consumer texts such as children's magazines, dictionaries, encyclopedias, etc.
- *I Love Reading,* Theme 8, take-home books 78–79
- Little Readers for Guided Reading

Centers

- Classroom Management Kit
- Classroom Management activities, TE T174–T175
- Responding activities, TE T212–T213

Differentiated Instruction

- High-Frequency Word Review, TE T232
- Comprehension Review: Drawing Conlclusions, TE T228

Assessment

End-of-Week Assessment

- Weekly Skills Tests for Theme 8, Week 3
- Fluency Assessment, *Sam Sundown's Problem,* PL Theme 8, pp. 69–75, TE T229–T231
- Alternative Assessment, Teacher's Resource Blackline Master 111

End-of-Theme Assessment

- Integrated Theme Tests for Theme 8

TE = Teacher Edition; PB = Practice Book; Tr = Transparency; LR = Leveled Reader; PL = Phonics Library; VR = Vocabulary Reader; VR Guide = Vocabulary Readers Teacher's Manual; LBB = Little Big Book; TP = Theme Paperback

Theme 9 Overview

	Week 1
Reading and Comprehension	**Shared Reading** Main Selection: *When I Am Old with You* Technology Link: "Inventions Then and Now" Book Share **Comprehension** Strategy: Monitor/Clarify Skill: Noting Details Content Skill: Adjusting Your Reading Rate
Word Work	**Phonemic Awareness:** Manipulate Phonemes **Phonics:** Sounds for *y* **Phonics Review:** Base Words and Endings *-ed, -ing* **Vocabulary:** Sensory Words; Family Activity Words **High-Frequency Words:** *around, dance, else, ever, ocean, open, talk, though* **Spelling:** The Long *i* Spelling *y*
Options for Guided Reading	**Vocabulary Reader** *In the Country* **Leveled Readers:** Extra Support: *Come Play with Me* On Level: *Friends Online* Above Level: *The Story Box* ELL: *Let's Play Today!* **Phonics Library** *Fussy Gail* *Sunny's Buddy* *I Spy* Theme Paperbacks **Literature Circles**
Writing and Oral Language	**Shared Writing:** A Solution **Interactive Writing:** A Solution **Independent Writing:** Response to Literature **Grammar:** Using *Is* and *Are* **Listening and Speaking:** Evaluate and Assess
Assessment Options	• Weekly Skills Test for Theme 9, Week 1 • Fluency Assessment: Phonics Library

- Use **Launching the Theme** on pages T16–T17 of the Teacher's Edition to introduce the theme.
- Use the **Focus on Genre** section to help children explore the unique characteristics of folktales.

Week 2

Shared Reading
Main Selection: *The New Friend*
Poetry Link: Poems
Book Share

Comprehension
Strategy: Evaluate
Skill: Story Structure
Content Skill: How to Read a Poem

Phonemic Awareness: Manipulate Phonemes
Phonics: Base Words and Endings *-es, -ies*
Phonics: Prefixes *un-* and *re-*
Phonics Review: Sounds for *y*
Vocabulary: Synonyms; Feeling Words
High-Frequency Words: *after, before, buy, done, off, pretty, school, wash*
Spelling: Adding *-es* to Naming Words

Vocabulary Reader
Plan a Party

Leveled Readers:
Extra Support: *Knock, Knock*
On Level: *The Sleepover*
Above Level: *Friends Forever*
ELL: *New Friends*

Phonics Library
Bo's Bunnies
The Fleet Street Club
Peaches, Screeches

Literature Circles

Shared Writing: A Class Newsletter
Interactive Writing: A Class Newsletter
Independent Writing: Complete Sentences
Grammar: Using *Was* and *Were*
Speaking: Giving Information

- Weekly Skills Test for Theme 9, Week 2
- Fluency Assessment: Phonics Library

Week 3

Shared Reading
Main Selection: *The Surprise Family*
Science Link: "Watch Them Grow"
Book Share

Comprehension
Strategy: Question
Skill: Compare and Contrast
Content Skill: How to Read a Science Article

Phonemic Awareness: Manipulate Phonemes
Phonics: Vowel Pairs *oi, oy; aw, au*
Phonics: Suffixes *-ful, -ly, -y*
Phonics Review: Base Words and Endings *-es, -ies;* Prefixes *un-* and *re-*
Vocabulary: Possessive Pronouns; Bird Words
High-Frequency Words: *baby, edge, enough, garden, only, sharp, together, watched*
Spelling: The Vowel Sound in *coin*

Vocabulary Reader
Chickens on the Farm

Leveled Readers:
Extra Support: *Runaway Sandy*
On Level: *The Duck Pond*
Above Level: *Junk into Art*
ELL: *Sandy Runs Away*

Phonics Library
Jenny's Big Voice
Joy Boy
Shawn's Soy Sauce

Literature Circles

Shared Writing: Another Version
Interactive Writing: Another Version
Independent Writing: A Comparison
Grammar: Describing What We See
Listening and Speaking: Reader's Theater

- Weekly Skills Test, Theme 9, Week 3
- Fluency Assessment: Phonics Library

Day 1 Balanced Literacy Plan

Teacher Notes

Reading and Comprehension

20-30 minutes

Shared Reading of Daily Message, TE T28

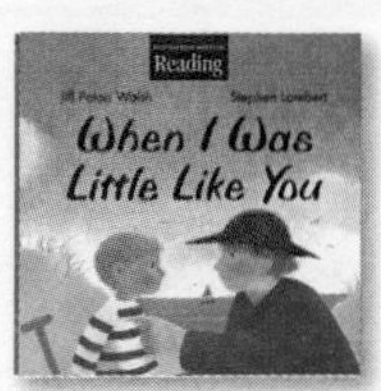

Shared Reading of Big Book

- Read aloud *When I Was Little Like You,* TE T17, R2.
- Model fluent reading; discuss the story.

Word Work

25-40 minutes

Phonemic Awareness/Phonics Instruction

Teach Deleting Phonemes, TE T29, T32

Teach Sounds for *y*, TE T32–T34

Practice Assign PB 195–196.

Spelling Instruction: The Long *i* Sound Spelled *y*

Pretest and Teach Spelling Principle, TE T38

Assign Take-Home Spelling Word List, PB 319

by my cry try fly why

Challenge: pry, multiply

Vocabulary Instruction

Teach Words That Rhyme with *my*, TE T38

Options for Guided Reading

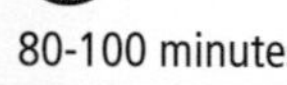
80-100 minutes

Extra Support

Before Reading Preview *Fussy Gail,* PL Theme 9, pp. 5–11. Model Phonics/Decoding Strategy. See TE T35–T37.

During Reading Coach as children read story.

After Reading Discuss story; have children find/read words with sounds for *y*. **Fluency Modeling:** Model fluent reading. Have partners reread story.

✓ = opportunity for ongoing assessment; adjust groups accordingly

On Level

Before Reading Preview *Fussy Gail,* PL Theme 9, pp. 5–11, and review TE T35–T37.

During Reading Have children begin story. **Fluency Modeling:** Model Phonics/Decoding Strategy and fluent reading.

After Reading Have children retell story so far and find/read words with sounds for y. **Fluency Practice:** Have partners finish story and reread for fluency.

Above Level

Before Reading Preview LR *The Story Box,* TE T88.

During Reading Have children read first half of story. **Fluency Modeling:** Model fluent reading.

After Reading Have children finish reading and write answers to Responding questions. ✓

Level K

English Language Learners

Before Reading Preview VR *In the Country.* See VR Guide, p. 30.

During Reading **Fluency Modeling:** Read aloud each page; have children do echo reading.

After Reading Discuss Responding pages. Have children reread with partners or audio CD.

Level D

4 WHOLE GROUP

Writing and Language

25-40 minutes

Writing

Teach Shared Writing: A Solution, TE T39

Practice Assign Writing Prompt, TE T29.

Listening and Speaking

Teach Discussing Conflict Resolution, TE T39

Optional Resources

Teacher Read Aloud

Reread the Big Book: *When I Was Little Like You,* TE T17, R2.

Read *Animal Helpers,* TE T30–T31.

Independent Work

Self-Selected Reading

Choose from

- classroom/school library
- Leveled Bibliography, TE T6–T7
- *I Love Reading,* Theme 9, take-home books 80–81
- Little Readers for Guided Reading

Centers

- Classroom Management Kit
- Classroom Management activities, TE T26–T27

Differentiated Instruction

- Phonics Reteaching or Extension: Sounds for *y,* TE R12–R13
- High-Frequency Words Review: Word Wall, TE T28

TE = Teacher Edition; PB = Practice Book; Tr = Transparency; LR = Leveled Reader; PL = Phonics Library; VR = Vocabulary Reader; VR Guide = Vocabulary Readers Teacher's Manual; LBB = Little Big Book; TP = Theme Paperback

Day 2 Balanced Literacy Plan

Teacher Notes

1 Reading and Comprehension

20-30 minutes

WHOLE GROUP

Shared Reading of *When I Am Old with You* (Part 1)

▼ Anthology Selection

- Build Background and Vocabulary; Introduce Story Vocabulary, TE T44–T45, Tr 9-2

canoe	cedar	Grandaddy	mind	tired
cards	field/s	imagine	remember	

- Introduce Comprehension Strategy and Skill: Monitor/Clarify, TE T46
  Noting Details, TE T46, TE T54
- Set Purpose, TE T47
- Read Anthology Selection pp. 17–28 (independent, partner, or audio CD).

Words to Know

around	though
dance	by
else	my
open	try
talk	cry
ever	any
ocean	Grandaddy

2 Word Work

25-40 minutes

WHOLE GROUP

Phonemic Awareness/Phonics Instruction

Teach Deleting Phonemes, TE T41

High-Frequency Word Instruction

Teach TE T42–T43, Tr 9-1; Practice PB 197–198.

Spelling Instruction

Review The Long *i* Sound Spelled *y*, TE T60

High-Frequency Words

around	ocean
dance	open
else	talk
ever	though

3 Options for Guided Reading

80-100 minutes

SMALL GROUP

● **Extra Support**

Before Reading Preview VR *In the Country.* See VR Guide, p. 30.

During Reading Read the book together; coach reading. Help children apply Monitor/Clarify Strategy.

After Reading Help children compare this book to *When I Am Old with You.* **Fluency Practice:** Have children reread VR. Assign *Sunny's Buddy,* PL Theme 9, pp. 12–20, for partner reading.

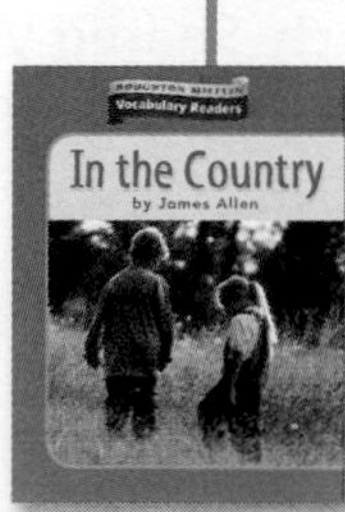

Level D

✓ = opportunity for ongoing assessment; adjust groups accordingly

▲ On Level

Before Reading Discuss PL *Fussy Gail,* TE T35. Preview LR *Friends Online,* TE T87.

During Reading Coach reading as children begin story. Have children model the Monitor/Clarify Strategy. **Fluency Modeling:** Model fluent reading, then have children model it.

After Reading Have children finish reading and write answers to Responding questions. ✓ Assign *Sunny's Buddy,* PL Theme 9, pp. 12–20, for partner reading.

Level I

■ Above Level

Before Reading Have children model the Monitor/Clarify Strategy and discuss Responding questions for LR *The Story Box,* TE T88.

During Reading **Fluency Check:** Monitor children's oral reading. ✓

After Reading Have children discuss the story with a partner. Assign *Sunny's Buddy,* PL Theme 9, pp. 12–20, for partner reading.

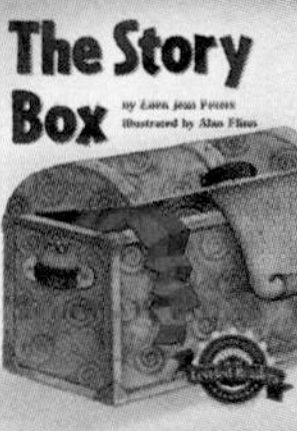

Level K

◆ English Language Learners

Before Reading To review VR vocabulary, have children demonstrate or give examples. See VR Guide, p. 30.

During Reading Model Monitor/Clarify Strategy. Help children apply the Monitor/Clarify Strategy. **Fluency Practice:** Have children reread book. Option: Preview and coach reading of *Fussy Gail,* PL Theme 9, pp. 5–11, TE T35–T37.

After Reading Help children summarize VR. Have partners discuss, draw, or write facts they learned. ✓

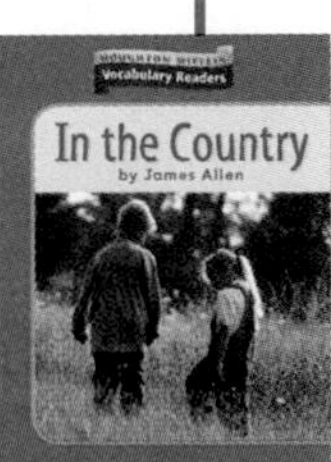

Level D

Optional Resources

Teacher Read Aloud

Reread Big Book: *When I Was Little Like You.* See TE T17, R2.

Independent Work

Self-Selected Reading

Choose from

- classroom/school library
- Leveled Bibliography, TE T6–T7
- *I Love Reading,* Theme 9, take-home books 80–81
- Little Readers for Guided Reading

Centers

- Classroom Management Kit
- Classroom Management activities, T26–T27

Differentiated Instruction

- High-Frequency Words
  - Word Wall, TE T40
  - Review, TE T60
  - Reteaching or Extension, TE R22–R23

4 WHOLE GROUP

Writing and Language

25-40 minutes

Writing

Teach Interactive Writing: A Solution, TE T61

Practice Assign Writing Prompt, TE T41.

TE = Teacher Edition; PB = Practice Book; Tr = Transparency; LR = Leveled Reader; PL = Phonics Library; VR = Vocabulary Reader; VR Guide = Vocabulary Readers Teacher's Manual; LBB = Little Big Book; TP = Theme Paperback

Day 3 Balanced Literacy Plan

Teacher Notes

Reading and Comprehension

20-30 minutes

▼ Anthology Selection

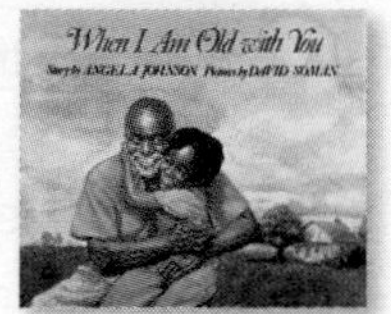

Shared Reading of *When I Am Old with You* (Part 2)

- Read Anthology Selection pp. 29–40 (independent, partner, or audio CD).
- Discuss questions, TE T64; have children cite text to support answers.

Comprehension Skill Instruction

Teach Noting Details, TE T66–T67, Tr 9-3

Practice Assign PB 201 or retelling of story.

Word Work

25-40 minutes

Phonemic Awareness Instruction

Teach Deleting Phonemes, TE T63

Spelling: The Long *i* Sound Spelled *y*

Practice Assign PB 202 or activity, TE T68.

Vocabulary Instruction

Teach Sensory Words, TE T68

Practice Assign PB 203.

Options for Guided Reading

80-100 minutes

Extra Support

Before Reading Discuss Responding questions from VR *In the Country.* See VR Guide, p. 30. Preview LR *Come Play With Me,* TE T86.

During Reading Coach as children read story. **Fluency Modeling:** Model fluent reading; have children model.

After Reading **Fluency Practice:** Have partners reread story. Have children write answers to Responding questions. ✓

Level D

✓ = opportunity for ongoing assessment; adjust groups accordingly

On Level

Before Reading Discuss Responding questions for LR *Friends Online,* TE T87.

During Reading **Fluency Check:** Ask individuals to read story aloud. ✓

After Reading Create a Noting Details Chart; see TE T66, Tr 9-3 for format. Have children suggest details in their LR. Complete the chart together.

Level I

Above Level

Before Reading Preview TP *Max Found Two Sticks.* See TE R5.

During Reading **Fluency Modeling:** Model fluent reading, then have children model it. Have them read first half of story independently.

After Reading Ask questions; have children cite text to support answers. Create a Noting Details Chart; see TE T66, Tr 9-3 for format. Have children suggest details in their TP. Complete the chart together.

Level K

English Language Learners

Before Reading Preview *Sunny's Buddy,* PL Theme 9, pp. 12–20. Model Phonics/Decoding Strategy.

During Reading **Fluency Modeling:** Read aloud each page; have children do echo reading.

After Reading Discuss story; help children find/read words with sounds for *y.* Have children use illustrations to retell story to partners.

Writing and Language

30-40 minutes

Writing

Practice Assign Write a Message, Anthology p. 43.

Grammar

Teach Using *Is* and *Are,* TE T69

Practice Assign PB 204.

Optional Resources

Teacher Read Aloud

Choose a book from your class/school library or from the Leveled Bibliography, TE T6–T7.

Suggestion: *The Best of Friends* by Pirkko Vainio

Independent Work

Self-Selected Reading

Choose from

- classroom/school library
- Leveled Bibliography, TE T6–T7
- *I Love Reading,* Theme 9, take-home books 80–81
- Little Readers for Guided Reading

Centers

- Classroom Management Kit
- Classroom Management activities, T26–T27
- Responding activities, TE T64–T65

Differentiated Instruction

- Comprehension Reteaching or Extension: Noting Details, TE R28–R29
- High-Frequency Word Review: Word Wall, TE T62

TE = Teacher Edition; PB = Practice Book; Tr = Transparency; LR = Leveled Reader; PL = Phonics Library; VR = Vocabulary Reader; VR Guide = Vocabulary Readers Teacher's Manual; LBB = Little Big Book; TP = Theme Paperback

Day 4 Balanced Literacy Plan

Teacher Notes

Reading and Comprehension

20-30 minutes

Shared Reading of Technology Link

- "Inventions Then and Now," Anthology pp. 44–47, TE T72–T73 (independent, partner, or group)
- Skill: Adjusting Your Reading Rate, Anthology p. 44, TE T72
- Introduce Concept Vocabulary, TE T72.

Concept Vocabulary

inventions
hourglasses
past
bulb

Word Work

25-40 minutes

Phonemic Awareness/Phonics Instruction

Teach Deleting Phonemes, TE T71

Review Base Words and Endings *-ed, -ing,* TE T74–T75

Spelling: The Long *i* Sound Spelled *y*

Practice Assign PB 205 or activity, TE T76.

Vocabulary Instruction

Teach Family Activity Words, TE T76

3 SMALL GROUP

Options for Guided Reading

80-100 minutes

Extra Support1

Before Reading Review Responding questions for LR *Come Play With Me,* TE T86. Begin a Noting Details Chart; see TE T66, Tr 9-3 for format. Help children suggest details in their LR.

During Reading Have children reread story. **Fluency Check:** Have individuals read aloud. ✓

After Reading Work with students to complete the Noting Details Chart. Have partners list other details in the story.

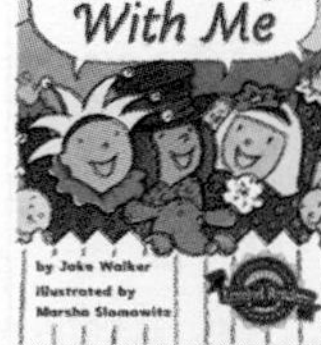

Level D

✓ = opportunity for ongoing assessment; adjust groups accordingly

▲ On Level

Before Reading Have children summarize LR *Friends Online.* ✓ Preview a teacher-selected book or TP *Mr. Santizo's Tasty Treats!,* TE R4.

During Reading Have children begin story and model Phonics/Decoding Strategy.

After Reading Discuss the story so far. Have children finish story.

Level J

■ Above Level

Before Reading Review first half of TP *Max Found Two Sticks,* TE R5. Have children make predictions about second half.

During Reading Have children finish book.

After Reading Discuss how book connects to theme. Have children write journal entries to connect it to personal experience or other reading.

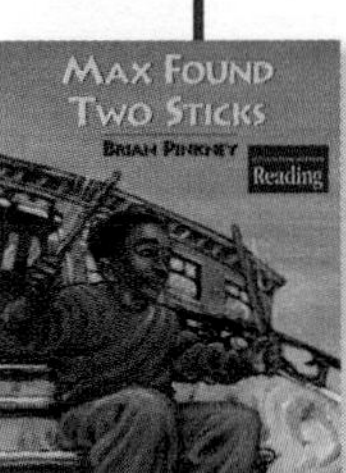

Level K

◆ English Language Learners

Before Reading Build background and preview LR *Let's Play Today!,* TE T89.

During Reading Read story. **Fluency Modeling:** Reread each page; have children do echo reading. Reinforce Phonics/Decoding Strategy.

After Reading Discuss Responding questions, TE T89. **Fluency Practice:** Have children reread with partners or audio CD.

Level D

Optional Resources

Teacher Read Aloud

Continue selected Read Aloud book from Day 3 or choose a new one from your class or school library.

Independent Work

Self-Selected Reading

Choose from

- classroom/school library
- Leveled Bibliography, TE T6–T7
- children's magazines
- *I Love Reading,* Theme 9, take-home books 80–81
- Little Readers for Guided Reading

Centers

- Classroom Management Kit
- Classroom Management activities, TE T26–T27
- Responding activities, TE T64–T65

Differentiated Instruction

- Writer's Craft: Using Headings, TE T73
- High-Frequency Words: Word Wall, TE T70
- Study Skills: Using a Dictionary, TE R34

4 WHOLE GROUP

Writing and Language

30-40 minutes

Writing

Teach Response to Literature, TE T77

Practice Assign PB 206.

TE = Teacher Edition; PB = Practice Book; Tr = Transparency; LR = Leveled Reader; PL = Phonics Library; VR = Vocabulary Reader; VR Guide = Vocabulary Readers Teacher's Manual; LBB = Little Big Book; TP = Theme Paperback

Day 5 Balanced Literacy Plan

Teacher Notes

Reading and Comprehension

20-30 minutes

Book Share

- Ask children to give examples of how they applied the comprehension skill and strategy to books they have read this week.
- Help children use genre and text features to compare and contrast what they have read.
- As a class, discuss one *how, why,* or *what if* question. See examples on Blackline Master 1 to use as a guide.

Word Work

25-40 minutes

Phonemic Awareness Instruction

Teach Deleting Phonemes, TE T79

High-Frequency Words

Cumulative Review Word Wall, TE T78

Spelling

Test See TE T84.

Options for Guided Reading

80-100 minutes

Extra Support

Before Reading Preview *I Spy,* PL Theme 9, pp. 21–27. Have children find/read words with sounds for *y.* See TE T81–T83.

During Reading Have children read and model Phonics/ Decoding Strategy. **Fluency Check:** Have individuals reread aloud. ✓

After Reading Have partners make connections between the story and LR *Come Play With Me.* Assign On My Way Practice Reader *The Ant and the Dove* for partner reading.

✓ = opportunity for ongoing assessment; adjust groups accordingly

◆ English Language Learners

Level D

Before Reading Review LR *Let's Play Today!*, TE T89.

During Reading Coach rereading of book. **Fluency Check:** Have individuals reread aloud. ✓

After Reading Help children summarize LR. Have children draw/caption a picture about a book they read this week. ✓

●▲■◆ Mixed Ability Levels

Literature Circles Form small, mixed-ability groups. Ask groups to discuss the main Anthology selection, Link, Leveled Readers, and other books they have read this week. Pose questions or topics for each group, and circulate among groups to offer support. Suggested group activities:

- Respond to specific Literature Discussion questions on Blackline Master 1.
- Discuss story or text elements, authors' choice of language, and/or illustrations.
- Connect book topics or themes to personal experiences or other reading.

Writing and Language

30-40 minutes

Writing

Practice Assign Writing Prompt, TE T79.

Grammar

Review Using *Is* and *Are*, TE T85

Listening and Speaking

Teach Evaluate and Assess, TE T85

Optional Resources

Teacher Read Aloud

Choose a nonfiction book related to Social Studies or Science unit.

Independent Work

Self-Selected Reading

Choose from
- classroom/school library
- Leveled Bibliography, TE T6–T7
- children's magazines
- consumer texts such as books about inventions/inventors, articles about new technology, etc.

Centers
- Classroom Management Kit
- Classroom Management activities, TE T26–T27
- Responding activities, TE T64–T65

Differentiated Instruction

- High-Frequency Word Review, TE T84
- Comprehension Review: Noting Details, TE T80

End-of-Week Assessment

- Weekly Skills Tests for Theme 9, Week 1
- Fluency Assessment, *I Spy*, PL Theme 9, pp. 21–27, TE T81–T83
- Alternative Assessment, Teacher's Resource Blackline Master 119

TE = Teacher Edition; PB = Practice Book; Tr = Transparency; LR = Leveled Reader; PL = Phonics Library; VR = Vocabulary Reader; VR Guide = Vocabulary Readers Teacher's Manual; LBB = Little Big Book; TP = Theme Paperback

Day 1 Balanced Literacy Plan

Teacher Notes

Reading and Comprehension

20-30 minutes

Shared Reading of Daily Message, TE T112

Listening Comprehension

- Read aloud *Frog Helps Snake,* TE T114–T115.
- Model fluent reading; discuss the story.

Word Work

25-40 minutes

Phonemic Awareness/Phonics Instruction

Teach Deleting Phonemes, TE T113, T116

Teach Base Words and Endings *-es, -ies;* Prefixes *un-* and *re-,* TE T116–T117, T118

Practice Assign PB 209, 210.

Spelling Instruction: Adding *-es* to Naming Words

Pretest and Teach Spelling Principle, TE T122

Assign Take-Home Spelling Word List, PB 319

dishes dresses boxes beaches wishes kisses

Challenge: brushes, classes

Vocabulary Instruction

Teach Base Words with the Ending *-es,* TE T122

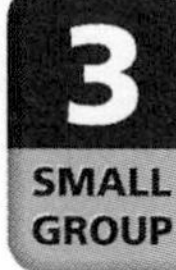

Options for Guided Reading

80-100 minutes

Extra Support

Before Reading Preview *Bo's Bunnies,* PL Theme 9, pp. 29–35. Model Phonics/Decoding Strategy. See TE T119–T121.

During Reading Coach as children read story.

After Reading Discuss story; have children find/read words with endings *-es* and *-ies* and prefixes *un-* and *re-*. **Fluency Modeling:** Model fluent reading. Have partners reread story.

✓ = opportunity for ongoing assessment; adjust groups accordingly

▲ On Level

Before Reading Preview *Bo's Bunnies,* PL Theme 9, pp. 29–35, and review TE T119–T121.

During Reading Have children begin story. **Fluency Modeling:** Model Phonics/Decoding Strategy and fluent reading.

After Reading Have children retell story so far and find/read words with endings *-es* and *-ies* and prefixes *un-* and *re-*. **Fluency Practice:** Have partners finish story and reread for fluency.

■ Above Level

Before Reading Preview LR *Friends Forever,* TE T170.

During Reading Have children read first half of story. **Fluency Modeling:** Model fluent reading.

After Reading Have children finish reading and write answers to Responding questions. ✓

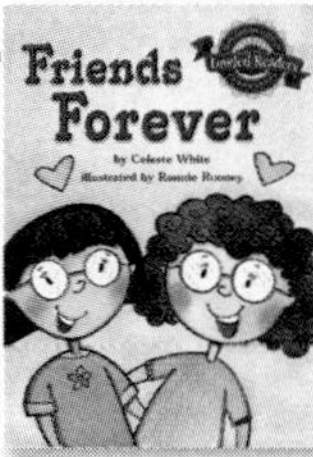

Level K

◆ English Language Learners

Before Reading Preview VR *Plan a Party.* See VR Guide, p. 31.

During Reading **Fluency Modeling:** Read aloud each page; have children do echo reading.

After Reading Discuss Responding pages. Have children reread with partners or audio CD.

Level E

4 WHOLE GROUP

Writing and Language

25-40 minutes

Writing

Teach Shared Writing: A Class Newsletter, TE T123

Practice Assign Writing Prompt, TE T113.

Listening and Speaking

Teach Having a Conversation, TE T123

Optional Resources

Teacher Read Aloud

Reread *Frog Helps Snake,* TE T114–T115.

Independent Work

Self-Selected Reading

Choose from

- classroom/school library
- Leveled Bibliography, TE T6–T7
- *I Love Reading,* Theme 9, take-home books 82–83
- Little Readers for Guided Reading

Centers

- Classroom Management Kit
- Classroom Management activities, TE T110–T111

Differentiated Instruction

- Phonics Reteaching or Extension: Base Words and Endings *-es, -ies,* TE R14–R15
- Phonics Reteaching or Extension: Prefixes *un-, re-,* TE R16–R17
- High-Frequency Words Review: Word Wall, TE T112

TE = Teacher Edition; PB = Practice Book; Tr = Transparency; LR = Leveled Reader; PL = Phonics Library; VR = Vocabulary Reader; VR Guide = Vocabulary Readers Teacher's Manual; LBB = Little Big Book; TP = Theme Paperback

Day 2 Balanced Literacy Plan

Teacher Notes

Reading and Comprehension

20-30 minutes

Shared Reading of *The New Friend* (Part 1)

➤ Build Background and Vocabulary; Introduce Story Vocabulary, TE T128–T129, Tr 9-8

birthday	cookies	party	soccer
city	empty	seventh	years

➤ Introduce Comprehension Strategy and Skill:
Evaluate, TE T130
Story Structure, TE T130, T136

➤ Set Purpose, TE T131

➤ Read Anthology Selection pp. 54–60 (independent, partner, or audio CD).

▼ Anthology Selection

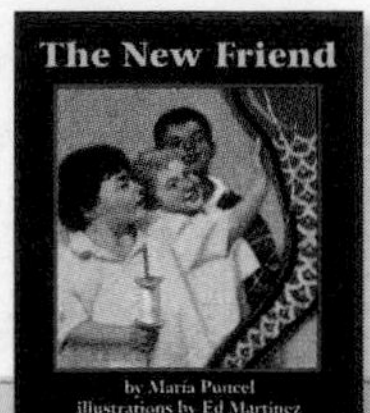

Words to Know

after	brushes
before	wishes
school	boxes
pretty	families
done	unloaded
buy	unpack
off	repaid
wash	

Word Work

25-40 minutes

Phonemic Awareness/Phonics Instruction

Teach Deleting Phonemes, TE T125

High-Frequency Word Instruction

Teach TE T126–T127, Tr 9-7; Practice PB 211–212.

High-Frequency Words

after	off
before	pretty
buy	school
done	wash

Spelling Instruction

Review Adding *-es* to Naming Words, TE T142

3
SMALL
GROUP

Options for Guided Reading

80-100 minutes

● **Extra Support**

Before Reading Preview VR *Plan a Party.* See VR Guide, p. 31.

During Reading Read the book together; coach reading. Help children apply Evaluate Strategy.

After Reading Help children compare this book to *The New Friend.* **Fluency Practice:** Have children reread VR. Assign *The Fleet Street Club,* PL Theme 9, pp. 36–44, for partner reading.

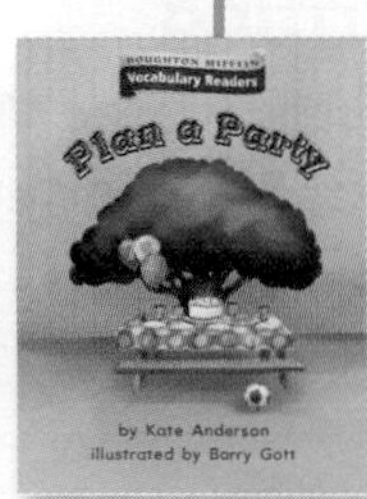

Level E

✓ = opportunity for ongoing assessment; adjust groups accordingly

 **On Level**

Before Reading Discuss PL *Bo's Bunnies,* TE T119. Preview LR *The Sleepover,* TE T169.

During Reading Coach reading as children begin story. Have children model the Evaluate Strategy. **Fluency Modeling:** Model fluent reading; have children model.

After Reading Have children finish reading and write answers to Responding questions. ✓ Assign *The Fleet Street Club,* PL Theme 9, pp. 36–44, for partner reading.

Level H

 **Above Level**

Before Reading Have children model the Evaluate Strategy and discuss Responding questions for LR *Friends Forever,* TE T170.

During Reading **Fluency Check:** Monitor children's oral reading. ✓

After Reading Have children discuss the story with a partner. Assign *The Fleet Street Club,* PL Theme 9, pp. 36–44, for partner reading.

Level K

 **English Language Learners**

Before Reading To review VR vocabulary, have children demonstrate or give examples. See VR Guide, p. 31.

During Reading Model Evaluate Strategy. Help children apply the Evaluate Strategy. **Fluency Practice:** Have children reread book. Option: Preview and coach reading of *Bo's Bunnies,* PL Theme 9, pp. 29–35, TE T119–T121.

After Reading Help children summarize VR. Have partners discuss, draw, or write facts they learned. ✓

Level E

Writing and Language

25-40 minutes

Writing

Teach Interactive Writing: A Class Newsletter, TE T143

Practice Assign Writing Prompt, TE T125.

TE = Teacher Edition; PB = Practice Book; Tr = Transparency; LR = Leveled Reader; PL = Phonics Library; VR = Vocabulary Reader; VR Guide = Vocabulary Readers Teacher's Manual; LBB = Little Big Book; TP = Theme Paperback

Optional Resources

Teacher Read Aloud

Choose a book from your class/school library or from the Leveled Bibliography, TE T6–T7.

Suggestion: *Extraordinary Friends* by Fred Rogers

Independent Work

Self-Selected Reading

Choose from
- classroom/school library
- Leveled Bibliography, TE T6–T7
- *I Love Reading,* Theme 9, take-home books 82–83
- Little Readers for Guided Reading

Centers
- Classroom Management Kit
- Classroom Management activities, TE T110–T111

Differentiated Instruction

- High-Frequency Words
  - Word Wall, TE T124
  - Review, TE T142
  - Reteaching or Extension, TE R24–R25

Day 3 Balanced Literacy Plan

Teacher Notes

Reading and Comprehension

Shared Reading of *The New Friend* (Part 2)

▼ Anthology Selection

- Read Anthology Selection pp. 61–71 (independent, partner, or audio CD).
- Discuss questions, TE T146; have children cite text to support answers.

Comprehension Skill Instruction

Teach Story Structure, TE T148–T149, Tr 9-9

Practice Assign PB 215 or retelling of story.

Word Work

Phonemic Awareness Instruction

Teach Deleting Phonemes, TE T145

Spelling: Adding *-es* to Naming Words

Practice Assign PB 216 or activity, TE T150.

Vocabulary Instruction

Teach Synonyms, TE T150

Practice Assign PB 217.

3 SMALL GROUP

Options for Guided Reading

80-100 minutes

Extra Support

Before Reading Discuss Responding questions from VR *Plan a Party.* See VR Guide, p. 31. Preview LR *Knock, Knock,* TE T168.

During Reading Coach as children read story. **Fluency Modeling:** Model fluent reading; have children model.

After Reading **Fluency Practice:** Have partners reread story. Have children answer Responding questions. ✓

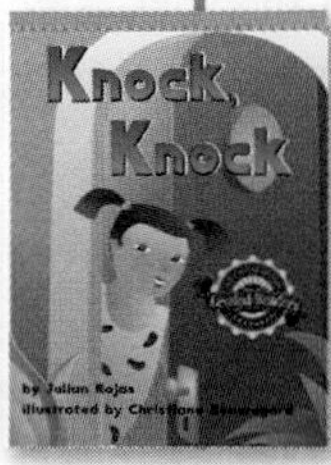

Level E

✓ = opportunity for ongoing assessment; adjust groups accordingly

 **On Level**

Before Reading Discuss Responding questions for LR *The Sleepover,* TE T169.

During Reading **Fluency Check:** Ask individuals to read story aloud. ✓

After Reading Create a Story Map; see TE T148, Tr 9-9 for format. Have children identify the important parts of their LR. Complete the Story Map together.

Level H

 **Above Level**

Before Reading Preview teacher-selected book such as *Best Friends Together Again.* See TE R8.

During Reading **Fluency Modeling:** Model fluent reading, then have children model it. Have them read first half of story independently.

After Reading Ask questions; have children cite text to support answers. Create a Story Map; see TE T148, Tr 9-9 for format. Have children identify the important parts of the teacher-selected book. Complete the Story Map together.

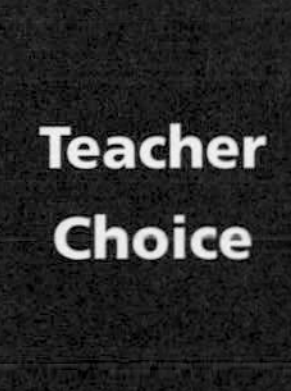

 **English Language Learners**

Before Reading Preview *The Fleet Street Club,* PL Theme 9, pp. 36–44. Model Phonics/Decoding Strategy.

During Reading **Fluency Modeling:** Read aloud each page; have children do echo reading.

After Reading Discuss story; help children find/read words with endings *-es* and *-ies* and prefixes *un-* and *re-*. Have children use illustrations to retell story to partners.

Writing and Language

 30-40 minutes

Writing

Practice Assign Write an Invitation, Anthology p. 73.

Grammar

Teach Using *Was* and *Were,* TE T151

Practice Assign PB 218.

Optional Resources

Teacher Read Aloud

Continue selected Read Aloud book from Day 2 or choose a new one from your class or school library.

Independent Work

Self-Selected Reading

Choose from

- classroom/school library
- Leveled Bibliography, TE T6–T7
- *I Love Reading,* Theme 9, take-home books 82–83
- Little Readers for Guided Reading

Centers

- Classroom Management Kit
- Classroom Management activities, TE T110–T111
- Responding activities, TE T146–T147

Differentiated Instruction

- Comprehension Reteaching or Extension: Story Structure, TE R30–R31
- High-Frequency Word Review: Word Wall, TE T144

TE = Teacher Edition; PB = Practice Book; Tr = Transparency; LR = Leveled Reader; PL = Phonics Library; VR = Vocabulary Reader; VR Guide = Vocabulary Readers Teacher's Manual; LBB = Little Big Book; TP = Theme Paperback

Day 4 Balanced Literacy Plan

Teacher Notes

Reading and Comprehension

Shared Reading of Poetry Link

- Poems, Anthology pp. 74–75, TE T154–T155 (independent, partner, or group)
- Skill: How to Read a Poem, Anthology p. 74, TE T154.
- Introduce Concept Vocabulary, TE T154.

Concept Vocabulary

halfway
hope
decide
lonely

Word Work

Phonemic Awareness/Phonics Instruction

Teach Deleting Phonemes, TE T153

Review Sounds for *y,* TE T156–T157

Spelling: Adding *-es* to Naming Words

Practice Assign PB 219 or activity, TE T158.

Vocabulary Instruction

Teach Feeling Words, TE T158

3 SMALL GROUP

Options for Guided Reading

80-100 minutes

Extra Support

Before Reading Review Responding questions for LR *Knock, Knock,* TE T168. Begin a Story Map; see TE T148, Tr 9-9 for format. Help children identify the important parts of the LR.

During Reading Have children reread story. **Fluency Check:** Have individuals read aloud. ✓

After Reading Work with students to complete the Story Map. Have partners identify other story elements.

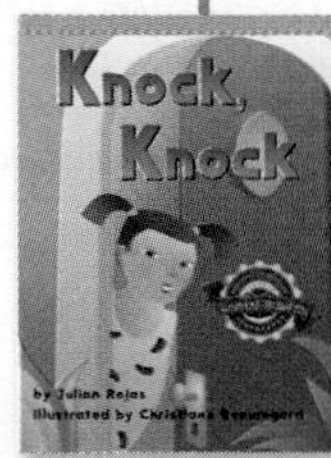

Level E

✓ = opportunity for ongoing assessment; adjust groups accordingly

▲ On Level

Before Reading Have children summarize LR *The Sleepover.* ✓ Preview a teacher-selected book such as *For Pete's Sake,* TE R7.

During Reading Have children begin story and model Phonics/Decoding Strategy.

After Reading Discuss the story so far. Have children finish story.

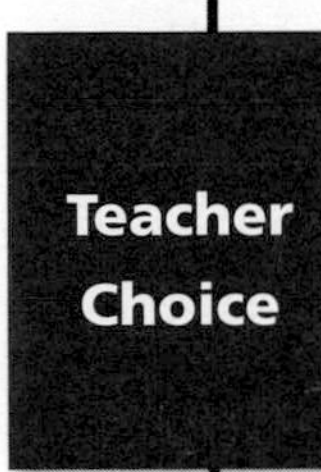

■ Above Level

Before Reading Review first half of selected book. Have children make predictions about second half.

During Reading Have children finish book.

After Reading Discuss how book connects to theme. Have children write journal entries to connect it to personal experience or other reading.

◆ English Language Learners

Before Reading Build background and preview LR *New Friends,* TE T171.

During Reading Read story. **Fluency Modeling:** Reread each page; have children do echo reading. Reinforce Phonics/Decoding Strategy.

After Reading Discuss Responding questions, TE T171. **Fluency Practice:** Have children reread with partners or audio CD.

Level E

4 WHOLE GROUP Writing and Language

30-40 minutes

Writing

Teach Complete Sentences, TE T159

Practice Assign PB 220.

Optional Resources

Teacher Read Aloud

Choose a new book from your class or school library.

Independent Work

Self-Selected Reading

Choose from

- classroom/school library
- Leveled Bibliography, TE T6–T7
- children's magazines
- *I Love Reading,* Theme 9, take-home books 82–83
- Little Readers for Guided Reading

Centers

- Classroom Management Kit
- Classroom Management activities, TE T110–T111
- Responding activities, TE T146–T147

Differentiated Instruction

- Writer's Craft: Writing with *I,* TE T155
- High-Frequency Words: Word Wall, TE T152
- Study Skills: Using a Dictionary, TE R34

TE = Teacher Edition; PB = Practice Book; Tr = Transparency; LR = Leveled Reader; PL = Phonics Library; VR = Vocabulary Reader; VR Guide = Vocabulary Readers Teacher's Manual; LBB = Little Big Book; TP = Theme Paperback

Day 5 Balanced Literacy Plan

Teacher Notes

Reading and Comprehension

20-30 minutes

Book Share

- Ask children to give examples of how they applied the comprehension skill and strategy to books they have read this week.
- Help children use genre and text features to compare and contrast what they have read.
- As a class, discuss one *how, why,* or *what* if question. See examples on Blackline Master 13 to use as a guide.

Word Work

25-40 minutes

Phonemic Awareness Instruction

Teach Deleting Phonemes, TE T161

High-Frequency Words

Cumulative Review Word Wall, TE T160

Spelling

Test See TE T166.

Options for Guided Reading

80-100 minutes

Extra Support

Before Reading Preview *Peaches, Screeches,* PL Theme 9, pp. 45–51. Have children find/read words with endings *-es* and *-ies* and prefixes *un-* and *re-*. See TE T163–T165.

During Reading Have children read and model Phonics/Decoding Strategy. **Fluency Check:** Have individuals reread aloud. ✓

After Reading Have partners make connections between the story and LR *Knock, Knock.* Assign On My Way Practice Reader *Pen Pals* for partner reading.

✓ = opportunity for ongoing assessment; adjust groups accordingly

◆ English Language Learners

Before Reading Review LR *New Friends,* TE T171.

During Reading Coach rereading of book. **Fluency Check:** Have individuals reread aloud. ✓

After Reading Help children summarize LR. Have children draw/caption a picture about a book they read this week. ✓

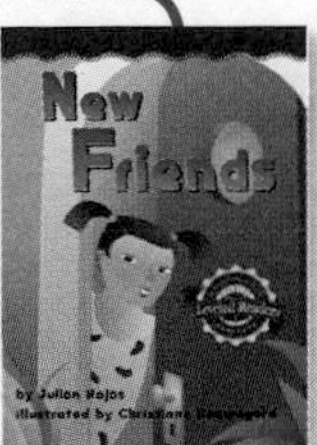

Level E

●▲■◆ Mixed Ability Levels

Literature Circles Form small, mixed-ability groups. Ask groups to discuss the main Anthology selection, Link, Leveled Readers, and other books they have read this week. Pose questions or topics for each group, and circulate among groups to offer support. Suggested group activities:

- Respond to specific Literature Discussion questions on Blackline Master 1.
- Discuss story or text elements, authors' choice of language, and/or illustrations.
- Connect book topics or themes to personal experiences or other reading.

Writing and Language

30-40 minutes

Writing

Practice Assign Writing Prompt, TE T161.

Grammar

Review Using *Was* and *Were,* TE T167

Speaking

Teach Giving Information, TE T167

Optional Resources

Teacher Read Aloud

Choose a nonfiction book related to Social Studies or Science unit.

Independent Work

Self-Selected Reading

Choose from

- classroom/school library
- Leveled Bibliography, TE T6–T7
- children's magazines
- consumer texts such as poetry books, dictionaries, etc.

Centers

- Classroom Management Kit
- Classroom Management activities, TE T110–T111
- Responding activities, TE T146–T147

Differentiated Instruction

- High-Frequency Word Review, TE T166
- Comprehension Review: Story Structure, TE T162

End-of-Week Assessment

- Weekly Skills Tests for Theme 9, Week 2
- Fluency Assessment, *Peaches, Screeches,* PL Theme 9, pp. 45–51, TE T163–T165
- Alternative Assessment, Teacher's Resource Blackline Master 122

TE = Teacher Edition; PB = Practice Book; Tr = Transparency; LR = Leveled Reader; PL = Phonics Library; VR = Vocabulary Reader; VR Guide = Vocabulary Readers Teacher's Manual; LBB = Little Big Book; TP = Theme Paperback

Day 1 Balanced Literacy Plan

Teacher Notes

Reading and Comprehension

20-30 minutes

Shared Reading of Daily Message, TE T182

Listening Comprehension

- Read aloud *Natural Habits,* TE T184–T185.
- Model fluent reading; discuss the story.

Word Work

25-40 minutes

Phonemic Awareness/Phonics Instruction

Teach Deleting Phonemes, TE T183, T186

Teach Vowel Pairs *oy, oi; aw, au,* Suffixes *-ful, -ly, -y,* TE T186–T187, T188

Practice Assign PB 221–222, 223.

Spelling Instruction: The Vowel Sound in *coin*

Pretest and Teach Spelling Principle, TE T192

Assign Take-Home Spelling Word List, PB 321

coin soil boy oil toy point

Challenge: moist, destroy

Vocabulary Instruction

Teach Words with *aw, oy,* TE T192

Options for Guided Reading

80-100 minutes

Extra Support

Before Reading Preview *Jenny's Big Voice,* PL Theme 9, pp. 53–59. Model Phonics/Decoding Strategy. See TE T189–T191.

During Reading Coach as children read story.

After Reading Discuss story; have children find/read words with *oy, oi, aw, au.* **Fluency Modeling:** Model fluent reading. Have partners reread story.

✓ = opportunity for ongoing assessment; adjust groups accordingly

▲ On Level

Before Reading Preview *Jenny's Big Voice,* PL Theme 9, pp. 53–59, and review TE T189–T191.

During Reading Have children begin story. **Fluency Modeling:** Model Phonics/Decoding Strategy and fluent reading.

After Reading Have children retell story so far and find/read words with *oy, oi, aw, au.* **Fluency Practice:** Have partners finish story and reread for fluency.

■ Above Level

Before Reading Preview LR *Junk into Art,* TE T246.

During Reading Have children read first half of story. **Fluency Modeling:** Model fluent reading.

After Reading Have children finish reading and write answers to Responding questions. ✓

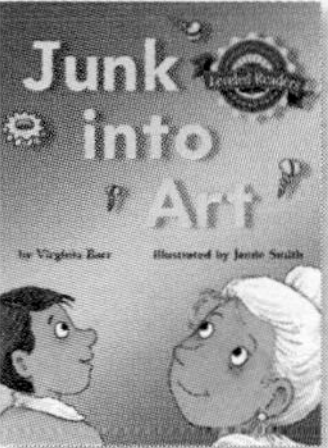

Level K

◆ English Language Learners

Before Reading Preview VR *Chickens on the Farm.* See VR Guide, p. 32.

During Reading **Fluency Modeling:** Read aloud each page; have children do echo reading.

After Reading Discuss Responding pages. Have children reread with partners or audio CD.

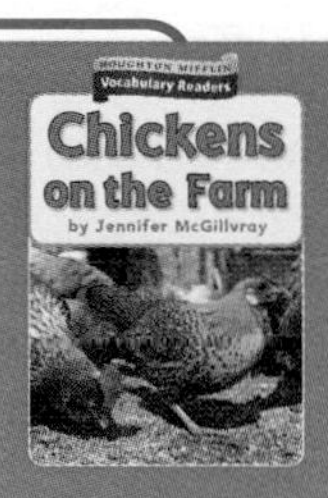

Level F

4 WHOLE GROUP

Writing and Language

25-40 minutes

Writing

Teach Shared Writing: Another Version, TE T193

Practice Assign Writing Prompt, TE T183.

Listening

Teach Visualizing, TE T193

Optional Resources

Teacher Read Aloud

Reread *Natural Habits,* TE T184–T185.

Independent Work

Self-Selected Reading

Choose from

- classroom/school library
- Leveled Bibliography, TE T6–T7
- *I Love Reading,* Theme 9, take-home books 84–87
- Little Readers for Guided Reading

Centers

- Classroom Management Kit
- Classroom Management activities, TE T180–T181

Differentiated Instruction

- Phonics Reteaching or Extension: Vowel Pairs *oi, oy; aw, au,* TE R18–R19
- Phonics Reteaching or Extension: Suffixes *-ful, -ly, -y,* TE R20–R21
- High-Frequency Words Review: Word Wall, TE T182

TE = Teacher Edition; PB = Practice Book; Tr = Transparency; LR = Leveled Reader; PL = Phonics Library; VR = Vocabulary Reader; VR Guide = Vocabulary Readers Teacher's Manual; LBB = Little Big Book; TP = Theme Paperback

Day 2 Balanced Literacy Plan

Teacher Notes

Reading and Comprehension

Shared Reading of *The Surprise Family* (Part 1)

▼ Anthology Selection

- Build Background and Vocabulary; Introduce Story Vocabulary, TE T198–T199, Tr 9-14

built	danger	feathers	gizzard/s	vacuum cleaner
chicken/s	expected	gathered	taught	

- Introduce Comprehension Strategy and Skill: Question, TE T200
  Compare and Contrast, TE T200, T215
- Set Purpose, TE T201
- Read Anthology Selection pp. 79–90 (independent, partner, or audio CD).

Words to Know

only	boy
together	pointed
watched	saw
baby	hawk
edge	taught
enough	fluffy
garden	fuzzy
sharp	

Word Work

Phonemic Awareness/Phonics Instruction

Teach Deleting Phonemes, TE T195

High-Frequency Word Instruction

Teach TE T196–T197, Tr 9-13; Practice PB 224–225.

High-Frequency Words

baby	only
edge	sharp
enough	together
garden	watched

Spelling Instruction

Review The Vowel Sound in *coin,* TE T218

Options for Guided Reading

Extra Support

Before Reading Preview VR *Chickens on the Farm.* See VR Guide, p. 32.

During Reading Read the book together; coach reading. Help children apply Question Strategy.

After Reading Help children compare this book to *The Surprise Family.* **Fluency Practice:** Have children reread VR. Assign *Joy Boy,* PL Theme 9, pp. 60–68, for partner reading.

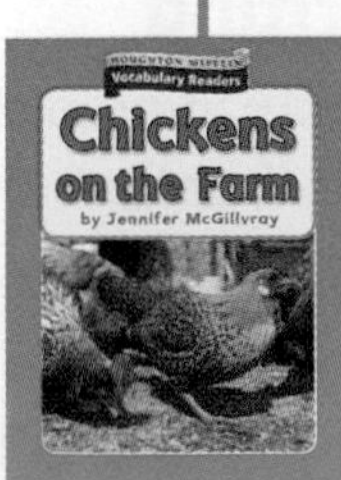

Level F

✓ = opportunity for ongoing assessment; adjust groups accordingly

▲ On Level

Before Reading Discuss PL *Jenny's Big Voice,* TE T189. Preview LR *The Duck Pond,* TE T245.

During Reading Coach reading as children begin story. Have children model the Question Strategy. **Fluency Modeling:** Model fluent reading, then have children model it.

After Reading Have children finish reading and write answers to Responding questions. ✓ Assign *Joy Boy,* PL Theme 9, pp. 60–68, for partner reading.

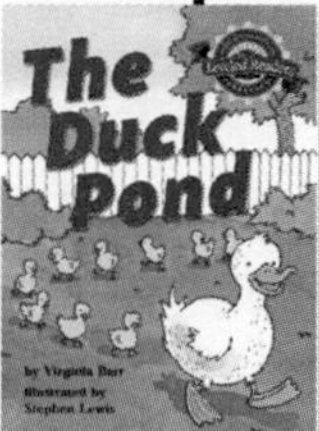

Level G

■ Above Level

Before Reading Have children model the Question Strategy and discuss Responding questions for LR *Junk into Art,* TE T246.

During Reading **Fluency Check:** Monitor children's oral reading. ✓

After Reading Have children discuss the story with a partner. Assign *Joy Boy,* PL Theme 9, pp. 60–68, for partner reading.

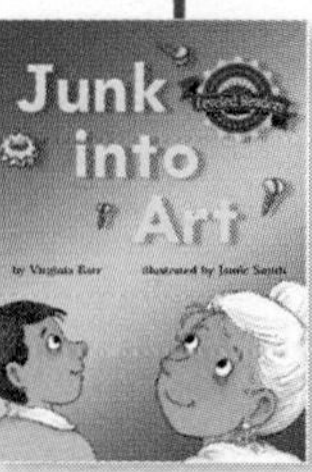

Level K

◆ English Language Learners

Before Reading To review VR vocabulary, have children demonstrate or give examples. See VR Guide, p. 32.

During Reading Model Question Strategy. Help children apply the Question Strategy. **Fluency Practice:** Have children reread book. Option: Preview and coach reading of *Jenny's Big Voice,* PL Theme 9, pp. 53–59, TE T189–T191.

After Reading Help children summarize VR. Have partners discuss, draw, or write facts they learned. ✓

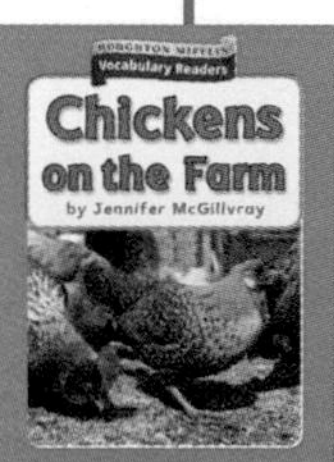

Level F

4 WHOLE GROUP Writing and Language

25-40 minutes

Writing

Teach Interactive Writing: Another Version, TE T219

Practice Assign Writing Prompt, TE T195.

Optional Resources

Teacher Read Aloud

Choose a book from your class/school library or from the Leveled Bibliography, TE T6–T7.

Suggestion: *You and Me* by Salley Mavor

Independent Work

Self-Selected Reading

Choose from

- classroom/school library
- Leveled Bibliography, TE T6–T7
- *I Love Reading,* Theme 9, take-home books 84–87
- Little Readers for Guided Reading

Centers

- Classroom Management Kit
- Classroom Management activities, TE T180–T181

Differentiated Instruction

- High-Frequency Words
  - Word Wall, TE T194
  - Review, TE T218
  - Reteaching or Extension, TE R26–R27

TE = Teacher Edition; PB = Practice Book; Tr = Transparency; LR = Leveled Reader; PL = Phonics Library; VR = Vocabulary Reader; VR Guide = Vocabulary Readers Teacher's Manual; LBB = Little Big Book; TP = Theme Paperback

Day 3 Balanced Literacy Plan

Teacher Notes

Reading and Comprehension

20-30 minutes

▼ Anthology Selection

Shared Reading of *The Surprise Family* (Part 2)

- Read Anthology Selection pp. 91–108 (independent, partner, or audio CD).
- Discuss questions, TE T222; have children cite text to support answers.

Comprehension Skill Instruction

Teach Compare and Contrast, TE T224–T225, Tr 9-15

Practice Assign PB 228 or retelling of story.

Word Work

25-40 minutes

Phonemic Awareness Instruction

Teach Deleting Phonemes, TE T221

Spelling: The Vowel Sound in *coin*

Practice Assign PB 229 or activity, TE T226.

Vocabulary Instruction

Teach Possessive Pronouns, TE T226

Practice Assign PB 230.

Options for Guided Reading

80-100 minutes

● Extra Support

Before Reading Discuss Responding questions from VR *Chickens on the Farm.* See VR Guide, p. 32. Preview LR *Runaway Sandy,* TE T244.

During Reading Coach as children read story. **Fluency Modeling:** Model fluent reading; have children model.

After Reading **Fluency Practice:** Have partners reread story. Have children answer Responding questions. ✓

Level E

✓ = opportunity for ongoing assessment; adjust groups accordingly

 On Level

Before Reading Discuss Responding questions for LR *The Duck Pond,* TE T245.

During Reading **Fluency Check:** Ask individuals to read story aloud. ✓

After Reading Create a Venn Diagram; see TE T224, Tr 9-15 for format. Have children compare/contrast story elements in their LR. Complete the diagram together.

Level G

 Above Level

Before Reading Preview teacher-selected book such as *Friends!* See TE R11.

During Reading **Fluency Modeling:** Model fluent reading, then have children model it. Have them read first half of story independently.

After Reading Ask questions; have children cite text to support answers. Create a Venn Diagram; see TE T224, Tr 9-15 for format. Have children compare/contrast story elements in the teacher-selected book. Complete the diagram together.

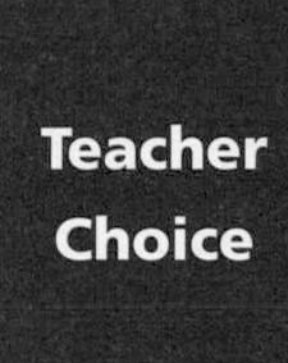

◆ English Language Learners

Before Reading Preview *Joy Boy,* PL Theme 9, pp. 60–68. Model Phonics/Decoding Strategy.

During Reading **Fluency Modeling:** Read aloud each page; have children do echo reading.

After Reading Discuss story; help children find/read words with *oy, oi, aw, au.* Have children use illustrations to retell story to partners.

Writing and Language  30-40 minutes

Writing

Practice Assign Write a Newspaper Article, Anthology p. 111.

Grammar

Teach Describing What We See, TE T227

Practice Assign PB 231.

Optional Resources

Teacher Read Aloud

Continue selected Read Aloud book from Day 2 or choose a new one from your class or school library.

Independent Work

Self-Selected Reading

Choose from

- classroom/school library
- Leveled Bibliography, TE T6–T7
- *I Love Reading,* Theme 9, take-home books 84–87
- Little Readers for Guided Reading

Centers

- Classroom Management Kit
- Classroom Management activities, TE T180–T181
- Responding activities, TE T222–T223

Differentiated Instruction

- Comprehension Reteaching or Extension: Compare and Contrast, TE R32–R33
- High-Frequency Word Review: Word Wall, TE T220

TE = Teacher Edition; PB = Practice Book; Tr = Transparency; LR = Leveled Reader; PL = Phonics Library; VR = Vocabulary Reader; VR Guide = Vocabulary Readers Teacher's Manual; LBB = Little Big Book; TP = Theme Paperback

Day 4 Balanced Literacy Plan

Teacher Notes

Reading and Comprehension

20-30 minutes

Shared Reading of Science Link

- "Watch Them Grow," Anthology pp. 112–115, TE T230–T231 (independent, partner, or group)
- Skill: How to Read a Science Article, Anthology p. 112, TE T230
- Introduce Concept Vocabulary, TE T230.

Concept Vocabulary
heading
hatching
duckling
eggs

Word Work

25-40 minutes

Phonemic Awareness/Phonics Instruction

Teach Deleting Phonemes, TE T229

Review Base Words and Endings *-es, -ies,* TE T232; Prefixes *un-, re-,* TE T233

Spelling: The Vowel Sound in *coin*

Practice Assign PB 232 or activity, TE T234.

Vocabulary Instruction

Teach Bird Words, TE T234

3 SMALL GROUP

Options for Guided Reading

80-100 minutes

Extra Support

Before Reading Review Responding questions for LR *Runaway Sandy,* TE T244. Begin a Venn Diagram; see TE T224, Tr 9-15 for format. Have children compare/contrast story elements in their LR.

During Reading Have children reread story. **Fluency Check:** Have individuals read aloud. ✓

After Reading Work with students to complete the Venn Diagram. Have partners compare/contrast other story elements.

Level E

✓ = opportunity for ongoing assessment; adjust groups accordingly

▲ On Level

Before Reading Have children summarize LR *The Duck Pond.* ✓ Preview a teacher-selected book such as *Titch and Daisy,* TE R10.

During Reading Have children begin story and model Phonics/Decoding Strategy.

After Reading Discuss the story so far. Have children finish story.

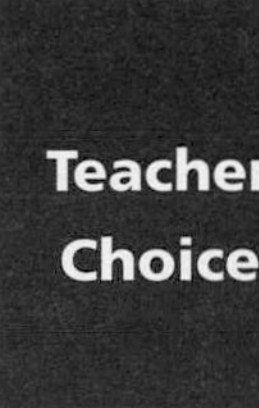

■ Above Level

Before Reading Review first half of selected book. Have children make predictions about second half.

During Reading Have children finish book.

After Reading Discuss how book connects to theme. Have children write journal entries to connect it to personal experience or other reading.

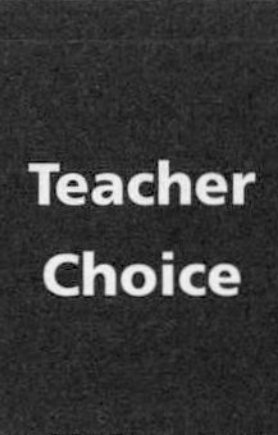

◆ English Language Learners

Before Reading Build background and preview LR *Sandy Runs Away,* TE T247.

During Reading Read story. **Fluency Modeling:** Reread each page; have children do echo reading. Reinforce Phonics/Decoding Strategy.

After Reading Discuss Responding questions, TE T247. **Fluency Practice:** Have children reread with partners or audio CD.

Level E

Optional Resources

Teacher Read Aloud

Choose a new book from your class or school library.

Independent Work

Self-Selected Reading

Choose from

- classroom/school library
- Leveled Bibliography, TE T6–T7
- children's magazines
- *I Love Reading,* Theme 9, take-home books 84–87
- Little Readers for Guided Reading

Centers

- Classroom Management Kit
- Classroom Management activities, TE T180–T181
- Responding activities, TE T222–T223

Differentiated Instruction

- Visual Literacy: Viewing Photographs, TE T231
- High-Frequency Words: Word Wall, TE T228
- Study Skills: Using a Dictionary, TE R34

Writing and Language

30-40 minutes

Writing

Teach Writing a Comparison, TE T235

Practice Assign PB 233.

TE = Teacher Edition; PB = Practice Book; Tr = Transparency; LR = Leveled Reader; PL = Phonics Library; VR = Vocabulary Reader; VR Guide = Vocabulary Readers Teacher's Manual; LBB = Little Big Book; TP = Theme Paperback

Day 5 Balanced Literacy Plan

Teacher Notes

Reading and Comprehension

20-30 minutes

Book Share

- Ask children to give examples of how they applied the comprehension skill and strategy to books they have read this week.
- Help children use genre and text features to compare and contrast what they have read.
- As a class, discuss one *how, why,* or *what if* question. See examples on Blackline Master 1 to use as a guide.

Word Work

25-40 minutes

Phonemic Awareness Instruction

Teach Deleting Phonemes, TE T237

High-Frequency Words

Cumulative Review Word Wall, TE T236

Spelling

Test See TE T242.

Options for Guided Reading

80-100 minutes

Extra Support

Before Reading Preview *Shawn's Soy Sauce*, PL Theme 9, pp. 69–75. Have children find/read words with *oi, oy, aw, au* and suffixes *-ful, -ly, -y.* See TE T239–T241.

During Reading Have children read and model Phonics/Decoding Strategy. **Fluency Check:** Have individuals reread aloud. ✓

After Reading Have partners make connections between the story and LR *Runaway Sandy.* Assign On My Way Practice Reader *Pet Shop* for partner reading.

✓ = opportunity for ongoing assessment; adjust groups accordingly

◆ English Language Learners

Before Reading Review LR *Sandy Runs Away,* TE T247.

During Reading Coach rereading of book. **Fluency Check:** Have individuals reread aloud. ✓

After Reading Help children summarize LR. Have children draw/caption a picture about a book they read this week. ✓

Level E

●▲■◆ Mixed Ability Levels

Literature Circles Form small, mixed-ability groups. Ask groups to discuss the main Anthology selection, Link, Leveled Readers, and other books they have read this week. Pose questions or topics for each group, and circulate among groups to offer support. Suggested group activities:

- Respond to specific Literature Discussion questions on Blackline Master 1.
- Discuss story or text elements, authors' choice of language, and/or illustrations.
- Connect book topics or themes to personal experiences or other reading.

Writing and Language

30-40 minutes

Writing

Practice Assign Writing Prompt, TE T237.

Grammar

Review Describing What We See, TE T243

Listening and Speaking

Teach Reader's Theater, TE T243

Optional Resources

Teacher Read Aloud

Choose a nonfiction book related to Social Studies or Science unit.

Independent Work

Self-Selected Reading

Choose from

- classroom/school library
- Leveled Bibliography, TE T6–T7
- children's magazines
- consumer texts such as books about baby animals, articles about nature, etc.

Centers

- Classroom Management Kit
- Classroom Management activities, TE T180–T181
- Responding activities, TE T222–T223

Differentiated Instruction

- High-Frequency Word Review, TE T242
- Comprehension Review: Compare and Contrast, TE T238

Assessment

End-of-Week Assessment

- Weekly Skills Tests for Theme 9, Week 3
- Fluency Assessment, *Shawn's Soy Sauce,* PL Theme 9, pp. 69–75, TE T239–T241
- Alternative Assessment, Teacher's Resource Blackline Master 126

End-of-Theme Assessment

- Integrated Theme Tests for Theme 9

TE = Teacher Edition; PB = Practice Book; Tr = Transparency; LR = Leveled Reader; PL = Phonics Library; VR = Vocabulary Reader; VR Guide = Vocabulary Readers Teacher's Manual; LBB = Little Big Book; TP = Theme Paperback

Theme 10 Overview

	Week 1
Reading and Comprehension	**Shared Reading** Main Selection: *Two Greedy Bears* Math Link: "Fraction Action" Book Share **Comprehension** Strategy: Predict/Infer Skill: Making Predictions Content Skill: How to Read a Cartoon
Word Work	**Phonemic Awareness:** Manipulate Phonemes **Phonics:** *r*-Controlled Vowels: *or, ore* **Phonics:** *r*-Controlled Vowels: *er, ir, ur* **Phonics Review:** Vowel Pairs *oi, oy; aw, au;* Suffixes *-ful, -ly, -y* **Vocabulary:** Math Words; Ordinal Number Words **High-Frequency Words:** *began, break, divide, head, laugh, second, sure* **Spelling:** The Vowel + *r* Sound in *store*
Options for Guided Reading	**Vocabulary Reader** *Polar Bears* **Leveled Readers:** Extra Support: *This Piece or That Piece?* On Level: *Why Rabbit's Tail Is Short* Above Level: *Why Bear Sleeps All Winter* ELL: *The Treat* **Phonics Library** *Sport Gets a Bath* *Home Run* *Pet Store* **Theme Paperbacks** **Literature Circles**
Writing and Oral Language	**Shared Writing:** An Opinion **Interactive Writing:** An Opinion **Independent Writing:** A Book Report **Grammar:** Describing What We Hear **Speaking:** Giving a Book Report
Assessment Options	• Weekly Skills Test for Theme 10, Week 1 • Fluency Assessment: Phonics Library

Use **Launching the Theme** on pages T16–T17 of the Teacher's Edition to introduce the theme.

Week 2

Shared Reading
Main Selection: *Fireflies for Nathan*
Poetry Link: "The Firefly"
Book Share

Comprehension
Strategy: Summarize
Skill: Sequence of Events
Content Skill: How to Read a Poem

Phonemic Awareness: Manipulate Phonemes
Phonics: *r*-Controlled Vowels: *ar*
Review: *r*-Controlled Vowels: *or, ore; r*-Controlled Vowels: *er, ir, ur*
Vocabulary: Prefixes *dis-, re-;* Comparing with Figurative Language
High-Frequency Words: *above, against, already, begin, caught, minute*
Spelling: The Vowel + *r* Sound in *car*

Vocabulary Reader
Fireflies

Leveled Readers:
Extra Support: *The New Sled*
On Level: *Cliff Can't Come*
Above Level: *Carla's Corner*
ELL: *The Sled*

Phonics Library
Big Star's Gifts
Car Trip
Mark's Part

Literature Circles

Shared Writing: A Class Poem
Interactive Writing: A Class Poem
Independent Writing: Writing Clearly with Describing Words
Grammar: Describing Words: Taste, Smell, Feel
Listening and Speaking: Listening to Retell

- Weekly Skills Test for Theme 10, Week 2
- Fluency Assessment: Phonics Library

Week 3

Shared Reading
Main Selection: *Days With Frog and Toad*
Science Link: "Is It a Frog or a Toad?"
Book Share

Comprehension
Strategy: Monitor/Clarify
Skill: Cause and Effect
Content Skill: How to Read a Chart

Phonemic Awareness: Manipulate Phonemes
Phonics: Base Words and Endings *-er, -est*
Phonics Review: Base Words and Endings *-er, -est*
Vocabulary: Suffix *-ly;* Clothing Words
High-Frequency Words: *able, eye, present, thoughts*
Spelling: Adding *-er* or *-est* to Words

Vocabulary Reader
At the Zoo

Leveled Readers:
Extra Support: *The Sweetest Present*
On Level: *Faster! Faster!*
Above Level: *Dog's Party*
ELL: *The Birthday Present*

Phonics Library
Ice-Cold Drinks
The Best Pie
Don't Ask Me

Literature Circles

Shared Writing: An Alternate Ending
Interactive Writing: An Alternate Ending
Independent Writing: A Thank-You Note
Grammar: Comparing (*-er, -est*)
Speaking and Listening: Giving and Following Directions

- Weekly Skills Test, Theme 10, Week 3
- Fluency Assessment: Phonics Library

Day 1 Balanced Literacy Plan

Teacher Notes

Reading and Comprehension

20-30 minutes

Shared Reading of Daily Message, TE T28

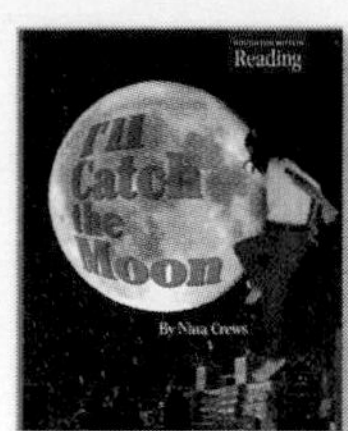

Shared Reading of Big Book

- Read aloud *I'll Catch the Moon,* TE T17, R2.
- Model fluent reading; discuss the story.

Word Work

25-40 minutes

Phonemic Awareness/Phonics Instruction

Teach Substitute Phonemes, TE T29, T32

Teach *r*-Controlled Vowels: *or, ore,* TE T32–T34

Practice Assign PB 238–239.

Spelling Instruction: The Vowel + *r* Sound in *store*

Pretest and Teach Spelling Principle, TE T38

Assign Take-Home Spelling Word List, PB 323

store more corn or for morning

Challenge: afford, before

Vocabulary Instruction

Teach Spelling Patterns *-ore, -or,* TE T38

Options for Guided Reading

80-100 minutes

Extra Support

Before Reading Preview *Sport Gets a Bath,* PL Theme 10, pp. 5–11. Model Phonics/Decoding Strategy. See TE T35–T37.

During Reading Coach as children read story.

After Reading Discuss story; have children find/read words with *or, ore.* **Fluency Modeling:** Model fluent reading. Have partners reread story.

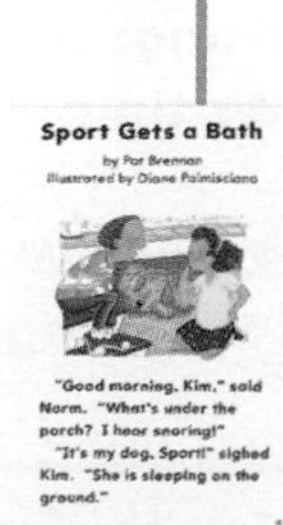

✓ = opportunity for ongoing assessment; adjust groups accordingly

 **On Level**

Before Reading Preview *Sport Gets a Bath,* PL Theme 10, pp. 5–11, and review TE T35–T37.

During Reading Have children begin story. **Fluency Modeling:** Model Phonics/Decoding Strategy and fluent reading.

After Reading Have children retell story so far and find/read words with *or, ore.* **Fluency Practice:** Have partners finish story and reread for fluency.

■ **Above Level**

Before Reading Preview LR *Why Bear Sleeps All Winter,* TE T90.

During Reading Have children read first half of story. **Fluency Modeling:** Model fluent reading.

After Reading Have children finish reading and write answers to Responding questions. ✓

Level L

 **English Language Learners**

Before Reading Preview VR *Polar Bears.* See VR Guide, p. 33.

During Reading **Fluency Modeling:** Read aloud each page; have children do echo reading.

After Reading Discuss Responding pages. Have children reread with partners or audio CD.

Level E

Writing and Language

 25-40 minutes

Writing

Teach Shared Writing: An Opinion, TE T39

Practice Assign Writing Prompt, TE T29.

Listening

Teach Assess/Evaluate, TE T39

Optional Resources

Teacher Read Aloud

Reread the Big Book: *I'll Catch the Moon,* TE T17, R2.

Read *The Pumpkin in a Jar,* TE T30–T31.

Independent Work

Self-Selected Reading

Choose from

- classroom/school library
- Leveled Bibliography, TE T6–T7
- *I Love Reading,* Theme 10, take-home book 88–89
- Little Readers for Guided Reading

Centers

- Classroom Management Kit
- Classroom Management activities, TE T26–T27

Differentiated Instruction

- Phonics Reteaching or Extension: *r*-Controlled Vowels *or, ore,* TE R12–R13
- High-Frequency Words Review: Word Wall, TE T28

TE = Teacher Edition; PB = Practice Book; Tr = Transparency; LR = Leveled Reader; PL = Phonics Library; VR = Vocabulary Reader; VR Guide = Vocabulary Readers Teacher's Manual; LBB = Little Big Book; TP = Theme Paperback

Day 2 Balanced Literacy Plan

Teacher Notes

Reading and Comprehension

20-30 minutes

Shared Reading of *Two Greedy Bears* (Part 1)

- Build Background and Vocabulary; Introduce Story Vocabulary, TE T46–T47, Tr 10-2

appetite	bigger	hungrier	larger	thirstier
argued/ing	equal	journey	stomachache	

- Introduce Comprehension Strategy and Skill: Predict/Infer, TE T48
Making Predictions, TE T48, T58
- Set Purpose, TE T49
- Read Anthology Selection pp. 144–154 (independent, partner, or audio CD).

▼ Anthology Selection

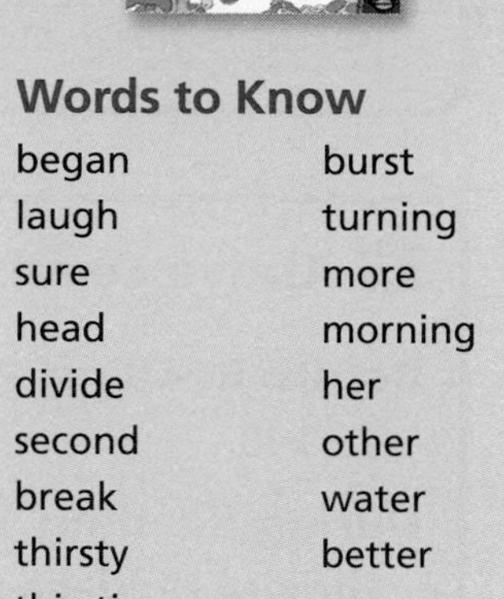

Words to Know

began	burst
laugh	turning
sure	more
head	morning
divide	her
second	other
break	water
thirsty	better
thirstier	

Word Work

25-40 minutes

Phonemic Awareness/Phonics Instruction

Teach Substitute Phonemes; *r*-Controlled Vowels *er, ir, ur,* TE T41, T42, T43;
Practice Assign PB 240–241.

High-Frequency Word Instruction

Teach TE T44–T45, Tr 10-1; Practice PB 242, 243.

Spelling Instruction

Review The Vowel + *r* Sound in *store,* TE T62

High-Frequency Words

began	sure
divide	break
second	laugh
head	

Options for Guided Reading

80-100 minutes

Extra Support

Before Reading Preview VR *Polar Bears,* VR Guide, p. 33.

During Reading Read the book together; coach reading. Help children apply Predict/Infer Strategy.

After Reading Help children compare this book to *Two Greedy Bears.* **Fluency Practice:** Have children reread VR. Assign *Home Run,* PL Theme 10, pp. 12–20, for partner reading.

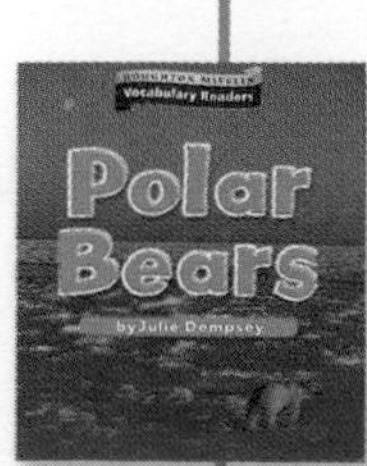

Level E

✓ = opportunity for ongoing assessment; adjust groups accordingly

▲ On Level

Before Reading Discuss PL *Sport Gets a Bath,* TE T36. Preview LR *Why Rabbit's Tail Is Short,* TE T89.

During Reading Coach reading as children begin story. Have children model the Predict/Infer Strategy. **Fluency Modeling:** Model fluent reading; have children model.

After Reading Children finish reading and write answers to Responding questions. ✓ Assign *Home Run,* PL Theme 10, pp. 12–20, for partner reading.

Level G

■ Above Level

Before Reading Have children model the Predict/Infer Strategy and discuss Responding questions for LR *Why Bear Sleeps All Winter,* TE T90.

During Reading **Fluency Check:** Monitor children's oral reading. ✓

After Reading Have children discuss the story with a partner. Assign *Home Run,* PL Theme 10, pp. 12–20, for partner reading.

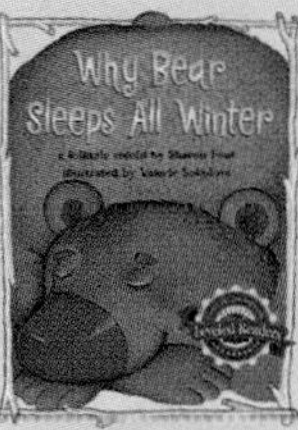

Level L

◆ English Language Learners

Before Reading To review VR vocabulary, have children demonstrate or give examples. See VR Guide, p. 33.

During Reading Model Predict/Infer Strategy. Help children apply the Predict/Infer Strategy. **Fluency Practice:** Have children reread book. Option: Preview and coach reading of *Sport Gets a Bath,* PL Theme 10, pp. 5–11, TE T35–T37.

After Reading Help children summarize VR. Have partners discuss, draw, or write facts they learned. ✓

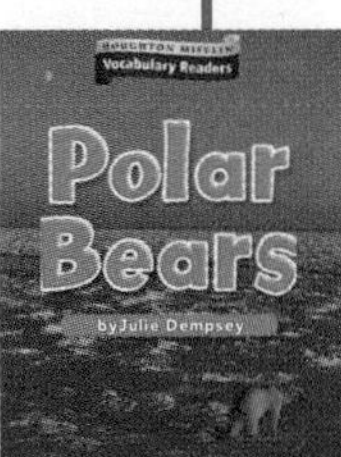

Level E

4 WHOLE GROUP Writing and Language

25-40 minutes

Writing

Teach Interactive Writing: An Opinion, TE T63

Practice Assign Writing Prompt, TE T41.

Optional Resources

Teacher Read Aloud

Reread Big Book: *I'll Catch the Moon.* See TE T17, R2.

Independent Work

Self-Selected Reading

Choose from

- classroom/school library
- Leveled Bibliography, TE T6–T7
- *I Love Reading,* Theme 10, take-home books 88–89, 90–92
- Little Readers for Guided Reading

Centers

- Classroom Management Kit
- Classroom Management activities, TE T26–T27

Differentiated Instruction

- Phonics Reteaching or Extension: *r*-Controlled Vowels *or, ore,* TE R12–R13
- Phonics Reteaching or Extension: *r*-Controlled Vowels *er, ir, ur,* TE R14–R15
- High-Frequency Words
  - Word Wall, TE T40
  - Review, TE T62
  - Reteaching or Extension, TE R20–R21

TE = Teacher Edition; PB = Practice Book; Tr = Transparency; LR = Leveled Reader; PL = Phonics Library; VR = Vocabulary Reader; VR Guide = Vocabulary Readers Teacher's Manual; LBB = Little Big Book; TP = Theme Paperback

Day 3 Balanced Literacy Plan

Teacher Notes

Reading and Comprehension

Shared Reading of *Two Greedy Bears* (Part 2)

▼ **Anthology Selection**

- Read Anthology Selection pp. 155–164 (independent, partner, or audio CD).
- Discuss questions, TE T66; have children cite text to support answers.

Comprehension Skill Instruction

Teach Making Predictions, TE T68–T69

Practice Assign PB 247 or retelling of story.

Word Work

Phonemic Awareness Instruction

Teach Substitute Phonemes, TE T65

Spelling: The Vowel + *r* Sound in *store*

Practice Assign PB 248 or activity, TE T70.

Vocabulary Instruction

Teach Math Words, TE T70

Practice Assign PB 249.

Options for Guided Reading

● Extra Support

Before Reading Discuss Responding questions from VR *Polar Bears.* See VR Guide, p. 33. Preview LR *This Piece or That Piece?,* TE T88.

During Reading Coach as children read story. **Fluency Modeling:** Model fluent reading; have children model.

After Reading **Fluency Practice:** Have partners reread story. Have children answer Responding questions. ✓

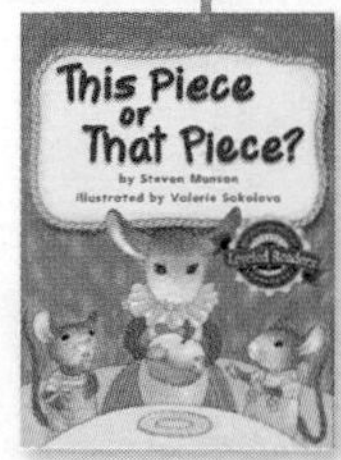

Level E

✓ = opportunity for ongoing assessment; adjust groups accordingly

▲ On Level

Before Reading Discuss Responding questions for LR *Why Rabbit's Tail Is Short,* TE T89.

During Reading **Fluency Check:** Ask individuals to read story aloud. ✓

After Reading Have children predict what might happen if the author continued the LR story or the same characters were in new situations.

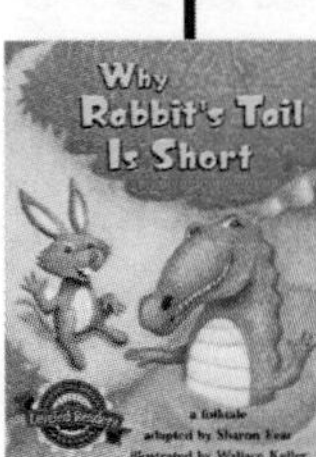

Level G

■ Above Level

Before Reading Preview TP *Fireman Small.* See TE R5.

During Reading **Fluency Modeling:** Model fluent reading, then have children model it. Have them read first half of story independently.

After Reading Ask questions; have children cite text to support answers. Have children predict what might happen if the author continued the LR story or the same characters were in new situations.

Level K

 English Language Learners

Before Reading Preview *Home Run,* PL Theme 10, pp. 12–20. Model Phonics/Decoding Strategy.

During Reading **Fluency Modeling:** Read aloud each page; have children do echo reading.

After Reading Discuss story; help children find/read words with *or, ore, er, ir, ur.* Have children use illustrations to retell story to partners.

4 WHOLE GROUP

Writing and Language

30-40 minutes

Writing

Practice Assign Write Sentences, Anthology p. 167.

Grammar

Teach Describing What We Hear, TE T71

Practice Assign PB 250.

Optional Resources

Teacher Read Aloud

Choose a book from your class/school library or from the Leveled Bibliography, TE T6–T7.

Suggestion: *Science Fair Bunnies* by Kathryn Lasky

Independent Work

Self-Selected Reading

Choose from

- classroom/school library
- Leveled Bibliography, TE T6–T7
- *I Love Reading,* Theme 10, take-home books 88–89, 90–92
- Little Readers for Guided Reading

Centers

- Classroom Management Kit
- Classroom Management activities, TE T26–T27
- Responding activities, TE T66–T67

Differentiated Instruction

- Comprehension Reteaching or Extension, *r*-Controlled Vowels *or, ore,* TE R12–R13
- Comprehension Reteaching or Extension, *r*-Controlled Vowels *er, ir, ur,* TE R14–R15
- High-Frequency Word Review: Word Wall, TE T64

TE = Teacher Edition; PB = Practice Book; Tr = Transparency; LR = Leveled Reader; PL = Phonics Library; VR = Vocabulary Reader; VR Guide = Vocabulary Readers Teacher's Manual; LBB = Little Big Book; TP = Theme Paperback

Day 4 Balanced Literacy Plan

Teacher Notes

Reading and Comprehension

20-30 minutes

Shared Reading of Math Link

- "Fraction Action," Anthology pp. 168–171, TE T74–T75 (independent, partner, or group)
- Skill: How to Read a Cartoon, Anthology p. 168, TE T74
- Introduce Concept Vocabulary, TE T74.

Concept Vocabulary

fraction
equal
whole
one half

Word Work

25-40 minutes

Phonemic Awareness/Phonics Instruction

Teach Substitute Phonemes, TE T73

Review Vowel Pairs *oi, oy, aw, au,* TE T76; Suffixes *-ful, -ly, -y,* TE T77

Spelling: The Vowel + *r* Sound in *store*

Practice Assign PB 251 or activity, TE T78.

Vocabulary Instruction

Teach Original Number Words, TE T78

3 SMALL GROUP

Options for Guided Reading

80-100 minutes

Extra Support

Before Reading Review Responding questions for LR *This Piece or That Piece?,* TE T88. Help children predict events in the LR story.

During Reading Have children reread story. **Fluency Check:** Have individuals read aloud. ✓

After Reading Help children predict what might happen if the author continued the LR story or the same characters were in new situations.

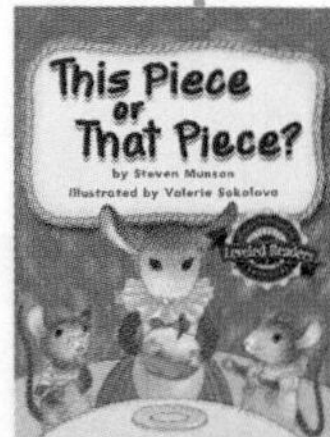

Level E

✓ = opportunity for ongoing assessment; adjust groups accordingly

 **On Level**

Before Reading Have children summarize LR *Why Rabbit's Tail Is Short.* ✓ Preview a teacher-selected book or TP *Bunny Cakes,* TE R4.

During Reading Have children begin story and model Phonics/Decoding Strategy.

After Reading Discuss the story so far. Have children finish story.

Level K

 **Above Level**

Before Reading Review first half of TP *Fireman Small,* TE R5. Have children make predictions about second half.

During Reading Have children finish book.

After Reading Discuss how book connects to theme. Have children write journal entries to connect it to personal experience or other reading.

Level K

 **English Language Learners**

Before Reading Build background and preview LR *The Treat,* TE T91.

During Reading Read story. **Fluency Modeling:** Reread each page; have children do echo reading. Reinforce Phonics/Decoding Strategy.

After Reading Discuss Responding questions, TE T91. **Fluency Practice:** Have children reread with partners or audio CD.

Level E

Writing and Language

 30-40 minutes

Writing

Teach A Book Report, TE T79

Practice Assign PB 252.

Optional Resources

Teacher Read Aloud

Continue selected Read Aloud book from Day 3 or choose a new one from your class or school library.

Independent Work

Self-Selected Reading

Choose from

- classroom/school library
- Leveled Bibliography, TE T6–T7
- children's magazines
- *I Love Reading,* Theme 10, take-home books 88–89, 90–92
- Little Readers for Guided Reading

Centers

- Classroom Management Kit
- Classroom Management activities, TE T26–T27
- Responding activities, TE T66–T67

Differentiated Instruction

- Writer's Craft: Speech Balloons, TE T75
- High-Frequency Words: Word Wall, TE T72
- Study Skills
  – Reading a Chart, TE R32

TE = Teacher Edition; PB = Practice Book; Tr = Transparency; LR = Leveled Reader; PL = Phonics Library; VR = Vocabulary Reader; VR Guide = Vocabulary Readers Teacher's Manual; LBB = Little Big Book; TP = Theme Paperback

Day 5 Balanced Literacy Plan

Teacher Notes

Reading and Comprehension

20-30 minutes

Book Share

- Ask children to give examples of how they applied the comprehension skill and strategy to books they have read this week.
- Help children use genre and text features to compare and contrast what they have read.
- As a class, discuss one *how, why,* or *what if* question. See examples on Blackline Master 1 to use as a guide.

Word Work

25-40 minutes

Phonemic Awareness Instruction

Teach Phoneme Substitutions, TE T81

High-Frequency Words

Cumulative Review Word Wall, TE T80

Spelling

Test See TE T86.

Options for Guided Reading

80-100 minutes

Extra Support

Before Reading Preview *Pet Store*, PL Theme 10, pp. 21–27. Have children find/read words with *or, ore.* See TE T83–T85.

During Reading Have children read and model Phonics/Decoding Strategy. **Fluency Check:** Have individuals reread aloud. ✓

After Reading Have partners make connections between the story and LR *This Piece or That Piece?* Assign On My Way Practice Reader *You Can Help, Too!* for partner reading.

✓ = opportunity for ongoing assessment; adjust groups accordingly

 **English Language Learners**

Before Reading Review LR *The Treat,* TE T91.

During Reading Coach rereading of book. **Fluency Check:** Have individuals reread aloud. ✔

After Reading Help children summarize LR. Have children draw/caption a picture about a book they read this week. ✔

Level E

 **Mixed Ability Levels**

Literature Circles Form small, mixed-ability groups. Ask groups to discuss the main Anthology selection, Link, Leveled Readers, and other books they have read this week. Pose questions or topics for each group, and circulate among groups to offer support. Suggested group activities:

- Respond to specific Literature Discussion questions on Blackline Master 1.
- Discuss story or text elements, authors' choice of language, and/or illustrations.
- Connect book topics or themes to personal experiences or other reading.

Writing and Language

 30-40 minutes

Writing

Practice Assign Writing Prompt, TE T81.

Grammar

Review Describing What We Hear, TE T87

Speaking

Teach Giving a Book Report, TE T87

Optional Resources

Teacher Read Aloud

Choose a nonfiction book related to Social Studies or Science unit.

Independent Work

Self-Selected Reading

Choose from

- classroom/school library
- Leveled Bibliography, TE T6–T7
- children's magazines
- consumer text such as books about comics, books about math, etc.

Centers

- Classroom Management Kit
- Classroom Management activities, TE T26–T27
- Responding activities, TE T66–T67

Differentiated Instruction

- High-Frequency Word Review: TE T86
- Comprehension Review: Making Predictions, TE T82

End-of-Week Assessment

- Weekly Skills Tests for Theme 10, Week 1
- Fluency Assessment, *Pet Store,* PL Theme 10, pp. 21–27, TE T83–T85
- Alternative Assessment, Teacher's Resource Blackline Master 132

TE = Teacher Edition; PB = Practice Book; Tr = Transparency; LR = Leveled Reader; PL = Phonics Library; VR = Vocabulary Reader; VR Guide = Vocabulary Readers Teacher's Manual; LBB = Little Big Book; TP = Theme Paperback

Day 1 Balanced Literacy Plan

Teacher Notes

Reading and Comprehension

20-30 minutes

Shared Reading of Daily Message, TE T114

Listening Comprehension

- Read aloud *Stone Soup,* TE T116–T117.
- Model fluent reading; discuss the story.

Word Work

25-40 minutes

Phonemic Awareness/Phonics Instruction

Teach Substitute Phonemes, TE T115, T118

Teach *r*-Controlled Vowels: *ar,* TE T118–T120

Practice Assign PB 255–256.

Spelling Instruction: The Vowel + *r* Sound in *car*

Pretest and Teach Spelling Principle, TE T124

Assign Take-Home Spelling Word List, PB 323

arm far car start dark yard

Challenge: large, jar

Vocabulary Instruction

Teach Spelling Pattern *-ar,* TE T124

Options for Guided Reading

80-100 minutes

Extra Support

Before Reading Preview *Big Star's Gifts,* PL Theme 10, pp. 29–35. Model Phonics/Decoding Strategy. See TE T121–T123.

During Reading Coach as children read story.

After Reading Discuss story; have children find/read words with *ar*. **Fluency Modeling:** Model fluent reading. Have partners reread story.

✓ = opportunity for ongoing assessment; adjust groups accordingly

▲ On Level

Before Reading Preview *Big Star's Gifts,* PL Theme 10, pp. 29–35, and review TE T121–T123.

During Reading Have children begin story. **Fluency Modeling:** Model Phonics/Decoding Strategy and fluent reading.

After Reading Have children retell story so far and find/read words with *ar.* **Fluency Practice:** Have partners finish story and reread for fluency.

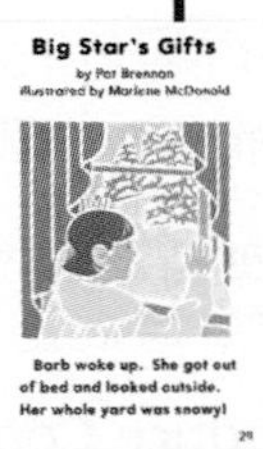

■ Above Level

Before Reading Preview LR *Carla's Corner,* TE T174.

During Reading Have children read first half of story. **Fluency Modeling:** Model fluent reading.

After Reading Have children finish reading and write answers to Responding questions. ✓

Level J

◆ English Language Learners

Before Reading Preview VR *Fireflies.* See VR Guide, p. 34.

During Reading **Fluency Modeling:** Read aloud each page; have children do echo reading.

After Reading Discuss Responding pages. Have children reread with partners or audio CD.

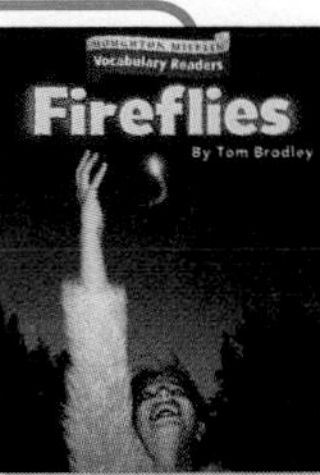

Level E

Writing and Language

25-40 minutes

Writing

Teach Shared Writing: A Class Poem, TE T125

Practice Assign Writing Prompt, TE T115.

Listening and Speaking

Teach Giving Directions, TE T125

Optional Resources

Teacher Read Aloud

Reread *Stone Soup,* TE T116–T117.

Independent Work

Self-Selected Reading

Choose from

- classroom/school library
- Leveled Bibliography, TE T6–T7
- *I Love Reading,* Theme 10, take-home book 93
- Little Readers for Guided Reading

Centers

- Classroom Management Kit
- Classroom Management activities, TE T112–T113

Differentiated Instruction

- Phonics Reteaching or Extension: *r*-Controlled Vowels *ar,* TE R16–R17
- High-Frequency Words Review: Word Wall, TE T114

TE = Teacher Edition; PB = Practice Book; Tr = Transparency; LR = Leveled Reader; PL = Phonics Library; VR = Vocabulary Reader; VR Guide = Vocabulary Readers Teacher's Manual; LBB = Little Big Book; TP = Theme Paperback

Day 2 Balanced Literacy Plan

Teacher Notes

Reading and Comprehension

20-30 minutes

Shared Reading of *Fireflies for Nathan* (Part 1)

▼ Anthology Selection

- Build Background and Vocabulary; Introduce Story Vocabulary, TE T130–T131, Tr 10-7

appear	favorite	monarch	warns
beacon	journey	promises	whispers

- Introduce Comprehension Strategy and Skill:
  Summarize, TE T132
  Sequence of Events, TE T132, TE T143
- Set Purpose, TE T133
- Read Anthology Selection pp. 177–190 (independent, partner, or audio CD).

Words to Know

above	minute
against	dark
already	star
caught	jar
begin	arm

Word Work

25-40 minutes

Phonemic Awareness/Phonics Instruction

Teach Substitute Phonemes, TE T127

High-Frequency Word Instruction

Teach TE T128–T129, Tr 10-6; **Practice** PB 257, 258.

Spelling Instruction

Review The Vowel + *r* Sound in *car,* TE T146

High-Frequency Words

above	caught
begin	already
against	minute

3
SMALL GROUP

Options for Guided Reading

80-100 minutes

 **Extra Support**

Before Reading Preview VR *Fireflies.* See VR Guide, p. 34.

During Reading Read the book together; coach reading. Help children apply Summarize Strategy.

After Reading Help children compare this book to *Fireflies for Nathan.* **Fluency Practice:** Have children reread VR. Assign *Car Trip,* PL Theme 10, pp. 36–44, for partner reading.

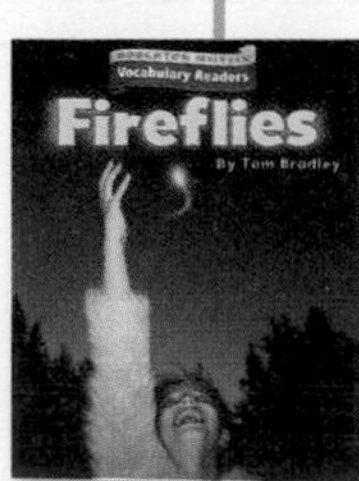

Level E

✓ = opportunity for ongoing assessment; adjust groups accordingly

▲ On Level

Before Reading Discuss PL *Big Star's Gifts,* TE T122. Preview LR *Cliff Can't Come,* TE T173.

During Reading Coach reading as children begin story. Have children model the Summarize Strategy. **Fluency Modeling:** Model fluent reading, then have children model it.

After Reading Children finish reading and write answers to Responding questions. ✓ Assign *Car Trip,* PL Theme 10, pp. 36–44, for partner reading.

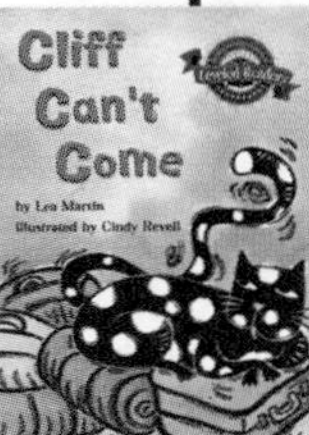

Level F

■ Above Level

Before Reading Have children model the Summarize Strategy and discuss Responding questions for LR *Carla's Corner,* TE T174.

During Reading **Fluency Check:** Monitor children's oral reading. ✓

After Reading Have children discuss the story with a partner. Assign *Car Trip,* PL Theme 10, pp. 36–44, for partner reading.

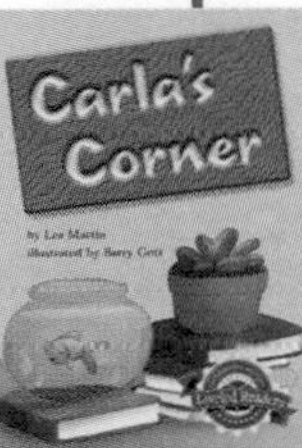

Level J

◆ English Language Learners

Before Reading To review VR vocabulary, have children demonstrate or give examples. See VR Guide, p. 34.

During Reading Model Summarize Strategy. Help children apply the Summarize Strategy. **Fluency Practice:** Have children reread book.
Option: Preview and coach reading of *Big Star's Gifts,* PL Theme 10, pp. 29–35, TE T121–T123.

After Reading Help children summarize VR. Have partners discuss, draw, or write facts they learned. ✓

Level E

4 WHOLE GROUP Writing and Language

25-40 minutes

Writing

Teach Interactive Writing: A Class Poem, TE T147

Practice Assign Writing Prompt, TE T127.

Optional Resources

Teacher Read Aloud

Choose a book from your class/school library or from the Leveled Bibliography, TE T6–T7.

Suggestion: *Mike Mulligan and His Steam Shovel* by Virginia Lee Burton

Independent Work

Self-Selected Reading

Choose from

- classroom/school library
- Leveled Bibliography, TE T6–T7
- *I Love Reading,* Theme 10, take-home book 93
- Little Readers for Guided Reading

Centers

- Classroom Management Kit
- Classroom Management activities, TE T112–T113

Differentiated Instruction

- Phonics Reteaching or Extension: *r*-Controlled Vowels *ar,* TE R16–R17
- High-Frequency Words
  - Word Wall, TE T126
  - Review, TE T146
  - Reteaching or Extension, TE R22–R23

TE = Teacher Edition; PB = Practice Book; Tr = Transparency; LR = Leveled Reader; PL = Phonics Library; VR = Vocabulary Reader; VR Guide = Vocabulary Readers Teacher's Manual; LBB = Little Big Book; TP = Theme Paperback

Day 3 Balanced Literacy Plan

Teacher Notes

Reading and Comprehension

20-30 minutes

Shared Reading of *Fireflies for Nathan* (Part 2)

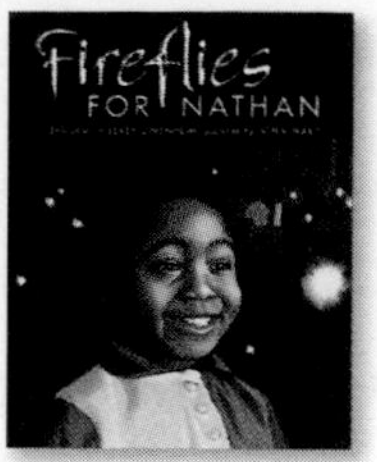

- Read Anthology Selection pp. 191–199 (independent, partner, or audio CD).
- Discuss Responding questions, TE T150; have children cite text to support answers.

Comprehension Skill Instruction

Teach Sequence of Events, TE T152–T153, Tr 10-8

Practice Assign PB 263 or retelling of story.

Word Work

25-40 minutes

Phonemic Awareness Instruction

Teach Substitute Phonemes, TE T149

Spelling: The Vowel + *r* Sound in *car*

Practice Assign PB 264 or activity, TE T154.

Vocabulary Instruction

Teach Prefixes *dis-, re-,* TE T154

Practice Assign PB 265.

Options for Guided Reading

80-100 minutes

Extra Support

Before Reading Discuss Responding questions from VR *Fireflies.* See VR Guide, p. 34. Preview LR *The New Sled,* TE T172.

During Reading Coach as children read story. **Fluency Modeling:** Model fluent reading; have children model.

After Reading **Fluency Practice:** Have partners reread story. Have children answer Responding questions. ✓

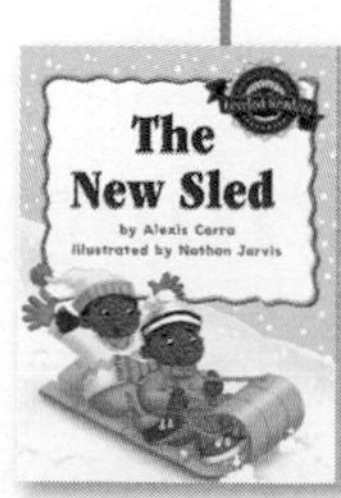

Level E

✓ = opportunity for ongoing assessment; adjust groups accordingly

 **On Level**

Before Reading Discuss Responding questions for LR *Cliff Can't Come,* TE T173.

During Reading **Fluency Check:** Ask individuals to read story aloud. ✓

After Reading Help children note sequence of events in LR. Complete list of events together.

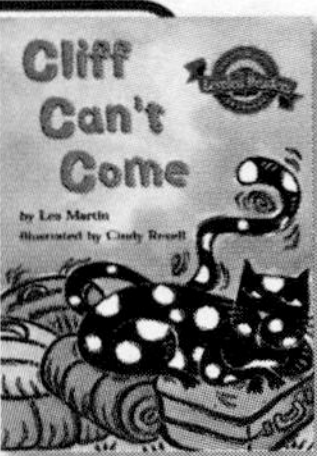

Level F

■ **Above Level**

Before Reading Preview new book, such as *Little Rat Sets Sail* by Monika Bang-Campbell. See TE R8.

During Reading **Fluency Modeling:** Model fluent reading, then have children model it. Have them read first half of story independently.

After Reading Ask questions; have children cite text to support answers. Help children map the sequence of events for selected book. Complete list of events together.

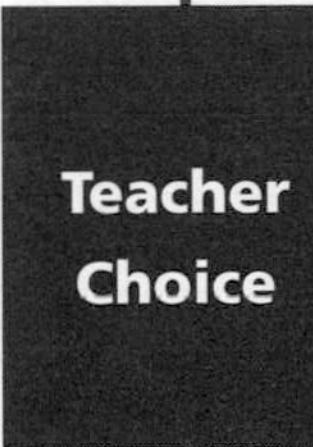

◆ **English Language Learners**

Before Reading Preview *Car Trip,* PL Theme 10, pp. 36–44. Model Phonics/Decoding Strategy.

During Reading **Fluency Modeling:** Read aloud each page; have children do echo reading.

After Reading Discuss story; help children find/read words with *ar.* Have children use illustrations to retell story to partners.

Writing and Language

30-40 minutes

Writing

Practice Assign Write a Character Sketch, Anthology p. 203.

Grammar

Teach Describing Words: Taste, Smell, Feel, TE T155

Practice Assign PB 266.

Optional Resources

Teacher Read Aloud

Continue selected Read Aloud book from Day 2 or choose a new one from your class or school library.

Independent Work

Self-Selected Reading

Choose from

- classroom/school library
- Leveled Bibliography, TE T6–T7
- *I Love Reading,* Theme 10, take-home book 93
- Little Readers for Guided Reading

Centers

- Classroom Management Kit
- Classroom Management activities, TE T112–T113
- Responding activities, TE T150–T151

Differentiated Instruction

- Comprehension Reteaching or Extension, *r*-Controlled Vowels *ar,* TE R16–R17
- High-Frequency Word Review: Word Wall, TE T148

TE = Teacher Edition; PB = Practice Book; Tr = Transparency; LR = Leveled Reader; PL = Phonics Library; VR = Vocabulary Reader; VR Guide = Vocabulary Readers Teacher's Manual; LBB = Little Big Book; TP = Theme Paperback

Day 4 Balanced Literacy Plan

Teacher Notes

Reading and Comprehension

20-30 minutes

Shared Reading of Poetry Link

- "The Firefly," Anthology pp. 204–205, TE T158–T159 (independent, partner, or group)
- Skill: How to Read a Poem, Anthology p. 204, TE T158
- Introduce Concept Vocabulary, TE T158.

Concept Vocabulary

August
batteries
blink

Word Work

25-40 minutes

Phonemic Awareness/Phonics Instruction

Teach Substitute Phonemes, TE T157

Review *r*-Controlled Vowels: *or, ore,* TE T160; *r*-Controlled Vowels: *ar, er, ir, ur,* TE T161

Spelling: The Vowel + *r* Sound in *car*

Practice Assign PB 267 or activity, TE T162.

Vocabulary Instruction

Teach Comparing with Figurative Language, TE T162

3 SMALL GROUP

Options for Guided Reading

80-100 minutes

Extra Support

Before Reading Review Responding questions for LR *The New Sled,* TE T172. Help children note sequence of events in LR.

During Reading Have children reread story. **Fluency Check:** Have individuals read aloud. ✓

After Reading Have partners complete a numbered list of events in the LR.

Level E

✓ = opportunity for ongoing assessment; adjust groups accordingly

▲ On Level

Before Reading Have children summarize LR *Cliff Can't Come.* ✓ Preview a teacher-selected book such as *I Can Read with My Eyes Shut!,* TE R7.

During Reading Have children begin story and model Phonics/Decoding Strategy.

After Reading Discuss the story so far. Have children finish story.

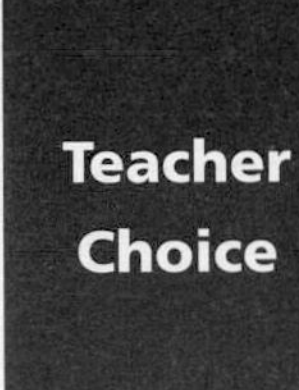

■ Above Level

Before Reading Review first half of selected book. Have children make predictions about second half.

During Reading Have children finish book.

After Reading Discuss how book connects to theme. Have children write journal entries to connect it to personal experience or other reading.

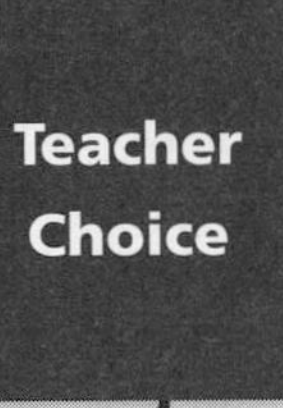

◆ English Language Learners

Before Reading Build background and preview LR *The Sled,* TE T175.

During Reading Read story. **Fluency Modeling:** Reread each page; have children do echo reading. Reinforce Phonics/Decoding Strategy.

After Reading Discuss Responding questions, TE T75. **Fluency Practice:** Have children reread with partners or audio CD.

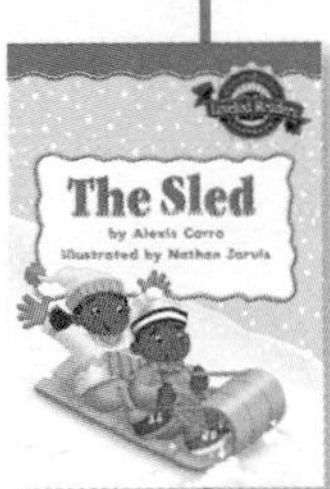

Level D

Optional Resources

Teacher Read Aloud

Choose a new book from your class or school library.

Independent Work

Self-Selected Reading

Choose from

- classroom/school library
- Leveled Bibliography, TE T6–T7
- children's magazines
- *I Love Reading,* Theme 10, take-home book 93
- Little Readers for Guided Reading

Centers

- Classroom Management Kit
- Classroom Management activities, TE T112–T113
- Responding activities, TE T150–T151

Differentiated Instruction

- Writer's Craft: Using Poetic Language, TE T159
- High-Frequency Words: Word Wall, TE T156
- Study Skills
  – Reading a Chart, TE R32

4 WHOLE GROUP

Writing and Language

30-40 minutes

Writing

Teach Writing Clearly with Describing Words, TE T163

Practice Assign PB 268.

TE = Teacher Edition; PB = Practice Book; Tr = Transparency; LR = Leveled Reader; PL = Phonics Library; VR = Vocabulary Reader; VR Guide = Vocabulary Readers Teacher's Manual; LBB = Little Big Book; TP = Theme Paperback

Day 5 Balanced Literacy Plan

Teacher Notes

Reading and Comprehension

20-30 minutes

Book Share

- Ask children to give examples of how they applied the comprehension skill and strategy to books they have read this week.
- Help children use genre and text features to compare and contrast what they have read.
- As a class, discuss one *how, why,* or *what if* question. See examples on Blackline Master 1 to use as a guide.

Book Share

Word Work

25-40 minutes

Phonemic Awareness Instruction

Teach Substitute Phonemes, TE T165

High-Frequency Words

Cumulative Review Word Wall, TE T164

Spelling

Test See TE T170.

Options for Guided Reading

80-100 minutes

Extra Support

Before Reading Preview *Mark's Part,* PL Theme 10, pp. 45–51. Have children find/read words with *ar.* See TE T167–T169.

During Reading Have children read and model Phonics/Decoding Strategy. **Fluency Check:** Have individuals reread aloud. ✓

After Reading Have partners make connections between the story and LR *The New Sled.* Assign On My Way Practice Reader *A Storm at the Farm* for partner reading.

✓ = opportunity for ongoing assessment; adjust groups accordingly

◆ English Language Learners

Before Reading Review LR *The Sled,* TE T175.

During Reading Coach rereading of book. **Fluency Check:** Have individuals reread aloud. ✓

After Reading Help children summarize LR. Have children draw/caption a picture about a book they read this week. ✓

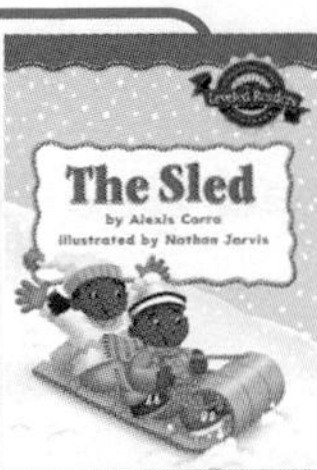

Level D

Mixed Ability Levels

Literature Circles Form small, mixed-ability groups. Ask groups to discuss the main Anthology selection, Link, Leveled Readers, and other books they have read this week. Pose questions or topics for each group, and circulate among groups to offer support. Suggested group activities:

- Respond to specific Literature Discussion questions on Blackline Master 1.
- Discuss story or text elements, authors' choice of language, and/or illustrations.
- Connect book topics or themes to personal experiences or other reading.

Literature Circle

Writing and Language

30-40 minutes

Writing

Practice Assign Writing Prompt, TE T165.

Grammar

Review Describing Words: Taste, Smell, Feel, TE T171

Listening and Speaking

Teach Listening to Retell, TE T171

Optional Resources

Teacher Read Aloud

Choose a nonfiction book related to Social Studies or Science unit.

Independent Work

Self-Selected Reading

Choose from
- classroom/school library
- Leveled Bibliography, TE T6–T7
- children's magazines
- consumer text such as books about poetry, books about fireflies, etc.

Centers
- Classroom Management Kit
- Classroom Management activities, TE T112–T113
- Responding activities, TE T150–T151

Differentiated Instruction
- High-Frequency Word Review: TE T170
- Comprehension Review: Sequence of Events, TE T166

End-of-Week Assessment

- Weekly Skills Tests for Theme 10, Week 2
- Fluency Assessment, *Mark's Part,* PL Theme 10, pp. 45–51, TE T167–T169
- Alternative Assessment, Teacher's Resource Blackline Master 136

TE = Teacher Edition; PB = Practice Book; Tr = Transparency; LR = Leveled Reader; PL = Phonics Library; VR = Vocabulary Reader; VR Guide = Vocabulary Readers Teacher's Manual; LBB = Little Big Book; TP = Theme Paperback

Day 1 Balanced Literacy Plan

Teacher Notes

Reading and Comprehension

20-30 minutes

Shared Reading of Daily Message, TE T186

Listing Comprehension

- Read aloud *Frog Tricks Loud Rabbit,* TE T188–T189.
- Model fluent reading; discuss the story.

Word Work

25-40 minutes

Phonemic Awareness/Phonics Instruction

Teach Substitute Phonemes, TE T187, T190

Teach Base Words and Endings *-er, -est,* TE T190–T192

Practice Assign PB 269.

Spelling Instruction: Adding *-er* or *-est* to Words

Pretest and Teach Spelling Principle, TE T196

Assign Take-Home Spelling Word List, PB 325

deepest newer faster richer highest warmest

Challenge: kindest, smaller

Vocabulary Instruction

Teach Spelling Patterns *-er, -est,* TE T196

Options for Guided Reading

80-100 minutes

Extra Support

Before Reading Preview *Ice-Cold Drinks,* PL Theme 10, pp. 53–59. Model Phonics/Decoding Strategy. See TE T193–T195.

During Reading Coach as children read story.

After Reading Discuss story; have children find/read words with *-er, -est.* **Fluency Modeling:** Model fluent reading. Have partners reread story.

Ice-Cold Drinks

Rose and Bruce set up a selling stand. Bruce wrote this:
Ice-cold drinks for sale.
Sweetest, coolest drinks in town!
Just ten cents!

✓ = opportunity for ongoing assessment; adjust groups accordingly

▲ On Level

Before Reading Preview *Ice-Cold Drinks,* PL Theme 10, pp. 53–59, and review TE T193–T195.

During Reading Have children begin story. **Fluency Modeling:** Model Phonics/Decoding Strategy and fluent reading.

After Reading Have children retell story so far and find/read words with *-er, -est.* **Fluency Practice:** Have partners finish story and reread for fluency.

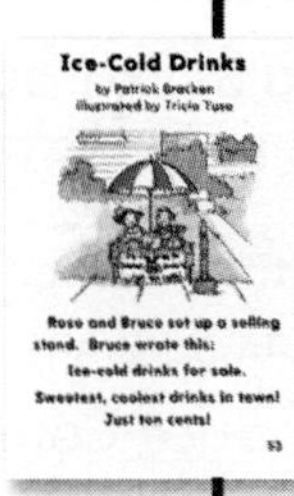

■ Above Level

Before Reading Preview LR *Dog's Party,* TE T240.

During Reading Have children read first half of story. **Fluency Modeling:** Model fluent reading.

After Reading Have children finish reading and write answers to Responding questions. ✓

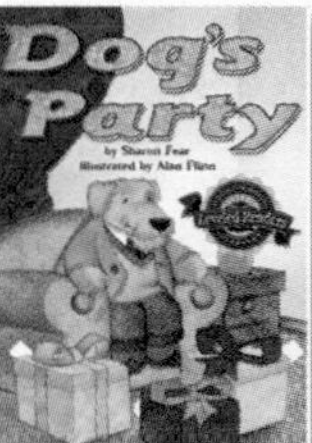

Level I

◆ English Language Learners

Before Reading Preview VR *At the Zoo.* See VR Guide, p. 35.

During Reading **Fluency Modeling:** Read aloud each page; have children do echo reading.

After Reading Discuss Responding pages. Have children reread with partners or audio CD.

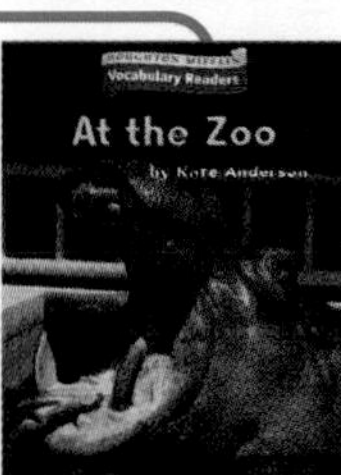

Level E

Optional Resources

Teacher Read Aloud

Reread *Frog Tricks Loud Rabbit,* TE T188–T189.

Independent Work

Self-Selected Reading

Choose from

- classroom/school library
- Leveled Bibliography, TE T6–T7
- *I Love Reading,* Theme 10, take-home books 94–95
- Little Readers for Guided Reading

Centers

- Classroom Management Kit
- Classroom Management activities, TE T184–T185

Differentiated Instruction

- Phonics Reteaching or Extension: Base Words and Endings (*-er*, *-est*), TE R18–R19
- High-Frequency Words Review: Word Wall, TE T186

4 WHOLE GROUP

Writing and Language

25-40 minutes

Writing

Teach Shared Writing: An Alternate Ending, TE T197

Practice Assign Writing Prompt, TE T187.

Listening and Speaking

Teach Compare/Contrast Stories, TE T197

TE = Teacher Edition; PB = Practice Book; Tr = Transparency; LR = Leveled Reader; PL = Phonics Library; VR = Vocabulary Reader; VR Guide = Vocabulary Readers Teacher's Manual; LBB = Little Big Book; TP = Theme Paperback

Day 2 Balanced Literacy Plan

Teacher Notes

Reading and Comprehension

20-30 minutes

Shared Reading of *The Hat* (Part 1)

▼ Anthology Selection

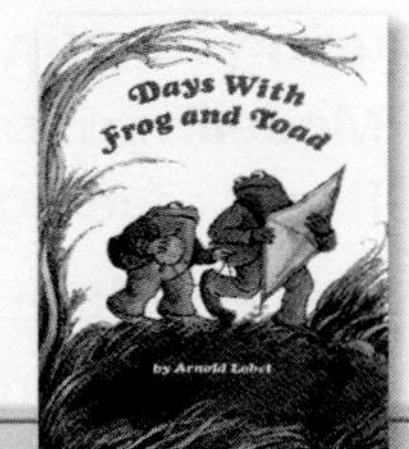

- Build Background and Vocabulary; Introduce Story Vocabulary, TE T202–T203, Tr 10-14

beautiful	delighted	pleasant	sorry
birthday	giant	smaller	

- Introduce Comprehension Strategy and Skill: Monitor/Clarify, TE T204
  Cause and Effect, TE T204, TE T209
- Set Purpose, TE T205
- Read Anthology Selection pp. 210–214 (independent, partner, or audio CD).

Words to Know

able	smaller
eyes	larger
present	biggest
thoughts	

2 WHOLE GROUP

Word Work

25-40 minutes

High-Frequency Words

able	eyes
thoughts	present

Phonemic Awareness/Phonics Instruction

Teach Substituting Phonemes, TE T199

High-Frequency Word Instruction

Teach TE T200–T201, Tr 10-13; **Practice** PB 270, 271.

Spelling Instruction

Review Adding *-er* or *-est* to Words, TE T212

3 SMALL GROUP

Options for Guided Reading

80-100 minutes

● Extra Support

Before Reading Preview VR *At the Zoo,* VR Guide, p. 35.

During Reading Read the book together; coach reading. Help children apply Monitor/Clarify Strategy.

After Reading Help children compare this book to *The Hat.* **Fluency Practice:** Have children reread VR. Assign *The Best Pie,* PL Theme 10, pp. 60–68, for partner reading.

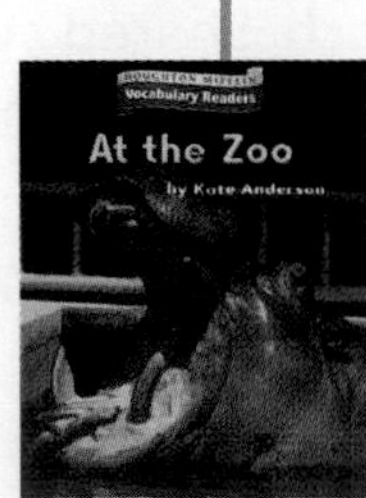

Level E

✓ = opportunity for ongoing assessment; adjust groups accordingly

▲ On Level

Before Reading Discuss PL *Ice-Cold Drinks,* TE T194. Preview LR *Faster! Faster!,* TE T239.

During Reading Coach reading as children begin story. Have children model the Monitor/Clarify Strategy. **Fluency Modeling:** Model fluent reading, then have children model it.

After Reading Children finish reading and write answers to Responding questions. ✓ Assign *The Best Pie,* PL Theme 10, pp. 60–68, for partner reading.

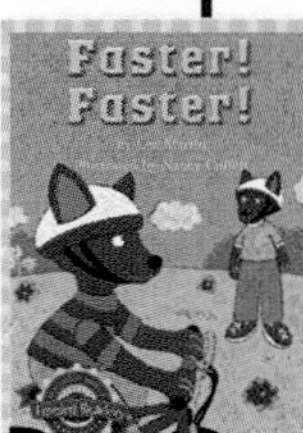

Level H

■ Above Level

Before Reading Have children model the Monitor/Clarify Strategy and discuss Responding questions for LR *Dog's Party,* TE T240.

During Reading **Fluency Check:** Monitor children's oral reading. ✓

After Reading Have children discuss the story with a partner. Assign *The Best Pie,* PL Theme 10, pp. 60–68, for partner reading.

Level I

◆ English Language Learners

Before Reading To review VR vocabulary, have children demonstrate or give examples. See VR Guide, p. 35.

During Reading Model Monitor/Clarify Strategy. Help children apply the Monitor/Clarify Strategy. **Fluency Practice:** Have children reread book. Option: Preview and coach reading of *Ice-Cold Drinks,* PL Theme 10, pp. 53–59, TE T193–T195.

After Reading Help children summarize VR. Have partners discuss, draw, or write facts they learned. ✓

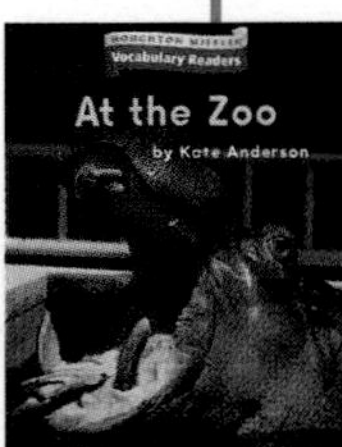

Level E

Optional Resources

Teacher Read Aloud

Choose a book from your class/school library or from the Leveled Bibliography, TE T6–T7.

Suggestion: *Curious George Gets a Medal* by H.A. Rey

Independent Work

Self-Selected Reading

Choose from
- classroom/school library
- Leveled Bibliography, TE T6–T7
- *I Love Reading,* Theme 10, take-home books 94–95
- Little Readers for Guided Reading

Centers
- Classroom Management Kit
- Classroom Management activities, TE T184–T185

Differentiated Instruction
- Phonics Reteaching or Extension: Base Words and Endings (*-er, -est*), TE R18–R19
- High-Frequency Words
  - Word Wall, TE T198
  - Review, TE T212
  - Reteaching or Extension, TE R24–R25

4 WHOLE GROUP

Writing and Language

25-40 minutes

Writing

Teach Interactive Writing: An Alternate Ending, TE T213

Practice Assign Writing Prompt, TE T199.

TE = Teacher Edition; PB = Practice Book; Tr = Transparency; LR = Leveled Reader; PL = Phonics Library; VR = Vocabulary Reader; VR Guide = Vocabulary Readers Teacher's Manual; LBB = Little Big Book; TP = Theme Paperback

Day 3 Balanced Literacy Plan

Teacher Notes

Reading and Comprehension

20-30 minutes

▼ Anthology Selection

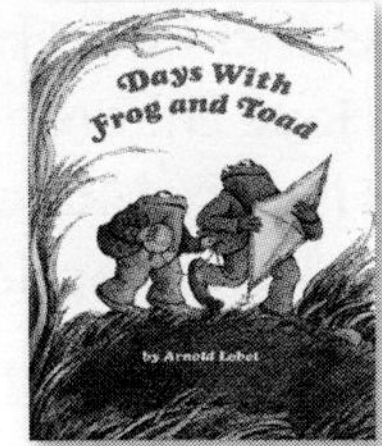

Shared Reading of *The Hat* (Part 2)

- ➤ Read Anthology Selection pp. 215–219 (independent, partner, or audio CD).
- ➤ Discuss questions, TE T216; have children cite text to support answers.

Comprehension Skill Instruction

Teach Cause and Effect, TE T218–T219, Tr 10-15

Practice Assign PB 274 or retelling of story.

Word Work

25-40 minutes

Phonemic Awareness Instruction

Teach Substituting Phonemes, TE T215

Spelling: Adding *-er* or *-est* to Words

Practice Assign PB 275 or activity, TE T220.

Vocabulary Instruction

Teach Suffix *-ly*, TE T220

Practice Assign PB 276.

Options for Guided Reading

80-100 minutes

Extra Support

Before Reading Discuss Responding questions from VR *At the Zoo.* See VR Guide, p. 35. Preview LR *The Sweetest Present,* TE T238.

During Reading Coach as children read story. **Fluency Modeling:** Model fluent reading; have children model.

After Reading **Fluency Practice:** Have partners reread story. Have children answer Responding questions. ✓

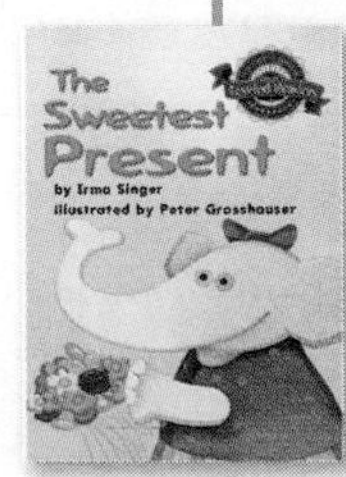

Level E

✓ = opportunity for ongoing assessment; adjust groups accordingly

▲ On Level

Before Reading Discuss Responding questions for LR *Faster! Faster!*, TE T239.

During Reading **Fluency Check:** Ask individuals to read story aloud. ✓

After Reading Create a Cause and Effect Chart; see TE T218, Tr 10-15. Help children examine the cause and effect elements in the LR. Complete the chart together.

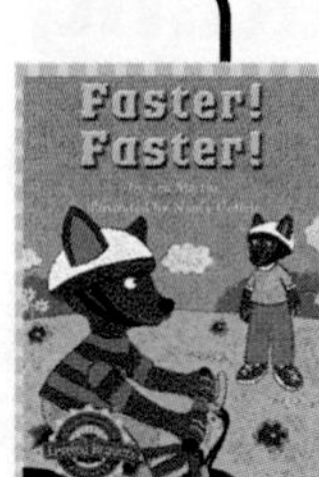

Level H

■ Above Level

Before Reading Preview a teacher-selected book, such as *The Wright Brothers*, TE R11.

During Reading **Fluency Modeling:** Model fluent reading, then have children model it. Have them read first half of story independently.

After Reading Ask questions; have children cite text to support answers. Create a Cause and Effect Chart; see TE T218, Tr 10-15. Help children examine the cause and effect elements in the selected book. Complete the chart together.

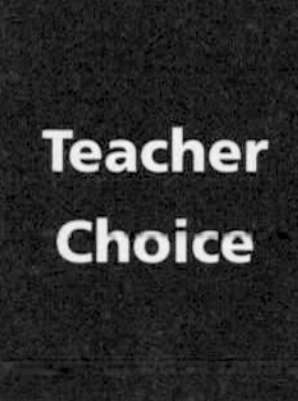

◆ English Language Learners

Before Reading Preview *The Best Pie*, PL Theme 10, pp. 60–68. Model Phonics/Decoding Strategy.

During Reading **Fluency Modeling:** Read aloud each page; have children do echo reading.

After Reading Discuss story; help children find/read words with *-er, -est.* Have children use illustrations to retell story to partners.

Writing and Language

30-40 minutes

Writing

Practice Assign Write a Book Report, Anthology p. 221.

Grammar

Teach Comparing (*-er, -est*), TE T221

Practice Assign PB 277.

Optional Resources

Teacher Read Aloud

Continue selected Read Aloud book from Day 2 or choose a new one from your class or school library.

Independent Work

Self-Selected Reading

Choose from

- classroom/school library
- Leveled Bibliography, TE T6–T7
- *I Love Reading*, Theme 10, take-home books 94–95
- Little Readers for Guided Reading

Centers

- Classroom Management Kit
- Classroom Management activities, TE T184–T185
- Responding activities, TE T216–T217

Differentiated Instruction

- Comprehension Reteaching or Extension, Cause and Effect, TE R30–R31
- High-Frequency Word Review: Word Wall, TE T214

TE = Teacher Edition; PB = Practice Book; Tr = Transparency; LR = Leveled Reader; PL = Phonics Library; VR = Vocabulary Reader; VR Guide = Vocabulary Readers Teacher's Manual; LBB = Little Big Book; TP = Theme Paperback

Day 4 Balanced Literacy Plan

Teacher Notes

Reading and Comprehension

20-30 minutes

Shared Reading of Science Link

- "Is It a Frog or a Toad?", Anthology pp. 222–223, TE T224–T225 (independent, partner, or group)
- Skill: How to Read a Chart, Anthology p. 222, TE T224
- Introduce Concept Vocabulary, TE T224.

Concept Vocabulary
ridges
plump
slender
clumps
rows

Word Work

25-40 minutes

Phonemic Awareness/Phonics Instruction

Teach Substituting Phonemes, TE T223

Review Base Words and Endings *-er, -est,* TE T226

Spelling: Adding *-er* or *-est* to Words

Practice Assign PB 278 or activity, TE T228.

Vocabulary Instruction

Teach Clothing Words, TE T228

3 SMALL GROUP

Options for Guided Reading

80-100 minutes

Extra Support

Before Reading Review Responding questions for LR *The Sweetest Present,* TE T238. Create a Cause and Effect Chart; TE T218, Tr 10-15. Help children examine the cause and effect elements in the LR.

During Reading Have children reread story. **Fluency Check:** Have individuals read aloud. ✓

After Reading Work with children to complete the Cause and Effect Chart. Have partners look at the cause and effect of other story elements.

Level E

✓ = opportunity for ongoing assessment; adjust groups accordingly

▲ On Level

Before Reading Have children summarize LR *Faster! Faster!* ✓ Preview a teacher-selected book such as *Bernard On His Own*, TE R10.

During Reading Have children begin story and model Phonics/Decoding Strategy.

After Reading Discuss the story so far. Have children finish story.

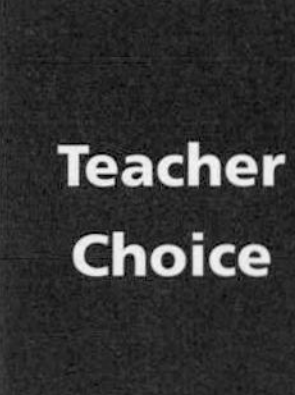

■ Above Level

Before Reading Review first half of selected book. Have children make predictions about second half.

During Reading Have children finish book.

After Reading Discuss how book connects to theme. Have children write journal entries to connect it to personal experience or other reading.

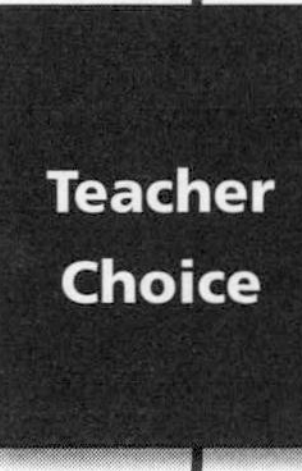

◆ English Language Learners

Before Reading Build background and preview LR *The Birthday Present,* TE T241.

During Reading Read story. **Fluency Modeling:** Reread each page; have children do echo reading. Reinforce Phonics/Decoding Strategy.

After Reading Discuss Responding questions, TE T241. **Fluency Practice:** Have children reread with partners or audio CD.

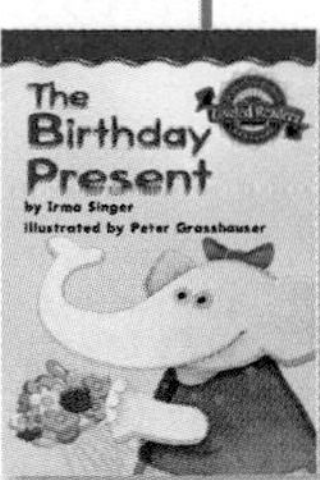

Level E

Optional Resources

Teacher Read Aloud

Choose a new book from your class or school library.

Independent Work

Self-Selected Reading

Choose from

- classroom/school library
- Leveled Bibliography, TE T6–T7
- children's magazines
- *I Love Reading,* Theme 10, take-home books 94–95
- Little Readers for Guided Reading

Centers

- Classroom Management Kit
- Classroom Management activities, TE T184–T185
- Responding activities, TE T216–T217

Differentiated Instruction

- High-Frequency Words: Word Wall, TE T222
- Study Skills
  – Reading a Chart, TE R32

Writing and Language

30-40 minutes

Writing

Teach A Thank-You Note, TE T229

Practice Assign PB 279.

TE = Teacher Edition; PB = Practice Book; Tr = Transparency; LR = Leveled Reader; PL = Phonics Library; VR = Vocabulary Reader; VR Guide = Vocabulary Readers Teacher's Manual; LBB = Little Big Book; TP = Theme Paperback

Day 5 Balanced Literacy Plan

Teacher Notes

Reading and Comprehension

20-30 minutes

Book Share

- Ask children to give examples of how they applied the comprehension skill and strategy to books they have read this week.
- Help children use genre and text features to compare and contrast what they have read.
- As a class, discuss one *how, why,* or *what if* question. See examples on Blackline Master 1 to use as a guide.

Word Work

25-40 minutes

Phonemic Awareness Instruction

Teach Substituting Phonemes, TE T231

High-Frequency Words

Cumulative Review Word Wall, TE T230

Spelling

Test See TE T236.

Options for Guided Reading

80-100 minutes

Extra Support

Before Reading Preview *Don't Ask Me,* PL Theme 10, pp. 69–75. Have children find/read words with *-er, -est.* See TE T233–T235.

During Reading Have children read and model Phonics/Decoding Strategy. **Fluency Check:** Have individuals reread aloud. ✓

After Reading Have partners make connections between the story and LR *The Sweetest Present.* Assign On My Way Practice Reader *Wind and Sun* for partner reading.

Don't Ask Me

"Happy birthday, Marge!" said Mom. "Did Dad tell you where we are going?"

"Not yet!" blurted Marge.

"We are going to Fred's farm," laughed Dad.

69

✓ = opportunity for ongoing assessment; adjust groups accordingly

◆ English Language Learners

Before Reading Review LR *The Birthday Present,* TE T241.

During Reading Coach rereading of book. **Fluency Check:** Have individuals reread aloud. ✓

After Reading Help children summarize LR. Have children draw/caption a picture about a book they read this week. ✓

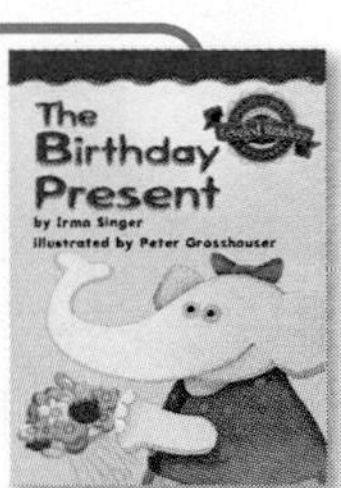

Level E

●▲■◆ Mixed Ability Levels

Literature Circles Form small, mixed-ability groups. Ask groups to discuss the main Anthology selection, Link, Leveled Readers, and other books they have read this week. Pose questions or topics for each group, and circulate among groups to offer support. Suggested group activities:

- Respond to specific Literature Discussion questions on Blackline Master 1.
- Discuss story or text elements, authors' choice of language, and/or illustrations.
- Connect book topics or themes to personal experiences or other reading.

Writing and Language

30-40 minutes

Writing

Practice Assign Writing Prompt, TE T231.

Grammar

Review Comparing (*-er, -est*), TE T237

Speaking and Listening

Teach Giving and Following Directions, TE T237

Optional Resources

Teacher Read Aloud

Choose a nonfiction book related to Social Studies or Science unit.

Independent Work

Self-Selected Reading

Choose from

- classroom/school library
- Leveled Bibliography, TE T6–T7
- children's magazines
- consumer text such as books about toads, books about frogs, etc.

Centers

- Classroom Management Kit
- Classroom Management activities, TE T184–T185
- Responding activities, TE T216–T217

Differentiated Instruction

- High-Frequency Word Review: TE T236
- Comprehension Review: Cause and Effect, TE T232

Assessment

End-of-Week Assessment

- Weekly Skills Tests for Theme 10, Week 3
- Fluency Assessment, *Don't Ask Me,* PL Theme 10, pp. 69–75, TE T233–T235
- Alternative Assessment, Teacher's Resource Blackline Master 139

End-of-Theme Assessment

- Integrated Theme Tests for Theme 10

TE = Teacher Edition; PB = Practice Book; Tr = Transparency; LR = Leveled Reader; PL = Phonics Library; VR = Vocabulary Reader; VR Guide = Vocabulary Readers Teacher's Manual; LBB = Little Big Book; TP = Theme Paperback

Ideas for Literature Discussion Questions

For Fiction

1. If you could spend a day with a story character, what questions would you ask? What would you do together?
2. How are the characters like real people? How are they different?
3. Do you think the author wrote a good ending for the story? Why do you think so?
4. What is the problem in the story? How is it solved?
5. How is this story like something that happened to you?
6. What might the characters do in their next story?

For Nonfiction

1. What is the topic of this book? How does the author tell you that?
2. What did you already know about the topic?
3. What facts did you learn from the book?
4. What did you learn from the pictures?
5. Would you tell a friend to read this book? Why or why not?

Blackline Master 1